Austin Allegro Owners Workshop Manual

by J H Haynes

Member of the Guild of Motoring Writers

and B L Chalmers - Hunt

T Eng (CEI), AMIMI, AMIRTE, AMVBRA

Models covered
Austin Allegro 1100 and 1300 (1973 to 1975)
Austin Allegro 2 1100 and 1300 (1975 to 1979)
Austin Allegro 3 1.1 and 1.3 (1979 to 1980)

ISBN 0 85696 592 8

HAYNES PUBLISHING GROUP
SPARKFORD YEOVIL SOMERSET ENGLAND
distributed in the USA by
HAYNES PUBLICATIONS INC
861 LAWRENCE DRIVE
NEWBURY PARK
CALIFORNIA 91320
USA

Acknowledgements

Thanks are due to BL Cars Limited for their assistance with technical material, to Castrol Limited for lubrication data and to the Champion Sparking Plug Company who supplied the illustrations showing various spark plug conditions.

The bodywork repair photographs used in this manual were provided by Holt Lloyd Limited who supply 'Turtle Wax', 'Dupli-color Holts' and other Holts range products.

Special thanks are due to F. J. Chalke and Son of Mere, Wiltshire, who were extremely helpful in providing much of the detailed information on the latest Series 3 models, and to all those people at Sparkford who helped produce this book; Brian Horsfall who carried out the mechanical work, Les Brazier who took the photographs and Stanley Randolph who planned the layout of each page. Philip Methuen wrote the updated supplement on the latest Series 3 models and Paul Hansford edited the text.

About this manual

Its aim

The aim of this manual is to help you get the best value from your car. It can do so in several ways. It can help you decide what work must be done (even should you choose to get it done by a garage), provide information on routine maintenance and servicing, and give a logical course of action and diagnosis when random faults occur. However, it is hoped that you will use the manual by tackling the work yourself. On simpler jobs it may even be quicker than booking the car into a garage and going there twice to leave and collect it. Perhaps most important, a lot of money can be saved by avoiding the costs the garage must charge to cover its labour and overheads.

The manual has drawings and descriptions to show the function of the various components so that their layout can be understood. Then the tasks are described and photographed in a step-by-step sequence so that even a novice can do the work.

Its arrangement

The manual is divided into thirteen Chapters, each covering a logical sub-division of the vehicle. The Chapters are each divided into Sections, numbered with single figures, eg 5; and the Sections into paragraphs (or sub-sections), with decimal numbers following on from the Section they are in, eg 5.1, 5.2, 5.3 etc.

It is freely illustrated, especially in those parts where there is a detailed sequence of operations to be carried out. There are two forms of illustration: figures and photographs. The figures are numbered in sequence with decimal numbers, according to their position in the Chapter — eg Fig. 6.4 is the fourth drawing/illustration in Chapter 6. Photographs carry the same number (either individually or in related groups) as the Section or sub-section to which they relate.

There is an alphabetical index at the back of the manual as well as a contents list at the front. Each Chapter is also preceded by its own individual contents list.

References to the 'left' or 'right' of the vehicle are in the sense of a person in the driver's seat facing forwards.

Unless otherwise stated, nuts and bolts are removed by turning anti-clockwise, and tightened by turning clockwise.

Vehicle manufacturers continually make changes to specifications and recommendations, and these when notified are incorporated into our manuals at the earliest opportunity.

Whilst every care is taken to ensure that the information in this manual is correct, no liability can be accepted by the authors or publishers for loss, damage or injury caused by any errors in, or omissions from, the information given.

Contents

Introduction to the Austin Allegro

The Austin Allegro range of models was introduced in May 1973, being powered by either an 1100cc or 1300cc overhead valve engine, or a 1500cc or 1750cc overhead camshaft engine, the former type of model being the subject of this manual. The 1500, 1750, 1.5 and 1.7 models are covered in a separate Haynes Owners Workshop Manual.

When the Allegro was announced, it made motoring history as being the first car with a 'square' steering wheel, or 'quartic' as it was called. This was phased out in 1975 and replaced by a conventional circular one. The squat shape of the car, however, has remained unchanged, although trim and exterior fittings have altered considerably; the most notable changes being in the Mk 3 models introduced at the end of 1979.

In 1975, a 1300 3-door Estate model was announced as an addition to the range. Again, the styling does not suit everyone, but the load carrying area is considerable for a small Estate car, as the loading area is not reduced by a sloping tailgate, or roofline.

Modifications to the engine mountings, suspension and driveshafts, a new steering rack and a new alternator were also introduced with the Mk 2 in 1975, and the radiator grille was standardised on the type used in the 1500/1750 models. New front seats (allowing more leg room) were introduced, and the rubber flooring gave way to carpet. The ventilation system was also improved. Although the Estate model was given a brake servo unit when it was introduced in 1975, this was not fitted as standard to Saloon models until 1977.

In September 1979, the new Allegro 3 models were announced. The designations of 1100 and 1300 were changed to 1.1 and 1.3 respectively, although the engines remain the same at 1098cc and 1275cc respectively. The Allegro range was considerably increased in size, more in the 1.3 sector than anywhere else. There are now seven 1.3 variants, including a Standard and L version of the Estate. The range now consists of Standard models, L models or HL models to choose from, although there is no HL model in 1.1 form. Both the 1.1 and 1.3 Saloon models are available in 2- or 4-door form, and although all 1.1 and 1.3 models are produced with manual gearboxes as standard, the 1.3 model can be ordered with an automatic gearbox as an optional extra.

The most significant changes in the Allegro Mk 3 models lie in the interior trim and fittings and in their exterior appearance. In the interior, a completely new facia and instrument binnacle with improved sound insulation has been fitted, not to mention the face level ventilation. The seats have fabric facings. In all Saloon models, provision is made for fitting child safety seats in the rear.

From the outside, the Mk 3 cars are easily identifiable by their matt black bumpers and front air spoiler. All L and HL models have full size 'alloy' style roadwheel trims, while all HL models have twin circular headlamps on each side, not to mention twin fog lamps. The rear lamp assemblies have been altered to incorporate reversing lamps, the number plate is now mounted on the boot lid and all models are fitted with a red rear fog guard lamp.

Buying spare parts
and vehicle identification numbers

Buying spare parts

Spare parts are available from many sources, for example: BL garages, other accessory shops, and motor factors. Our advice regarding spare parts is as follows:

Officially appointed BL garages — This is the best source of parts which are peculiar to your car and otherwise not generally available (eg complete cylinder heads, internal gearbox components, badges, interior trim etc). It is also the only place at which you should buy parts if your car is still under warranty; non-BL parts may invalidate the warranty. To be sure of obtaining the correct parts it will always be necessary to give the storeman your car's engine and chassis number, and if possible, to take the old part along for positive identification. Many parts are available under a factory exchange scheme — any parts returned should always be clean. It obviously makes good sense to go straight to the specialists on your car for this type of part for they are best equipped to supply you.

Other garages and accessory shops — These are often very good places to buy material and components needed for the maintenance of your car (eg oil filters, spark plugs, bulbs, drivebelts, oils and grease, touch-up paint, filler paste etc). They also sell accessories, usually have convenient opening hours, charge lower prices and can often be found not far from home.

Motor factors — Good factors stock all of the more important components which wear out relatively quickly (eg clutch components, pistons and liners, valves, exhaust systems, brake pipes/seals and pads, etc). Motor factors will often provide new or reconditioned components on a part exchange basis — this can save a considerable amount of money.

Vehicle identification numbers

Modifications are a continuing and unpublished process in vehicle manufacture quite apart from major model changes. Spare parts manuals and lists are compiled upon a numerical basis, the individual vehicle numbers being essential to correct identification of the component required.

When ordering spare parts, always give as much information as possible. Quote the car model, year of manufacture, body and engine numbers as appropriate.

Commission number: Located on a plate mounted on the right-hand side of the bonnet lock platform.

Car number: Located on a plate mounted on the right hand side of the bonnet lock platform.

Engine number: Stamped on the cylinder block or on a metal plate secured to the cylinder block between the ignition coil and distributor.

Body number: Stamped on a plate fixed to the left-hand side of the bonnet lock platform.

Allegro 1100 De luxe

Allegro 3 1.1

H15968

Recommended lubricants and fluids

Component or system	Lubricant type or specification	Castrol product
Engine (1)	SAE 20w/50 multigrade oil	GTX
Final drive	SAE 20w/50 multigrade oil	GTX
Gearbox (including automatic transmission) (1)	SAE 20w/50 multigrade oil	GTX
Steering rack (6)	SAE EP 90 gear oil	Hypoy
Carburettor dashpot (2)	SAE 20w/50 multigrade oil	GTX
Accelerator pedal fulcrum (3)	SAE 20w/50 multigrade oil	GTX
Distributor cam and weights (3)	SAE 20w/50 multigrade oil	GTX
Steering joints and swivels (4)	Lithium grease NLGI No 2	LM Grease
Handbrake cable ends (5)	Lithium grease NLGI No 2	LM Grease
Rear and front wheel bearings	Lithium grease NLGI No 2	LM Grease
Brake master cylinder	SAE 1703c fluid	Girling Universal Brake and Clutch Fluid
Clutch master cylinder	SAE 1703c fluid	Girling Universal Brake and Clutch Fluid

Tools and working facilities

Introduction

A selection of good tools is a fundamental requirement for anyone contemplating the maintenance and repair of a motor vehicle. For the owner who does not possess any, their purchase will prove a considerable expense, offsetting some of the savings made by doing-it-yourself. However, provided that the tools purchased are of a good quality, they will last for many years and prove an extremely worthwhile investment.

To help the average owner to decide which tools are needed to carry out the various tasks detailed in this manual, we have compiled three lists of tools under the following headings: Maintenance and minor repair, Repair and overhaul, and Special. The newcomer to practical mechanics should start off with the 'Maintenance and minor repair' tool kit and confine himself to the simpler jobs around the vehicle. Then, as his confidence and experience grows, he can undertake more difficult tasks, buying extra tools as and when they are needed. In this way, a 'Maintenance and minor repair' tool kit can be built up into a 'Repair and overhaul' tool kit over a considerable period of time without any major cash outlays. The experienced do-it-yourselfer will have a tool kit good enough for most repair and overhaul procedures and will add tools from the special category when he feels the expense is justified by the amount of use these tools will be put to.

It is obviously not possible to cover the subject of tools fully here. For those who wish to learn more about tools and their use there is a book entitled 'How to Choose and Use Car Tools' available from the publishers of this manual.

Maintenance and minor repair tool kit

The tools given in this list should be considered as a minimum requirement if routine servicing and minor repair operations are to be undertaken. We recommend the purchase of combination wrenches (ring one end, open-ended the other); although more expensive than open-ended ones, they do give the advantages of both types of spanner.

Combination wrenches - 3/8, 7/16, ½, 9/16, 5/8 in AF
Adjustable wrench - 9 inch
Engine sump/gearbox drain plug key
Spark plug wrench (with rubber insert)
Spark plug gap adjustment tool
Set of feeler gauges
Brake adjuster wrench (where applicable)
Brake bleed nipple spanner
Screwdriver - 4 in long x ¼ in dia (plain)
Screwdriver - 4 in long x ¼ in dia (crosshead)
Combination pliers - 6 inch
Hacksaw, junior
Tyre pump
Tyre pressure gauge
Grease gun (where applicable)
Oil can

Fine emery cloth (1 sheet)
Wire brush (small)
Funnel (medium size)

Repair and overhaul tool kit

These tools are virtually essential for anyone undertaking any major repairs to a motor vehicle, and are additional to those given in the basic lists. Included in this list is a comprehensive set of sockets. Although these are expensive they will be found invaluable as they are so versatile - particularly if various drives are included in the set. We recommend the ½ inch square drive type, as this can be used with most proprietary torque wrenches. If you cannot afford a socket set, even bought piecemeal, then inexpensive tubular box wrenches are a useful alternative.

The tools in this list will occasionally need to be supplemented by tools from the Special list.

Sockets (or box wrenches) to cover range ½ to 1 1/8 AF
Reversible ratchet drive (for use with sockets)
Extension piece, 10 inch (for use with sockets)
Universal joint (for use with sockets)
Torque wrench (for use with sockets)
'Mole' wrench - 8 inch
Ball pein hammer
Soft-faced hammer, plastic or rubber
Screwdriver - 6 in long x 5/16 in dia (plain)
Screwdriver - 2 in long x 5/16 dia (plain) Screwdriver - 1½ in long x ¼ in dia (crosshead)
Screwdriver - 3 in long x 1/8 in dia (electricians)
Pliers - electricians side cutters
Pliers - needle nosed
Pliers - circlip (internal and external)
Cold chisel - ½ inch
Scriber (this can be made by grinding the end of a broken hacksaw blade)
Scraper (this can be made by flattening one end of a piece of copper pipe)
Centre punch
Pin punch
Hacksaw
Valve grinding tool
Steel rule/straight edge
Allen keys
Selection of files
Wire brush (large)
Axle stands
Jack (strong scissor or hydraulic type)

Special tools

The tools in this list are those which are not used regularly, are expensive to buy or which need to be used in accordance with their manufacturer's instructions. Unless relatively difficult mechanical jobs are undertaken frequently, it will not be ecconomic to buy

many of these tools. Where this is the case, you could consider clubbing together with friends (or a motorists club) to make a joint purchase, or borrowing the tools against a deposit from a local garage or tool hire specialist.

The following list contains only those tools and instruments freely available to the public, and not those special tools produced by the vehicle manufacturer specifically for its dealer network. You will find occassional references to these manufacturers special tools in the text of this manual. Generally, an alternative method of doing the job without the manufacturer's special tool is given. However, sometimes there is no alternative to using them. Where this is the case and the relevant tool cannot be bought or borrowed you will have to entrust the work to a franchised repair station.

> Valve spring compressor
> Piston ring compressor
> Ball joint separator
> Universal hub/bearing puller
> Impact screwdriver
> Micrometer and/or vernier gauge
> Carburettor flow balancing device (where applicable)
> Dial gauge
> Stroboscopic timing light
> Dwell angle meter/tachometer
> Universal electrical multi-meter
> Cylinder compresssion gauge
> Lifting tackle
> Trolley jack
> Light with extension lead

Buying tools

For practically all tools, a tool factor is the best source since he will have a very comprehensive range compared with the average repair station or accessory store. Having said that, accessory stores often offer excellent quality tools at discount prices, so it pays to shop around.

Remember, you do not have to buy the most expensive items on the shelf, but it is always advisable to steer clear of the very cheap tools. There are plenty of good tools around, at reasonable prices, so ask the proprietor or manager of the shop for advice, before making a purchase.

Care and maintenance of tools

Having purchased a reasonable tool kit, it is necessary to keep the tools in a clean and serviceable condition. After use, always wipe off any dirt, grease and metal particles using a clean, dry cloth, before putting the tools away. Never leave them lying around after they have been used. A simple tool rack on the garage or workshop wall, for items such as screwdrivers and pliers is a good idea. Store all normal spanners and sockets in a metal box. Any measuring instruments, gauges, meters etc must be carefully stored where they cannot be damaged or become rusty.

Take a little care when the tools are used. Hammer heads inevitably become marked and screwdrivers lose the keen edge of their blades from time-to-time. A little timely attention with emery cloth or a file will soon restore items like this to a good serviceable finish.

Working facilities

Not to be forgotten when discussing tools, is the workshop itself, if anything more than routine maintenance is to be carried out, some form of suitable working area becomes essential.

It is appreciated that many an owner mechanic is forced by circumstances to remove an engine or similar item, without the benefit of a garage or workshop. Having done this, any repairs should always be done under the cover of a roof.

Whenever possible, any dismantling should be done on a clean flat workbench or table at a suitable working height.

Any workbench needs a vice; one with a jaw opening of 4 in (100 mm) is suitable for most jobs. As mentioned previously some dry clean storage space is also requried for tools, as well as the lubricants, cleaning fluids, touch up paints and so on which soon become necessary.

Another item which may be required, and which has a much more than general usage is an electric drill with a chuck capacity of at least 5/16 in (8 mm). This together with a good range of twist drills, is virtually essential for fitting accessories such as wing mirrors and reversing lights.

Last, but not least always keep a supply of old newspapers and clean, lint free rags available, and try to keep any working areas as clean as possible.

Spanner jaw gap comparison table

Jaw gap (in)	Spanner size
0.250	1/4 in. AF
0.275	7 mm AF
0.312	5/16 in. AF
0.315	8 mm AF
0.340	11/32 in. AF/1/8 in. Whitworth
0.354	9 mm AF
0.375	3/8 in. AF
0.393	10 mm AF
0.433	11 mm AF
0.437	7/16 in. AF
0.445	3/16 in. Whitworth/1/4in. BSF
0.472	12 mm AF
0.500	1/2 in. AF
0.512	13 mm AF
0.525	1/4in. Whitworth/5/16 in. BSF
0.551	14 mm AF
0.562	9/16 in. AF
0.590	15 mm AF
0.600	5/16 in. Whitworth/3/8 in. BSF
0.625	5/8 in. AF
0.629	16 mm AF
0.669	17 mm AF
0.687	11/16 in. AF
0.708	18 mm AF
0.710	3/8 in. Whitworth/7/16 in. BSF
0.748	19 mm AF
0.750	3/4 in. AF
0.812	13/16 in. AF
0.820	7/16 in. Whitworth/1/2 in. BSF
0.866	22 mm AF
0.875	7/8 in AF
0.920	1/2 in. Whitworth/9/16 in. BSF
0.937	15/16 in AF
0.944	24 mm AF
1.000	1 in. AF
1.010	9/16 in. Whitworth/5/8 in. BSF
1.023	26 mm AF
1.062	1 1/16 in. AF/27 mm AF
1.100	5/8 in. Whitworth/11/16 in. BSF
1.125	1 1/8 in. AF
1.181	30 mm AF
1.200	11/16 in. Whitworth/3/4 in. BSF
1.250	1 1/4 in. AF
1.259	32 mm AF
1.300	3/4 in. Whitworth/7/8 in. BSF
1.312	1 5/16 in. AF
1.390	13/16 in. Whitworth/15/16 in. BSF
1.417	36 mm AF
1.437	1 7/16 in. AF
1.480	7/8 in. Whitworth/1 in. BSF
1.500	1 1/2 in. AF
1.574	40 mm AF/15/16 in. Whitworth
1.614	41 mm AF
1.625	1 5/8 in. AF
1.670	1 in. Whitworth/1 1/8 in. BSF
1.687	1 11/16 in. AF
1.611	46 mm AF
1.812	1 13/16 in. AF
1.860	1 1/8 in. Whitworth/1 1/4 in. BSF
1.875	1 7/8 in. AF
1.968	50 mm AF
2.000	2 in. AF
2.050	1 1/4in. Whitworth/1 3/8 in. BSF
2.165	55 mm AF
2.362	60 mm AF

Routine maintenance

Introduction

1 In the schedule that follows this introduction, the routine servicing that should be carried out on the car is tabulated. This work has two important functions: First: is that of adjusting and lubricating to ensure the least wear and greatest efficiency. Second, is inspection; this function could almost be the more important of the two - for by looking your car over, on top and underneath, you have the opportunity to check that all is in order.

2 Examine the whole car systematically, for obvious faults and other indications of trouble to come. Some faults will be clearly seen such as: leaks (oil and water), rusting. Others, will be less obvious, such as: electrical cables chafing, cracking of the dirt surrounding a nut (indicating that the nut is loose) etc. All must be found and rectified before they bring about failure on the road, or a more expensive repair.

3 The tasks to be done on the car are in general those recommended by the manufacturer. We have also put in some additional ones. For someone having his servicing done at a garage it may be more economical to purchase, and fit, a new or reconditioned component. Your garage proprietor has many things to consider when giving you a quote for any work, eg; labour, costs, availability of his labour force, overheads etc - you may therefore make considerable savings in time and costs provided that you are capable of tackling a job, and are prepared to do it. To leave an obviously developing fault "until the next service" - may prove costly and even disastrous - do it now!

4 When you are checking the car, if something looks wrong, look it up in the appropriate chapter. If something seems to be working badly look in the fault finding section.

5 Always road test after a repair, and inspect the work after it, and check nuts etc for tightness. Check again after about 150 miles (250 kms).

Every 250 miles (400 km), weekly or before a long journey

Check tyre pressures (when cold).
Examine tyres for wear and damage, and check wheel nuts.
Check steering for smooth and accurate operation.
Check brake reservoir fluid level. If this has fallen noticeably, check for fluid leakage.
Check for satisfactory brake operation.
Check operation of all lights.
Check operation of windscreen wipers and washers.
Check that the horn operates.
Check that all instruments and gauges are operating.
Check all mirrors for clarity and crazing.
Check the engine oil level; top-up if necessary.
Check radiator coolant level.
Check battery electrolyte level.
Check wind screen washer reservoir level.

3000 mile (5000 km) or 3 months interval

Carry out daily and weekly service plus:
1 Check water pump drive belt tension and adjust if necessary.

2 Check steering and suspension system for oil leaks.
3 Check steering unit joints for security, backlash and gaiter (oil seal) condition.
4 Visually inspect brake hydraulic pipes and unions for signs of chafing, leaks or corrosion.
5 Check brake pedal travel and handbrake operation. Adjust as necessary.
6 Check operation of horns and windscreen wipers.
7 Check specific gravity of battery electrolyte.
8 Check headlight beam alignment and reset as necessary.
9 Check windscreen wiper blades and renew if worn or perished.
10 Visually inspect clutch hydraulic pipes and unions for signs of chafing, leaks or corrosion, and check reservoir fluid level.
11 Check exhaust system for security and also for leaks.
12 Check condition and security of seats and seat belts.
13 Check brake servo hose for wear or damage.
14 Check fuel system and pipes, including filler, for leaks.

6,000 mile (10,000 km) or 6 months interval

Carry out 3,000 mile (5,000 km) service plus:
1 Drain and renew the engine/transmission oil.
2 Fit a new oil filter element or cartridge.
3 Top up the carburettor piston damper with oil.
4 Check the carburettor settings and adjust as necessary.
5 Carefully examine all cooling system hoses, including the heater hoses, for perishing or leaks. Check and tighten all hose clips.
6 Lubricate accelerator control linkage and pedal fulcrum.
7 Clean and adjust the spark plugs.
8 Check the condition of the contact breaker points. Clean and re-set or renew as necessary.
9 Lubricate distributor.
10 Check and re-set ignition timing using a stroboscopic light.
11 Check clutch return stop clearance and adjust as necessary.
12 Lubricate automatic gearbox exposed selector linkage (where fitted).
13 Check front wheel alignment and adjust as necessary.
14 Lubricate all steering and suspension grease points, but not hubs.
15 Inspect brake pads for wear.
16 Check the condition of the brake discs.
17 Lubricate handbrake cables and linkage.
18 Check the tightness of all battery connections. Clean off any corrosion and smear the terminals with vaseline or petroleum jelly.
19 Lubricate all door locks, bonnet and boot lock, and hinges with a little oil; check that they open and shut correctly. Wipe off any excess.
20 Check the condition of the seat belts. They should have no tears and should not be twisted. If inertia belts are fitted, check that the reels operate smoothly.
21 Check the front seat mountings and runners for security and lightly lubricate the runners.
22 Carry out a quick road test to ensure that everything functions correctly.

12,000 miles (20,000 km) or 12 months interval

Carry out 6,000 mile (10,000 km) service plus:
1   Renew the air cleaner element.
2   Renew the engine breather filter/oil filler cap.
3   Check the valve clearances and adjust as necessary.
4   Renew the spark plugs.
5   Adjust the rear wheel bearing endfloat. (Note that there must be play in the bearings or they will seize up).
6   Inspect the brake pads and linings for wear and the condition of the drums and discs. Clean out any brake lining dust from the drums.
7   Check all HT and LT leads for damage, and secure connections.

36,000 mile (60,000 Km) or 3 years interval

Carry out 12,000 mile service, plus

1   Fit new brake servo filter element.
2   Discuss with BLMC garage about changing all brake hydraulic seals and fluid.

Other aspects of Routine maintenance

1 Wheel nuts

These should be cleaned and lightly smeared with grease as necessary to keep them moving freely. If the nuts are stubborn to undo, due to dirt and overtightening, it may be necessary to prevent the wheel from rotating by lowering the jack, until the wheel rests on the ground. Normally if the wheel brace is used across the hub centre, a foot or knee held against the tyre will prevent the wheel from turning, and so save the wheels and nuts from wear if the nuts are slackened with weight on the wheel. After replacing a wheel make a point of later rechecking the nuts again for tightness.

2 Safety

Whenever working, even partially, under the car, put an extra strong box or piece of timber underneath onto which the car will fall rather than onto you.

3 Cleanliness

Whenever you do any work, allow time for cleaning. When some component is in pieces or parts removed to improve access to other areas, use the opportunity for a thorough clean-up. This cleanliness will allow you to cope with a crisis on the road without getting yourself too dirty. During bigger jobs when you expect a bit of dirt it is less extreme and can be tolerated at least whilst removing a component. When an item is being taken to pieces there is less risk of ruinous grit finding its way inside. The act of cleaning focuses your attention onto parts and you are more likely to spot trouble. Dirt on the ignition system is a common cause of poor starting. Large areas such as the engine compartment inner wings or bulkhead should be brushed thoroughly with a cleansing solvent, allowed to soak and then very carefully hosed down. Water in the wrong places, particularly the carburettor or electrical components, will do more harm than dirt. Use petrol or paraffin and a small paintbrush to clean the more inaccessible places.

4 Waste disposal

Old oil and cleaning paraffin must be destroyed. Although it makes a good base for a bonfire the practice is dangerous. It is also illegal to dispose of oil and paraffin via domestic drains. By buying your new engine oil in one gallon cans you can refill with old oil and take back to the local garage who have facilities for disposal. The garage should be pleased to help as they normally sell their old oil for re-cycling.

5 Long journeys

Before taking your car on long journeys, particularly such trips as Continental holidays make sure that the car is given a full visual inspection well in advance so that any faults found can be rectified in time.

Jacking and towing

Towing

Serious body distortion can result if Allegro models are not jacked up correctly. Always abide by the following information.

Standard car jack

Front: The jack supplied with the car must be placed under the front slinging bracket at either side of the car with the peg on the top face of the jack registered in the outer hole in the slinging bracket and the lugs of the jack head located around the bracket.

Rear: Position the jack under the rear suspension reinforcement channel with the rear face of the jack head butting against the rear tongue of the reinforcement channel and the lugs of the jack head located around the inner and outer faces of the channel. **Do not** use the rear slinging brackets as the jacking points.

Workshop jack

When using a trolley jack the following may be used as jacking points

Front

a) Suspension wishbones at their outer ends.

b   Front longitudinal reinforcements using a shaped block on the jack saddle.

Note Do not use the front slinging bracket as it will be damaged stopping use of the jack supplied with the car.

Rear

Rear reinforcement channel, provided that a wooden block is made to fit inside the channel.

Towing

Towing eyes are provided at the front of the car only (see Fig. 5). They are an integral part of the front suspension tie-bar brackets.

Note: *The eyes at the rear of the car are not for towing. They are designed for lashing the car down only.*

On cars with automatic transmission, the car must only be towed with the front wheels off the ground if the distance involved is more than 20 miles. Due to the construction of the Allegro, this suspension of the front wheels must be by means of a trailer type 'ambulance' and not by a normal suspended tow. Better still, use a full size recovery trailer and lash the car to it using the front towing hooks and rear eyes.

For short distances, however, select Neutral (N) and tow the car slowly. Do not exceed 30 mph (48 kmh). Ensure, before starting off, that the engine oil level is correct.

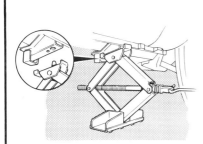

Fig. 1 Use of jack for raising front of car

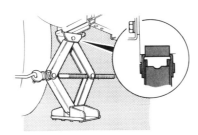

Fig. 2 Use of jack for raising rear of car

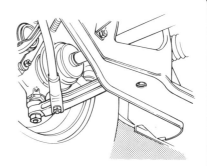

Fig. 3 Jacking point for workshop jack - front (use wooden block between jack and body member)

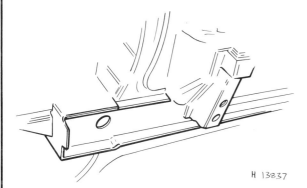

Fig. 4 Jacking point for workshop jack - rear (use wooden block between jack and body member)

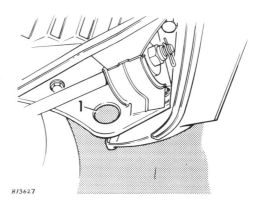

Fig. 5 Front towing eye (1)
The eyes at the rear are for lashing only, not towing

Chapter 1 Engine

For modifications, and information applicable to later models, see Supplement at end of manual

Contents

Specifications

1100 cc Engine (manufacturer's type: 10H)

Type	4 cylinder-in-line
Bore	2.543 in (64.58 mm)
Stroke	3.296 in (83.72 mm)
Cubic capacity	67.0 cu in (1,098 cc)
Compression ratio	8.5 : 1
Oversize bore	Max: 0.020 in (.508 mm)
	Min: 0.010 in (.254 mm)
Brake mean effective pressure	135 lb/sq in at 2,500 rpm
Maximum torque	60 lb/f. ft at 2,450 rpm
Firing order	1 3 4 2
Location of No 1 cylinder	Water pump end

Camshaft and camshaft bearings:

The camshaft is driven from the crankshaft by a single roller chain. The camshaft is supported by three renewable white metal lined shell bearings pressed into, and reamed in position in the block.

Camshaft bearing clearance	0.001 to 0.002 in (0.0254 to 0.0508 mm)
Inside bearing diameter reamed when fitted:	
Front bearing	1.667 to 1.6675 in. (42.342 to 42.355 mm)
Centre bearing	1.6242 to 1.6247 in. (41.256 to 41.269 mm)
Rear bearing	1.3745 to 1.3750 in. (34.912 to 34.925 mm)
End float	0.003 to 0.007 in. (0.076 to 0.178 mm)
Journal diameters: Front	1.6655 to 1.666 in. (42.304 to 42.316 mm)
Centre	1.62275 to 1.62325 in. (41.218 to 41.231 mm)
Rear	1.3725 to 1.3735 in. (34.862 to 34.887 mm)
Clearance	0.0001 to 0.002 in. (o.025 to 0.051 mm)

Connecting rods and big-end bearings:

Length between centres	5.75 in. (14.605 cm)
Big-end bearings	Steel-backed, lead indium lined
Side clearance	0.008 to 0.012 in. (0.203 to 0.305 mm)
Bearing internal diameter clearance	0.001 to 0.0025 in. (0.025 to 0.063 mm)

Crankshaft and main bearings:

Main journal diameter	1.7505 to 1.7510 in. (44.46 to 44.47 mm)
Minimum main journal regrind diameter	1.7105 in. (43.45 mm)
Crankpin journal diameter	1.6254 to 1.6259 in. (41.28 to 41.30 mm)
Minimum crankpin regrind diameter	1.5854 in. (40.27 mm)
Main bearings	White metal, steel backed liners, 3 shelf type
End float	0.002 to 0.003 in. (0.051 to 0.076 mm)
Side thrust	Taken by thrust washers located on either side of centre main bearing
Undersizes available	−0.010 in. (−0.254 mm), −0.020 in. (−0.508 mm) −0.030 in. (−0.762 mm), −0.040 in. (−1.02 mm)

Cylinder block

Type	Cylinder cast integral with top half of crankcase
Water jackets	Full length

Cylinder head:

Type	Cast iron with vertical valves. Siamised inlet ports, 2
Combustion chamber capacity with valves fitted	24.5 cc

Gudgeon pins

Type	Fully floating
Fit to piston	Hand push fit − 0.0001 to 0.00035 in. (0.0025 to 0.009 mm)
Fit in connecting rod	Hand push fit − 0.0001 to 0.0006 in. (0.0025 to 0.015 mm)
Diameter (outer)	.6244 to .6246 in. (15.86 to 15.865 mm)

Lubrication system:

Type	Pressure feed. Pressure fed bearings: Main, camshaft and connecting rods. Reduced pressure to rocker shaft. Piston pin and cylinder wall lubrication - splash
Oil filter	Full flow
Crankcase ventilation	Air filter integral with oil filler cap
Manual transmission/sump capacity (including filter) ...	8.5 pints (4.83 litres)
Oil pump: Type	Eccentric rotor or vane
Oil pump relief pressure	60 lbs/sq in.
Oil pressure: Normal	30 to 60 lbs/sq in.
Idling	15 to 25 lbs/sq in.
Relief valve spring: Free length	2.859 in. (72.63 mm)
Fitted length	2.156 in. (54.77 mm)

Pistons:

Type	Solid skirt, anodised aluminium alloy 3 compression rings, 1 oil control ring
Clearance of piston: Top of skirt	0.0021 to 0.0037 in. (0.053 to 0.094 mm)
Bottom of skirt	0.0005 to 0.0011 in. (0.013 to 0.028 mm)
Pistons oversizes available	+0.010 in. (+0.254 mm) +0.020 in. (+0.508 mm)

Piston rings:

Top compresssion ring	Plain
2nd and 3rd compression ring	Tapered
Fitted gap:	0.007 to 0.012 in. (0.178 to 0.30 mm)
Groove clearance	0.0015 to 0.0035 in. (0.038 to 0.089 mm)
Oil control ring	Slotted scraper
Clearance in groove	0.0015 to 0.0035 in. (0.038 to 0.089 mm)

Tappets (Cam followers)

Type	Bucket
Length	1.505 in. (38.23 mm)
Diameter	0.8120 in. (20.62 mm)

Valves:

Head diameter: Inlet	1.151 to 1.156 in. (29.23 to 29.36 mm)
Exhaust	1.000 to 1.005 in. (25.40 to 25.53 mm)
Later twin carburettor engines: Inlet	1.213 to 1.218 in. (30.81 to 30.94 mm)
Valve lift	0.312 in. (7.925 mm)
Seat angle	Inlet and Exhaust: 45º
Valve clearance	0.012 in. (0.305 mm)
Stem diameter: Inlet	0.2793 to 0.2798 in. (7.094 to 7.107 mm)
Exhaust	0.2788 to 0.2793 in. (7.081 to 7.094 mm)
Valve stem to guide clearance: Inlet	0.0015 to 0.0025 in. (0.038 to 0.063 mm)
Exhaust	0.002 to 0.003 in. (0.051 to 0.076 mm)
Valve rocker bush bore (reamed)	0.5630 to 0.5635 in. (14.30 to 14.31 mm)

Valve guides:

Length: Inlet and Exhaust	1.531 in. (38.89 mm)
Diameter: Inlet and exhaust: Outside	0.4695 to 0.470 in. (11.92 to 11.94 mm)
Inside	0.2813 to 0.2818 in. (7.145 to 7.177 mm)
Fitted height above head	19/32 in. (15.1 mm)

Valve timing

Inlet valve: opens 5º BTDC	Exhaust valve: opens 51º BBDC
closes 45º ABDC	closes 21º ATDC
Valve timing marks	Dimples on crankshaft and camshaft sprockets, Marks on flywheel
Chain pitch and No. of pitches	3/8 in. (9.52 mm) 52 pitches
Valve rocker clearance: timing	0.029 in. (0.74 mm)

Valve springs:

Type	Single valve springs
No. of coils	4½
Free length: Inlet and Exhaust	1.750 in. (44.45 mm)
Valve spring pressure with valves open	85 lb
Valve spring pressure with valves closed	52.5 lb

1300 cc Engine (manufacturer's type: 12H)

The engine specification is identical to the 1100 cc unit except for the differences listed below.

Bore	2.78 in. (70.61 mm)
Stroke	3.2 in. (81.28 mm)
Cubic capacity	77.8 cu in. (1274.86 cc)
Compression ratio	8.8 : 1
Brake mean effective pressure	134 lb/sq in. (9.4 kg/cm^2) at 3,500 rpm
Maximum torque	69.5 lb f. ft at 3,500 rpm

Crankshaft and main bearings :

Main journal diameter	2.0005 to 2.0010 in. (50.81 to 50.82 mm)
Crankpin journal diameter	1.7504 to 1.7509 in. (44.45 to 44.47 mm)
Undersizes available	0.020 in. (0.51 mm) − 0.040 in. (1.02 mm)

Gudgeon pin:

Fit in connecting rod	0.0008 to 0.0015 in. (0.02 to 0.04 mm) interference
Diameter (outer)	0.8123 to 0.8125 in. (20.63 to 20.64 mm)

Lubrication system:

Oil pump relief pressure	50 lb/sq. in. (5.3 kg/cm^2)
Automatic transmission/sump capacity (including filter) ...	9 pints (5.1 litres)

Pistons:

Type		Solid skirt, aluminium, dished crown
Clearance of piston:	Top of skirt	0.0029 to 0.0037 in. (0.07 to 0.09 mm)
	Bottom of skirt	0.0015 to 0.0021 in. (0.04 to 0.05 mm)

Piston rings:

Top compression ring	Internally chamfered chrome
2nd and 3rd compression rings	Tapered cast iron
Fitted gap: Top ring	0.011 to 0.016 in. (0.28 to 0.50 mm)
2nd and 3rd rings	0.008 to 0.013 in. (0.20 to 0.33 mm)
Oil control ring	Duraflex 61
Fitted gap - rails and side spring	0.012 to 0.028 in. (0.30 to 0.70 mm)

Valves:

Head diameter:	Inlet	1.307 to 1.312 in. (33.2 to 33.21 mm)
	Exhaust	1.1515 to 1.565 in. (29.24 to 29.37 mm)
Valve stem to guide clearance:	Inlet and Exhaust ...	0.0015 to 0.0025 in. (0.04 to 0.08 mm)
Valve lift		0.318 in. (8.07 mm)

Valve guides:

Length:	Inlet	1.6875 in. (42.87 mm)
	Exhaust ,..	1.8437 in. (46.83 mm)
Fitted height above head		0.540 in. (13.72 mm)

Valve springs:

Free length	1.95 in. (49,13 mm)
Fitted length	1.383 in. (34.175 mm)
Load at fitted length	79.5 lb (36.03 kg)
Load at top of lift	124 lb (56.3 kg)

Valve timing:

Valve rocker clearance	0.012 in (0.31 mm)

Torque wrench settings:

	lb f. ft	kg fm
Cylinder head stud nuts	50	6.91
Connecting rod big-end bolts	37	5.11
Main bearing bolts	63	8.70
Flywheel centre-bolt	113	15.61
Rocker bracket nuts	24	3.32
Cylinder side cover bolt	4	0.55
Timing cover - ¼ in. UNF bolt	6	0.83
5/16 in. UNF bolt	12	1.66
Water pump bolts	16	2.21
Water outlet elbow nuts	8	1.10
Oil filter centre bolt	14	1.94
Oil filter head nuts	14	1.94
Oil pump bolts	8	1.10
Manifold to cylinder head nuts	14	1.94
Rocker cover nuts	4	0.55
Crankshaft pulley nut	75	10.37
Sump drain plug	25	3.46
Flywheel housing bolts and stud nuts	18	2.5

1 General description

The engine is a four cylinder overhead valve type and is mounted on the transmission unit.

Two valves per cylinder are mounted vertically in the cast iron cylinder head and run in pressed-in valve guides. They are operated by rocker arms and pushrods from the camshaft which is located at the base of the cylinder bores in the left hand side of the engine (viewed from the clutch end).

The cylinder head has all five inlet and exhaust ports on the left-hand side. Cylinders 1 and 2 share a siamised inlet port and also cylinders 3 and 4. Cylinders 1 and 4 have individual exhaust ports and cylinders 2 and 3 share a siamised exhaust port.

The cylinder block and the upper half of the crankcase are cast together. The bottom half of the crankcase consists of a combined tranmission casing and oil sump.

The pistons are made from anodised aluminium alloy and unlike some other 'A' series engines all models have solid skirts. Three compression rings and an oil control ring are fitted on all models.

The gudgeon pin on 1100 models is retained by circlips in the piston whereas on 1300 models it is a press fit.

At the front of the engine a single or double row chain drives the camshaft via the camshaft and crankshaft chain wheels.

The camshaft is supported by three steel-backed white metal bearings. If these are replaced it is necessary to ream the bearings in position.

The overhead valves are operated by means of rocker arms mounted on the rocker shaft running along the top of the cylinder head. The rocker arms are activated by pushrods and tappets which in turn rise and fall in accordance with the cams on the camshaft. The valves are held closed by small powerful springs.

The statically and dynamically balanced forged steel crankshaft is supported by three renewable main bearings. Crankshaft end float is controlled by four semi-circular thrust washers, two of which are located on either side of the centre main bearing.

The centrifugal water pump is driven together with the alternator, from the crankshaft pulley wheel by a rubber/fabric belt. The distributor is mounted towards the rear of the right hand side of the cylinder block and advances and retards the ignition timing by mechanical and vacuum means. The distributor is driven at half crankshaft speed by a short shaft and skew gear from the skew gear on the camshaft. The oil pump is driven from the rear of the camshaft.

2 Major operations with engine in place

Not very many major operations can be carried out on the engine with it in situ because it is not possible to drop the sump as can be done with most cars. The following operations are possible however:
1 Removal and replacement of the cylinder head assembly.
2 Removal and replacement of the timing chain and gears.
3 Removal and replacement of the clutch/flywheel.
4 Removal and replacement of the engine mountings.

3 Major operations necessitating engine removal

The following major operations can be carried out with the engine out of the body frame and on the bench or floor:
1 Removal and replacement of the main bearings.
2 Removal and replacement of the crankshaft.
3 Removal and replacement of the oil pump.
4 Removal and replacement of the big end bearings.
5 Removal and replacement of the pistons and connecting rods.
6 Removal and replacement of the camshaft.

4 Engine and manual gearbox assembly - removal

1 The combined engine and manual gearbox unit may be removed by one person using an overhead hoist but, the services of a second person will certainly make the task easier.
2 Open the bonnet and mark the outline of the hinges relative to the bonnet. Undo and remove the securing nuts, bolts and washers (photo). (Assistance will be necessary to support the bonnet).
3 With the help of a second person lift away the bonnet and put it in a safe place. (photo)
4 Refer to Chapter 3 and remove the air cleaner assembly. (photo)
5 Refer to Chapter 2 and completely drain the cooling system. Do not forget to remove the filler plug from the top of the thermostat housing. (photo)
6 Refer to Chapter 2 and remove the radiator and fan motor assembly. (photo)
7 Undo the terminal securing screws and detach the terminals from the battery. (photo)
8 Release the battery clamp bar securing nuts; lift away the clamp bar.
9 Carefully remove the battery ensuring it is kept vertical. (photo)
10 Undo and remove the screws securing the expansion chamber to the battery support. (photo)
11 Move the expansion chamber and hang over the engine compartment crossmember.
12 Undo and remove the bolts and washers securing the battery support to the inner wing panel. Detach the horn cables and lift away. (photo)
13 Slacken the top hose to water outlet hose clip and detach the hose. (photo)
14 Slacken the clip securing the bottom hose to water inlet connection on the water pump and detach the hose. (photo).
15 Slacken the heater hose connection clip on the bulkhead and detach the hose. (photo).
16 Slacken the clip securing the bottom hose to the radiator cross tube and remove the bottom hose. (photo)
17 Release the clip and detach the fuel inlet hose from the fuel pump. (photo)
18 Make a note of the carburettor control cable connections and detach from the carburettor. Further information will be found in Chapter 3. (photo)
19 Slacken the clip and detach the hose from the metal pipe located beside the master cylinders. (photo)
20 Disconnect the clutch release lever return spring. Note which way round it is fitted. (photo)
21 Undo and remove the two bolts and spring washers securing the clutch slave cylinder to the flywheel housing. Move the slave cylinder to one side having carefully detached from the pushrod. (photo)
22 Release the clip and detach the terminal connector from the rear of the alternator. (photo)
23 Detach the terminal connector from the thermal transmitter located just above the alternator. (photo)
24 Detach the ignition cable terminal connector located at the rear of the alternator. (photo).
25 Make a note of the terminal connections on the ignition coil and detach. Move the cable out of the way. (photo)
26 Detach the twin cable connection from the starter relay switch. (photo)
27 Detach the terminal connector from the oil pressure switch located to the left of the distributor. Move the cable out of the way. (photo).
28 Undo and remove the nuts and spring washers securing the tie-rod to the body. (photo)
29 Undo and remove the nut bolt and washer securing the tie-rod to the engine mounted bracket. (photo)

4.2 Bonnet to hinge securing nuts, bolts and washers

4.3 Lifting away bonnet

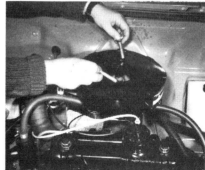

4.4 Removal of air cleaner

4.5 Cooling system filler plug

4.6 Fan and motor assembly removal

4.7 Disconnecting battery terminals

4.9 Lifting away battery

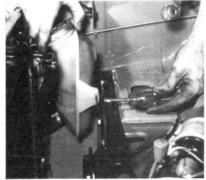
4.10 Expansion chamber removal

4.12 Battery support removal

4.13 Top hose removal

4.14 Bottom hose removal from pump

4.15 Heater hose removal

4.16 Lifting away bottom hose

4.17 Removal of inlet hose from fuel pump

4.18 Carburettor controls

4.19 Hose removal

4.20 Clutch release lever return spring removal

4.21 Clutch slave cylinder removal

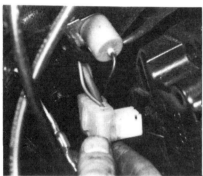

4.22 Terminal connector removal from rear of alternator

4.23 Terminal connector removal from thermal transmitter

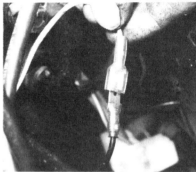

4.24 Ignition cable terminal connector

4.25 Low tension cable connections to ignition coil

4.26 Starter relay switch

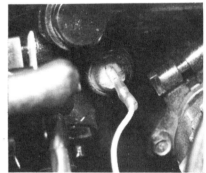

4.27 Oil pressure switch terminal connector

4.28 Tie-rod to body mounting

4.29 Tie-rod to engine mounting

4.31 Engine left hand mounting

30 Using an overhead hoist and chains or strong rope support the weight of the engine and transmission assembly.
31 Undo and remove the left-hand mounting to body securing nuts and bolts. Also remove the two mounting to adaptor through bolts, nuts and spring washer. Leave the bolts in position until later (paragraph 40). (photo)
32 If not already done, remove the drain plug and drain the oil into a suitable sized container. (photo)

33 This photo (4.33) shows how much metallic swarf can be trapped by the special magnetic drain plug.
34 Unscrew the speedometer drive connection at the transmission unit. (photo)
35 This photo shows the underside of the remote gear change lever. The two rods are disconnected at the transmission unit end. (photos) Note the exhaust downpipe clamp bracket has been detached.

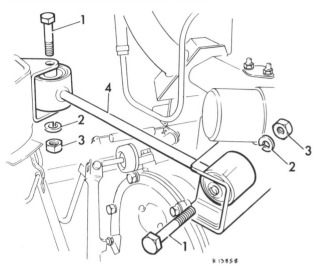
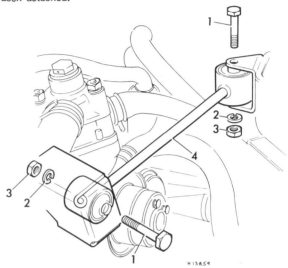

Fig. 1.1. Right-hand tie-rod

1 Bolt   3 Nut
2 Spring washer   4 Tie-rod

Fig. 1.2. Left-hand tie-rod

1 Bolt   3 Nut
2 Spring washer   4 Tie-rod

4.32 Draining oil from transmission unit

4.33 Efficient function of magnetic drain plug

4.34 Speedometer cable connection at transmission unit

4.35a Gear change lever remote control

4.35b Remote gearchange selector rods

4.36 Exhaust manifold to downpipe clamp

4.37 Detaching upper selector rod

4.38 Lifting away spring pin

4.39 Earth lead attached to transmission unit

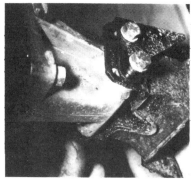

4.40a Removal of left-hand mounting through bolts

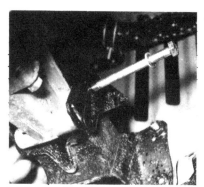

4.40b Note the plain washer

4.41 Detaching right-hand engine mounting

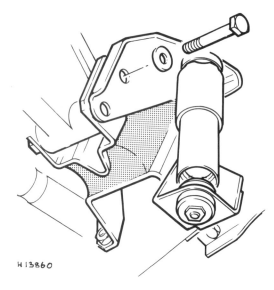

H13860

Fig. 1.3. Later type left-hand engine mounting

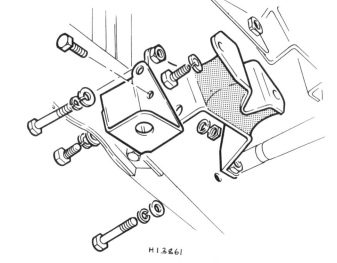

H13861

Fig. 1.4. Later type right-hand engine mounting

36 Undo and remove the two exhaust manifold to downpipe clamp nuts, bolts and washers and lift away the clamp. (photo)

37 Undo and remove the nut and bolt securing the upper selector rod yoke to the transmission unit. (photo)

38 Using a parallel pin punch carefully remove the spring pin securing the lower selector rod from the collar. Tie the two rods out of the way. (photo)

39 Undo and remove the bolt and washer securing the earth lead to the transmission unit. (photo)

40 Remove the two through bolts from the left-hand engine mounting (photo). Note that on later models a damper type engine mounting is used (Fig. 1.3).

41 Undo and remove the right-hand mounting securing bolts and washers (photo). Note that on some later models two nuts and bolts must be removed to release the damper mounting bracket from the engine mounting (Fig. 1.4).

42 The left-hand mounting may now be eased out of its position. (photo)

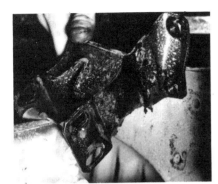

4.42 Lifting away left-hand engine mounting

4.43. Lifting away right-hand engine mounting

4.44 Releasing drive shaft from differential

4.45 Detaching drive shaft

4.46 Nylon water/dust deflector on end of drive shaft

4.47 Location of spring clip

4.48a Commencing engine removal

4.48b Make sure all cables and controls are out of the way

4.48c The underside of the transmission must clear the front cross panel

43 Lift away the right-hand mounting. (photo)
44 The drive shafts must now be released from the differential. For full information refer to Chapter 7. (photo)
45 Check that all cables, hoses and controls have been detached from the engine/transmission unit and then raise by a few inches. The left-hand drive shaft may now be detached from the differential. Note on this photo the rubber boot clip is missing. This should be in position.
46 The right-hand drive shaft may now be detached. Note the water/dust deflector. (photo)
47 This photo shows the spring clip that locks the drive shaft in position. It is this clip that has to be compressed before the drive shaft can be detached from the differential.
48 The engine/transmission unit may now be lifted from the engine compartment. Take care that no cable or pipe becomes caught. Push the car rearwards or draw the hoist forwards and

lower the unit to the ground. (photos)
49 Check that the engine compartment and floor area around the car are clear of loose nuts, bolts and tools.

5 Engine and automatic transmission assembly - removal

The sequence for removal of the complete engine and automatic transmission unit is basically identical to that for the manual type transmission as described in Section 4. The major difference will be the disconnection of the selector cable from the transmission unit. Full information will be found in Chapter 6. Do not forget that the cable must be adjusted once it has been reconnected.

6 Separating the engine from manual transmission - flywheel removal

Before the engine can be stripped right down it is essential to separate the transmission casing from the cylinder block. Until this is done it is not possible to remove the pistons, connecting rods, or crankshaft. Before the transmission casing/sump can be removed it is necessary to take off the clutch, flywheel, and flywheel housing. The clutch and flywheel are best removed together because of their unusual construction.

1 Remove the clutch cover, as described in Chapter 5.
2 Remove the clutch thrust plate by undoing the three nuts which hold it to the spring pressure plate.
3 Before removing the flywheel it is most important to turn the crankshaft so that the slots in the crankshaft end and in the flywheel are horizontal. If this is not done, the C-washer which holds the primary gear in place may fall out resulting in damage or an inability to remove the flywheel and clutch assembly.
4 The flywheel is held in position on the tapered end of the crankshaft by a single centre retaining bolt which will have been tightened to a torque of 113 lb f ft (15.61 kg fm). Knock back the tab on the lock washer, and if a spanner large enough to undo the retaining bolt is not available, then chisel it round three or four times using a suitable cold chisel on the ends of the flats.
5 To pull the flywheel off the taper on the end of the crankshaft, will involve the use of a special puller. This is BLMC service tool "18G 304" which is used with adaptor "18G 304N". It is hardly worth while making up this tool as it involves drilling and cutting steel at least ½ in. thick. It is far better to borrow this tool from your local BLMC garage.
6 To operate the puller, screw the three studs into the three tapped holes in the flywheel. Place the puller plate over the

studs and then screw the nuts onto the studs keeping the plate parallel with the flywheel. Screw in the short centre screw and tighten till the flywheel breaks free from the crankshaft. If it proves very difficult to break the flywheel from the taper, tap the centre bolt with a hammer while the bolt is tightened down hard. This will jar the flywheel loose.
7 As soon as the taper has been broken, remove the puller tool, unscrew the retaining bolt and take off the flywheel.

7 Separating the engine from the transmission - flywheel housing removal

With the flywheel and clutch removed the flywheel housing (which is effectively the engine end plate) can be separated from the transmission casing/engine as follows:
1 Knock back the tabs on the lock washers inside the housing.
2 Undo and remove the nine nuts from tne studs on the transmission casing.
3 Undo and remove the six bolts from the cylinder block. Note the positions from which the shorter bolts are removed.

8 Separating the engine from transmission

Before the engine can be stripped right down it is essential to separate the transmission unit from the cylinder block. Until this is done it is not possible to remove the pistons, connecting rods or crankshaft.

Manual transmission
1 Refer to Sections 6 and 7, and remove the flywheel and clutch assembly and also the flywheel housing.
2 Undo and remove the nuts, bolts and washers that secure

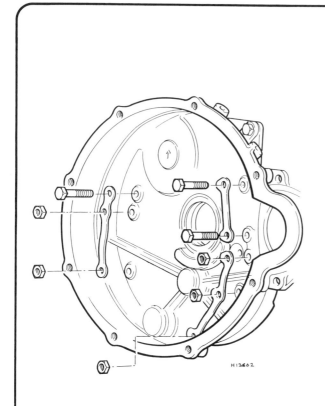

Fig. 1.5. Flywheel housing attachments

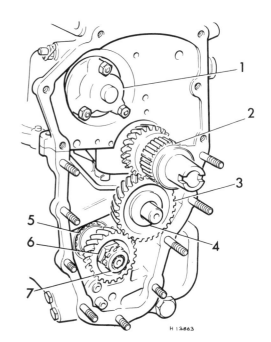

Fig. 1.6. End view of tne transfer gears with the clutch flywheel and housing removed

1 Oil pump	5 First motion shaft bearing
2 Crankshaft primary gear	6 First motion shaft gear-wheel
3 Idler or transfer gear	
4 Thrust washer	7 Roller bearing

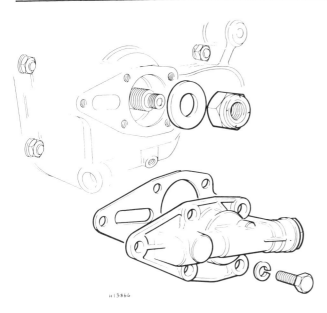

H13864

Fig. 1.7. Pressure valve assembly

the transmission unit to the underside of the cylinder block.

3 The engine may now be lifted from the transmission unit.

4 The housing can now be carefully pulled off. The flywheel housing oil seal should always be renewed when the housing is removed. If for any reason this is not possible, then wrap adhesive tape round the primary gear splines before pulling off the housing, so that the splines do not damage the oil seal.

Automatic transmission

1 Refer to Section 24, and remove the oil filter.

2 Refer to Chapter 10, and remove the starter motor.

3 Undo and remove the nuts, bolts and washers that secure the converter end cover. Lift away the end cover.

4 Using a chisel knock back the lock washer on the converter retaining bolt.

5 A special tool (part number 18G 587) is now required to undo and remove the converter retaining bolt. Alternatively a large socket may be used. It will be necessary to hold the converter whilst the bolt is being undone.

6 Remove the key plate that locates the converter relative to the crankshaft.

7 Carefully turn the converter until the end slot is horizontal.

8 Knock back the locking tabs and remove three equally spaced setscrews from the centre of the torque converter. It is important not to remove all six setscrews at one time.

9 Another special tool is required (part number 18G 1086) to draw the converter from the end of the crankshaft. If it is not available a very sturdy flange puller can be used.

10 Locate the plug adaptor of the tool into the end of the crankshaft. Screw the tool onto the converter and hold the converter firmly. Screw in the centre bolt to release the converter from the crankshaft taper.

11 The converter may now be lifted away. Take care as it will contain some oil.

12 Remove the low pressure valve retaining screws and detach the valve.

13 Hold the converter output gear and remove the input gear self locking nut and washer.

14 Undo and remove the two setscrews that secure the bell crank lever to the converter housing.

15 Remove the rubber grommet from the converter housing.

16 Undo and remove the setscrews, nuts and spring washers securing the converter housing to the engine.

17 Wrap some tape over the converter output gear and then withdraw the converter housing.

18 Disconnect the external engine oil feed pipe from the adaptor on the gearbox casing.

19 Carefully lever the main oil feed pipe from the oil pump and gearbox casing.

20 Undo and remove the nuts and setscrews that secure the two major units together.

21 The engine may now be lifted from the transmission unit.

9 Dismantling the engine - general

1 It is obviously best to mount the engine on a dismantling stand, but as this is not likely to be available, stand the engine on a strong bench to be at a comfortable working height. It can be dismantled on the floor but this is not desirable.

2 During the dismantling process take great care to keep the exposed parts free from dirt. Firstly, thoroughly clean down the outside of the engine, removing all traces of oil and congealed dirt. Use paraffin or cleansing solvent. The latter will make the job much easier for, after the solvent has been applied and allowed to stand for a time, water can be used to wash off the solvent with all the dirt. If the dirt is thick and deeply embedded, work the solvent into it with a wire brush. Finally, wipe down the exterior of the engine with a rag and only then, when it is quite clean, should the dismantling process begin. As the engine is stripped, clean each part in a bath of paraffin or petrol.

3 Never immerse parts with oilways in paraffin (for example, the crankshaft). To clean them, wipe down carefully with a petrol dampened cloth. Oilways can be cleaned with nylon pipe cleaners. If an airline is available, all parts can be blown dry and the oilways blown through as an added precaution.

4 Re-use of old engine gaskets is false economy and will lead to oil and water leaks, if nothing worse. Always use new gaskets throughout. However, do not throw the old gaskets away, for it may happen that an immediate replacement cannot be found and the old gasket is then very useful as a template. Hang up the old gaskets as they are removed, on a suitable hook.

5 To strip the engine it is best to work from the top down. The underside of the crankcase when supported on wood blocks acts as a firm base. When the stage where the crankshaft and connecting rods have to be removed, is reached, the engine can be turned on its side and all other work carried out with it in this position.

6 Wherever possible, replace nuts, bolts and washers finger tight from wherever they were removed. This helps avoid loss and muddle later. If they cannot be replaced lay them out in such a fashion that it is clear from whence they came.

Reference should be made to the photographs on page 43 to 49 covering engine dismantling and re-assembly.

10 Ancillary engine components - removal

Before basic engine dismantling begins it is necessary to strip it of ancillary components as follows:

Alternator
Distributor
Thermostat
Oil filter cartridge
Inlet/exhaust manifold and carburettor
Mechanical fuel pump

It is possible to strip all these items with the engine in the car if it is merely the individual items that require attention. Presuming the engine to be out of the car and on the bench, and that the item mentioned is still on the engine, follow this procedure:

1 Slacken off the dynamo/alternator retaining bolts and remove the unit with its adjustment link.

2 To remove the distributor first disconnect the vacuum advance/retard pipe from the side of the distributor. Undo and

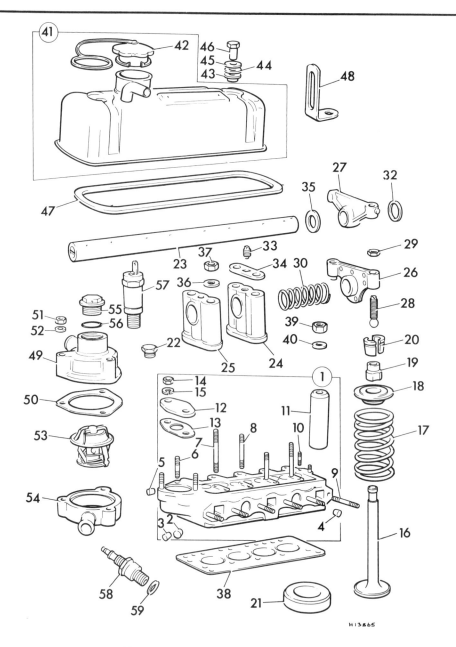

Fig. 1.8. Exploded view of the cylinder head

1 Cylinder head assembly
2 Oil hole plug
3 Water hole plug
4 Water and dowel hole plug
5 Cleaning hole plug
6 Water outlet elbow stud
7 Rocker bracket stud - long
8 Rocker bracket stud - short
9 Inlet and exhaust manifold stud
10 Cover plate or heater tap boss stud
11 Valve guide
12 Plate
13 Gasket
14 Nut
15 Washer
16 Valve
17 Valve spring
18 Valve spring cup
19 Inlet valve oil seal

20 Valve cotter
21 Valve seat insert
22 Cylinder head blanking plug
23 Rocker shaft
24 Rocker shaft bracket - tapped
25 Rocker shaft bracket - oil hole
26 Rocker arm - pressed steel
27 Rocker arm - forged
28 Tappet adjusting screw
29 Locknut
30 Spring
32 Distance piece
33 Locating screw
34 Plate
35 Washer
36 Washer
37 Nut
38 Cylinder head gasket
39 Cylinder head nut
40 Washer

41 Rocker cover assembly
42 Oil filler cap
43 Rubber bush
44 Washer
45 Distance piece
46 Nut
47 Rocker cover gasket
48 Bracket
49 Water outlet elbow
50 Gasket
51 Nut
52 Washer
53 Thermostat
54 Sandwich plate
55 Plug
56 O - ring
57 Water temperature sender unit
58 Spark plug
59 Spark plug washer

remove the two screws with spring and plain washers that secure the distributor clamp flange to the cylinder block and lift away the distributor and clamp flange.
3 Remove the thermostat cover by undoing and removing the three nuts and spring washers which hold it in position. Lift away the cover and gasket, followed by the thermostat itself.
4 Remove the oil filter cartridge by simply unscrewing it from the housing on the side of the cylinder block.
5 Undo and remove the six nuts and washers that secure the inlet/exhaust manifold assembly to the side of the cylinder head. If the carburettor is still mounted on the inlet manifold release it from the petrol feed pipe from the pump. Lift off the manifold assembly and recover the gasket.
6 Remove the mechanical fuel pump by unscrewing the two retaining nuts and spring washers which hold it to the block. Release it from the petrol feed pipe to the carburettor float chamber and lift away.
   The engine is now stripped of all ancillary components and is ready for major dismantling to begin.

11 Cylinder head removal - engine in car

1 Drain the cooling system as described in Chapter 2.
2 Detach the distributor vacuum pipe from the carburettor.
3 Undo and remove the two rocker cover securing bolts, lifting brackets and washers and lift away the rocker cover and its gasket.
4 Disconnect the top water hose and the heater hose from the water outlet pipe and thermostat housing.
5 Undo and remove the three nuts and spring washers securing the thermostat cover to the top of the cylinder head. Lift the cover from the three studs and recover the gasket. The thermostat may now be lifted out from its location.
6 Detach the thermal transmitter cable from the unit on the side of the cylinder head.
7 Slacken the hose clips and remove the breather hose and fuel hose from the carburettor. Then undo and remove the two nuts and spring washers securing the carburettor to the inlet manifold. Lift the carburettor from the studs and recover the metal heat shield.
8 Undo and remove the one manifold nut that secures the metal heater pipe support bracket. Slacken the hose clips on

either end of the metal heater pipe and detach the hoses. Lift away the metal heater pipe. Recover the one manifold washer from the stud. Undo and remove the two nuts securing the exhaust manifold to downpipe clamp. Part and lift away the two halves of the clamp. Undo and remove the remaining nuts and washers securing the manifold assembly to the side of the cylinder head. Lift away the manifold assembly and recover the gasket.
9 Slacken the heater hose clip on the union at the rear of the cylinder head. Pull the hose off the union.
10 Mark the spark plug HT leads to ensure correct refitting and detach the leads from the spark plugs. Spring back the distributor cap spring clips and lift off the distributor cap. Place to one side of the engine compartment.
11 Slacken the eight nuts securing the rocker shaft pedestals to the cylinder head in a progressive manner. Remove the eight nuts and washers.
12 Slacken the remaining cylinder head nuts using the reverse order of the tightening sequence shown in Fig. 1.9.
13 Recover the locking tab from No. 2 rocker shaft bracket.
14 Lift the rocker shaft from the top of the cylinder head.
15 Remove the pushrods, keeping them in the order in which they were removed. The easiest way to do this is to push them through a sheet of thin card in the correct sequence.
16 The cylinder head can now be removed by lifting upwards. If the head is jammed, try to rock it to break the seal. Under no circumstances try to prise it apart from the block with a screwdriver or cold chisel as damage will be done to the faces of the head or block. If the head will not readily free, turn the engine over using the starter motor as the compression in the cylinders will often break the cylinder head joint. If this fails to work, strike the head sharply with a plastic headed or wooden hammer, or with a metal hammer onto a piece of wood on the head. Under no circumstances hit the head directly with a metal hammer as this may cause the iron casting to fracture. Several sharp taps with a hammer at the same time pulling upwards, should free the head. Lift the head off and place on one side.

12 Cylinder head removal - engine on bench

   The sequence for removal of the cylinder head with the

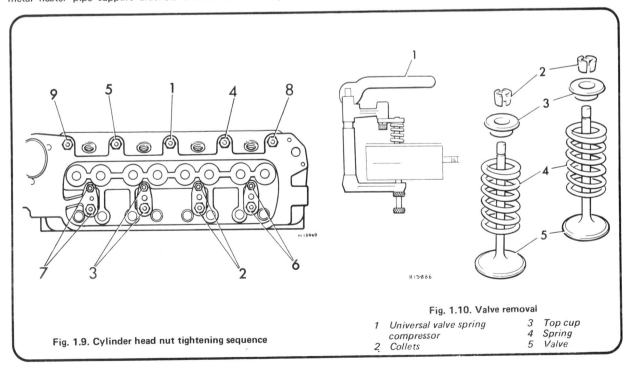

Fig. 1.9. Cylinder head nut tightening sequence

Fig. 1.10. Valve removal

1 Universal valve spring compressor
2 Collets
3 Top cup
4 Spring
5 Valve

engine on the bench is basically identical to the later operations for removal with the engine in the car. Refer to Section 11 and follow the instructions given in paragraphs 2 to 5, 7 to 10, 12, and 14 to 16.

13 Valve removal

1 The valves are easily removed from the cylinder head. Compress each spring in turn with a valve spring compressor until the two halves of the collets can be removed. Release the compressor and lift away the two collets, spring top cups, the spring oil seal (inlet valves only) and the valve (Fig. 1.10).
2 If, when the valve spring compressor is screwed down, the valve spring top cup refuses to free and expose the split collet, do not continue to screw down on the compressor as there is a likelihood of damaging it. Gently tap the top of the tool directly over the cup with a light hammer. This should free the cup. To avoid the compressor jumping off the valve retaining cap when it is tapped, hold the compressor firmly in position with one hand.
3 It is essential that the valves are kept in their correct sequence unless they are so badly worn that they are to be renewed. If they are going to be re-used, place them in a sheet of card having eight holes numbered 1 to 8 corresponding with the relative positions. Also keep the valve springs, cups etc. in this same order.

14 Valve guide - removal

Valve guide removal is a simple task but it is not recommended that you should do this because their replacement is too difficult to do accurately. Leave their removal and insertion to a specialist engineering shop.

15 Rocker assembly - dismantling

1 To dismantle the rocker assembly, release the rocker shaft locating screw, remove the split pins, flat and spring washers from each end of the shaft and slide from the shaft the shims, pedestals, rocker arms and rocker spacing springs.
2 From the end of the shaft undo the plug which gives access to the inside of the rocker, which can now be cleaned of sludge etc. Ensure the rocker arm lubricating holes are clear.

16 Timing cover, gears and chain - removal

1 Bend back the locking tab of the crankshaft pulley locking washer under the crankshaft pulley retaining bolt, and with a large socket remove the bolt and lock washer.
2 Placing two large screwdrivers, or tyre levers, behind the crankshaft pulley wheel at 180° to each other, carefully lever off the pulley. It is preferable to use a proper extractor if this is available, but damage will not occur if care is taken.
3 Remove the woodruff key from the crankshaft nose with a pair of pliers and note how the groove in the pulley is designed to fit over it. Place the woodruff key in a glass jar for it is very small. Store carefully.
4 Unscrew the bolts holding the timing cover to the block. **Note:** that three different sizes of bolt are used, and that each block makes use of a large flat washer as well as a spring washer.
Note: *Refer to Chapter 13 for later models with crankcase breather.*
5 Pull off the timing cover and gasket. With the timing cover off take off the oil thrower. Note which way round the oil thrower is fitted.
6 Undo and remove the pivot screw and plain washer retaining the tensioner to the front engine plate. Lift away the tensioner and the second plain washer.

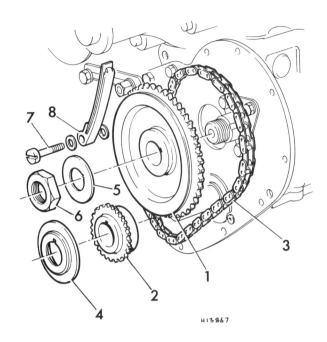

Fig. 1.11. Timing gear and chain assembly (typical)

1 Camshaft gear	5 Lock washer
2 Crankshaft gear	6 Nut
3 Timing chain	7 Tensioner retaining bolt
4 Oil thrower	8 Tensioner

7 To remove the camshaft and crankshaft timing wheel complete with chain, first bend back the camshaft gear retaining nut lock washer and unscrew the nut and lift away the nut and lock washer. Ease each wheel forward a little at a time levering behind each gear wheel in turn with two large screwdrivers or tyre levers at 180° to each other. If the gear wheels are locked solid, then it will be necessary to use a proper gear wheel and pulley extractor, and if one is available this should be used anyway in preference to levers. With both gear wheels safely off, remove the woodruff keys from the crankshaft and camshaft with a pair of pliers and place them in a jar for safe keeping. Note the number of very thin packing washers behind the crankshaft gear wheel and remove them very carefully.

17 Camshaft - removal

The camshaft can only be removed with the engine on the bench. The timing cover, gears and chain, must be removed as described in Section 16. It is also necessary to remove the distributor drive shaft as described in Section 18. With the drive gear out of the way proceed:
1 Undo and remove the three bolts and spring washers which hold the camshaft locating plate to the block. The bolts are normally covered by the camshaft gear wheel. Remove the plate. Recover the tappets if they are still in place and keep in the correct order as fitted in the engine.
2 The camshaft can now be withdrawn. Take great care to remove the camshaft gently, and in particular ensure that the cam peaks do not damage the camshaft bearings as the shaft is pulled forward.

18 Distributor drive - removal

To remove the distributor drive with the transmission unit

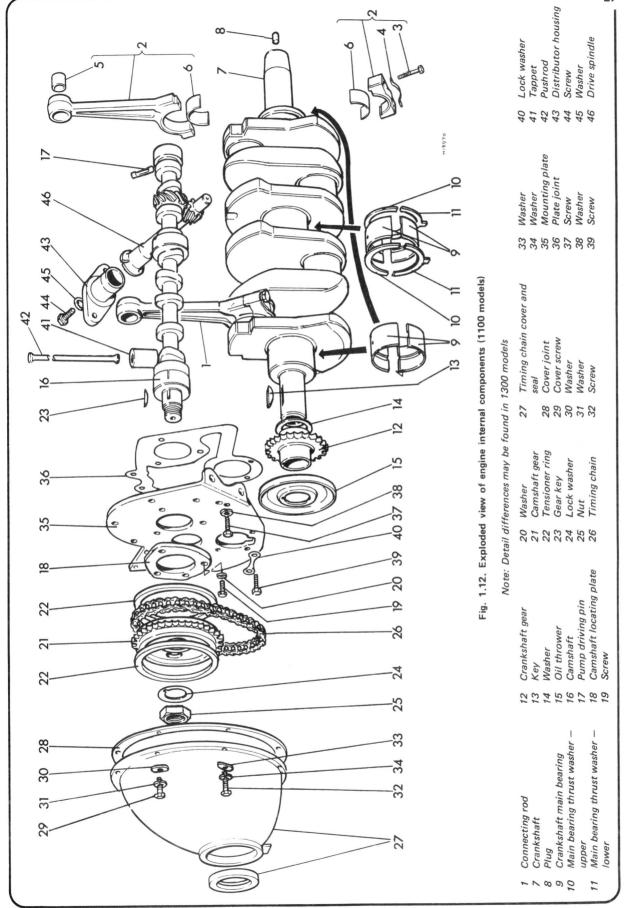

Fig. 1.12. Exploded view of engine internal components (1100 models)

Note: Detail differences may be found in 1300 models

1	Connecting rod	12	Crankshaft gear	27	Timing chain cover and	
7	Crankshaft	13	Key		seal	
8	Plug	14	Washer	28	Cover joint	
9	Crankshaft main bearing	15	Oil thrower	29	Cover screw	
10	Main bearing thrust washer —	16	Camshaft	30	Washer	
	upper	17	Pump driving pin	31	Washer	
11	Main bearing thrust washer —	18	Camshaft locating plate	32	Screw	
	lower	19	Screw			
		20	Washer	33	Washer	40 Lock washer
		21	Camshaft gear	34	Washer	41 Tappet
		22	Tensioner ring	35	Mounting plate	42 Pushrod
		23	Gear key	36	Plate joint	43 Distributor housing
		24	Lock washer	37	Screw	44 Screw
		25	Nut	38	Washer	45 Washer
		26	Timing chain	39	Screw	46 Drive spindle

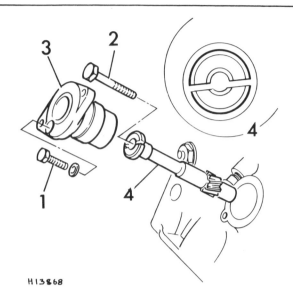

H13868

Fig. 1.13. Distributor drive shaft and housing

1 Distributor housing securing bolt and
   shakeproof washer
2 0.312 inch UNF bolt, 3.5 inch (90
   mm) long for shaft removal
3 Distributor drive housing
4 Distributor drive shaft
Inset: Final fitted position of slot

still in position it is necessary first to remove one of the tappet cover bolts. With the distributor and the distributor clamp plate already removed, this is achieved as follows:

1 Unscrew the single retaining bolt and spring washer to release the distributor housing. With the distributor housing removed, if the sump is still in position, screw into the end of the distributor drive shaft a 5/16 inch UNF bolt. A tappet cover bolt is ideal for this purpose. The drive shaft can then be lifted out, the shaft being turned slightly in the process to free the shaft skew gear from the camshaft skew gear (Fig. 1.13).

2 If the transmission unit has already been removed, then it is a simple matter to push the drive shaft out from inside the crankcase.

19 Pistons, connecting rods and big-end bearings - removal

1 Undo and remove the big end cap retaining nuts using a socket and remove the big end caps one at a time, taking care to keep them in the right order and the correct way round. Also ensure that the shell bearings are also kept with their correct connecting rods and caps for inspection. Normally, the numbers 1 to 4 are stamped on adjacent sides of the big end caps and connecting rods, indicating which cap fits on which rod and which way round the cap fits. If no numbers or lines can be found then scratch mating marks across the joint from the rod to the cap with a sharp screwdriver. One line for connecting rod number 1, two for connecting rod number 2 and so on. This will ensure there is no confusion later for it is most important that the caps go back in the position on the connecting rods from which they were removed.

   If the big end caps are difficult to remove they may be gently tapped with a soft hammer.

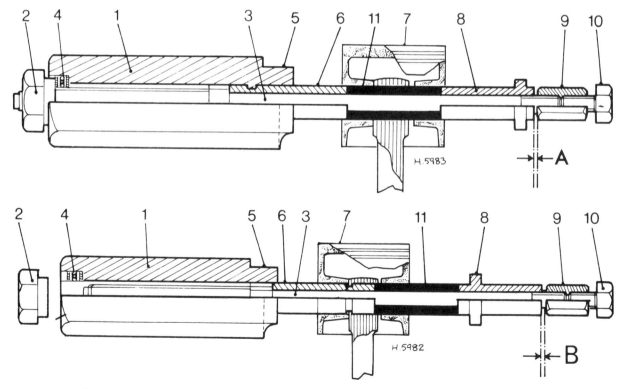

Fig. 1.14. Using service tool '18G 1150' to remove (upper illustration) and refit (lower illustration) gudgeon pin

1 Hexagon body	4 Thrust race	7 Piston	10 Lock screw
2 Large nut	5 Adaptor	8 Service tool bush	11 Gudgeon pin
3 Centre screw	6 Parallel sleeve	9 Stop nut	Dimension A and B = 1/32 in (0.8 mm)

2 To remove the shell bearings, press the bearing opposite the groove in both the connecting rod and the connecting rod cap, and the bearings will slide out easily.

3 Withdraw the pistons and connecting rods upwards and ensure they are kept in the correct order, for replacement in the same bore. Refit the connecting rod caps and bearings to the rods for inspection and correct re-location.

20 Gudgeon pins - removal

Fully floating gudgeon pins are fitted to 1100 models. They are retained in position by circlips which fit into recesses in the pistons at each end of the hole for the gudgeon pin. To extract the pin, remove the circlip from one end of the gudgeon pin hole and push the pin out. Make sure that the pins are kept with the pistons from which they were removed as they must be replaced the same way round in the same piston.

A press type gudgeon pin is used on 1300 models and requires a special BLMC tool number "18G 1150" with adaptor "18G 1150A" to remove and replace the pin. This tool is shown in Fig. 1.14 and must be used in the following manner:

1 Securely hold the hexagonal body in a firm vice and screw back the large nut until it is flush with the end of the main centre screw.

Well lubricate the screw and large nut as they have to withstand high loading. Now push the centre screw in until the nut touches the thrust race.

2 Fit the adaptor number 18G 1150A onto the main centre screw with the piston ring cutaway positioned uppermost. Then slide the parallel sleeve with the groove end first onto the centre screw.

3 Fit the piston with the "FRONT" or "V" mark on towards the adaptor on the centre screw. This is important because the gudgeon pin bore is offset and irreparable damage will result if fitted the wrong way round. Next fit the remover/replacer bush on the centre screw with the flange end towards the gudgeon pin.

4 Screw the stop nut onto the main centre screw and adjust it until approximately 0.032 inch (0.8 mm) end play ("A" in Fig. 1.14) exists, and lock the stop nut securely with the lock screws. Now check that the remover/replacer bush and parallel sleeve are positioned correctly in the bore on both sides of the piston. Also check that the curved face of the adaptor is clean and slide the piston onto the tool so it fits into the curved face of the adaptor with the piston rings over the cut-away.

5 Screw the large nut up to the thrust race and holding the lock screw turn the large nut with a ring spanner or long socket until the piston pin is withdrawn from the piston.

21 Piston rings - removal

1 To remove the piston rings, slide them carefully over the top of the piston, taking care not to scratch the alloy off the piston. Never slide them off the bottom of the piston skirt. It is very easy to break piston rings if they are pulled off roughly. This operation should be done with extreme caution. It is helpful to use an old 0.020 inch feeler gauge, to ease their removal.

2 Lift one end of the piston ring to be removed, out of its groove and insert the end of the feeler gauge under it. Turn the feeler gauge slowly round the piston and as the ring comes out of its groove it rests on the land above. It can then be eased off the piston with the feeler gauge stopping it from slipping into any empty grooves, if it is any but the top piston ring that is being removed.

22 Crankshaft and main bearings - removal

Removal of the crankshaft can only be attempted with the engine on the bench.

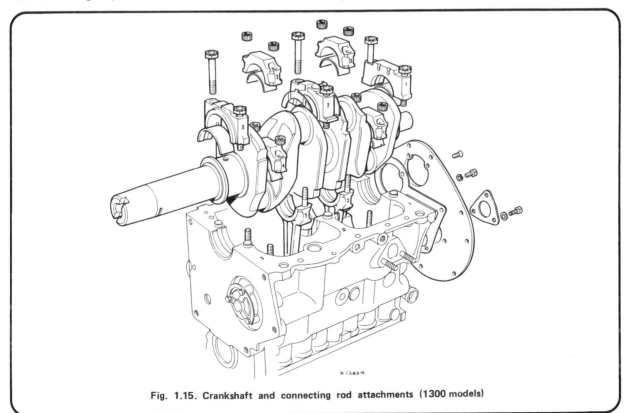

Fig. 1.15. Crankshaft and connecting rod attachments (1300 models)

Drain the engine oil, remove the timing gears and remove the transmission casing and the big end bearings, flywheel and flywheel housing as has already been described.

1 Release the locking tabs from the six bolts which hold the three main bearing caps in place.

2 Unscrew the bolts and remove them together with the locking plates.

3 Remove the two bolts which hold the front main bearing cap against the engine front plate.

4 Remove the main bearing caps and the bottom half of each bearing shell, taking care to keep the bearing shells in the right caps.

5 When removing the centre bearing cap, **Note:** the bottom semi-circular halves of the thrust washers, one half lying on either side of the main bearing. Lay them with the centre bearing along the correct side.

6 Slightly rotate the crankshaft to free the upper halves of the bearing shells and thrust washers which should now be extracted and placed over the correct bearing cap.

7 Remove the crankshaft by lifting it away from the crankcase.

23 Lubrication system - description

A forced feed system of lubrication is fitted with oil circulated round the engine from the transmission casing/sump. The level of engine oil in the sump is indicated on the dipstick which is fitted on the right-hand side of the engine. It is marked to indicate the optimum level which is the maximum mark. The level of oil in the sump, ideally, should not be above or below this line. Oil is replenished via the filter cap on the front of the rocker cover.

The oil in the transmission casing/sump is also used to lubricate the gearbox and differential, the total capacity including the filter being 8½ pints (4.83 litres).

The oil pump is mounted at the end of the crankcase and is driven by the camshaft. Two different makes of oil pump have been fitted. These are either the Holbourn Eaton or the Concentric (Engineering) Ltd. concentric rotor type. All are of the non-draining variety to allow rapid pressure build-up when starting the engine after it has been standing for some time.

Oil is drawn from the sump through a gauze screen in the oil strainer and is sucked up the pick-up pipe and drawn into the oil pump. From the oil pump it is forced under pressure along a gallery on the right-hand side of the engine, and through drillings to the big end, main and camshaft bearings. A small hole in each connecting rod allows a jet of oil to lubricate the cylinder wall with each revolution.

From the camshaft front bearing oil is fed through drilled passages in the cylinder block and head to the front rocker pedestal where it enters the hollow rocker shaft. Holes drilled in the shaft allow for the lubrication of the rocker arms, and the valve stems and pushrod ends. This oil is at a reduced pressure to the oil delivered to the crankshaft bearings. Oil from the front camshaft bearing also lubricates the timing gears and the timing chain. Oil returns to the sump by various passages, the tappets being lubricated by oil returning via the pushrod drillings in the block.

On all models a full flow oil filter is fitted, and all oil passes through this filter before it reaches the main oil gallery. The oil is passed directly from the oil pump across the block to an external pipe on the right-hand side of the engine which feeds into the filter head.

24 Oil filter - removal and refitment

The external oil filter is of the disposable cartridge type and is located on the right-hand side of the engine (Fig. 1.16).

To renew the oil filter unscrew the old cartridge from the filter head and discard it. Smear the seal on the new filter with a little oil and position it on the filter head. Screw it on and

tighten with the hands only. Do not attempt to tighten with a spanner or strap wrench. If the filter proves to be excessively tight it can be pierced and tapped off.

25 Oil pump - removal and dismantling

Oil pump removal is an operation which can only be carried out with the engine out of the car. Prior to removing the pump it is necessary to remove the clutch, flywheel, and flywheel housing. The oil pump is connected to the camshaft via a shaped coupling inserted in the rear of the camshaft.

1 Bend back the locking tabs on the securing bolts that hold the pump to the block. Unscrew the bolts and remove them complete with shaped tab washers.

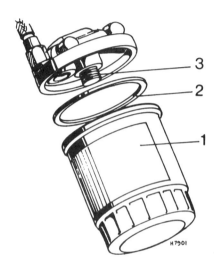

Fig. 1.16. Oil filter assembly

1 Canister   3 Screw thread
2 Seal

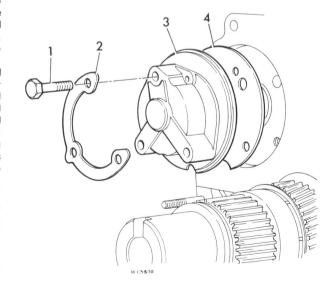

Fig. 1.17. Oil pump attachment (1100 models)

1 *Oil pump securing bolt*   3 *Oil pump*
2 *Tab washer*   4 *Gasket - Note cut-out*
                                      at bottom

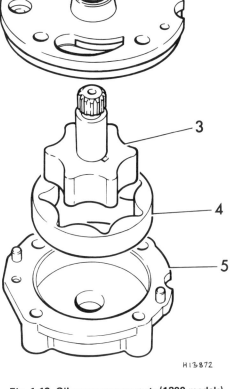

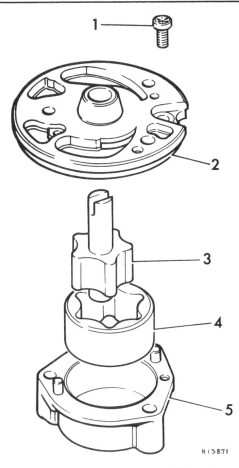

Fig. 1.18. Oil pump components (1100 models)

1	Screw	4	Outer rotor
2	Cover	5	Body
3	Inner rotor		

Fig. 1.19. Oil pump components (1300 models)

1	Screw	4	Outer rotor
2	Cover	5	Body
3	Inner rotor		

2 The oil pump cover can now be removed, complete with drive shaft and inner rotor and coupling.

3 To dismantle the oil pump undo the one screw securing the two halves of the pump body together. Carefully ease the pump cover from the two dowels on the pump body and lift out the rotors.

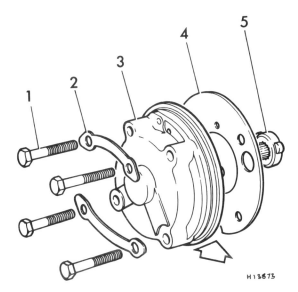

Fig. 1.20. Oil pump attachment (1300 models)

1	Oil pump securing bolt	4	Gasket - Note cut-out
2	Tab washer	5	Oil pump coupling
3	Oil pump		

26 Oil pressure relief valve - removal and refitment

To prevent excessive oil pressure - for example when the engine oil is thick and cold - an oil pressure relief valve is built into the right-hand side of the engine at the rear. The relief valve is identified externally by a large 9/16 inch domed hexagon nut (Fig. 1.21).

To dismantle the valve unscrew the domed nut and remove it complete with sealing washer. The relief spring and valve can then be easily extracted.

In position the valve fits over the opposite end of the relief valve spring resting in the dome of the hexagon nut, and bears against a machining in the block. When the oil pressure exceeds 70 lb/sq in. (4.92 kg/cm^2), the valve is forced off its seat and the oil bypasses it and returns via a drilling directly into the sump.

Check the tension of the spring by measuring its length. If it is shorter than 2.86 inch (72.64 mm) it should be replaced with a new spring.

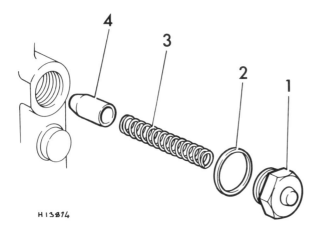

H13874

Fig. 1.21. Oil pressure relief valve

1 Dome nut   3 Spring
2 Sealing washer   4 Valve

Examine the valve for signs of pitting and, if evident, it should be carefully lapped in using cutting paste. Remove all traces of paste when a good seating has been obtained.

Reassembly of the relief valve is the reverse sequence to removal.

27 Engine - examination and renovation - general

1 With the engine stripped down and all parts thoroughly clean, it is now time to examine everything for wear. The following items should be checked and where necessary renewed or renovated, as described in the following sections.

28 Crankshaft - examination and renovation

Examine the crankpin and main journal surfaces for signs of scoring or scratches and check the ovality of the crankpins at different positions with a micrometer. If more than 0.001 inch (0.0254 mm) out of round, the crankpin will have to be reground. It will also have to be reground if there are any scores or scratches present. Also check the journals in the same fashion. BLMC 'A' series engine centre main bearings are prone to failure. This is not always immediately apparent, but slight vibration in an otherwise normally smooth engine and a very slight drop in oil pressure under normal conditions are clues. If the centre main bearing is suspected of failure it should be investigated immediately, by dropping the sump and removing the centre main bearing cap. Failure to do this will result in badly scored centre main journal. If it is necessary to regrind the crankshaft and fit new bearings, an engineering works will be able to decide how much metal to grind off and be able to supply the correct undersize shells to fit.

29 Big-end and main bearings - examination and renovation

1 Big-end bearing failure is accompanied by a noisy knocking from the crankcase and a slight drop in oil pressure. Main bearing failure is accompanied by vibration which can be quite severe as the engine speed rises and falls, and a drop in oil pressure.
2 Bearings which have not broken up, but are badly worn will give rise to low oil pressure and some vibration. Inspect the big-ends, main bearings and thrust washers for signs of general wear, scoring, pitting and scratches. The bearings should be matt grey in colour. With lead-indium bearings

should a trace of copper colour be noticed the bearings are badly worn as the lead bearing material has worn away to expose the indium underlay. Renew the bearings if they are in this condition or if there is any sign of scoring or pitting.
3 The undersizes available are designed to correspond with the regrind sizes, i.e. 0.010 bearings are correct for a crankshaft reground - 0.010 undersize. The bearings are in fact, slightly more than the stated undersize as running clearances have been allowed for during their manufacture.
4 Very long engine life can be achieved by changing big-end bearings at intervals of 30,000 miles and main bearings at intervals of 50,000 miles, irrespective of bearing wear. Normally, crankshaft wear is infinitesimal and regular changes of bearings will ensure mileages of between 100,000 to 120,000 miles before crankshaft regrinding becomes necessary. Crankshafts normally have to be reground because of scoring due to bearing failure.

30 Cylinder bores - examination and renovation

1 The cylinder bores must be examined for taper, ovality, scoring and scratches. Start by carefully examining the top of the cylinder bores. If they are at all worn a very slight ridge will be found on the thrust side. This marks the top of the piston travel. The owner will have a good indication of the bore wear prior to dismantling the engine, or removing the cylinder head. Excessive oil consumption accompanied by blue smoke from the exhaust is a sure sign of worn cylinder bores and piston rings.
2 Measure the bore diameter just under the ridge with a micrometer and compare it with the diameter at the bottom of the bore, which is not subject to wear. If the difference between the two measurements is more than .006 inch then it will be necessary to fit special piston rings or have the cylinders rebored and fit oversize pistons and rings. If no micrometer is available remove the rings from a piston and place the piston in each bore in turn about ¾ inch (19 mm) below the top of the bore. If an 0.010 inch feeler gauge can be slid between the piston and the cylinder wall on the thrust side of the bore then remedial action must be taken. Oversize pistons are available in the following sizes:-

+0.010 inch (0.254 mm),   +0.020 inch (0.508 mm)
+0.030 inch (0.762 mm),   +0.040 inch (1.016 mm)

3 These are accurately machined to just below these measurements so as to provide correct running clearances in bores bored out to the exact oversize dimensions.
4 If the bores are slightly worn but not so badly worn as to justify reboring them, special oil control rings can be fitted to the existing pistons which will restore compression and stop the engine burning oil. Several different types are available and the manufacturer's instructions concerning their fitting must be followed closely.

31 Pistons and piston rings - examination and renovation

1 If the old pistons are to be refitted carefully remove the piston rings and then thoroughly clean them. Take particular care to clean out the piston ring grooves. Do not scratch the aluminium in any way. If new rings are to be fitted to the old pistons, then the top ring should be stepped, so as to clear the ridge left above the previous top ring. If a normal but oversize new ring is fitted it will hit the ridge and break, because the new ring will not have worn in the same way as the old.
2 Before fitting the rings on the pistons each should be inserted approximately 3 inches (76 mm) down the cylinder bore and the gap measured with a feeler gauge as shown in Fig. 1.22. This should be between the limits given in the specifications at the beginning of this Chapter. It is essential that the gap is measured at the bottom of the ring travel, for

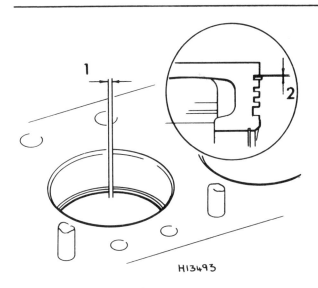

Fig. 1.22. Measurement of piston ring end gap and clearance

1   Ring gap measurement   2   Ring groove measurement

if it is measured at the top of a worn bore and gives a perfect fit, it could easily seize at the bottom. If the ring gap is too small rub down the ends of the ring with a very fine file until the gap is correct when fitted. To keep the rings square in the bore for measurement, line each one up in turn with an old piston in the bore upside down, and use the piston to push the ring down about 3 inches (76 mm). Remove the piston and measure the piston ring gap.

3   When fitting new pistons and rings to a rebored engine the ring gap can be measured at the top of the bore as the bore will now not taper. It is not necessary to measure the side clearance in the piston ring grooves with rings fitted, as the groove dimensions are accurately machined during manufacture. When fitting new oil control rings to the pistons it may be necessary to have the grooves widened by machining to accept the new under rings. In this instance the manufacturer will make this quite clear and will supply the address to which the pistons must be sent for machining.

4   When new pistons are fitted, take great care to be sure to fit the exact size best suited to the particular bore of your engine. BLMC go one stage further than merely specifying one size piston for all standard bores. Because of very slight differences in cylinder machining during production it is necessary to select just the right piston for the bore. A range of different sizes are available either from the piston manufacturer or from the local BLMC stores.

5   Examination of the cylinder block face will show adjacent to each bore, a small diamond shaped box with a number stamped in the metal. Careful examination of the piston crown will show a matching diamond and number. These are the standard piston sizes and will be the same for all bores. If the standard pistons are to be refitted or standard low compression pistons changed to standard high compression pistons, then it is essential that only pistons with the same number in the diamond are used. With larger pistons, the amount of oversize is stamped in an elipse on the piston crown.

6   On engines with tapered second and third compression rings, the top narrow side of the ring is marked with a "T". Always fit this side uppermost and carefully examine all rings for this mark before fitting.

32 Camshaft and camshaft bearings - examination and renovation

1   Carefully examine the camshaft bearings for wear. If the bearings are obviously worn or pitted or the metal underlay just showing through, then they must be renewed. This is an operation for your local BLMC garage or engineering works as it demands the use of specialised equipment. The bearings are removed using a special drift after which the new bearings are pressed in, care being taken that the oil driving in the bearings line up with those in the block. With another special tool the bearings are then reamed in position.

2   The camshaft itself should show no sign of wear, but, if very slight, scoring marks can be removed by gently rubbing down with very fine emery cloth or an oil stone. The greatest care must be taken to keep the cam profiles smooth.

33 Valves and seats - examination and renovation

1   Examine the heads of the valves for pitting or burning, especially the heads of the exhaust valves. The valve seatings should be examined at the same time. If the pitting on the valves is very slight the marks can be removed by grinding the seats and valves together with coarse, and then fine, valve grinding paste. Where bad pitting has occurred to the valve seats, it will be necessary to recut them and fit new valves. If the valve seats are so worn that they cannot be recut then it will be necessary to fit new valve seat inserts. These latter two jobs should be entrusted to a BLMC garage or engineering works. In practice it is very seldom that the seats are so badly worn that they require renewal. Normally it is the valve that is too badly worn, and you can easily purchase a new set of valves and match them to the seats by valve grinding.

2   Valve grinding is easily carried out. Place the cylinder head upside down on a bench with a block of wood at each end to give clearance for the valve stems. Alternatively place the head at 45° to a wall with the combustion chambers facing away from the wall.

3   Smear a trace of coarse carborundum paste on the seat face and apply a suction grinding tool to the valve head as shown in Fig. 1.23. With a semi-rotary action, grind the valve head to its seat, lifting the valve occasionally to redistribute the grinding paste. When a dull matt even surface finish is produced on both the valve seat and the valve, then wipe off the paste and repeat the process with fine carborundum paste, lifting and turning the valve to redistribute the paste as before. A light spring placed under the valve head will greatly ease this operation. When a smooth unbroken ring of light grey matt finish is produced, on both valve and valve seat faces, the grinding operation is complete.

4   Scrape away all carbon from the valve head and the valve

Fig. 1.23. Grinding in valve

stem. Carefully clean away every trace of grinding compound, taking great care to leave none in the ports or in the valve guides. Clean the valves and valve seats with a paraffin soaked rag then wipe with clean rag. (If an air line is available blow clean).

34 Timing gear and chain - examination and renovation

1 Examine the teeth on both the crankshaft gear wheel and the camshaft gear wheel for wear. Each tooth forms an inverted "V" with the gear wheel periphery and, if worn, the side of each tooth under tension will be slightly concave in shape when compared with the other side of the tooth i.e. one side of the inverted "V" will be concave when compared with the other.
2 Examine the links of the chain for side slackness and renew the chain if any slackness is noticeable when compared with a new chain. It is a sensible precaution to renew the chain every 30,000 miles (48,000 km) and at a lesser mileage if the engine is stripped down for a major overhaul. The actual rollers on a very badly worn chain may be slightly grooved.

35 Rocker and rocker shaft - examination and renovation

1 Remove the threaded plug with a screwdriver from the end of the rocker shaft and thoroughly clean out the shaft. As it acts as the oil passages for the valve gear, clean out these passages and make sure they are quite clear. Check the shaft for straightness by rolling it on a flat surface. It is most unlikely that it will deviate from normal, but, if it does, you must purchase a new shaft. The surface of the shaft should be free from any worn ridges caused by the rocker arms. If any wear is present, renew the rocker shaft. Wear is likely to have occurred only if the rocker shaft oil holes have become blocked.
2 Check the rocker arms for wear of the rocker bushes, at the rocker arm face which bears on the valve stem, and of the adjusting ball ended screws. Wear in the rocker arm bush can be checked by gripping the rocker arm tip and holding the

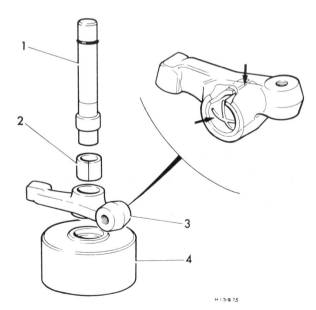

Fig. 1.24. Correct fitment of rocker bush

1 Suitable diameter drift	*4 Firm base*
2 Bush	*Inset: Correct location of*
3 Rocker	*bush in rocker*

rocker arm in place on the shaft, noting if there is any lateral rocker arm shake. If any shake is present, and the arm is very loose on the shaft, remedial action must be taken. It is recommended that if a forged type of rocker arm is fitted it be taken to your local BLMC garage or engineering works to have the old bush drawn out and a new bush fitted. The correct placement of the bush is shown in Fig. 1.24. If a pressed steel rocker arm is fitted, rebushing must not be undertaken but a new rocker arm obtained.
3 Check the tip of the rocker arm where it bears on the valve head, for cracking or serious wear on the case hardening. If none is present the rocker arm may be refitted. Check the pushrods for straightness by rolling them on a flat surface. If bent they must be renewed.

36 Tappets (cam followers) - examination and renovation

Examine the bearing surface of the tappets which lie on the camshaft. Any indentation in this surface or any cracks indicate serious wear and the tappets should be renewed. Thoroughly clean them out, removing all traces of sludge. It is most unlikely that the sides of the tappets will prove worn, but, if they are a very loose fit in their bores and can be readily rocked, they should be discarded and new tappets fitted. It is very unusual to find worn tappets and any wear present is likely to occur only at very high mileages.

37 Flywheel starter ring gear - examination and renovation

1 If the teeth on the flywheel starter ring gear are badly worn, or if some are missing, then it will be necessary to remove the ring. This is achieved by splitting the old ring using a cold chisel. The greatest care must be taken not to damage the flywheel during this process.
2 To fit a new ring gear, heat it gently and evenly with an oxyacetylene flame until a temperature of approximately 350° C is reached. This is indicated by a light metallic blue surface colour. With the ring gear at this temperature, fit it to the flywheel with the front of the teeth facing the flywheel register. The ring gear should be either pressed or lightly tapped gently onto its register and left to cool naturally when the contraction of the metal on cooling will ensure that it is a secure and permanent fit. Great care must be taken not to overheat the ring gear, as if this happens the temper of the ring gear will be lost.
3 Alternatively, your local BLMC garage or automobile engineering works may have a suitable oven in which the ring gear can be heated. The normal domestic oven will give a temperature of about 250° C only, at the very most, except for the latest self cleaning type which will give a higher temperature. With the former it may just be possible to fit the ring gear with it at this temperature, but it is unlikely and no great force should have to be used.

38 Oil pump - examination and renovation

1 Thoroughly clean all the component parts in petrol and then check the rotor end float and lobe clearances in the following manner:
2 Position the rotors in the pump and place the straight edge of a steel rule across the joint face of the pump. Measure the gap between the bottom of the straight edge and the top of the rotors with a feeler gauge as shown in Fig. 1.25. If the measurement exceeds 0.005 inch (0.127 mm) then check the lobe clearances as described in the following paragraph. If the lobe clearances are correct then remove the dowels from the joint face of the pump body and lap joint the inner face on a sheet of plate glass.
3 Measure the gaps between the peaks of the lobes and the peaks in the pump body with a feeler gauge, and if the gap

exceeds 0.010 inch (0.254 mm) then fit a replacement pump. This measurement is shown in Fig. 1.25.

39 Cylinder head - decarbonisation

1 This operation can be carried out with the engine either in or out of the car. With the cylinder head off, carefully remove with a wire brush and blunt scraper all traces of carbon deposits from the combustion spaces and the ports. The valve stems and valve guides should also be freed from any carbon deposits. Wash the combustion spaces and ports down with petrol and scrape the cylinder head surface free of any foreign matter with the side of a steel rule or a similar article. Take care not to scratch the surfaces.

2 Clean the pistons and top of the cylinder bores. If the pistons are still in the cylinder bores then it is essential that great care is taken to ensure that no carbon gets into the cylinder bores as this could scratch the cylinder walls or cause damage to the piston and rings. To ensure that this does not happen, first turn the crankshaft so that two of the pistons are at the top of the bores. Place clean non-fluffy rag into the other two bores or seal them off with paper and masking tape. The water ways and pushrod holes should also be covered with a small piece of masking tape to prevent particles of carbon entering the cooling system and damaging the water pump, or entering the cooling system and damaging the water pump, or entering the lubrication system and causing damage to a bearing surface.

3 There are two schools of thought as to how much carbon ought to be removed from the piston crown. One is that a ring of carbon should be left around the edge of the piston and on the cylinder bore wall as an aid to keep oil consumption low. Although this is probably true for early engines with worn bores, on later engines however, the tendency is to remove all traces of carbon during decarbonisation.

4 If all traces of carbon are to be removed, press a little grease into the gap between the cylinder walls and the two pistons which are to be worked on. With a blunt scraper carefully scrape away the carbon from the piston crown, taking care not to scratch the aluminium. Also scrape away the carbon from the surrounding lip of the cylinder wall. When all carbon has been removed, scrape away the grease which will now be contaminated with carbon particles, taking care not to press any into the bores. To assist prevention of carbon build-up the piston crown can be polished with a metal polish such as Brasso. Remove the rags or masking tape from the other two cylinders and turn the crankshaft so that the two pistons which were at the bottom are now at the top. Place non-fluffy rag into the other two bores or seal them off with paper and masking tape. Do not forget the waterways and oilways as well. Proceed as previously described.

5 If a ring of carbon is going to be left round the piston then this can be helped by inserting an old piston ring into the top of the bore to rest on the piston and ensure that carbon is not accidently removed. Check that there are no particles of carbon in the cylinder bores. Decarbonising is now complete.

40 Valve guides - examination and renovation

Examine the valve guides internally for wear. It the valves are a very loose fit in the guides and there is the slightest suspicion of lateral rocking, then new guides will have to be fitted, their correct location being shown in Fig. 1.26. If the valve guides have been removed compare them internally by visual inspection with a new guide as well as testing them for rocking with the valves.

41 Engine - re-assembly - general

1 To ensure maximum life with minimum trouble from a

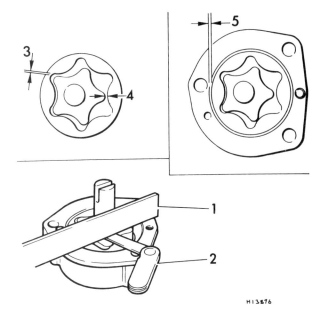

Fig. 1.25. Oil pump wear checks

1 Straight edge	4 Inner rotor lobe clearance
2 Feeler gauge	5 Outer rotor to body
3 Inner rotor side clearance	clearance

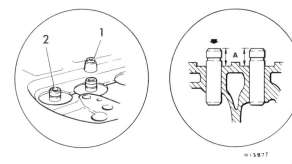

Fig. 1.26. Location of valve guides

1 Oil seal (inlet valve only)
2 Valve guide
Dimension A   = 0.540 in. (13.72 mm)

rebuilt engine, not only must everything be correctly assembled, but everything must be spotlessly clean, all the oilways must be clear, locking washers and spring washers must always be fitted where indicated and all bearing and other working surfaces must be thoroughly lubricated during assembly. Before assembly begins renew any bolts or studs the threads of which are in any way damaged, and whenever possible use new spring washers.

2 Apart from your normal tools, a supply of clean rag, an oil can filled with engine oil (an empty plastic detergent bottle thoroughly cleaned and washed out, will invariably do just as well), a new supply of assorted spring washers, a set of new gaskets, and preferably a torque spanner, should be collected together.

42 Camshaft - refitment

1 Lightly lubricate the tappets and fit them into the same bores from which they were removed.

2 Wipe the camshaft bearings and generously lubricate them with engine oil.
3 Temporarily refit the camshaft gear wheel and locating plate and secure with the retaining nut. Using feeler gauges, check the end float which should not exceed 0.003 to 0.007 inch (0.07 to 0.18 mm). If this maximum limit is exceeded obtain a new locating plate.
4 Remove the camshaft gear wheel retaining nut, gear wheel and locating plate.
5 Insert the camshaft into the crankcase gently, taking care not to damage the camshaft bearing with the sharp edges of the cams. Take care, the camshaft lobe edges are sharp.

43 Crankshaft - refitment

1 Ensure that the crankcase and that all oilways are clear. A thin twist drill is useful for cleaning oilways out. If possible, blow them out with compressed air. Inject engine oil into the crankshaft oilways, now.
2 Replace the crankshaft rear main bearing oil deflector and secure with the three bolts and spring washers.
3 Carefully clean away all traces of the protective grease with which new bearings are coated.
4 Fit the upper halves of the main bearing shells to their location in the crankcase. Note the tag which engages into the locating grooves.
5 With the three upper bearing shells securely in place, wipe the lower bearing cap housings and fit the three lower shell bearings to their caps.
6 Wipe the recesses either side of the centre main bearing which locate the upper halves of the thrust washer.
7 Generously lubricate the crankshaft journals and the upper and lower main bearing shells. Apply a little grease to either side of the centre main bearing so as to retain the upper halves of the thrust washers.
8 Refit the upper thrust washers (the halves without tabs) to either side of the centre main bearing with the oil grooves outwards from the bearing.
9 Carefully lower the crankshaft into position, making sure it is the correct way round.
10 During removal of the crankshaft gear wheel it should have been noted that there are shims behind the gear wheel. Replace the shims and then the Woodruff key.
11 Apply a little non-hardening sealer to the rear of the crankcase to which the rear main bearing cap fits.
12 Replace the rear main bearing cap and lightly tighten the two securing bolts.
13 Smear a little grease onto the thrust washer locations on either side of the centre main bearing cap and refit the lower halves of the thrust washers (the halves with tabs), with the lubrication grooves facing outwards. Refit the centre and front main bearing caps and lightly tighten the securing bolts.
14 Test the crankshaft for freedom of rotation. Should it be very stiff to turn or possess high spots a most careful inspection must be made, with a micrometer to trace the cause of the trouble. It is very seldom that any trouble of this nature will be experienced when fitting the crankshaft.
15 Tighten the main bearing bolts using a torque wrench set to 60 lb ft (8.3 kg fm). Recheck the crankshaft for freedom of rotation.

44 Pistons and connecting rods - re-assembly

If the same pistons are being used, then they must be mated to the same connecting rod with the same gudgeon pin. If new pistons are being fitted it does not matter which connecting rod they are used with, but the gudgeon pins are not to be interchanged. As the gudgeon pin is a press fit on 1300 models a special BLMC tool "18G 1150" with adaptor "18G 1150A" is required to fit the gudgeon pin as shown in Fig. 1.14 and should be used as follows:

1 Unscrew the large nut and withdraw the centre screw from the body a few inches. Well lubricate the screw thread and correctly locate the piston support adaptor.
2 Carefully slide the parallel sleeve with the groove end last onto the centre screw, up as far as the shoulder. Lubricate the gudgeon pin and its bores in the connecting rod and piston with a graphited oil.
3 Fit the connecting rod and piston, side marked "Front" or "V" to the tool with the connecting rod entered on the sleeve up to the groove. Fit the gudgeon pin into the piston bore up to the connecting rod. Next fit the remover/replacer bush flange end towards the gudgeon pin.
4 Screw the stop nut onto the centre screw and adjust the nut to give a 0.032 inch (0.8 mm) end play, "B" as shown in Fig. 1.14. Lock the nut securely with the lock screw. Ensure that the curved face of the adaptor is clean and slide the piston on the tool so that it fits into the curved face of the adaptor with the piston rings over the adaptor cut-away.
5 Screw the large nut up the thrust race. Adjust the torque wrench to a setting of 16 lb ft (2.2 kg fm) if of the 'click' type which will represent the minimum load for an acceptable fit. Use the torque wrench previously set on the large nut, and a ring spanner on the lock screw. Pull the gudgeon pin into the piston until the flange of the remover/replacer bush is 0.032 inch (0.8 mm) from the piston skirt. It is critically important that the flange is **not** allowed to contact the piston. Finally withdraw the BLMC service tool.
6 Should the torque wrench not 'click' or reach 16 lb ft (2.2 kg fm) throughout the pull, the fit of the gudgeon pin in the connecting rod is not within limits and the parts must be renewed.
7 Ensure that the piston pivots freely on the gudgeon pin and is free to slide sideways. Should stiffness exist wash the assembly in paraffin, lubricate the gudgeon pin with graphited oil and recheck. Again if stiffness exists, dismantle the assembly and check for signs of ingained dirt or damage.
8 1100 models: Insert the gudgeon pin and retain with the circlips. Make sure they are securely fitted.

45 Piston rings - refitment

1 Check that the piston ring grooves and oilways are thoroughly clean and unblocked. Piston rings must always be fitted over the head of the piston and never from the bottom.
2 Refitment is the exact opposite procedure to removal, see Section 21.
3 Set all ring gaps 90° to each other.

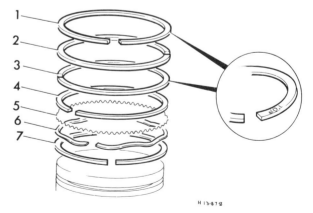

Fig. 1.27. Piston ring identification (1100 models)

1 Chrome plated compression ring
2 Taper compression ring
3 Taper compression ring
4 Top rail
5 Expander
6 Side spring
7 Bottom rail

4 An alternative method is to fit the rings by holding them slightly open with the thumbs and both your index fingers. This method requires a steady hand and great care for it is easy to open the ring too much and break it.

5 The special oil control ring requires a special fitting procedure. First fit the bottom rail of the oil control ring to the piston and position it below the bottom groove. Refit the oil control expander into the bottom groove and move the bottom oil control ring rail up into the bottom groove. Fit the top oil control rail into the bottom groove.

6 Inspect that the ends of the expander are butting and not overlapping.

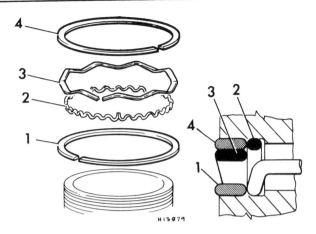

Fig. 1.28. Correct assembly of oil control ring (1300 models)

1 Bottom rail	3 Oil control ring rail
2 Expander	4 Top rail

46 Pistons - refitment

Fit pistons, complete with connecting rods, to the cylinder bores as follows:

1 Wipe the cylinder bores clean with clean non-fluffy rag.

2 The pistons, complete with connecting rods, must be fitted to their bores from above. As each piston is inserted into the bore, ensure that it is the correct piston/connecting rod assembly for that particular bore and that the front of the piston is towards the front of the bore, assuming that the connecting rod is fitted correctly i.e., towards the front of the engine. Lubricate the piston well with clean engine oil.

3 Check that the piston ring gaps are 90° to each other.

4 The piston will slide into the bore only as far as the oil control ring and then it will be necessary to compress the piston rings into a clamp. The piston ring compressor should be fitted to the piston before it is inserted into the bore. If a proper piston ring clamp is not available then a suitable jubilee clip will do. Guide the piston into the bore until it reaches the ring compressor. Gently tap the piston into the cylinder bore with a wooden or plastic hammer.

47 Connecting rod to crankshaft - re-assembly

1 Wipe the connecting rod half of the big-end bearing location and the underside of the shell bearing clean, (as for the main bearing shells) and fit the shell bearing in position with its locating torque engaged with the corresponding groove in the connecting rod. Always fit new shells.

2 Generously lubricate the crankpin journals with engine oil and turn the crankshaft so that the crankpin is in the most advantageous position for the connecting rod to be drawn onto it.

3 Fit the bearing shell to the connecting rod cap in the same way as with the connecting rod itself.

4 Generously lubricate the shell bearing and offer up the connecting rod bearing cap to the connecting rod. Fit the connecting rod cap retaining nuts. It will be observed that these are special twelve sided nuts.

5 Tighten the retaining nuts to a torque wrench setting of 37 lb ft (5.11 kg fm).

48 Oil pump and coupling - refitment

1 Fit the coupling to the oil pump splined drive.

2 Make sure the mating face of the oil pump is clean and fit a new gasket. Make sure it is fitted the correct way round.

3 Wipe the location of the oil pump at the rear of the cylinder block and offer the oil pump up into position. Make sure that it is fitted correctly with the cutaway towards the bottom of the rear of the cylinder block.

4 Refit the oil pump securing bolts and two shaped locking washers and tighten these bolts to a torque wrench setting of 9 lb ft (1.2 kg fm).

5 Using a pair of pliers bend over the locking tabs.

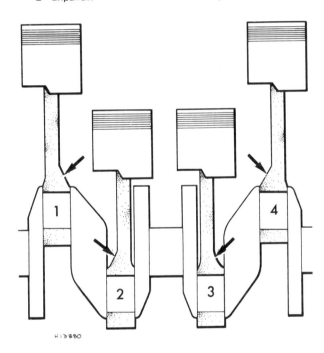

Fig. 1.29. The correct positions of the offsets on the connecting rod big ends

49 Oil pressure relief valve and switch - refitment

1 Assemble the valve components in the order of: valve, spring and domed nut with new washer.

2 Carefully insert the assembly into its location at the rear of the cylinder block. Tighten the domed nut fully.

3 Locate the oil pressure switch in its drilling in the side of the cylinder block just above the oil pressure relief valve and tighten firmly using an open ended spanner.

50 Engine front plate, timing gears, tensioner and cover - refitment

1 Wipe the mating faces of the front plate and cylinder block and smear the new gasket with a little grease. Attach the gasket to the rear of the front plate and offer up into position.

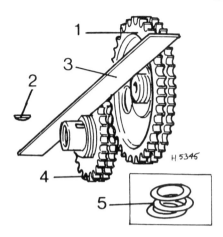

Fig. 1.30. Timing gear alignment

1	Camshaft gear	4	Crankshaft gear
2	Woodruff key	5	Inset: shims
3	Straight edge		

2 Refit the two special screws located to the bottom of the crankshaft and tighten with an Allen key.

3 Replace the two front plate to cylinder block securing bolts and spring washers.

4 Refit the camshaft retainer to the front plate with the thrust face towards the camshaft. The hole should be to the bottom of the cylinder block. Secure in position with the three bolts and spring washers.

5 Check that the packing washers are in place on the crankshaft nose. If new gear wheels are being fitted it may be necessary to fit additional washers as described in paragraph 12. These washers ensure that the crankshaft gear wheel lines up correctly with the camshaft gear wheel.

6 Replace the woodruff key in its slot in the camshaft. If the edges of this key or the one fitted to the crankshaft are burred they must be cleaned with a fine file.

7 Lay the camshaft and crankshaft gear wheels on a clean surface so that the two timing marks - dot of camshaft gear wheel and a shaped protrusion on the hub of the crankshaft gear wheel, are adjacent to each other. Check the gear alignment as shown in Fig. 1.30.

8 Rotate the crankshaft so that the woodruff key is at TDC.

9 Rotate the camshaft so that when viewed from the front the woodruff key is at one o'clock position.

10 Fit the timing chain and gear wheel assembly onto the camshaft and crankshaft keeping the timing marks adjacent.

11 If the camshaft and crankshaft have been positioned accurately it will be found that the keyways on the gear wheels will match the position of the keys, although it may be necessary to rotate the camshaft a fraction to ensure accurate lining up of the camshaft gear wheel.

12 Press the gear wheels into position on the crankshaft and camshaft as far as they will go. **Note :** If new gear wheels are being fitted they should be checked for alignment before finally fitting to the engine. Place the gear wheels in position without the timing chain and place the straight edge of a steel rule from the side of the camshaft gear teeth to the crankshaft gear wheel and measure the gap between the steel rule and the crankshaft gear wheel. Add or subtract shims to this thickness located on the crankshaft nose (see Fig. 1.30).

13 Refit the camshaft gear wheel retaining lock washer and nut and tighten this nut fully.

14 Using a chisel bend over the lock washer on one flat.

15 If a tensioner is fitted, assemble the pivot screw, washer, tensioner and second washer and fit to the front of the cylinder block.

16 Fit the crankshaft oil thrower onto the crankshaft nose. The thrower should be fitted with the letter "F" facing towards the front of the engine.

17 Wipe the cover mating face and the front end plate and smear a little grease onto the end plate. Fit a new gasket and align all the holes. les.

18 If oil leaked from the seal in the front cover this should be levered out using a screwdriver, and a new one fitted. The lip when fitted faces inwards.

19 Generously oil the chain, gear wheels, and cover oil seal.

20 Offer up the front cover taking care not to dislodge the gasket and retain in position with the bolts and spring washers. Bolts of different sizes are used and they must go back in their original fitted position as was noted during dismantling. Do not tighten yet.

21 Using the pulley centralise the cover and tighten as many bolts as possible.

22 Remove the pulley again and tighten the three lower bolts.

23 With the pulley back on the crankshaft nose again, refit the pulley retaining bolt and lock washer.

24 Using a chisel bend up the lock washer to one flat.

51 Water and fuel pump - refitment

1 Make sure the mating faces of the water pump and cylinder block are free of old gasket or jointing compound.

2 Smear a little grease onto the water pump and place on a new gasket.

3 Fit the water pump to the cylinder block mating it to the dowels in the cylinder block face.

4 Refit and tighten the four securing bolts and spring washers.

5 Clean the mating faces of the crankcase and fuel pump and fit a new set of gaskets to the spacer. Slide the spacer and gaskets over the studs.

6 Refit the fuel pump and secure with the two nuts and spring washers.

52 Valves and valve springs - re-assembly

1 Rest the cylinder head on its side, or if the manifold studs are still fitted with the gasket surface downwards.

2 Fit each valve and valve spring in turn, wiping down and lubricating each valve stem as it is inserted into the same valve guide from which it was removed.

3 As each inlet valve is inserted slip on the oil seal and push it down over the valve guide.

4 Move the cylinder head towards the edge of the work bench if it is facing downwards and slide it partially over the edge of the bench, so as to fit the bottom half of the valve spring compressor to the valve head.

5 Slip the valve spring over the valve stem and down onto its seating.

6 Refit the spring cap to the top of the valve spring.

7 With the base of the valve spring compressor on the valve head, compress the valve spring until the cotters can be slipped into place in the spring cap. Gently release the compressor. Check that the cotters are correctly located in the spring cap.

8 Repeat for all eight valve assemblies.

53 Rocker shaft - re-assembly

To re-assemble the rocker shaft fit the split pin, flat washer, and spring washer at the rear end of the shaft and then slide on the rocker arms, rocker shaft pedestals, and spacing springs in the same order in which they were removed (Fig. 1.31).

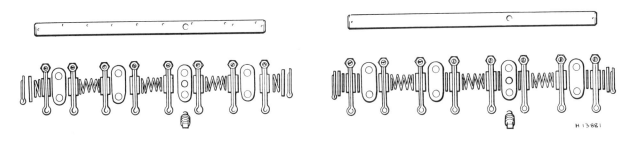

Fig. 1.31. Valve rocker reassembly order (left) 1100 models (right) 1300 models

With the front pedestal in position screw in the rocker shaft locating screw and slip the locating plate into position. Finally fit to the front of the shaft, the spring washer, plain washer, and split pin, in that order.

54 Cylinder head - replacement

1 After checking that both the cylinder block and cylinder head mating faces are perfectly clean, generously lubricate each cylinder with engine oil.
    Always use a new cylinder head gasket. The old gasket will be compressed and incapable of giving a good seal. It is also easier at this stage to refit the small hose from the water pump to the cylinder head.
2 Never smear on gasket cement either side of the gasket, for pressure leaks may blow through it.
3 The cylinder head gasket is marked **Front** and **Top** and should be fitted in position according to the markings. The copper side will be uppermost.
4 Carefully lower the gasket into position ensuring that the stud threads do not damage the side of the holes through which they pass.
5 The cylinder head may now be lowered over the studs until it rests on the cylinder head gasket.
6 With the cylinder head in position, fit the pushrods in the same order in which they were removed. Ensure that they locate properly in the stems of the tappets.
7 Refit the two tappet covers with new cork gaskets and tighten the two securing bolts and washers.
8 The rocker shaft assembly can now be lowered over its eight locating studs. Take care that the rocker arms are the right way round. Lubricate the ball joints, and insert the rocker arm ball joints into the pushrod cups. Note: Failure to place the ball joints in the cups can result in the ball joints seating on the edge of a pushrod or outside it when the head and rocker assembly is pulled down tight.
9 Fit the lock plate to the second pedestal.
10 Fit the four rocker pedestal nuts and washers, and then the four cylinder head stud nuts and washers which also hold down the rocker pedestals. Pull the nuts down evenly, but without tightening them right up.
11 Fit the remaining nuts and washers to the cylinder head studs.
12 When all are in position, tighten the rocker pedestal nuts to a torque wrench setting of 25 lb ft (3.4 kg fm) and the cylinder head nuts to a torque wrench setting of 40 lb ft (5.5 kg fm). The correct order is that shown in Fig. 1.9.
13 Finally tighten the water pump bypass hose clip.

55 Rocker arm/valve - adjustment

1 The valve adjustments should be made with the engine cold. The importance of correct rocker arm/valve stem clearances cannot be overstressed as they vitally affect the performance.

2 If the clearances are set too wide, the efficiency of the engine is reduced as the valves open late and close earlier than was intended. If the clearances are set too close there is a danger that the stem and pushrods upon expansion when hot, will not allow the valves to close properly which will cause burning of the valve head and possibly warping.
3 If the engine is in the car, to get at the rockers, it is merely necessary to remove the two holding down dome shaped nuts from the rocker cover, and then to lift the rocker cover and gasket away.
4 It is important that the clearance is set when the tappet of the valve being adjusted is on the heel of the cam (i.e. opposite the peak). This can be done by carrying out the adjustments in the following order, which also avoids turning the crankshaft more than necessary.

Valve fully open	Check and adjust
Valve No. 8	Valve No. 1
Valve No. 6	Valve No. 3
Valve No. 4	Valve No. 5
Valve No. 7	Valve No. 2
Valve No. 1	Valve No. 8
Valve No. 3	Valve No. 6
Valve No. 5	Valve No. 4
Valve No. 2	Valve No. 7

5 The correct valve clearance is given in the Specifications at the beginning of this Chapter. It is obtained by slackening the hexagonal locknut with a spanner while holding the ball pin against rotation with a screwdriver. Then still pressing down with the screwdriver, insert a feeler gauge of the required thickness between the valve stem and head and the rocker arm and adjust the ball pin until the feeler gauge will just move in and out without nipping. Then, still holding the ball pin in the correct position, tighten the locknut.
6 An alternative method is to set the gaps with the engine running at idle speed. Although this method may be faster, more practice is needed and it is no more reliable.
7 Refit the rocker cover and gasket, and secure with the dome nuts and washers.

56 Distributor and distributor drive - refitment

    It is important to set the distributor drive correctly otherwise the ignition timing will be incorrect. It is easy to set the distributor drive in apparently the right position, but in fact exactly 180° out, by omitting to select the correct cylinder which must not only be at TDC but must also be on the firing stroke with both valves closed. The distributor drive should therefore not be fitted until the cylinder head is in position and the valves can be observed. Alternatively, if the timing chain cover has not been replaced, the distributor drive can be replaced when the marks on the timing wheels are adjacent to each other.
1 Rotate the crankshaft so that No. 1 piston is at TDC, and on its firing stroke (the marks in the timing gears will be adjacent to each other). When No. 1 piston is at TDC the inlet

valve on No. 4 cylinder is just opening and the exhaust valve closing.

2 When the marks "1/4" on the flywheel are at TDC or when the dimple on the crankshaft pulley wheel is in line with the TDC pointer on the timing gear cover, then Nos. 1 and 4 pistons are at TDC.

3 Screw the tappet cover bolt into the head of the distributor drive (any 5/16 inch UNF bolt).

4 Insert the distributor drive into its housing so that when fully home the smaller half of the offset distributor drive head is in the eleven o'clock position. To allow for rotation of the distributor drive as its skew gear meshes with the skew gear on the camshaft, the drive should be inserted with the slot vertical and the smaller offset towards the front of the engine. As the drive is pushed right home, the skew gears will turn the drive shaft anti-clockwise to the eleven o'clock position.

5 Remove the tappet cover bolt from the drive shaft.

6 Replace the distributor housing and lock it in position with the single bolt and lock washer.

7 The distributor can now be replaced and the two securing bolts and spring washers which hold the distributor clamping plate to the distributor housing, tightened. If the clamp bolt on the clamping plate was not previously loosened and the distributor body was not turned in the clamping plate, then the ignition timing will be as previously set. If the clamping bolt has been loosened, then it will be necessary to re-time the ignition as described in Chapter 4.

8 Tighten the two distributor clamping plate securing bolts firmly.

57 Flywheel housing oil seal - removal

If the sharp edges of the oil seal in the flywheel housing are at all damaged it is a simple matter to carefully prise it out. Keep it on one side to assist with the replacement of the new seal.

58 Flywheel housing oil seal - refitment

The new seal goes into position from the flywheel side of the flywheel housing. Ensure it enters the housing tensioning spring side first. Keep the oil seal square in the housing, and use the old seal to protect the new one as it is tapped or pressed gently into position.

59 Refitting the engine to the transmission casing - flywheel housing refitment

Carefully scrape away all traces of the old gaskets from the crankcase to transmission case joint and the engine/transmission to flywheel housing joints. **Note:** If it has been necessary to fit new transfer gears then it is essential to check the end float of the idler gear in the transmission casing before proceeding any further. See Chapter 6 for details.

1 Fit a new front bearing cork oil seal and position the crankcase to transmission casing gaskets carefully. Ensure the "O" ring on the top transmission casing flange is in place.

2 Lower the engine onto the transmission casing and ensure the cork oil seal and the gaskets do not slip.

3 Replace and tighten down the 10 set bolts and 2 nuts which hold the transmission casing to the engine. Use a torque of 6 lb ft (0.83 kg fm).

4 Ensure that the primary gear thrust washer is fitted next to the crankshaft with its bevelled edge against the crankshaft flange. Replace the "C" washer which locks the primary gear in place. Measure the primary gear end float which should be between 0.003 in. and 0.006 in. (0.0762 and 0.1524 mm). If this is incorrect, measure the gap without the thrust washer in position. The width of the gap will determine the washer that

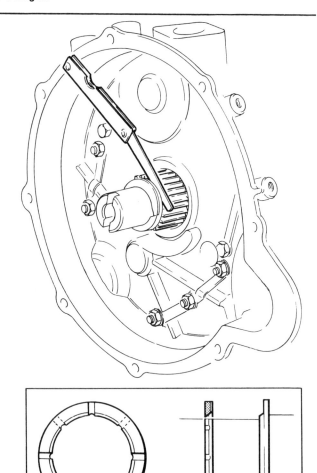

H13882

**Fig. 1.32. Measurement of primary gear end float
Inset shows thrust washer**

should be used to give the ideal clearance of 0.0045 in. (0.1016 mm).

Gap width	Washer thickness
0.1295 to 0.1315 in. (3.27 to 3.34 mm)	0.125 to 0.127 in. (3.17 to 3.22 mm)
0.1315 to 0.1335 in. (3.34 to 3.39 mm)	0.127 to 0.129 in. (3.22 to 3.27 mm)
0.1335 to 0.1345 in. (3.39 to 3.42 mm)	0.129 to 0.131 in. (3.27 to 3.32 mm)

5 Before fitting the flywheel housing make sure that a new flywheel housing oil seal has been fitted, and cover the splines of the crankshaft primary gear with the special thin sleeve used by BLMC garages. Alternatively, wrap a piece of tinfoil, tape or waxed paper tightly over the splines so no damage will be done to the oil seal by the sharp edges on the splines. Lubricate the seal prior to refitting the housing.

6 Fit a new gasket in position on the end of the engine/transmission casing. **Note:** The cut out on the outer edge. This is to allow a measurement to be taken with a feeler gauge when the housing bolts/nuts have been fully tightened down. This is to check that the gasket has compressed to the correct thickness of 0.030 in. (0.762 mm).

7 Carefully fit the housing in position. If the small roller bearing on the outer end of the first motion shaft will not

enter the housing, on no account try to force the housing on. Turn the bearing a quarter of a turn and try again. The rollers can be held in position with grease if wished. The second or third attempts are invariably successful.

8 Fit new locking tabs, and tighten down the nine nuts and six bolts evenly to a torque of 18 lb ft (2.49 mm). Make certain that the correct short bolt is fitted in the top right-hand position. Too long a bolt may damage the main oil gallery in the cylinder block.

60 Flywheel refitment

1 Turn the crankshaft so that cylinders 1 and 4 are at TDC and the grooves in the sides of the crankshaft are vertical.
2 Check that the curved portion of the "C" washer which holds the primary gear in place is at the top of the crankshaft, and that the sides of the washer fit in the crankshaft grooves.
3 Carefully clean the mating tapers in the flywheel and on the end of the crankshaft and make quite certain there are no traces of oil, grease, or dirt present. Sparingly lubricate the edges of the oil seal, where an oil seal is fitted - early models only.
4 Replace the flywheel on the end of the crankshaft with the 1/4 TDC markings at the top and then replace the driving washer which positively locates the flywheel.
5 Fit a new lock washer under the head of the flywheel securing bolt. Insert the bolt in the centre of the flywheel and tighten it to 110 to 115 lb ft. (15.20 to 15.89 kg fm)
6 Tap down the side of the lock washer against the driving plate, and tap up the other side of the washer against the retaining bolt head.
7 Fit the thrust plate.

61 Refitting the engine to the automatic transmission casing

1 Apply a little grease to the joint faces of the engine crankcase and locate a new joint washer in position.
2 Position the front main bearing cap oil seal on the transmission case.
3 Carefully lower the engine onto the transmission unit and start the retaining nuts and spring washers on the studs before completely lowering the engine onto the unit.
4 Tighten all retaining nuts evenly and with a sharp knife trim off any excess joint washer from the rear of the unit.
5 Reconnect and tighten the external oil feed pipe.
6 Refit the internal oil feed pipe into its locations in the oil pump and cylinder block.
7 Fit a new converter housing joint washer to the power unit.
8 Apply some tape to the splines on the converter output gear. Smear with a little grease.
9 Refit the converter housing, ensuring that the converter outlet pipe is in alignment with the nylon guide, so that the pipe will enter the valve block pipe chest.
10 Tighten the converter housing nuts and bolts to a torque wrench setting of 18 lb ft (2.5 kg fm). It is important that the UNC threaded screws locate in the transmission casing. Also the screw, with the copper washer, is fitted adjacent to the transverse selector rod.
11 Refit the input shaft washer and nyloc nut. Hold the converter output gear and tighten the retaining nut to a torque wrench setting of 70 lb ft (9.68 kg fm).
12 Refit the low pressure valve with a new joint washer.
13 Remove each pair of bolts in turn from the converter centre and refit them with new locking plates. Tighten the bolts to a torque wrench setting of 24 lb ft (3.32 kg fm). It is important that all six bolts are not removed at once.
14 Refit the converter and align the offset slot with that on the crankshaft. Replace the locating key plate.
15 Refit the converter retaining bolt with a new lock washer, hold the converter from turning and tighten the bolt to a torque wrench setting of 114 lb ft (15.75 kg fm).

16 Carefully bend over the lock washer tab.
17 Insert the rubber grommet into its location in the converter housing and refit the converter end cover.
18 The gear selector bell crank lever should next be refitted.
19 Refer to Chapter 10 and refit the starter motor.
20 Refer to Section 24 and refit the oil filter.
21 The unit is now ready for refitting to the car.

62 Final assembly

1 Refit the rocker cover, using a new cork gasket, and secure in position with the two domed nuts.
2 Fit the two tappet cover plates, using new gaskets and tighten the tappet chest bolts to a torque wrench setting of 2 lb ft (0.3 kg fm). Do not exceed this figure or the covers will distort and leak oil.
3 Fit a new manifold gasket over the studs taking care not to rip it as it passes over the stud threads.
4 Replace the manifold and secure in position with the six nuts, spring and large plain washers.
5 Insert the thermostat into its housing making sure the word "Front" marked on the flange is towards the front of the engine.
6 Fit a new gasket taking care not to rip the gasket as it passes over the threads of the three studs. Then refit the thermostat housing cover and secure with the three nuts and spring washers.
7 If the dipstick guide tube was removed this should next be inserted into its drilling in the side of the crankcase.
8 Fit a new oil filter canister (see Section 24).
9 It should be noted that in all cases it is best to reassemble the engine as far as possible before refitting it to the car. This means that the alternator, fan belt and other minor attachments should be replaced at this stage.

63 Engine refitment

Although the engine and transmission unit can be replaced by one man and a suitable hoist, it is easier if two are present; one to lower the unit into the engine compartment, and the other to guide the unit into position and to ensure it does not foul anything. Generally replacement is the reverse sequence to removal (see Sections 4 and 5). In addition however:
1 Ensure all the loose leads, cables etc., are tucked out of the way. It is easy to trap one and cause much additional work after the engine is replaced.
2 Carefully lower the unit into position. Then refit the following:

   (a) *Mounting nuts, bolts and washers*
   (b) *Drive shafts*
   (c) *Reconnect the clutch pipe to the slave cylinder and bleed the system (see Chapter 5)*
   (d) *Speedometer cable*
   (e) *Gear change lever linkage*
   (f) *Carpets (if removed)*
   (g) *Oil pressure switch cable*
   (h) *Water temperature indicator sender unit cable*
   (i) *Wire to coil, distributor and alternator*
   (j) *Carburettor controls and air cleaner*
   (k) *Exhaust manifold to down pipe*
   (l) *Earth and starter motor cables*
   (m) *Radiator, hoses and fan motor*
   (n) *Heater hoses*
   (o) *Engine closed circuit breather hoses*
   (p) *Vacuum advance and retard pipe*
   (q) *Battery (if removed)*
   (r) *Fuel lines to carburettor and pump*
   (s) *Bonnet*

3 Finally check that the drain taps are closed and refill the cooling system with water and the engine with oil.

64 Engine - initial start-up after overhaul or major repair

Make sure that the battery is fully charged and that all lubricants, coolants and fuel are replenished. (photo)

64a Refilling engine/transmission unit with oil

If the fuel system has been dismantled, it will require several revolutions of the engine on the starter motor to pump petrol up to the carburettor. An initial 'prime' of about 1/3 cup full of petrol down the air intake of the carburettor will help the engine to fire quickly, thus relieving the load on the battery. Do not overdo this however, as flooding may result.

As soon as the engine fires and runs, keep it going at a fast tickover only (no faster) and bring it up to normal working temperature.

As the engine warms up, there will be odd smells and some smoke from parts getting hot and burning off oil deposits. Look for leaks of water or oil which will be obvious if serious. Check also the clamp connection of the exhaust pipe to the manifold as these do not always 'find' their exact gas tight position until the warmth and vibration have acted on them, and it is almost certain that they will need tightening further. This should be done, of course, with the engine stopped.

When the engine running temperature has been reached, adjust the idling speed as described in Chapter 3.

Stop the engine and wait a few minutes to see if any lubricant or coolant drips out.

Road test the car to check that the timing is correct and giving the necessary smoothness and power. Do not race the engine - if new bearings and/or pistons and rings have been fitted, it should be treated as a new engine and run in at reduced revolutions for 500 miles (800 km).

For 'Fault diagnosis' see page 50.

7.2 After removing the flywheel casing by undoing the casing to crankcase bolts, the crankcase is separated from the gearbox casing.

11.16 Take off the rocker cover, tappet chest covers, rocker gear and pushrods and lift off the head.

16.2 The crankshaft fan belt pulley wheel can be gently eased off after the retaining bolt has been removed.

16.7a To prevent the camshaft gear wheel from turning, wedge the crankshaft with a length of wood - such as the hammer handle shown.

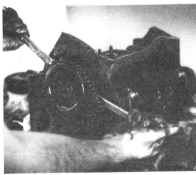

16.7b The gear wheels can be removed by judicious levering with spanners or broad screwdrivers as illustrated. Move each wheel a little in turn so as not to strain the chain.

17.2 The camshaft is removed from the front of the block. Make sure the peaks of the cams do not damage the white metal bearings.

18.2a The lower end of the drive fits into a recess in the block and the skew gear meshes with a similar gear on the camshaft.

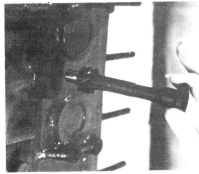

18.2b The next step is to remove the distributor drive. This can be removed by hand provided the sump is off.

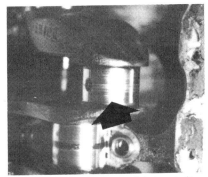

28A If a bearing begins to disintegrate it will soon mark the crankshaft. The ridges on the journals can be easily seen and also felt with a fingernail.

28B Check the diameter of the crankshaft journals with a micrometer. If the journals are oval or badly worn the crank must be reground.

29.2a Examine the shell bearings for wear. This one is in dreadful condition. The surface is worn and has actually started to break-up.

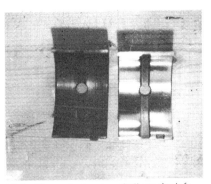

29.2b The main bearing shell on the left is worn and scored. Compare it with the condition of the new bearing on the right! Renew the bearing if worn.

30.2a Measure the wear in the cylinder bore with a micrometer. Your local engineering works will be able to do this for you.

30.2b If the bores are badly worn they must be rebored.

31.1 Carefully examine the piston and piston rings for wear. In this instance replacement of the complete piston is essential as the top ring has completely broken up and has damaged the piston.

31.3 Measure each piston ring gap in turn with a feeler gauge with the rings fitted in the bore.

37.1A Another item to check is the flywheel starter ring. The teeth may be chipped or just badly worn ...

37.1B ... as shown in this photograph. If damaged or badly worn the ring gear must be cut off and a new gear heated and shrunk on.

41.1 Before reassembly commences, the cylinder block must be thoroughly cleaned; both internally and externally.

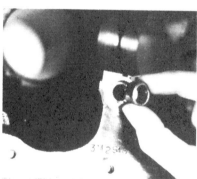
43.0 Before fitting the main bearings and crankshaft make sure the bearing cap locating dowels are in place.

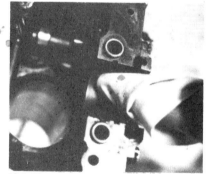
43.1 Thoroughly clean the bearing housings and the oilways in the block.

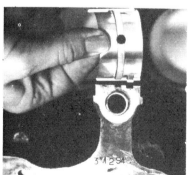
43.4 The next step is to fit the main bearing shells so that the lip on each shell engages with the machined slot in each bearing housing.

43.5 Thoroughly clean the main bearing cap and fit the shell bearing so the notch lies in the groove in the cap.

43.7 With the new shells fitted to the block, lubricate them generously with new engine oil. An old plastic detergent bottle makes a handy oilcan.

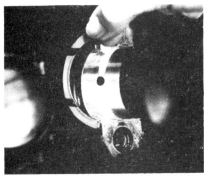

43.8 Next place a thrust washer, grooves facing outwards, on either side of the centre main bearing housing. Hold the washer to the block with a dab of grease.

43.9 Check that everything is scrupulously clean. Lubricate the main journals with engine oil before fitting the crankshaft to the crankcase.

43.13a With the shell bearing in place in the centre main bearing cap, fit the lower halves of the thrust washer, grooves facing outwards.

43.13b Fit the main bearing caps. When fitting the centre cap, ensure that the thrust washers are not dislodged.

43.14 Turn the crankshaft over with the aid of a screwdriver as shown to make sure there are no tight spots.

43.15a Tighten the main bearing cap bolt to a torque wrench setting of 60 lb f ft (8.3 kg f cm).

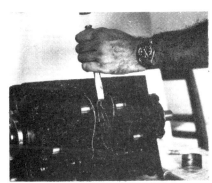

43.15b If locking tabs are fitted to the main bearing bolts, they should be knocked up against one of the 'flats' on the bolt head.

43.16 With the main bearing caps fitted check the crankshaft end float between the thrust washers and the crank with a feeler gauge. A 0.003 in. (0.0762 mm) end float is correct.

44.3 In this illustration the rods are correctly fitted to the pistons with the offsets the right way round.

46.2 Each piston is clearly marked 'Front'. Fit it this way round. The '3' in the diamond stamped on the block and piston crown indicates the grade of piston fitted.

46.4 When compressing the piston rings there is no need to use an expensive piston ring compressor. A Jubilee clip will do.

47.1 The connecting rod big end cap must be perfectly clean. The bearing shell can then be fitted with its lip locating in the groove in the rod.

47.3 Fit the big end cap bearing shell in the same way and make sure you replace the big end cap to the same connecting rod from which it was removed.

47.5 The next step is to tighten the big end bolts to a torque wrench setting of 45 lb f ft (6.22 kg f m) and then knock up the tab on the locking washer (where fitted).

48.2 Make sure a new gasket is properly positioned between the pump and the block. The slot in the rotor engages a raised lip in the end of the camshaft.

48.4 The pump is now securely fitted.

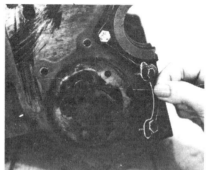

48.4a With the pump in place, fit the securing bolts and remember to turn up the tabs on the lockwasher.

49.2 The oil pressure relief valve fits into the threaded hole on the right-hand side of the engine at the rear.

50.1a The next step is to thoroughly clean the face of the block and fit a new front end plate gasket.

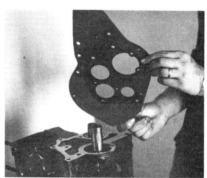

50.1b The front end plate must be carefully cleaned and then fitted to the block. Hold it in place with several bolts screwed in finger tight.

50.3 Fit the locking tab to the end plate as shown, and fit the two bolts. Turn up the tabs on the locking plate (if fitted).

50.4a With the front end plate in place the camshaft retaining plate can be fitted.

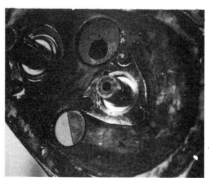

50.4b Fit and tighten down the three camshaft retaining plate bolts. Remember to fit spring washers,

50.5 If the original crankshaft is being fitted check the washers are in place on the crankshaft nose. They ensure the gear wheels lie in the same plane.

50.10 Fit the timing chain/gear wheel assembly onto the camshaft and crankshaft - keeping the timing marks adjacent.

50.13a Next, place the camshaft locking washer with its tag in the gear wheel keyway. Then fit the securing nut.

50.13b Tighten the camshaft gear wheel nut holding the crankshaft stationary with a spanner as shown. Make sure plenty of rag is placed between the spanner and the crankshaft.

50.14a Next bend back the camshaft locking washer to lock the camshaft gear wheel nut in place.

50.14b The gear wheels and timing chain are now in place and correctly positioned.

50.16 Place the oil thrower concave side down on the nose of the crankshaft. Remember to position the thrower so it fits over the crankshaft key.

50.17 The flange on the timing gear case must be carefully cleaned and scraped and a new gasket laid on the front end plate.

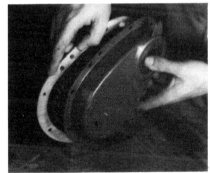

50.20 Replace the timing chain cover over the chain and gear wheels. Fit the retaining bolts and washers and tighten securely. Smear the edge of the oil seal with oil.

50.23a Next fit the crankshaft pulley wheel. Note that the wheel will only go on in one position with the crankshaft key entering the pulley groove.

50.23b Although correctly lined up, when a new oil seal has been fitted it is sometimes necessary to drive the wheel into place as shown.

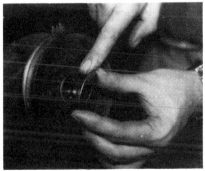

50.23c With the crankshaft pulley wheel in place fit the lockwasher so the tab locks into the pulley wheel groove.

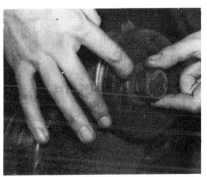

50.23d Next screw in the pulley wheel bolt. This is the largest bolt on the engine and it may be necessary to borrow a 1¼ in. AF socket.

50.23e Hold the crankshaft from turning by inserting a square section bar or similar in the slot at the flywheel end. Then tighten the bolt to the correct torque.

50.24 When the bolt is correctly tightened knock up the lockwasher against one of the flats on the bolt.

51.3 Now fit the water pump to the front of the engine. Make sure the mating surfaces are clean and that a new gasket is fitted.

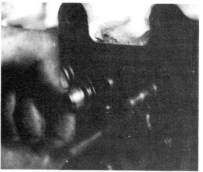

52.3 The next step is to fit the valves and valve springs to the cylinder head. Then fit the valve guide strouds in place.

52.7a Next fit each valve, oil seal and valve spring. Compress the spring with a compressor and make sure the head of the compressor does not slip.

52.7b Now fit the split collets. A trace of grease will help hold them to the valve stem recess. This job calls for care as the collets are small and easily dropped.

52.7c Slacken off the spring compressor until the collets are firmly held by the valve spring cup. Fit a circlip (where used) to the collets to make sure they stay together.

52.8 This is what the completed built-up valve and valve spring assembly should look like.

53.0 Next reassemble the rocker gear on the rocker shaft. Make sure that the oil holes are clear in the rocker shaft.

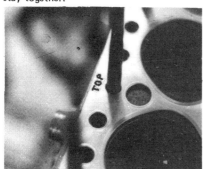

54.3 The next step is to thoroughly clean the face of the block and cylinder head. Fit a new cylinder head gasket with the side marked 'top' upwards.

54.5 The cylinder head can now be fitted. Keep the head and block parallel to each other so the head does not bind on the cylinder head studs.

54.6 Next fit the push rods with the mushroom shaped end fed into the block first. Make sure the push rods seat properly in the tappets.

54.9 Make sure that the rocker pedestal locking plate is fitted before replacing the rocker pedestal and cylinder head nuts.

54.12 The cylinder head and rocker bracket washers and nuts are now fitted. Tighten the nuts to the correct torque in the order shown in Fig. 1.14.

55.5 The next step is to set the valve clearances. Unlock the nut and screw the tappet adjusting screw up or down until the arm just nips the blade.

56.6a Next the distributor drive retaining plate is placed in position with the recessed hole lining up with the threaded hole in the flange on the block.

56.6b Screw in the retaining bolt and lock washer to secure the plate.

62.5 Fit the thermostat and thermostat cover and replace the spring washers and do up the three nuts.

62.6a Clean the thermostat housing flange and then fit a new gasket in place.

65 Fault diagnosis - engine

Symptom	Reason/s	Remedy
Engine will not turn over when starter switch is operated	Flat battery Bad battery connections Bad connections at solenoid switch and/or starter motor	Check that battery is fully charged and that all connections are clean and tight.
	Starter motor jammed	Rock car back and forth with a gear engaged. If ineffective remove starter (not automatic)
	Defective solenoid	Remove and check solenoid.
	Starter motor defective	Remove starter and overhaul.
Engine turns over normally but fails to fire and run	No spark at plugs	Check ignition system according to procedures given in Chapter 4.
	No fuel reaching engine	Check fuel system according to procedures given in Chapter 3.
	Too much fuel reaching the engine (flooding)	Check fuel system if necessary as described in Chapter 3.
Engine starts but runs unevenly and misfires	Ignition and/or fuel system faults	Check the ignition and fuel systems as though the engine had failed to start.
	Incorrect valve clearances	Check and reset clearances.
	Burnt out valves	Remove cylinder head and examine and overhaul as necessary.
Lack of power	Ignition and/or fuel system faults	Check the ignition and fuel systems for correct ignition timing and carburettor settings.
	Incorrect valve clearances	Check and reset the clearances.
	Burnt out valves	Remove cylinder head and examine and overhaul as necessary.
	Worn out piston or cylinder bores	Remove cylinder head and examine pistons and cylinder bores. Overhaul as necessary.
Excessive oil consumption	Oil leaks from crankshaft oil seal, rocker cover gasket, drain plug gasket, sump plug washer	Identify source of leak and repair as appropriate.
	Worn piston rings or cylinder bores resulting in oil being burnt by engine. Smoky exhaust is an indication	Fit new rings or rebore cylinders and fit new pistons, depending on degree of wear.
	Worn valve guides and/or defective valve stem seals	Remove cylinder head and recondition valve guides and valves and seals as necessary.
Excessive mechanical noise from engine	Wrong valve to rocker clearances	Adjust valve clearances.
	Worn crankshaft bearings Worn cylinders (piston slap)	Inspect and overhaul where necessary.
Unusual vibration	Misfiring on one or more cylinders	Check ignition system.
	Loose mounting bolts	Check tightness of bolts and condition of flexible mountings.

NOTE: When investigating starting and uneven running faults do not be tempted into snap diagnosis. Start from the beginning of the check procedure and follow it through. It will take less time in the long run. Poor performance from an engine in terms of power and economy is not normally diagnosed quickly. In any event the ignition and fuel systems must be checked first before assuming any further investigation needs to be made.

Chapter 2 Cooling system

Contents

Specifications

Type	Pressurised radiator. Thermo siphon, pump assisted. Thermostatically controlled electrically driven fan
Thermostat:	
Type	Non pressure sensitive - wax
Setting	Stamped on base of thermostat bulb
Blow off pressure of expansion tank cap	13 lb f in.^{2} (0.9 kg f cm^2)
Fan belt tension	0.5 in. (13 mm) total deflection on longest belt run
Fan motor light running current (less fan)	3 amp (max.) at 13.5V - after 60 seconds from cold
Fan motor light running speed (less fan)	3500 - 4000 rpm at 13.5V - after 60 seconds from cold
Fan motor minimum brush length	0.1875 in. (4.76 mm)
Fan motor relay:	
Winding resistance	76 ohms
Bobbin core to underside of armature air gap:	
Contact points open	0.025 ± 0.005 in. (0.64 ± 0.13 mm)
Contact points closed	0.015 ± 0.003 in. (0.38 ± 0.08 mm)
Cut-in voltage	5 — 9V
Drop off voltage	2.5V minimum
Water pump:	
Type	Centrifugal, impeller
Spindle diameter	0.6262 - 0.6267 in. (15.91 - 15.92 mm)
Impeller bore	0.6244 - 0.6252 in. (15.86 - 15.88 mm)
Pulley hub bore	0.6230 - 0.6247 in. (15.82 - 15.87 mm)
Bearing assembly dimension (measured from bearing outer race to water seal seating face in pump body)	0.533 - 0.543 in. (13.54 - 13.79 mm)
Impeller vane to pump body clearance	0.020 - 0.030 in. (0.51 - 0.76 mm)
Pulley hub assembly dimension (measured from the hub pulley face to the pump body joint face)	3.712 - 3.732 in. (94.3 - 94.8 mm)
Cooling system capacity:	
Less heater	6.25 pints (3.5 litres)
Heater	1 pint (0.568 litre)
Coolant mixture	Water or water and antifreeze mixture. Antifreeze of ethylene glycol base to BS 3151 or 3152

Torque wrench settings:	lb f ft	kg fm
Fan motor through bolts	14	0.17
Cylinder head nuts	50	6.90
Water pump securing bolts	16	2.21
Water outlet elbow nuts	8	1.10

1 General description

The engine cooling water is circulated by a thermo syphon, water pump assisted system. The coolant is pressurised. This is primarily to prevent premature boiling in adverse conditions and also to allow the engine to operate at its most efficient running temperature, this being just under the boiling point of water. The overflow pipe from the radiator is connected to an expansion tank which makes topping up unnecessary. The coolant expands when hot, and instead of being forced down the overflow pipe and lost, it flows into the expansion tank. As the engine cools the coolant contracts and because of the pressure differential flows back into the radiator.

The cap on the expansion tank is set to a pressure of 13 lb f in^2 (0.9 kg f cm^2) which increases the boiling point of the coolant to approximately 230°F. If the water temperature exceeds this figure and the water boils, the pressure in the system forces the internal valve of the cap off its seat thus opening the expansion tank overflow pipe along which the steam from the boiling water escapes and so relieves the pressure. It is, therefore, important to check that the expansion tank cap is in good condition and that the spring behind the sealing washers has not weakened. Check that the rubber has not perished and its seating in the neck is clean to ensure a good seal. Most garages have a special tool which enables the pressure cap to be pressure tested.

The cooling system comprises the radiator, top and bottom hoses, metal piping, heater hoses, the water pump (mounted on the front of the engine), the thermostat and drain plugs.

The system functions in the following manner: Cold water from the bottom of the radiator circulates along the lower radiator hose to the pump where it is pushed along the water passages in the cylinder block, helping to keep the cylinder bores and pistons cool.

The water then travels up into the cylinder head and circulates round the combustion chambers and valve seats absorbing more heat. Then, when the engine is at its correct operating temperature, the water travels out of the cylinder head, past the open thermostat into the upper radiator hose, and so into the radiator. The water travels across the radiator where it is cooled primarily by the rush of cold air through the radiator core.

To ensure that the engine does not overheat a thermo-statically controlled electrically driven fan is located behind the radiator to create or assist air flow through the radiator core when the car is being driven very slowly or is stationary.

When the engine is cold the thermostat (a valve able to open and close according to the temperature) maintains the circulation of water in the engine by returning it via the by-pass to the cylinder block. Only when the correct minimum operating temperature has been reached does the thermostat begin to open, allowing water to return to the radiator.

2 Cooling sytem - draining

1 If the engine is cold first remove the filler plug located on the top of the engine water outlet elbow.
2 If the engine is hot, then turn the expansion tank pressure cap very slightly until pressure in the system has had time to release. Use a rag over the cap to protect your hand from escaping steam. If, with the engine very hot, the cap is released suddenly, the drop in pressure can result in the water boiling. With the pressure released the cap can be removed. Now the filler plug located on the top of the engine water outlet elbow may be removed.
3 When antifreeze is being used in the cooling system, drain it into a bowl having a capacity of at least 7.25 pints (4.068 litres) for re-use.
4 Undo and remove the drain plug from the cylinder block just below the air cleaner air intake.
5 Slacken the clips securing the bottom hose connecting pipe

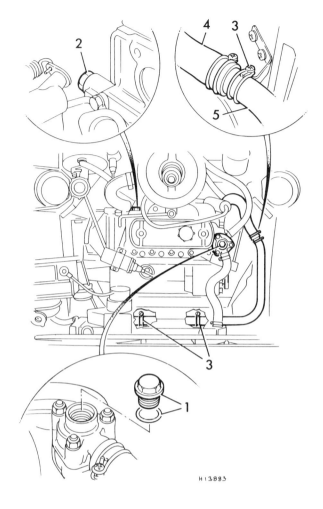

Fig. 2.1. Cooling system draining and refilling points

1 Filler plug and washer
2 Cylinder block drain plug
3 Hose clips
4 Water pump hose
5 Connecting pipe

to the front crossmember and wing valance.
6 Disconnect the water pump hose from the connecting pipe.
7 Detach the connecting pipe from the wing valance and push the connecting pipe downwards to complete the draining of the cooling system.
8 When the water has finished running, probe the drain plug orifice with a short piece of wire to dislodge any particles of rust or sediment which may be causing a blockage.
9 It is important to note that the heater cannot be fully drained so during cold weather an antifreeze solution must be used. Always use an antifreeze with an ethylene glycol or glycerine base.

3 Cooling system - flushing

With time the cooling system will gradually lose its efficiency as the radiator becomes choked with rust, scale deposits from the water, and other sediment. To clean the system; remove the top and bottom hoses from the radiator and leave a hose running first in the top hose connection of the radiator for about ten minutes and then reverse the flow by putting the hose into the bottom hose connection of the radiator.

The thermostat should then be removed and the engine

flushed out in both directions by placing the hose pipe in the top and bottom hoses. Pack it with rag. During this operation it would be advantageous to remove the cylinder block drain plug.

It is recommended that you place some polythene over the engine (if the engine is cool) to stop water finding its way into the ignition system.

4 Cooling system - refilling

1 Refit the water pump hose to the connecting pipe and tighten the clip.
2 Retighten the connecting pipe clips.
3 Refit the cylinder block drain plug.
4 The system should now be refilled. The total capacity (including heater) is 7.25 pints (4.068 litres). If antifreeze is to be used make up a solution to the ratio given in Section 20 of this Chapter.
5 The coolant should come up to the top of the filler plug hole in the engine water outlet elbow. Now refit the filler plug.
6 Fill the expansion tank with coolant up to the level mark on the side. Add a further 0.5 pint (250 cc) of coolant to the expansion tank to compensate for air trapped in the cooling system.
7 Refit the expansion tank filler cap.

5 Radiator - removal, inspection and cleaning

1 Refer to Section 2 and drain the cooling system.

2 For safety reasons disconnect the battery.
3 Disconnect the wiring harness plug and socket located at the rear of the fan motor.
4 Disconnect the wiring harness from the fan motor thermostatic switch located at the top hose end of the radiator.
5 Slacken the clip and disconnect the top hose from the radiator.
6 Release the expansion tank hose clip at the radiator end and disconnect the hose from the radiator.
7 Slacken the three clips, to release the bottom hose connecting pipe from the front crossmember and left-hand front wing valance.
8 Undo and remove the two set screws securing the two radiator top mounting brackets to the bonnet lock platform.
9 Carefully remove the radiator complete with fan motor, bottom hose and connecting pipe from the engine compartment.
10 Disconnect the two mounting brackets from the top of the radiator.
11 Release the clip and disconnect the bottom hose complete with connecting pipe from the radiator.
12 Undo and remove the four set screws securing the fan cowl and mounting bracket assembly to the radiator. Lift away the fan cowl assembly.
13 Release the two spring clips securing the thermostatic switch retaining plate to the radiator. Lift away the thermostatic switch complete with sealing bush from the radiator.
14 With the radiator away from the car any leaks can be soldered or repaired with a body filling compound such as 'Holts Cataloy'. Clean the inside of the radiator by flushing as described earlier in this Chapter. When the radiator is out of the car it is advantageous to reverse flush it. Clean the exterior

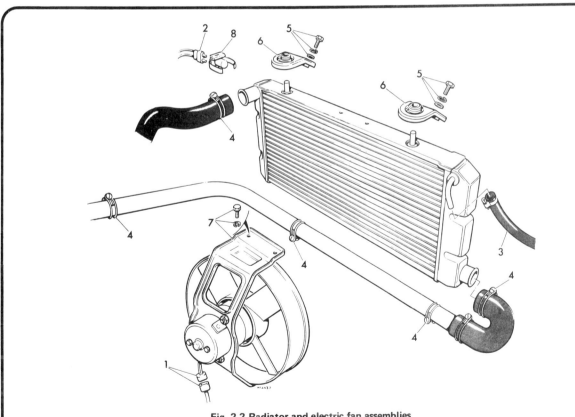

Fig. 2.2 Radiator and electric fan assemblies

1 Fan motor cable connections	3 Hose to expansion tank	plain washer
2 Thermostatic switch cable connector	4 Clip	6 Mounting bracket
	5 Setscrew, spring and	7 Setscrew and spring washer
		8 Thermostatic fan switch

of the radiator by carefully using a compressed air jet or a strong jet of water to clear away road dirt, flies etc.

15 Inspect the radiator hoses for cracks, internal or external perishing and damage by overtightening of the securing clips. Replace the hoses if suspect. Examine the radiator hose and expansion tank pipe clips and renew them if they are rusted or distorted.

6 Radiator - refitment

1 Refitting the radiator is the reverse sequence to removal (see Section 5).
2 If new hoses are to be used they can be a little difficult to fit, especially, to the radiator; lubricate them with a little soap.
3 Refill the cooling system as described in Section 4.

7 Thermostat - removal, testing and refitment

1 To remove the thermostat, first partially drain the cooling system (usually 4 pints (2.273 litres) is enough).
2 Undo and remove the filler plug located on the top of the engine water outlet elbow. Recover the sealing washer.
3 Undo and remove the three nuts and spring washers securing the engine water outlet pipe to the top of the sandwich plate on the cylinder head.
4 Lift away the engine water outlet pipe and its gasket.
5 Note which way round the thermostat is fitted and lift it away from the sandwich plate.
6 Test the thermostat for correct functioning by suspending it on a string in a saucepan of cold water together with a thermometer. Heat the water and note the temperature at which the thermostat begins to open. The nominal temperature in degrees C at which the thermostat opens is stamped on the base of the thermostat bulb. Continue heating the water until the thermostat is fully open. Then let it cool down naturally.
7 If the thermostat does not fully open in boiling water, or does not close down as the water cools, then it must be discarded and a new one fitted. Should the thermostat be stuck open when cold this will be apparent when removing it from the housing.
8 Refitting the thermostat is the reverse sequence to removal. Always ensure that the thermostat sandwich plate and engine water outlet pipe elbow mating faces are clean and flat. If the elbow is badly corroded and eaten away, fit a new elbow. Always use a new gasket.

8 Expansion tank - removal and refitment

1 Open the bonnet and disconnect the two battery terminals. Unscrew the battery clamp nuts, detach the clamp and lift away the battery.
2 If the engine is cold remove the expansion tank pressure cap. If the engine is hot turn the expansion tank pressure cap very slightly until pressure in the system has had time to release. Use a rag over the cap to protect your hand from escaping steam. If, with the engine very hot, the cap is released suddenly, the drop in pressure can result in the water boiling. With the pressure released the cap can be removed.
3 Unwind the hose clip and disconnect the hose from the expansion tank. Be prepared to collect the coolant as it flows from the underside of the expansion tank and hose.
4 Undo and remove the two screws securing the expansion tank to the battery retaining plate. Lift away the expansion tank.
5 Refitting the expansion tank is the reverse sequence to removal. Refill with coolant up to the level mark on the side of the tank.

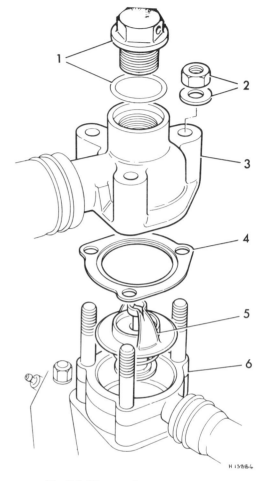

Fig. 2.3. Water outlet and thermostat

1 Filler plug and washer   4 Gasket
2 Nut and washer   5 Thermostat
3 Water outlet   6 Sandwich plate

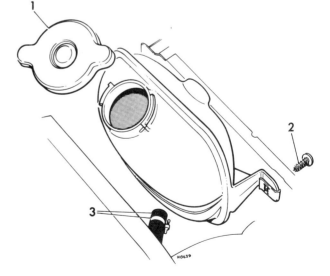

Fig. 2.4. Expansion tank and attachments

1 Expansion tank pressure   2 Self tapping screws
   cap   3 Hose and clip

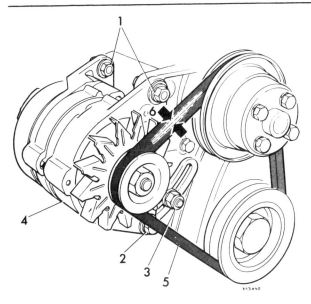

Fig. 2.5. Fan belt

1 *Alternator to bracket*
  securing nuts and bolts
2 *Alternator to slotted link*
  nut and bolt
3 *Slotted link securing nut*

4 *Alternator*
5 *Belt*
6 *Belt tension 0.5 in.*
  (13 mm) early models
  0.25 in (6 mm) later models

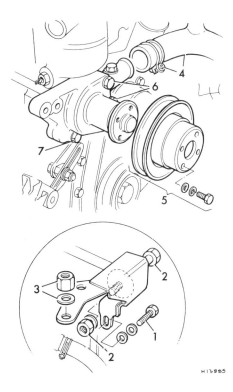

Fig. 2.6. Water pump and attachments

1 *Engine left-hand steady bracket to cylinder head bolt and*
  washers
2 *Engine steady to bracket nut and bolt*
3 *Nut and washer*
4 *Water pump hose and clip*
5 *Pulley to hub bolts and washers*
6 *Water pump securing bolts*
7 *Water pump lower bolt*

9 Fan belt - removal and refitment

If the belt is worn or has stretched badly it should be renewed. Often the reason for replacement is that the belt has broken in service, For this reason it is recommended that a spare belt is always carried in the car.

1 To remove the existing fan belt: slacken the alternator pivot bolts, and free the adjustment strap. Swing the alternator towards the cylinder block until the fan belt is slack enough to be removed.

2 Replacement is a reverse of the removal sequence, but as replacement is often due to breakage it is described below:

A Loosen the alternator pivot and slotted link nuts and bolts and move the alternator towards the engine.

B Carefully fit the new belt over the three pulleys and then adjust the belt as detailed in the following section and tighten the alternator mounting bolts. **Note**: after fitting a new belt it will require adjustment 250 miles (400 km) later.

10 Fan belt - adjustment

It is important to keep the belt correctly adjusted and it is considered that this should be a regular maintenance task (every 6,000 miles (10,000 km). If the belt is too loose, it will slip, wear rapidly and cause the water pump and alternator to malfunction. If the belt is too tight, the alternator and water pump bearings will wear rapidly, causing premature failure of these components.

The belt tension is correct when there is 0.5 inch (13 mm) of lateral movement at the mid point position of the longest belt run. This should be 0.25 in (6 mm) on Mk 2 and 3 models.

To adjust the belt, slacken the alternator securing bolts and nuts and move the alternator in or out until the correct tension is obtained. It is easier if the alternator bolts are only slackened a little so it requires some force to move the alternator. In this way the tension of the belt can be arrived at more quickly than by making frequent adjustments. If difficulty is experienced in moving the alternator away from the engine, a tyre lever or piece of wood placed behind the alternator and resting against the block gives good control so that the alternator can be held in position whilst the securing bolts are tightened.

11 Water pump - removal and refitment

1 Refer to Section 2 and drain the cooling system.

2 Release the alternator adjustment link nut and set screw.

3 Undo and remove the two alternator pivot bolts and nuts.

4 Undo and remove the bolt and washers that secure the engine left-hand steady bracket to the cylinder head.

5 Undo and remove the bolt and nut to release the engine left-hand steady from the bracket on the cylinder head.

6 Undo and remove the two cylinder head nuts to release the engine left-hand steady bracket..

7 Slacken the hose clip and detach the hose from the water pump body.

8 Undo and remove the four bolts spring and plain washers securing the drive pulley to the water pump spindle hub; lift away the pulley.

9 Undo and remove the four bolts securing the water pump to the front face of the cylinder block. Lift away the water pump and recover the gasket.

10 Refitting the water pump is the reverse sequence to removal, but the following additional points should be noted: noted:

a) Make sure the mating faces of the water pump and cylinder block are clean. Always use a new gasket.

b) Adjust the fan belt tension as described in Section 10.

c) Tighten the cylinder head nuts to a torque wrench setting of 50 lb f ft (6.90 kg fm).

d) Refill the cooling system as described in Section 4.

12 Water pump - dismantling and overhaul

Before undertaking the dismantling of a water pump to effect a repair check that all parts are available. It may be quicker and more economical to replace the complete unit.

1 Using a universal puller and suitable thrust block draw the pulley hub from the bearing and spindle assembly. If it is very tight a press will have to be used.

2 Suitably support the water pump body and drive out the bearing, spindle and impeller assembly from the pump body.

3 Using the universal puller and suitable thrust block draw the impeller from the bearing and spindle assembly. If it is very tight a press will have to be used.

4 The water seal may now be removed from the spindle. Note which way round it is fitted.

5 The spindle and bearing assembly is renewable as a unit which must be obtained if the bearing is worn, the impeller or hub loose on the spindle, or the bearing outer track a loose fit in the pump body.

6 To reassemble the water pump carefully drift the bearing and spindle assembly into the pump body until dimension A (Fig. 2.7) is obtained.

7 Lubricate the impeller sealing face with a little silicon based grease.

8 Carefully drift the impeller onto the bearing spindle so that the impeller to pump body clearance (dimension "B") is 0.020 - 0.030 in (0.51 - 0.76 mm).

9 Drift the pulley hub onto the bearing spindle so that the pulley hub assembled dimension ("C") is 3.712-3.732 in (94.3-94.8 mm). For this it is important that the spindle is supported and not the impeller or pump body.

13 Fan motor - removal and refitment

1 For safety reasons, disconnect the battery.

2 Locate and disconnect the wiring harness plug and socket at the rear of the fan motor.

3 Undo and remove the four set screws spring and plain washers securing the fan cowl and mounting bracket assembly to the radiator.

4 Lift away the fan cowl and mounting bracket complete with fan motor from behind the radiator.

5 If it is necessary to remove the fan blades undo the small grub screw in the fan hub and draw off the fan assembly.

6 To remove the fan motor undo and remove the three screws securing the motor to the cowl and mounting bracket. Lift away the motor.

7 Refitting the motor is the reverse sequence to removal.

14 Fan motor - testing and overhaul

1 Refer to Section 13 and remove the motor from the cowl and mounting bracket.

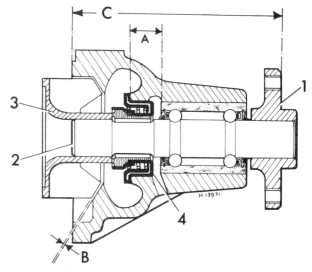

Fig. 2.7. Water pump cross sectional view

1 Pulley hub   3 Impeller
2 Spindle   4 Seal assembly
A Bearing assembly dimension *
B Impeller vane to pump body clearance *
C Pulley hub assembly dimension *
   * See specifications

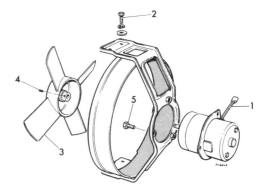

Fig. 2.8. Fan motor assembly

1 Fan motor cable connector
2 Fan cowl and mounting bracket securing setscrew, spring and plain washer
3 Fan blade assembly
4 Grub screw
5 Fan motor to cowl and mounting bracket securing screw

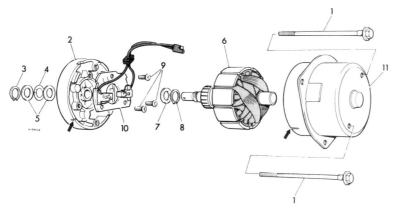

Fig. 2.9. Exploded view of fan motor

1   Through bolt
2   End cover
3   Circlip
4   Bowed spring washer
5   Shim washer
6   Armature
7   Thrust washer
8   Circlip
9   Brush carrier securing screws
10 Brush carrier
11 Yoke

2 Connect the motor, with the fan blades removed, to a 13.5 volt DC supply in series with a moving coil ammeter and check the light running current of the motor. This should be 3 amps after 60 seconds from cold. The light running speed should be 3500 - 4000 rev/min.
3 If it is observed that the current and speed are lower than specified it indicates that the commutator is dirty or the brush gear is faulty.
4 If after overhaul the current is high suspect misalignment of the end cover bearing. This may be corrected by applying a series of light blows to the side of the motor end cover - using a soft faced hammer. Should this not cure the trouble it is an indication that the armature is at fault.
5 To dismantle the motor; first undo and remove the two long through bolts.
6 Lift the end cover complete with armature from the motor yoke. Note the assembly marks on the end cover and yoke to ensure correct reassembly.
7 Using a pair of circlip pliers remove the circlip from the armature spindle and slide off the two shim washers and the bowed spring washer.
8 The armature assembly may now be separated from the end cover.
9 Recover the thrust washer from the armature spindle.
10 Again using circlip pliers remove the second circlip from the armature spindle.
11 Undo and remove the three screws securing the brush carrier assembly to the end cover. Lift away the brush carrier assembly.
12 Measure the length of the brushes, and if less than 0.1875 in. (4.7625 mm) the old brushes should be removed and new ones fitted.
13 If an armature fault is suspected, the armature should be taken to the local automobile electrical specialist who will be able to test it, using specialist equipment.
14 Clean the commutator with a petrol moistened cloth. If it is grooved it is possible to machine it using a lathe turning at high speed. Again this is a job for the local automobile electrical specialist. After skimming remove any copper swarf from the intersegment spaces. **Do not undercut the commutator segments.** Should the surface just be dirty it may be polished using a very fine glasspaper.
15 Reassembling the motor is the reverse sequence to dismantling. However the following additional points should be noted.
a) Sparingly lubricate the bearing bushes and the armature shaft bearing surfaces with Shell Turbo 41 oil.
b) Make sure the assembly marks on the yoke and the end cover are in alignment.
c) The bowed spring washers must be fitted between the two shim washers.
d) Tighten the two through bolts to a torque wrench setting of 14 lb f ft (0.17 kg f m).

15 Fan motor relay - testing

1 For this task an ohmmeter, a voltmeter, variable resistance and selection of bulbs will be required. If not available the unit should be taken to the local automobile electrical specialists.
2 Connect a 12 volt dc supply between the relay terminals "W1" and "W2" and a 12 volt 2.2 W test light in circuit with a 12 volt dc supply between terminals "C1" and "C2".
3 If the test light fails to light, the relay winding resistance should be checked using an ohmmeter connected between terminals "W1" and "W2". The correct resistance is 76 ohms. Should the resistance be incorrect the relay must be renewed.
4 If the resistance is correct the contacts may be adjusted. First uncrimp and remove the cover from the relay body.
5 Using feeler gauges measure the air gap between the relay bobbin core and underside of the armature. This should be 0.025 ± 0.005 in. (0.64 ± 0.13 mm). Bend the armature stop

plate to adjust the air gap when the points are open. When the contact points are closed the gap should be 0.015 ± 0.003 in. (0.38 ± 0.08 mm) and may be adjusted by bending the fixed contact post.
6 After any adjustment of the air gap, check the relay cut-in and drop off voltages in the following manner:
a) Connect a 24 volt battery and variable resistance between the relay terminals "W1" and "W2" and a 12 volt battery with test light in circuit between terminals "C1" and "C2".
b) Slowly raise the voltage from 0 to 15v and check that the light glows at the cut-in voltage of between 5 and 9 volts.
c) Now slowly lower the voltage from 15v to OV and check the drop-off voltage which should be a minimum of 2.5 volts.
d) If the above readings are not obtained refer to paragraph 5 and check the settings. Re-check once more.
7 Replace the relay cover and circlip over the cover lip.

16 Fan motor relay - removal and refitment

1 For safety reasons, disconnect the battery.
2 Make a note of their position and then disconnect the four terminal connectors from the underside of the relay.
3 Undo and remove the two screws securing the relay to the right-hand front wing valance. Lift away the relay.
4 Refitting the relay is the reverse sequence to removal.

17 Fan motor thermostatic switch - testing

1 Should the thermostatic switch operation be suspect it will be indicated by the cooling fan failing to operate when the engine coolant is at or very near to boiling point.
2 Before removing the switch check that the circuit is not at fault by disconnecting the wiring harness from the switch and bridging the two terminals in the wiring harness.
3 Switch on the ignition; if the wiring is in order the fan should operate. Otherwise check the circuit referring to the wiring diagram in Chapter 10.

18 Fan motor thermostatic switch - removal and refitmant

1 For safety reasons disconnect the battery.
2 Disconnect the wiring harness from the two terminals on the thermostatic switch.
3 Refer to Section 2 and partially drain the cooling system.
4 Release the two spring clips from the radiator and lift away the thermostatic switch retaining plate.
5 The thermostatic switch may now be withdrawn from the radiator.
6 Lift away the sealing bush from the thermostatic switch body.
7 Refitting the thermostatic switch is the reverse sequence to removal. Always use a new bush.

19 Temperature gauge sender unit - testing, removal and refitment

1 Should both fuel and temperature gauges record incorrect readings then the fault lies either in the battery or its connections, loose or bad earth connections or the voltage stabilizer or poorly earthed.
2 If the temperature gauge only, registers an incorrect reading then the fault lies in its own circuit, Check that all wiring connections are clean and secure and that all the relative parts are well earthed. The battery open circuit voltage should be checked and the resultant readings be over 11 volts.
3 If the voltage stabilizer is suspect, provide an alternative good earth for the unit and note any change in the fuel and temperature gauge readings. If it is still incorrect a new

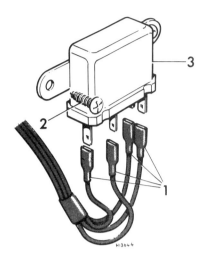

Fig. 2.10. Fan motor relay

1 Electrical terminal connectors
2 Relay securing screw
3 Relay

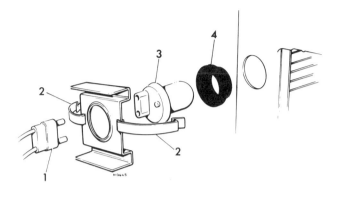

Fig. 2.11. Fan motor thermostatic switch

1 Terminal connector   3 Thermostatic switch
2 Spring clip   4 Sealing bush

stabilizer should be fitted.

4 Connect a wire between the sender unit terminal and the temperature gauge terminal and with the engine at normal operating temperature, note any change in the gauge reading. If the reading is correct with the additional wire connected then suspect faulty wiring or dirty terminal connections.

5 The best method of testing the sender unit is to substitute a new one. To remove the sender unit: first, partially drain the cooling system as described in Section 2.

6 Disconnect the electrical cable at its terminal and unscrew the sender unit from its location at the base of the thermostat housing.

7 Fitting a new sender unit is the reverse sequence to removal.

8 If the reading is still incorrect then a new temperature gauge should be fitted.

20 Antifreeze mixture

1 In circumstances where it is likely that the temperature will drop below freezing it is essential that some water is drained and an adequate amount of ethylene glycol based antifreeze is added to the cooling system.

2 Any antifreeze which conforms to specifications BS 3151 or BS 3152 can be used. Never use an antifreeze with an alcohol base as evaporation losses are too high.

3 Antifreeze with an anti-corrosion additive can be left in the cooling system for up to two years, but after six months it is advisable to have the specific gravity of the coolant checked at your local garage, and thereafter once every three months.

4 Add a 30% antifreeze solution (¼ pint - 0.142 litre) to the expansion tank to prevent freezing.

5 The table below gives the amount of antifreeze and the degree of protection.

Antifreeze	Commences to freeze		Frozen solid		Amount of antifreeze	
%	°C	°F	°C	°F	Pints	Litres
25	−13	+9	−26	−15	1.75	1.0
33.1/3	−19	−2	−36	−33	2.5	1.3
50	−36	−33	−48	−53	3.5	2.0

6 Never use antifreeze in the windscreen washer reservoir as it will cause damage to the paintwork.

21 Fault diagnosis - Cooling system

Symptom	Reason/s	Remedy
OVERHEATING Heat generated in cylinder not being successfully disposed of by radiator	Insufficient water in cooling system	Top up.
	Water pump belt slipping (accompanied by a shrieking noise on rapid engine acceleration)	Tighten belt to recommended tension or replace if worn.
	Radiator core blocked or radiator grille restricted	Reverse flush radiator, remove obstructions.
	Bottom water hose collapsed, impeding flow	Remove and fit new hose.
	Thermostat not opening properly	Remove and fit new thermostat.
	Ignition advance and retard incorrectly set (accompanied by loss of power and perhaps, misfiring)	Check and reset ignition timing.
	Carburettor incorrectly adjusted (mixture too weak)	Tune carburettor.
	Exhaust system partially blocked	Check exhaust pipe for constrictive dents and blockages.
	Oil level in sump too low	Top up sump to full mark on dipstick.
	Blown cylinder head gasket (water/steam being forced down the radiator overflow pipe under pressure)	Remove cylinder head, fit new gasket.
	Engine not yet run-in	Run-in slowly and carefully.
	Brakes binding	Check and adjust brakes if necessary.
	Electric fan not operating	Test thermostatic switch and circuit.
UNDERHEATING Too much heat being dispersed by radiator	Thermostat jammed open	Remove and renew thermostat.
	Incorrect grade of thermostat fitted allowing premature opening of valve	Remove and replace with new thermostat which opens at a higher temperature.
	Thermostat missing	Check and fit correct thermostat.
	Thermostatic switch operating too early	Fit new switch.
LOSS OF COOLING WATER Leaks in system	Loose clips on water hoses	Check and tighten clips if necessary.
	Top or bottom water hoses perished and leaking	Check and replace any faulty hoses.
	Radiator core leaking	Remove radiator and repair.
	Thermostat gasket leaking	Inspect and renew gasket.
	Pressure cap spring worn or seal ineffective	Renew pressure cap.
	Blown cylinder head gasket (Pressure in system forcing water/steam down overflow pipe.	Remove cylinder head and fit new gasket.
	Cylinder wall or head cracked	Dismantle engine, dispatch to engineering works for repair.

Chapter 3 Fuel system and carburation

For modifications, and information applicable to later models, see Supplement at end of manual

Contents

Specifications

Air cleaner:

Type	Replaceable paper element

Carburettor:

Type	SU HS4 horizontal
Specification:	
1100	AUD 608
1300	AUD 594
Piston spring	Red
Jet size	0.090 in. (2.29 mm)
Needle:	
1100	ABP
1300	ABB

Fuel pump:

Make	SU mechanical
Type	AUF 804 - lever operated
Suction (min.)	6.0 in. (152 mm) Hg
Pressure (max.)	4.0 lb f in.^{2} (0.2 kg f cm^2)

Engine idle speed:

1100	550 rpm
1300	650 rpm

Engine fast idle speed:

1100	1050 rpm
1300	1050 rpm

Fuel tank:

Type	Flat tank under rear floor between rear wheels
Capacity	10.5 gallons (47.67 litres)
Fuel octane rating:	
1100	95
1300	97

Torque wrench settings:	lb f ft	kg fm
Manifold to cylinder head nuts	8	1.10
Fuel pump to cylinder block	15	2.1

1 General description

The fuel system comprises a fuel tank at the rear of the car, a mechanical fuel pump and a single horizontally mounted SU carburettor. A renewable paper element air cleaner is fitted. Operation of the individual components is described elsewhere in this Chapter.

2 Fuel pump - general description

The mechanically operated fuel pump is located on the side of the crankcase and is operated by a seperate lobe on the camshaft. As the camshaft rotates the rocker lever is actuated, one end of which is connected to the diaphragm operating rod. When the rocker arm is moved by the cam lobe the diaphragm via the rocker moves downwards causing fuel to be drawn in, past the inlet valve and into the diaphragm chamber. As the cam lobe moves round, the diaphragm moves upwards under the action of the spring and fuel flows via the outlet valve to the carburettor float chamber.

When the float chamber has the requisite amount of fuel in it, the needle valve in the top of the float chamber shuts off the fuel supply, causing pressure in the fuel delivery line to hold the diaphragm down against the action of the diaphragm spring until the needle valve in the float chamber opens to admit more fuel.

3 Fuel pump - removal and refitment

1 Remove the fuel inlet and outlet connections from the fuel pump and plug the ends of the pipes to stop loss of fuel or dirt ingress.
2 Unscrew and remove the two pump mounting flange nuts and spring washers. Carefully slide the pump off the two studs followed by the insulating block assembly and gaskets.
3 Refitment is the reverse sequence to removal. Inspect the gaskets on each side of the insulating block and if damaged obtain, and fit new one.
4 Tighten the securing nuts to a torque wrench setting of 15 lb f ft (2.1 kg fm).

4 Fuel pump - overhaul

The fuel pump is a sealed unit and is serviced as an assembly. Should it develop a fault then a new pump will have to be obtained and fitted.

5 Fuel pump - testing

If the pump operation is suspect it may be dry tested by holding a finger over the inlet union and operating the rocker lever through three complete strokes. When the finger is released a suction noise should be heard. Next hold a finger over the outlet nozzle and press the rocker arm fully. The pressure generated should hold for a minimum of fifteen seconds.

6 Air cleaner - removal, refitment and element renewal

1 Undo and remove the two centre fixing wing nuts and lift away the air cleaner assembly from the carburettor air intake manifold (photos).
2 Carefully prise off the cover with a screwdriver inserted beneath one of the slots. Lift away the cover.

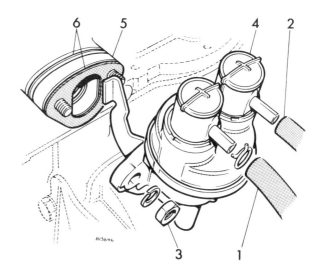

Fig. 3.1. Fuel pump removal

1 Inlet hose	4 Pump body
2 Outlet hose	5 Insulator
3 Nut	6 Joint washers

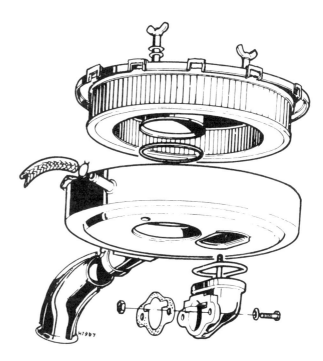

Fig. 3.2. Exploded view of air cleaner

3 Alternatively, the cover may be removed with the air cleaner body still on the air intake manifold.
4 The used element may now be lifted from the air cleaner body (photos).
5 Thoroughly clean the air cleaner body, cover, and air intake tube.
6 Make sure that the 'O' ring seal is in place in the main casing.
7 Fit a new element and replace the cover ensuring the arrow is aligned with the location lug on the air cleaner body (photo).

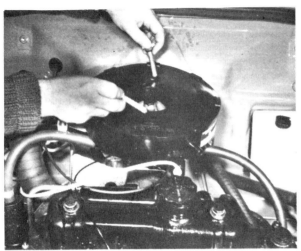
6.1a Centre fixing wing nuts removal

8 Make sure that the seal is correctly located on the carburettor air intake manifold.
9 Refit the air cleaner assembly and secure with the two wing nuts.
10 If necessary slacken the air intake clip and turn the intake to the necessary Winter or Summer position. Retighten the clip.

7 Carburettor - description

1 The variable choke SU carburettor, shown in component form is a relatively simple instrument. It differs from most other carburettors in that instead of having a number of various sized fixed jets for different conditions, only one variable jet is fitted to deal with all possible conditions.
2 Air passing rapidly through the carburettor draws petrol from the jet so forming the petrol/air mixture. The amount of petrol drawn from the jet depends on the position of the tapered carburettor needle which moves up and down the jet

6.1b Lifting away air cleaner assembly

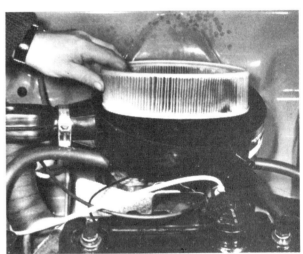
6.4a Lifting away element

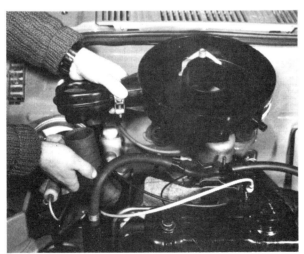
6.4b Lifting away air cleaner body

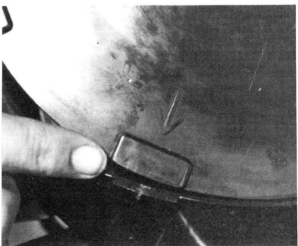
6.7 Cover arrow and locating lug alignment

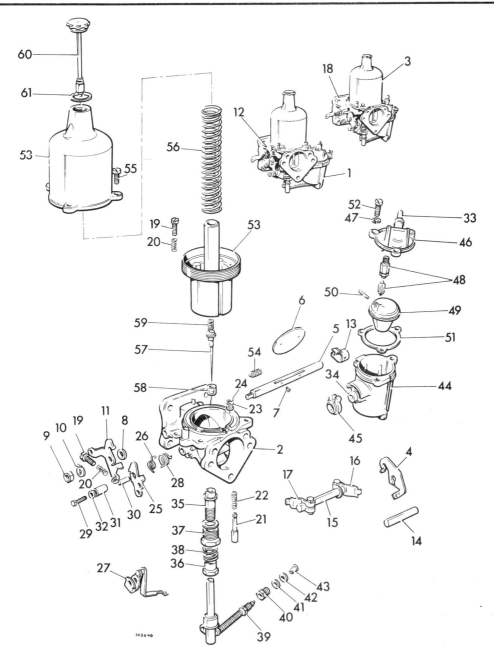

Fig. 3.3. Exploded view of carburettor - typical (twin carburettor set-up shown)

1	Float chamber assembly	16	Connecting lever	32	Washer	48	Needle and seat
2	Carburettor body	17	Connecting lever	33	Fuel inlet	49	Float
3	Dashpot assembly	18	Carburettor assembly	34	Fuel outlet	50	Hinge pin
4	Stop lever		(left)	35	Jet bearing	51	Gasket
5	Throttle plate shaft	19	Throttle stop screw	36	Adjusting screw	52	Screw
6	Throttle valve plate	20	Spring	37	Locking screw	53	Chamber and
7	Throttle plate screw	21	Piston lifting pin	38	Adjusting screw		piston
8	Washer	22	Spring		spring	54	Needle locking
9	Spindle nut	23	Neoprene washer	39	Jet assembly		screw
10	Tab washer	24	Circlip	40	Sleeve nut	55	Screw
11	Throttle lever	25	Cam lever	41	Washer	56	Piston spring
12	Carburettor assembly	26	Return spring	42	Gland	57	Jet needle
	(right)	27	Pick-up lever	43	Ferrule	58	Jet needle guide
13	Lost motion lever	28	Spring	44	Float chamber	59	Needle spring
14	Interconnecting rod	29	Pivot bolt	45	Float adaptor	60	Cap and damper
15	Interconnecting rod	30	Pivot tube inner	46	Float chamber lid	61	Washer
	assembly	31	Pivot tube outer	47	Washer		

'orifice according to the engine load and throttle opening, thus, effectively altering the size of jet so that exactly the right amount of fuel is metered for the prevailing conditions.

3 The position of the tapered needle in the jet is determined by the degree of inlet manifold depression (vacuum). The shank of the needle is held at its top end in a piston which slides up-and-down inside the dashpot in response to the degree of inlet manifold vacuum.

4 With the throttle fully open, the full effect of inlet manifold depression is felt by the piston, which has an air bleed into the choke tube on the outside of the throttle. This causes the piston to rise fully, bringing the needle with it. With the accelerator partially closed, only slight inlet manifold vacuum is felt by the piston (although, of course, on the engine side of the throttle the vacuum is greater), and the piston only rises a little, blocking most of the jet orifice with the metering needle.

5 To prevent the piston fluttering and giving a richer mixture when the accelerator pedal is suddenly depressed, an oil damper and light spring are fitted inside the dashpot.

6 The only portion of the piston assembly to come into contact with the piston chamber or dashpot is the actual piston rod. All other parts of the piston assembly, including the lower choke portion, have sufficient clearance to prevent any direct metal to metal contact which is essential if the carburettor is to function correctly.

7 The correct level of the petrol in the carburettor is determined by the level of petrol in the float chamber. When the level is correct the float rises and, by means of a raised portion on the top of the float closes the needle valve in the cover of the float chamber. This shuts off the supply of fuel from the pump. When the level in the float chamber drops as fuel is used in the carburettor, the float drops. As it does the float needle is unseated so allowing more fuel to enter the float chamber and restore the correct fuel level.

8 Carburettor - removal and refitment

1 Refer to Section 6 and remove the air cleaner assembly.
2 Ease the fuel feed pipe from the union on the float chamber cover. Plug the end to prevent dirt ingress.
3 Slacken the clip and ease off the engine breather pipe from the union on the carburettor body.
4 Carefully detach the vacuum advance pipe from the carburettor adaptor.
5 Make a note of how the throttle return spring is attached and then disconnect.
6 Slacken the throttle inner cable clamp and detach the inner cable. Release the outer cable clamp.
7 Disconnect the choke cable from the choke lever.
8 Undo and remove the four nuts and spring washers securing the carburettor to the manifold studs. Lift away the carburettor assembly.
9 Recover the insulator block and gaskets.
10 Refitting the carburettor is the reverse sequence to removal. Always fit new gaskets to the inlet manifold flange and insulator block. Refer to the relevant sections and adjust the choke control cable and throttle cable. If the carburettor has been dismantled it will be necessary to reset the jet.

9 Carburettor - dismantling and reassembly

1 Unscrew the piston damper and lift away from the suction chambers and piston assembly. Recover the fibre washer.
2 Using a screwdriver or small file, scratch identification marks on the suction chamber and carburettor body so that they may be fitted together again in their original relative positions. Remove the three suction chamber retaining screws and lift the suction chamber from the carburettor body leaving the suction chamber piston in-situ.
3 Lift the piston spring from the piston, noting which way

round it is fitted, and remove the piston. Invert it and allow the oil in the damper bore to drain out. Place the piston in a safe place so that the needle will not be touched or the piston roll back onto the floor. It is recommended that the piston be placed on the neck of a narrow jar with the needle inside so acting as a stand.

4 Mark the position of the float chamber cover relative to the body, and unscrew the three screws holding the float chamber cover to the float chamber body. Remove the cover and withdraw the pin thereby releasing the float. Using a socket or box spanner remove the needle valve assembly.

5 Release the pick-up lever return spring from its retaining lug.

6 Support the plastic moulded base of the jet and remove the screw retaining the jet pickup link and link bracket.

7 Carefully unscrew the flexible jet tube sleeve nut from the float chamber and lift away the jet assembly from the underside of the carburettor body. Note the gland, washer and ferrule at the end of the jet tube.

8 Undo and remove the jet adjustment nut and spring. Also unscrew the jet locknut and lift away together with the brass washer and jet bearing.

9 Unscrew and remove the lever pivot bolt and spacer. Detach the lever assembly and return springs noting the pivot bolt tubes, skid washer and the locations of the cam and pick-up lever springs.

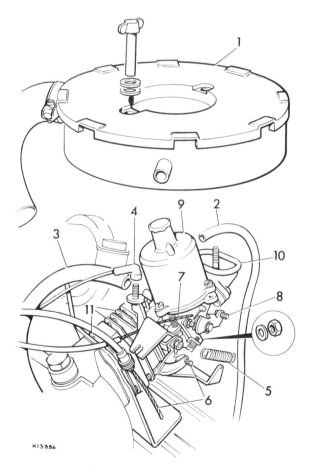

Fig. 3.4. Carburettor removal

1 Air cleaner	7 Choke control cable
2 Fuel hose	8 Choke control linkage
3 Engine breather pipe	9 Carburettor assembly
4 Vacuum advance pipe	10 Air intake adaptor
5 Throttle return spring	11 Gaskets
6 Throttle cable and linkage	

10 Close the throttle and lightly mark the relative position of the throttle disc and carburettor flange.

11 Unscrew the disc retaining screws, open the throttle and ease the disc from its slot in the throttle spindle.

12 Bend back the tab of the lock washer securing the spindle nut. Undo and remove the nut and detach the lever arm, washer and the throttle spindle.

13 Should it be necessary to remove the piston lifting pin, push it upwards and remove the securing clip. Lift away the pin and spring.

14 Reassembly is a straightforward reversal of the dismantling sequence and will present no problems provided that care was taken during dismantling.

10 Carburettor - examination and repair

The SU carburettor is most reliable but even so it may develop one of several faults which may not be readily apparent unless a careful inspection is carried out. The common faults the carburettor is prone to are:

1 Piston sticking
2 Float needle sticking
3 Float chamber flooding
4 Water and dirt in the carburettor.

In addition the following parts are susceptible to wear after high mileages and as they vitally affect the economy of the engine they should be checked and renewed where necessary, every 24,000 miles (40,000 km):

a) **Carburettor needle:** If this has been incorrectly fitted at some time so that it is not centrally located in the jet orifice, then the metering needle will have a tiny ridge worn on it. If a ridge can be seen then the needle must be renewed. SU carburettor needles are made to very fine tolerances and should a ridge be apparent, no attempt should be made to rub the needle down with fine emery paper. If it is wished to clean the needle, it can be polished lightly with metal polish.

b) **Carburettor jet:** If the needle is worn it is likely that the rim of the jet will be damaged where the needle has been striking it. It should be renewed, otherwise fuel consumption will suffer. The jet can also be badly worn or ridged where it has been sliding up and down between the jet housing every time the choke has been pulled out. Removal and renewal is the only answer.

c) Check the edges of the throttle and choke tube for wear. Renew if worn.

d) The washers fitted to the base of the jet and under the float chamber lid may leak after a time and can cause a great deal of fuel wastage. It is wisest to renew them automatically when the carburettor is stripped down.

e) After high mileages the float chamber needle and seat are bound to be ridged. They are not an expensive item to replace and must be renewed as a set. They should never be renewed separately.

11 Carburettor - piston sticking

1 The hardened piston rod which slides in the centre guide tube in the middle of the dashpot is the only part of the piston assembly (which comprises the jet needle, suction disc, and piston choke) which should make contact with the dashpot. The piston rim and the choke periphery are machined to very fine tolerances so that they will not touch the dashpot or the choke tube walls.

2 After high mileages wear in the centre guide tube may allow the piston to touch the dashpot wall. This condition is known as sticking.

3 If piston sticking is suspected and it is wished to test for this condition, rotate the piston about the centre guide tube at the same time as sliding it up and down inside the dashpot. If any portion of the piston makes contact with the dashpot

metal polish until clearance exists. In extreme cases, fine emery cloth can be used.

The greatest care should be taken to remove only the minimum amount of metal to provide the clearance as too large a gap will cause air leakage and upset the function of the carburettor. Clean down the walls of the dashpot and the piston rim and ensure that there is no oil on them. A trace of oil may be judiciously applied to the piston rod.

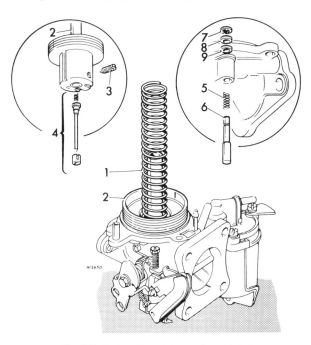

Fig. 3.5. Carburettor piston and associated parts

1 *Piston spring*
2 *Piston*
3 *Guide locking screw*
4 *Needle assembly*
5 *Spring*
6 *Piston lift pin*
7 *Circlip*
8 *Plain washer*
9 *Sealing washer*

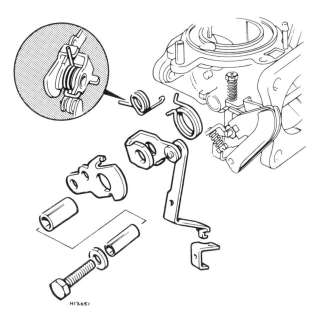

Fig. 3.6. Carburettor linkage

4 If the piston is sticking, under no circumstances try to clear it by trying to alter the tension of the light return spring.

12 Carburettor - float needle sticking

1 If the float needle sticks, the carburettor will soon run dry and the engine will stop, despite there being fuel in the tank.
2 The easiest way to check a suspected sticking float needle is to remove the inlet pipe at the carburettor and turn the engine over on the starter motor by pressing on the solenoid rubber button (manual gearbox) and operating the ignition/starter switch (automatic transmission). In the latter case remove the white lead from the ignition coil so that the engine does not start. If fuel spurts from the end of the pipe (direct it towards the ground, into a wad of cloth or into a jar) then the fault is almost certain to be a sticking float needle.
3 Remove the float chamber cover, dismantle the valve and clean the housing and float chamber out thoroughly.

13 Carburettor - float chamber flooding

If fuel emerges from the small breather hole in the cover of the float chamber this is known as flooding. It is caused by the float chamber needle not seating properly in its housing; normally, this is because a piece of foreign matter is jammed between the needle and needle housing. Alternatively the float may have developed a leak so that it is holding open the float chamber needle valve even though the chamber is full of petrol. Remove the float chamber cover, clean the needle assembly, check the float by shaking to verify if any petrol has leaked into it.

14 Carburettor - water contamination or dirt blockage

1 Because of the size of the jet orifice, water or dirt in the carburettor is normally cleared automatically. If dirt in the carburettor is suspected, lift the piston assembly and flood the float chamber. The normal level of the fuel should be about 0.0625 in (1.5875 mm) below the top of the jet, so that on flooding the carburettor the fuel should flow out of the jet hole.
2 If little or no petrol appears, start the engine (the jet is never completely blocked) and with the throttle butterfly fully open blank off the air intake. This will cause a partial vacuum in the choke tube and help suck out any foreign matter from the jet tube. Release the throttle as soon as the engine speed alters considerably. Repeat this procedure several times, stop the engine and then check the carburettor as described in the first paragraph of this Section.
3 If this failed to do the trick then there is no alternative but to remove and blow out the jet.

15 Carburettor - jet centering

1 This operation is always necessary if the carburettor has been dismantled. To check this on a carburettor in service first screw up the jet adjusting nut as far as it will go without forcing it. Lift the piston and then let it fall under its own weight. It should fall onto the bridge making a soft metallic click. Now repeat the above procedure but this time with the adjusting nut screwed right down. If the soft metallic click is not audible in either of the two tests proceed as follows:
2 Disconnect the jet link from the bottom of the jet, and the nylon flexible tube from the underside of the float chamber. Gently slide the jet and the nylon tube from the underside of the carburettor body. Next unscrew the jet adjusting nut and lift away the nut and the locking spring. Refit the adjusting nut without the locking spring and screw it up as far as

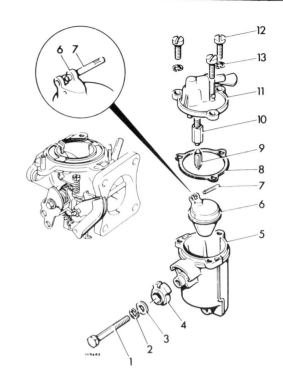

Fig. 3.7. Carburettor float chamber

1	Bolt	7	Pin
2	Spring washer	8	Gasket
3	Plain washer	9	Needle
4	Spacer	10	Seat
5	Float chamber alignment	11	Cover alignment mark
	mark	12	Screw
6	Float	13	Spring washer

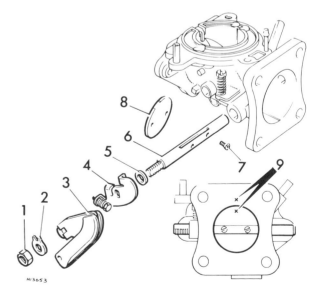

Fig. 3.8. Carburettor throttle disc

1	Nut	6	Spindle
2	Lockwasher	7	Screw
3	Lever	8	Disc
4	Cam	9	Assembly marks
5	Washer		

possible without forcing. Replace the jet and tube; there is no need to reconnect the tube.

3 Slacken the jet locking nut so that it may be rotated with the fingers only. Unscrew the piston damper and lift away the damper. Gently press the piston down onto the bridge and tighten the locknut. Lift the piston using the lifting pin and check that it is able to fall freely under its own weight. Now lower the adjusting nut and check once again. If this time there is a difference in the two metallic clicks, repeat the centering procedure until the sound is the same for both tests.

4 Gently remove the jet and unscrew the adjusting nut. Refit the locking spring and jet adjusting nut. Top up the damper with oil (if necessary) and replace the damper piston. Connect the nylon flexible tube to the underside of the float chamber and finally reconnect the jet link.

16 Carburettor - float chamber fuel level adjustment

1 It is essential that the fuel level in the float chamber is always correct as otherwise excessive fuel consumption may occur. Carburettors fitted to the models covered by this manual have non-adjustable floats.

2 With the carburettor fitted to the engine and the float chamber full of petrol remove the piston and suction chamber assembly.

3 Check that the level of fuel in the jet is about 0.0625 in (1.5875 mm) below the top of the jet. If it is above or below this level it may be adjusted by removing the needle and seat from the underside of the float chamber lid and either adding or removing washers so raising or lowering the relative position of the needle valve.

17 Carburettor - needle renewal

1 Should it be necessary to fit a new needle, first remove the piston and suction chamber assembly, marking the chamber for correct reassembly in its original position.

2 Slacken the needle clamping screw and withdraw the needle, guide and spring from the underside of the piston.

3 To refit the needle assembly, fit the spring and guide to the needle and insert the assembly into the piston making sure that the guide is fitted flush with the face of the piston and the flat on the guide positioned adjacent to the needle guide locking screw. Screw in the guide locking screw.

18 Carburettor - adjustment and tuning

1 To adjust and tune the SU carburettor proceed as follows: check the colour of the exhaust at idling speed with the choke fully in. If the exhaust tends to be black and the tailpipe interior is also black, it is a fair indication that the mixture is too rich, If the exhaust is colourless and the deposit in the exhaust pipe is very light grey it is likely that the mixture is too weak. This condition may also be accompanied by intermittent misfiring, while too rich a mixture will be accompanied by 'hunting'. Ideally, the exhaust should be colourless with a medium grey coloured pipe deposit.

2 The exhaust pipe deposit should only be checked after a good run of at least 20 miles. Idling in city traffic and stop/start motoring is bound to produce excessive dark exhaust pipe deposits.

3 Once the engine has reached its normal operating temperature, detach the carburettor air cleaner.

4 Only two adjustments are provided on the SU carburettor. Idling speed is governed by the throttle adjusting screw and the mixture strength by the jet adjusting nut. The SU carburettor is correctly adjusted for the whole of its engine revolution

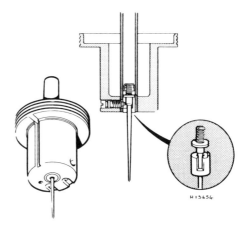

Fig. 3.9. Needle fitment to piston

range when the idling mixture strength is correct.

5 To adjust the mixture set the engine to run at about 1000 rpm by screwing in the throttle adjusting screw.

6 Check the mixture strength by lifting the piston of the carburettor approximately 0.0313 in (0.7937 mm) with the piston lifting pin so as to disturb the air flow as little as possible. If:

a) the speed of the engine increases appreciably the mixture is too rich.

b) the engine speed immediately decreases, the mixture is too weak.

c) the engine speed increases very slightly, the mixture is correct.

7 To enrich the mixture, screw the adjusting nut, which is at the bottom of the underside of the carburettor, down one flat at a time and check the mixture strength between each turn. It is likely that there will be a slight increase or decrease in rpm after the mixture adjustment has been made so the throttle idling screw should be turned so that the engine idles at the recommended speed.

19 Throttle cable - removal and refitment

1 Using two thin open ended spanners unscrew the cable trunnion screw.

2 Release the throttle return spring making a note of which way round it is fitted.

3 Detach the outer cable from the carburettor mounted bracket.

4 Disconnect the inner cable from the accelerator pedal by releasing the spring clip and lifting the cable from the slot.

5 Press in the plastic retainers on the inside of the bulkhead and ease the outer cable through the bulkhead.

6 Lift away the throttle cable assembly.

7 Refitting is the reverse sequence to removal but it is now necessary to adjust the effective length of the inner cable.

8 Pull down on the inner cable until all free movement of the throttle is eliminated.

9 Hold the cable in this position and raise the cam operating lever until it just contacts the cam.

10 Move the trunnion up the cable until it contacts the operating lever, and tighten the trunnion screw.

11 Depress the throttle pedal and make sure that the cable has 0.0625 in (1.588 mm) free movement before the cam operating lever begins to move.

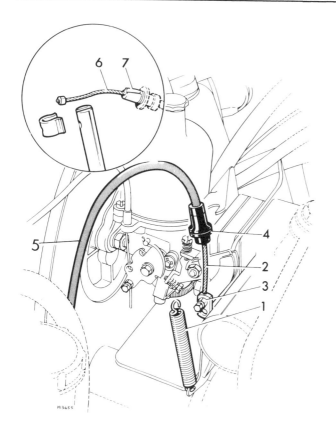

Fig. 3.10. Throttle cable attachments

1	Spring	5	Outer cable
2	Throttle cable	6	Inner cable
3	Trunnion	7	Retainer
4	Cable retainer		

Fig. 3.11. Choke cable attachments

1	Trunnion	4	Inner cable
2	Nut	5	Control knob
3	Washer		

20 Choke cable - removal and refitment

1 Using two thin open ended spanners slacken the cable trunnion screw.

2 Undo and remove the two self tapping screws securing the steering column top cowl. Lift away the top cowl.

3 Working from inside the bottom cowl unscrew the cable securing nut. Note there is a lock washer at the inner end.

4 Carefully pull the cable through the bulkhead grommet.

5 Refitting the choke cable is the reverse sequence to removal. However, it is now necessary to adjust the effective length of the inner cable as follows:

6 Set the position of the trunnion to give a free movement on the cable of 0.0625 in (1.588 mm) before the cam lever begins to move.

7 Pull out the control approximately 0.5 in (13 mm) until the linkage is just about to move the jet.

8 Start the engine and adjust the carburettor fast idle screw to give an engine speed of 1,050 rpm.

9 Push the control knob fully in, and check that there is a small gap between the end of the fast idle screw and cam.

21 Throttle pedal - removal and refitment

1 Refer to Fig. 3.12 and detach the throttle cable from the end of the pedal.

2 Undo and remove the two nuts, bolts, spring and plain washers securing the pedal bracket to the bulkhead panel. Lift away the pedal assembly.

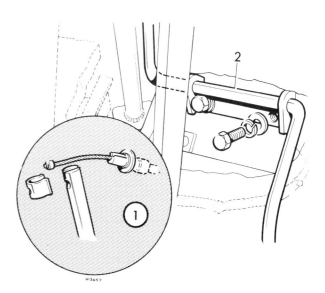

Fig. 3.12. Throttle pedal and attachments

1 Pedal to inner cable   2 Pedal support bracket

3 Refitting the throttle pedal is the reverse sequence to removal.

22 Fuel tank - removal and refitment

1 Disconnect the battery.
2 Chock the front wheels, raise the rear of the car and support on axle stands.
3 Unscrew the fuel tank drain plug and drain the contents of the fuel tank into a container of suitable capacity.
4 Detach the cable terminal from the fuel tank sender unit.
5 Slacken the clip and disconnect the filter hose from the fuel tank.
6 Release the clip and disconnect the fuel outlet hose from the fuel tank sender unit.
7 Suitably support the weight of the fuel tank.
8 Undo and remove the two self tapping screws, plain and spring washers securing the sides of the tank to the body.
9 Undo and remove the three screws, spring and plain washers securing the ends of the tank to the body.
10 Carefully lower the fuel tank and recover the seal from the filler neck.
11 Refitting the fuel tank is the reverse sequence to removal.

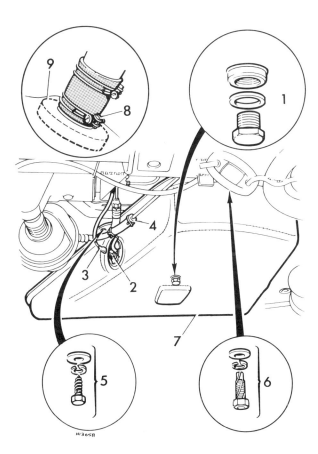

HI365B

Fig. 3.13. Fuel tank and attachments

1 Drain plug and washer	6 Securing bolt
2 Sender unit	7 Tank
3 Sender unit cable	8 Clip
4 Flexible hose	9 Packing/seal
5 Securing screw	

23 Fuel tank - cleaning and repair

1 With time it is likely that sediment will collect in the bottom of the fuel tank. Condensation (resulting in rust) and other impurities are sometimes found in the fuel tank of a car more than three or four years old.
2 With the tank removed it should be vigorously flushed out and turned upside down, and if facilities are available steam cleaned.
3 Repairs to the fuel tank to stop leaks are best carried out using resin adhesive and hardeners as supplied by most accessory shops. In cases of repairs being done to large areas, glass fibre mats or perforated zinc may be required to give the area support. If any soldering, welding or brazing is contemplated, the tank must be steamed out to remove any traces of petroleum vapour. It is dangerous to use naked flames in a fuel tank without this, even though it may have been lying empty for a considerable time.

24 Fuel tank sender unit - removal and refitment

1 The sender unit is mounted on the side of the fuel tank and may be removed with the fuel tank in the car.
2 If the fuel gauge does not work correctly then the fault is either in the sender unit, the gauge in the instrument panel, the wiring or the voltage regulator.
3 First test for operation: switch on the ignition and observe if the fuel and temperature gauges operate. If only one operates it can be assumed that the voltage regulator is satisfactory. However, if neither operates then check the regulator as described in Chapter 10.
4 To check the sender unit first disconnect the lead from the unit at the connector. Switch on the ignition and the gauge should read "Empty". Now connect the lead to earth and the gauge should read "Full". Allow 30 seconds for each reading.
5 If both the situations are correct then the fault lies in the sender unit.
6 If the gauge does not read "Empty" with the lead disconnected from the sender unit, the lead should then also be disconnected from the gauge to the sender unit.
7 If not, the gauge is faulty and should be renewed (for details see Chapter 10).
8 With the lead disconnected from the sender unit and earthed, if the gauge reads anything other than "Full" check the rest of the circuit (see Chapter 10 for the wiring diagram).
9 To remove the sender unit first disconnect the battery.
10 Disconnect the fuel gauge sender unit cable.
11 Unscrew the fuel tank drain plug and drain the contents of the fuel tank into a container of suitable capacity.
12 Detach the main fuel pipe from the sender unit by squeezing the ears of the clip with a pair of pliers and pulling off the hose.
13 Using two crossed screwdrivers, remove the fuel gauge tank unit by turning through approximately 30° and lift away from the tank. Take great care not to bend the float wire.
14 Refitting the fuel gauge tank unit is the reverse sequence to removal. Always fit a new sealing washer located between the unit and tank.

25 Fuel pipes - general inspection

1 Check all flexible hoses for signs of perishing, cracking or damage and replace if necessary.
2 Carefully inspect all metal fuel pipes for signs of corrosion, cracking, kinking or distortion and renew any pipe that is suspect. These pipes are clipped to the underbody.

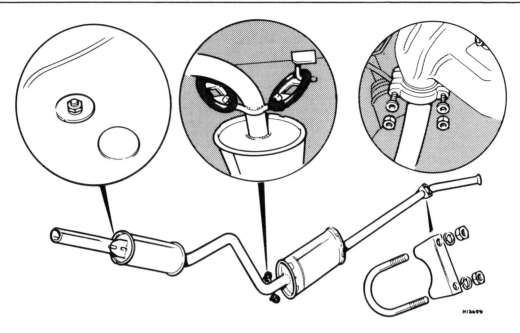

Fig. 3.14. Exhaust system and attachments

26 Exhaust system - removal and refitting

1   Place chocks in front of the front roadwheels and jack up the rear of the car. Then support the rear end of the car on axle stands. Alternatively, place the car in position over a pit, if one is available.
2   Remove the air cleaner from the engine as described in Section 6, and Section 5 of Chapter 13.
3   Remove the carburettor, distance piece and gaskets as described in Section 8, and Section 5 of Chapter 13.

4   Undo the two nuts and bolts which secure the exhaust pipe to manifold clamp and remove the clamp (See Fig. 3.14).
5   Next, undo the two nuts on the exhaust pipe clamp which is secured to the transmission casing.
6   Unscrew the nut which secures the rear rubber mounting bracket to the body and separate the mounting from the exhaust system (See Fig. 3.14).
7   Finally, unhook the two rubber rings from their hooks and withdraw the system complete from under the car.
8   Refitting is the reverse procedure to removal. Fit the whole system and align it before tightening up the mounting nuts and bolts.

27 Fault diagnosis - Fuel system

Symptom	Reason/s	Remedy
FUEL CONSUMPTION EXCESSIVE	Air cleaner choked and dirty giving rich mixture	Remove, clean and replace air cleaner.
	Fuel leaking from carburettor, fuel pumps, or fuel lines	Check for and eliminate all fuel leaks. Tighten fuel line union nuts.
	Float chamber flooding	Check and adjust float level.
	Generally worn carburettor	Remove, overhaul and replace.
	Distributor condenser faulty	Remove, and fit new unit.
	Balance weights or vacuum advance mechanism in distributor faulty	Remove, and overhaul distributor.
	Carburettor incorrectly adjusted, mixture too rich	Tune and adjust carburettor.
	Idling speed too high	Adjust idling speed.
	Contact breaker gap incorrect	Check and reset gap.
	Valve clearances incorrect	Check clearances and adjust as necessary.
	Incorrectly set spark plugs	Remove, clean, and regap.
	Tyres under-inflated	Check tyre pressures and inflate if necessary.
	Wrong spark plugs fitted	Remove and replace with correct units.
	Brakes dragging	Check and adjust brakes.
INSUFFICIENT FUEL DELIVERY OR WEAK MIXTURE DUE TO AIR LEAKS		
	Petrol tank air vent restricted	Remove petrol cap and clean out air vent.
	Partially clogged filters in pump and carburettor	Remove and clean filters.
	Dirt lodged in float chamber needle housing	Remove and clean out float chamber and needle valve assembly.
	Incorrectly seating valves in fuel pump	Remove, dismantle, and clean out fuel pump.
	Fuel pump diaphragm leaking or damaged	Remove, and overhaul fuel pump.
	Gasket in fuel pump damaged	Remove, and overhaul fuel pump.
	Fuel pump valves sticking due to petrol gumming	Remove, and thoroughly clean fuel pump.
	Too little fuel in fuel tank (Prevalent when climbing steep hills)	Refill fuel tank.
	Union joints on pipe connections loose	Tighten joints and check for air leaks.
	Split in fuel pipe on suction side of fuel pump	Examine, locate, and repair.
	Inlet manifold to block or inlet manifold to carburettor gasket leaking	Test by pouring oil along joints - bubbles indicate leak. Renew gasket as appropriate.

Chapter 4 Ignition system

For modifications, and information applicable to later models, see Supplement at end of manual

Contents

Specifications

Spark plugs:

Make	Champion
Type	N - 9Y
Size	14 mm
Gap	0.025 in. (0.65 mm)

Firing order: 1 3 4 2

Coil (either of two types may be fitted)

Type	Lucas LA12
Primary resistance at 20º C (68º F)	3.0 - 3.4 ohms
Comsumption:	
Ignition switched on	3.5 - 4.0 amp
At 2000 rpm	1 amp
Type	Lucas 16 C6 ballasted
Primary resistance at 20º C (68º F)	1.43 - 1.58 ohms (cold)
Consumption:	
Ignition switched on	4.5 - 5.0 amp
Ballast resistance	1.3 - 1.4 ohms

Distributor:

Type	Lucas 25D4
Serial number	41246 (1100) 41257 (1300)
Rotational direction of rotor	Anti clockwise
Contact breaker points gap	0.014 - 0.016 in. (0.35 - 0.40 mm)
When new	0.019 in. (0.48 mm)
Dwell angle	60º ± 3º
Condenser capacity	0.18 - 0.24 mf
Automatic advance	Vacuum and centrifugal

Note: *From 1976 onwards both 1100 and 1300 models may be fitted with a Lucas 45D4 or Ducellier distributor instead of a Lucas 25D4. Details of both alternative distributors are given in Chapter 13.*

1100

Centrifugal advance: (Crankshaft degrees and rpm. Vacuum disconnected)

Deceleration	... ...			
		20 - 24	at	6000 rpm
		14 - 18	at	4000 rpm
		9 - 13	at	2400 rpm
		6 - 10	at	1500 rpm
		0 - 1	at	900 rpm
		No advance below 800 rpm		

Vacuum advance:

Maximum (crankshaft degrees and rpm)	16º at 14 in Hg (356 mm Hg)
Starts	6 in. Hg (152 mm Hg)

1300
Centrifugal advance: (Crankshaft degrees and rpm. Vacuum disconnected)

Deceleration	18 - 22	at	5000 rpm
	11 - 15	at	2800 rpm
	4 - 8	at	1600 rpm
	No advance below 300 rpm		

Vacuum advance:
   Maximum (crankshaft degrees and rpm) ... ...   20º   at 10 in. Hg (250 mm Hg)
   Starts ... ...   3 in. Hg (80 mm Hg)

Ignition timing: (Vacuum advance/retard mechanism disconnected)
  Static:
    1100 ... ...   9º BTDC
    1300 ... ...   8º BTDC
  Stroboscopic - at 1000 rpm:
    1100 ... ...   12º BTDC
    1300 ... ...   13º BTDC

  Timing marks location   ... ...   Dimples on timing wheels; marks on flywheel
Note: *Later models have a timing mark on the crankshaft pulley with a pointer bracket attached to the crankcase. This is covered in Chapter 13.*

Torque wrench settings:

	lb f ft	kg fm
Distributor clamp plate	2.5	0.35
Distributor clamp bolt	3.0	0.41
Spark plug	14	1.9

1 General description

In order that the engine may run correctly it is necessary for an electrical spark to ignite the fuel/air mixture in the combustion chamber at exactly the right moment in relation to engine speed and load. The high tension voltage generated by the ignition system is powerful enough to jump the spark plug gap in the combustion chambers many times a second under high compression pressure, providing that the ignition system is in good working order and that all adjustments are correct.

The ignition system comprises two individual circuits known as the low tension circuit and the high tension circuit.

The low tension circuit (sometimes known as the primary circuit) comprises the battery, lead to ignition switch, lead to the low tension or primary coil windings and the lead from the low tension coil windings to the contact breaker points and condenser in the distributor.

The high tension circuit (sometimes known as the secondary circuit) comprises the high tension or secondary coil windings, the heavily insulated ignition lead from the centre of the coil to the centre of the distributor cap, the rotor arm, the spark plug leads and the spark plugs.

The complete ignition system operation is as follows:

Low tension voltage from the battery is changed within the ignition coil to high tension voltage by the opening and closing of the contact breaker points in the low tension circuit. High tension voltage is then fed via a contact in the centre of the distributor cap to the rotor arm of the distributor. The rotor arm revolves inside the distributor cap, and each time it comes in line with one of the four metal segments in the cap (these being connected to the spark plug leads) the opening and closing of the contact breaker points causes the high tension voltage to build up, jump the gap from the rotor arm to the appropriate metal segment and so, via the spark plug lead, to the spark plug where it finally jumps the gap between the two spark plug electrodes, one being connected to the earth system.

The ignition timing is advanced and retarded automatically to ensure the spark occurs at just the right instant for the particular load at the prevailing engine speed.

The ignition advance is controlled both mechanically and by a vacuum operated system. The mechanical governor mechanism comprises two weights which move out under centrifugal force from the central distributor shaft as the engine speed rises. As they move outwards they rotate the cams relative to the distributor shaft, and so advance the spark. The weights are held in position by two light springs, and it is the tension of the springs which is largely responsible for correct mechanical advancement.

The vacuum control comprises a diaphragm, one side of which is connected via a small bore tube to the carburettor, and the other side to the contact breaker plate. Depressions in the induction manifold and carburettor, which varies with engine speed and throttle opening, causes the diaphragm to move, so moving the control breaker plate and advancing or retarding the spark. A fine degree of control is achieved by a spring in the vacuum assembly.

2 Contact breaker points - adjustment

1 To adjust the contact breaker points so that the correct gap is obtained; first, release the two clips securing the distributor cap to the distributor body, and lift away the cap. Clean the inside and outside of the cap with a dry cloth. It is unlikely that the four segments will be badly burned or scored, but if they are the cap should be renewed. If only small deposits are on the segments they may be scraped away using a small screwdriver.
2 Push in the carbon brush, located in the top of the cap, several times to ensure that it moves freely. The brush should protrude by at least 0.25 in (6.35 mm).
3 Gently press the contact breaker points open to examine the condition of their faces. If they are rough, pitted or dirty it will be necessary to remove them for resurfacing, or for replacement points to be fitted.
4 Presuming the points are satisfactory, or that they have been cleaned or replaced, measure the gap between the points by turning the engine over until the contact breaker arm is on the peak of one of the four cam lobes A 0.014-0.016 in (0.36 - 0.41 mm) feeler gauge should now just fit between the points.
5 If the gap varies from the specified amount, slacken the control plate securing screw and adjust the contact gap by inserting a screwdriver in the notched hole at the end of the plate; turning clockwise to decrease, and anti-clockwise to increase, the gap. Tighten the securing screw and check the gap again.
6 Replace the rotor arm and distributor cap and clip the spring blade retainers into position.

3 Contact breaker points - removal, refitment and overhaul

1 If the contact breaker points are burned, pitted or badly worn, they must be removed and either replaced or their faces must be filed smooth.

2 To remove the points first detach the distributor cap and rotor arm. Unscrew the terminal nut and remove it together with the washer under its head. Remove the flanged nylon bush, the condenser lead and the low tension lead from the terminal pin. Lift off the contact breaker arm and remove the large fibre washer from the terminal pin.

3 The adjustable contact breaker plate is removed by unscrewing one screw and then withdrawing the plate.

4 To reface the points, rub the faces on a fine carborundum stone, or on fine emery paper. It is important that the faces are rubbed flat and parallel to each other so that there will be complete face to face contact when the points are closed. One of the points will be pitted and the other will have deposits on it.

5 It is necessary to completely remove the built up deposits, but unnecessary to rub the pitted point right to the stage where all the pitting has disappeared, though obviously, if this is done it will prolong the time before the operation of refacing the points has to be repeated.

6 To replace the points: first, position the adjustable contact breaker plate and secure it with its screw, spring and flat washer. Fit the fibre washer to the terminal pin and fit the contact breaker arm over it. Insert the flanged nylon bush with the condenser lead immediately under its head, and the low tension lead under that, over the terminal pin. Fit the steel washer and screw on the securing nut.

7 The points are now reassembled and the gap should be set as detailed in Section 2.

4 Condenser - removal, testing and refitment

1 The purpose of the condenser (sometimes known as a capacitor) is to ensure that when the contact breaker points open there is no sparking across them which would waste voltage and cause excessive wear.

2 The condenser is fitted in parallel with the contact breaker points. If it develops a short circuit, it will cause ignition failure, as the points will be prevented from interrupting the low tension circuit.

3 If the engine becomes very difficult to start, or begins to misfire after several miles running, and the breaker points show signs of excessive burning, then the condition of the condenser must be suspect. A further test can be made by separating the points by hand with the ignition switched on. If this is accompanied by a flash it is indicative that the condenser has failed.

4 Without special test equipment, the only sure way to diagnose condenser trouble is to replace a suspected unit with a new one and note if there is any improvement.

5 To remove the condenser from the distributor, remove the distributor cap and rotor arm. Unscrew the contact breaker arm terminal nut, remove the nut, washer and flanged nylon bush and release the condenser.

6 Undo and remove the condenser securing screw and lift away the condenser.

7 Replacement of the condenser is simply a reversal of the removal procedure. Take particular care that the condenser lead does not short circuit against any portion of the breaker plate.

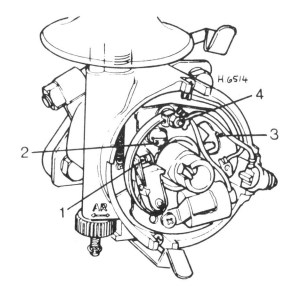

Fig. 4.1. Contact breaker points adjustment

1 Contact breaker points
2 Contact plate securing screw
3 Screwdriver slot
4 Moving contact spring and terminal securing nut

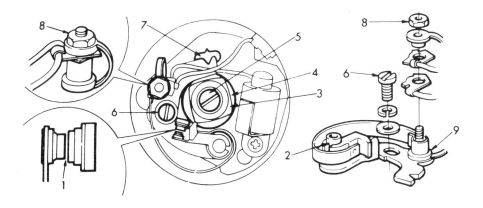

Fig. 4.2. Contact breaker points removal

1 Points
2 Pivot spindle
3 Cam
4 Lubrication hole
5 Screw head on cam
6 Contact plate securing screw
7 Adjustment notch
8 Terminal nut
9 Nylon bush

Measuring plug gap. A feeler gauge of the correct size (see ignition system specifications) should have a slight 'drag' when slid between the electrodes. Adjust gap if necessary

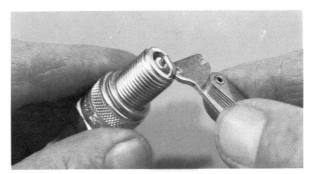

Adjusting plug gap. The plug gap is adjusted by bending the earth electrode inwards, or outwards, as necessary until the correct clearance is obtained. Note the use of the correct tool

Normal. Grey-brown deposits lightly coated core nose. Gap increasing by around 0.001 in (0.025 mm) per 1000 miles (1600 km). Plugs ideally suited to engine and engine in good condition

Carbon fouling. Dry, black, sooty deposits. Will cause weak spark and eventually misfire. Fault: over-rich fuel mixture. Check: carburettor mixture settings, float level and jet sizes; choke operation and cleanliness of air filter. Plugs can be re-used after cleaning

Oil fouling. Wet, oily deposits. Will cause weak spark and eventually misfire. Fault: worn bores/piston rings or valve guides; sometimes occurs (temporarily) during running-in period. Plugs can be re-used after thorough cleaning

Overheating. Electrodes have glazed appearance, core nose very white - few deposits. Fault: plug overheating. Check: plug value, ignition timing, fuel octane rating (too low) and fuel mixture (too weak). Discard plugs and cure fault immediately

Electrode damage. Electrodes burned away; core nose has burned, glazed appearance. Fault: initial pre-ignition. Check: as for 'Overheating' but may be more severe. Discard plugs and remedy fault before piston or valve damage occurs

Split core nose (may appear initially as a crack). Damage is self-evident, but cracks will only show after cleaning. Fault: pre-ignition or wrong gap-setting technique. Check: ignition timing, cooling system, fuel octane rating (too low) and fuel mixture (too weak). Discard plugs, rectify fault immediately

5 Distributor - lubrication

1 It is important that the distributor cam is lubricated with petroleum jelly at the specified mileages, and that the breaker arm, governor weights and cam spindle are lubricated every 6,000 miles (10,000 km). In practice it will be found that lubrication every 3,000 miles (5,000 km) is preferable although this is not recommended by the manufacturer's.
2 Great care should be taken not to use too much lubricant, as any excess that might find its way onto the contact breaker points could cause burning and misfiring.
3 To gain access to the cam spindle, lift away the rotor arm. Drop no more than two drops of engine oil onto the screw head within the shaft. This will run down the spindle when the engine is hot and lubricate the bearings. No more than **one** drop of oil should be applied to the pivot post.

6 Distributor - removal and refitment

1 Prior to removing the distributor, remove the flywheel housing timing aperture cover (if fitted). Determine which spark plug lead is attached to no 1 spark plug. This is the one at the front of the engine.
2 Release the clips securing the distributor cap to the body and lift away the distributor cap.
3 Slowly turn the crankshaft in the normal direction of rotation until the timing mark (with no 1 cylinder on the power stroke) is aligned with the housing pointer.
4 Release the low tension cable connector from the side of the distributor.
5 Detach the HT lead from the ignition coil. Suitably identify the spark plug HT leads and detach from the spark plugs. The distributor cap can now be completely removed.
6 Remove the vacuum advance/retard pipe at the distributor diaphragm housing.
7 Remove the two distributor clamp bolts and washers securing the clamp plate to the cylinder block. The distributor may now be lifted up with the clamp plate still attached.
8 If it is not wished to disturb the ignition timing, then under no circumstances should the clamp pinch bolt, which secures the distributor in its relative position in the clamp, be loosened. Providing the distributor is removed without the clamp being loosened from the distributor, and the engine is not turned, the ignition timing will not be lost.
9 Replacement is a reversal of the above sequence. If the engine has been turned, it will be necessary to re-time the ignition. This will also be necessary if the clamp pinch bolt has been loosened.

7 Distributor - dismantling

1 With the distributor removed from the engine and on the bench, remove the distributor cap and lift off the rotor arm. If very tight, lever it off gently with a screwdriver.
2 Remove the contact breaker points as described in Section 3.
3 Remove the condenser from the contact plate by releasing its securing screw.
4 Unlock the vacuum unit spring from its mounting pin on the moving contact plate.
5 Remove the rubber seals and the two screws to release the contact breaker base plate and the earthing lead from the distributor body. Lift away the contact breaker base plate
6 Turn the contact breaker base plate in a clockwise direction relative to the contact breaker moving plate and separate the two parts.
7 Note the position of the slot in the rotor arm drive in relation to the offset drive dog at the opposite end of the distributor. It is essential that this is re-assembled correctly as otherwise the timing will be 180° out.

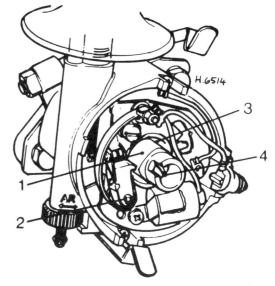

Fig. 4.3. Lubrication points for distributor

1 Contact breaker cam
2 Contact breaker pivot
3 Centrifugal mechanism lubrication point
4 Cam spindle and centre screw

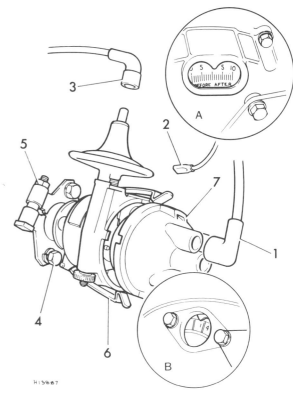

Fig. 4.4. Distributor removal

1 HT lead
2 LT lead terminal connector
3 Vacuum pipe connection
4 Clamp securing bolts and spring washers
5 Clamp nut and bolt
6 Spring clip
7 Distributor cap
Inset: Timing marks   A Automatic transmission
                         B Manual transmission

8 Unscrew the cam spindle retaining screw which is located in the centre of the rotor arm drive shaft cam.

9 Lift out the centrifugal weights together with their springs and then lift off the cam spindle.

10 To remove the vacuum unit, spring off the small circlip securing the advance adjustment knurled nut which should then be unscrewed. With the micrometer adjusting nut removed, release the spring and the micrometer adjusting nut lock spring clip. This is the clip that is responsible for the 'clicks' when the micrometer adjuster nut is turned. It is small so take care not to lose it and also the small circlip.

11 It is necessary to remove the distributor drive shaft or spindle only if it is thought to be excessively worn. With a thin parallel pin punch drive out the retaining pin from the driving tongue collar on the bottom end of the distributor drive shaft. The shaft can then be removed. Take care to recover the thrust washer(s) from the lower end and distance collar with steel washer(s) from the top end.

12 Carefully remove the 'O' ring from the distributor body.

8 Distributor - inspection and repair

1 Thoroughly wash all mechanical parts in petrol and wipe dry using a clean non-fluffy rag.

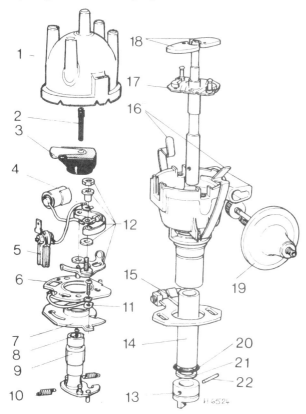

Fig. 4.5. Distributor component parts

1 Distributor cap	12 Contact breaker points
2 Brush and spring	13 Driving dog
3 Rotor arm	14 Bush
4 Condenser	15 Clamp plate
5 Terminal and lead	16 Cap retaining clips
6 Moving baseplate	17 Shaft and action plate
7 Fixed baseplate	18 Bob weights
8 Cam screw	19 Vacuum unit
9 Cam	20 O-ring oil seal
10 Advance spring	21 Thrust washer
11 Earth lead	22 Taper pin

2 Check the points that have been described previously. Check the distributor cap for signs of tracking, indicated by a thin black line between the segments. Replace the cap if any signs of tracking are found.

3 If the metal portion of the rotor arm is badly burned or loose, renew the arm. If slightly burnt, clean the arm with a fine file. Check that the carbon brush moves freely in the centre of the distributor cover.

4 Examine the fit of the contact breaker base and moving plate and also check the breaker arm pivot for looseness, or wear, and renew as necessary.

5 Examine the centrifugal weights and pivot pins for wear, and renew the weight or cam assembly if a degree of wear is found.

6 Examine the shaft and the fit of the cam assembly on the shaft. If the clearance is excessive compare the items with new units and renew either or both, if they show excessive wear.

7 If the shaft is a loose fit in the distributor bushes and can be seen to be worn, it will be necessary to fit a new shaft and bushes. The old bushes in the early distributor, or the single bush in the later ones, are simply pressed out. **Note**: Before inserting new bushes they should be immersed in engine oil for 24 hours.

8 Examine the length of the centrifugal weight springs and compare them with a new spring. If they have stretched they should be renewed.

9 Distributor - re-assembly

1 Re-assembly is a straightforward reversal of the dismantling process, but there are several points which should be noted in addition to those already given in Section 7.

2 Using engine oil lubricate the centrifugal weights and other parts of the mechanical advance mechanism, the distributor shaft and the portion of the shaft on which the cam bears, during re-assembly. Do not oil excessively but ensure these parts are adequately lubricated.

3 On re-assembly the cam driving pins with the centrifugal weights, check that they are in their correct position so that when viewed from above, the rotor arm should be at the six o'clock position, and the small offset on the driving dog must be on the right.

4 Check the action of the weights in the fully advanced and fully retarded positions and ensure they are not binding.

5 Tighten the micrometer adjusting nut to the central position on the timing scale.

6 If the oil seal has stretched or is damaged, obtain and fit a new one.

7 Finally set the contact breaker points gap to the correct clearance as described in Section 2.

10 Ignition timing

1 If the clamp plate pinch bolt has been loosened on the distributor and the static timing is lost, or if for any other reason it is wished to set the ignition timing, proceed as follows:

2 Refer to Section 2 and check the contact breaker points. Reset as necessary.

3 If the clamp plate has been removed then assemble the clamp plate to the distributor body but do not tighten the pinch bolt fully. If the distributor is still in position on the engine then slacken the clamp pinch bolt and also the two clamp bolts.

4 **Manual transmission models.** Remove the cover from the timing hole in the clutch cover/flywheel housing and rotate the crankshaft until the flywheel is at the correct static setting as indicated by the pointer cast in the timing hole. Do not forget No.1 cylinder must be commencing its power stroke.

5 **Automatic transmission models:** Remove the grommet from the timing hole in the converter cover and rotate the crank-

shaft until the converter is at the correct static setting as indicated by the pointer cast in the timing hole. Do not forget No.1 cylinder must be commencing power stroke.

6 Rotate the distributor shaft until the rotor is pointing towards No.1 HT lead segment in the distributor cap and offer up the distributor to the engine with the vacuum timing control unit in the position shown in Fig. 4.4.

7 Rotate the distributor body until the contact breaker points are just beginning to open and lightly tighten the securing plate clamp bolt and nut.

8 Refit the distributor cap and reconnect the spark plug leads. Do not forget the HT lead to the centre of the ignition coil.

9 If it was not found possible to align the rotor arm correctly, one of two things is wrong, either, the distributor drive shaft has been incorrectly refitted, in which case it must be removed and replaced correctly as described in Chapter 1, or the distributor has been dismantled and the distributor cam spindle refitted 180° out. To rectify, it will be necessary to partially dismantle the distributor, lift the camshaft pins from the centrifugal weight holes and turn the camshaft through 180°. Refit the pins into the weights and re-assemble.

10 It should be noted that this adjustment is nominal and the final adjustment should be made under running conditions.

11 First start the engine and allow to warm up to normal running temperature, and then accelerate in top gear from 30-50 mph, listening for heavy pinking of the engine. If this occurs, the ignition needs to be retarded slightly until just the faintest trace of pinking can be heard under these operating conditions.

12 Since the ignition advance adjustment enables the firing point to be related correctly to the grade of fuel used, the fullest advantage of any change of fuel will only be obtained by re-adjustment of the ignition settings.

13 This is done by varying the setting of the index scale on the vacuum advance mechanism by one or two divisions, checking to make sure that the best all round result is obtained.

14 Difficulty is sometimes experienced in determining exactly when the contact breaker points open. This can be ascertained most accurately by connecting a 12 volt bulb in parallel with the contact breaker points (one lead to earth and the other from the distributor low tension terminal). Switch on the ignition, and turn the advance and retard adjuster until the bulb lights up, indicating that the points have just opened.

11 Spark plugs and HT leads

1 The correct functioning of the spark plugs is vital for the proper running and efficiency of the engine.

2 At intervals of 6,000 miles (10,000 km) the spark plugs should be removed, examined, cleaned and if worn excessively, replaced. The condition of the spark plugs will also tell much about the general condition of the engine.

3 If the insulator nose of the spark plug is clean and white, with no deposits, this is indicative of a weak mixture, or too hot a plug (a hot plug transfers heat away from the electrode slowly - a cold plug transfers heat away quickly).

4 If the top and insulator nose is covered with hard black looking deposits, then this is indicative that the mixture is too rich. Should the plug be black and oily, then it is likely that the engine is fairly worn, as well as the mixture being too rich.

5 If the insulator nose is covered with light tan to greyish brown deposits, then the mixture is correct, and it is likely that the engine is in good condition.

6 If there are any traces of long brown tapering stains on the outside of the white portion of the plug, then the plug will have to be renewed, as this shows that there is a faulty joint between the plug body and the insulator, and compression is being allowed to leak away.

7 Plugs should be cleaned by a sand blasting machine, which will free them from carbon more efficiently than cleaning by hand. The machine will also test the condition of the plugs under compression. Any plug that fails to spark at the recommended pressure should be renewed.

8 The spark plug gap is of considerable importance, as, if it is too large or too small the size of the spark and its efficiency will be seriously impaired. The spark plug gap should be set to 0.025 in (0.65 mm) for the best results.

9 To set the gap measure it with a feeler gauge, and then bend open or close the outer plug electrode until the correct gap is achieved. The centre electrode must never be bent as this may crack the insulation and cause plug failure if nothing worse.

10 When replacing the spark plugs, remember to use new washers and replace the leads from the distributor in the correct firing order which is 1,3,4,2, cylinder No.1 being at the water pump end of the engine.

11 The plug leads require no routine maintenance other than being kept clean and wiped over regularly. At intervals of 6,000 miles (10,000 km) however, pull each lead off the plugs in turn and remove them from the distributor cap. Water can seep down these joints giving rise to a white corrosive deposit which must be carefully removed from the end of each cable.

12 Fault diagnosis - fault symptoms

There are two main symptoms indicating ignition faults. Either the engine will not start or fire, or the engine is difficult to start and misfires. If there is a regular misfire (ie the engine is only running on two or three cylinders) the fault is almost sure to be in the secondary, or high tension circuit. If the misfiring is intermittent, the fault could be in either the high or low tension circuits. If the engine stops suddenly, or will not start at all, it is likely that the fault is in the low tension circuit. Loss of power and overheating, apart from faulty carburation settings, are normally due to faults in the distributor, or incorrect ignition timing.

13 Fault diagnosis - engine fails to start

1 If the engine fails to start and the car was running normally when it was last used, first check that there is fuel in the petrol tank. If the engine turns over normally on the starter motor and the battery is evidently well charged, then the fault may be in either the high or low tension circuits. **Note**, if the battery is known to be fully charged, the ignition light comes on, and the starter motor fails to turn the engine, **check the tightness of the battery terminals** and the secureness of the earth lead to its connection to the body. It is quite common for the leads to have worked loose, even if they look and feel secure. If one of the battery terminal posts gets very hot when trying to operate the starter motor this is a sure indication of a faulty connection to that terminal.

2 One of the commonest reasons for bad starting is wet or damp spark plugs, leads, ignition coil and distributor. Remove the distributor cap. If condensation is visible internally, dry the cap with a rag and wipe over the leads. Replace the cap.

3 If the engine still fails to start, check that current is reaching the plugs, by disconnecting each plug lead in turn at the spark plug end and holding the end of the cable about 1/5 in (5 mm) away from the cylinder block. Spin the engine on the starter motor by pressing the rubber button on the starter motor solenoid switch located under the bonnet (This facility is not available on models with automatic transmission - an assistant will be required).

4 Sparking between the end of the cable and the block should be fairly strong with a regular blue spark. (Hold the lead with rubber to avoid electric shocks). If current is reaching the plugs, then remove them, clean and regap them to 0.25 in (0.65 mm). The engine should now start.

5 Switch on the ignition and remove the centre lead from the distributor and holding it within rubber spin the engine as

before when a rapid succession of blue sparks between the end of the lead and the block indicates that the coil is in order and that either the distributor cap is cracked or tracking, the carbon brush is stuck or worn, the rotor arm is faulty, or the contact points are burnt, pitted or dirty. If the points are in bad shape, clean and reset them as described in Section 3.

6 If there are no sparks ftom the end of the lead from the coil then check the connections of the lead to the coil and distributor cap, and if they are in order, check out the low tension circuit starting with the battery.

7 Switch on the ignition and turn the crankshaft so that the contact breaker points have fully opened. Then with either a 12 volt voltmeter or bulb and length of wire, check that current from the battery is reaching the starter solenoid switch. No reading indicates that there is a fault in the cable to the switch, or in the connections at the switch or at the battery terminals. Alternatively the battery earth lead may not be properly attached to the body.

8 Refer to the wiring diagram in Chapter 10 and with the ignition switched on systematically test the circuit at all points to the ignition coil. If no reading is obtained at any point recheck the last test point and this will show the wire or terminal failure.

9 Check the CB terminal on the ignition coil (this is the one connected to the distributor) and if no reading is recorded on the voltmeter then the coil has failed and must be renewed. The engine should start when a new coil has been fitted.

10 If a reading is obtained at the distributor cable connection at the coil, then check the low tension terminal on the side of the distributor. If no reading is obtained, check the wire for loose connections etc. If a reading is obtained then the final check on the low tension circuit is across the contact breaker points. No reading means a broken condenser which when renewed will enable the engine to be started.

14 Fault diagnosis - engine misfires

1 If the engine misfires regularly, run it at a fast idling speed, and short out each of the plugs in turn by placing a short screwdriver across the spark plug terminal to the cylinder head. Ensure the screwdriver has an insulated wooden or plastic handle.

2 No difference in engine running will be noticed when the plug in the defective cylinder is short circuited. Short circuiting the working plugs will accentuate the misfire.

3 Remove the plug lead from the end of the defective plug and hold it about 1/5 in (5 mm) from the cylinder head. Restart the engine. If sparking is fairly strong and regular the fault must lie in the spark plug.

4 The plug may be loose, the insulation may be cracked, or the points may have burnt away giving too wide a gap for the spark to jump. Worse still, one of the points may have broken off. Renew the plug, clean it and/or reset the gap - whichever is necessary and then test it.

5 If there is no spark at the end of the plug lead or if the spark is weak and intermittent check the ignition lead from the distributor to the plug. If the insulation is damaged renew the lead. Check connections at the distributor cap.

6 If there is still no spark, examine the distributor cap carefully for tracking. This can be recognised by a very thin black line running between two or more electrodes or between an electrode and some other part of the distributor. These lines are paths which now conduct electricity across the cap thus letting it run to earth. The only answer is to fit a new distributor cap.

7 Apart from the ignition timing being incorrect, other causes of misfiring have already been dealt with under Section 13.

8 If the ignition timing is too far retarded, it should be noted that the engine will tend to overheat and there will be quite a noticeable drop in power. If the engine is overheating and the power is down, and the ignition timing is correct, then the carburettor should be checked, as it is likely that this is where the fault lies. See Chapter 3 for details of this.

Chapter 5 Clutch

Contents

Specifications

Type	Diaphragm spring, single dry plate
Actuation	Hydraulically by pendant pedal
Clutch plate diameter	7.125 in. (181 mm)
Facing material	Wound yarn
Master cylinder diameter	0.70 in. (17.80 mm)
Slave cylinder diameter	0.875 in. (22.22 mm)
Clutch release lever clearance	0.020 in. (0.51 mm)
Clutch release bearing	Ball race
Clutch fluid	Unipart 550 brake fluid or Castrol Girling Universal Brake and Clutch Fluid

Torque wrench settings:	lb f ft	kg fm
Flywheel retaining bolt	110 - 115	15.2 - 15.9
Driving strap securing bolts	18	2.5
Diaphragm retaining bolts	15 - 18	2.1 - 2.5

1 General description

The main parts of the clutch assembly are: the clutch driven plate assembly, the flywheel/pressure plate assembly, and the release bearing assembly. When the clutch is in use the driven plate, being splined to the primary gear is under pressure from the diaphragm spring and the friction linings are hard against the flywheel and pressure plate. The driven plate is therefore rotated with the flywheel and the drive is transmitted to the splined primary gear and to the transmission unit input gear via an idler gear.

When the driver depresses the clutch pedal, hydraulic fluid passes from the clutch master cylinder under pressure to the clutch slave cylinder. The piston, within the slave cylinder, moves the clutch operating lever in such a manner that the release bearing is moved forwards. The diaphragm spring pressure is released from the driven plate and, therefore, the drive line is broken and engine torque is no longer transmitted to the transmission unit.

It will be seen from Fig. 5.7 that the primary gear also forms part of the hub of the driven plate. This hub and gear assembly is able to remain stationary, or rotate relative to the crankshaft. It is therefore possible for the crankshaft to rotate while the driven plate and gears within the transmission unit remain still.

As the friction linings on the clutch driven plate wear, the pressure plate automatically moves closer to the driven plate to compensate. This makes the centre of the diaphragm spring nearer to the release bearing, so descreasing the release bearing clearance but not the clutch free pedal travel, as, unless the master cylinder has been disturbed, this is automatically compensated for.

2 Bleeding the hydraulic system

Whenever the clutch hydraulic system has been overhauled, partially renewed, or the level in the reservoir is too low, air will have entered the system necessitating the bleeding operation to dispel the unwanted air. During this operation the level of hydraulic fluid in the reservoir should not be allowed to fall below half full, otherwise air will be drawn in again.

1 Obtain a clean dry jam jar, plastic tubing at least 12 in (30 cm) long and able to fit tightly over the bleed nipple of the slave cylinder, a supply of correct grade hydraulic fluid, and an assistant.

2 Ensure that the master cylinder fluid reservoir is full, and if not top it up. Note: The fluid reservoir must be kept at least 1/3 full throughout the whole bleeding operation. Pour sufficient brake/clutch fluid into the jar to provide a fluid depth of at least 1 in (2.5 cm).

3 Remove the rubber dust cap from the slave cylinder bleed nipple.

4 Connect one end of the rubber tube over the bleed nipple, and submerge the other end in the fluid in the jar. Note: the end of the tube must remain submerged throughout the bleeding operation. Using an open ended spanner, open the bleed nipple one turn.

5 The assistant should now push down the clutch pedal. At the end of each stroke the pedal must be held against the floor while the bleed nipple is closed - when the nipple is closed the pedal should be allowed to return without assistance.

6 Continue the above sequence until no more air bubbles appear and tighten the bleed screw during the next pedal downstroke.

7 Replace the rubber dust cap over the bleed nipple.

Note: Never re-use the fluid bled from the hydraulic system.

3 Slave cylinder (hydraulic system) - removal and refitment

1 It is not necessary to drain the clutch master cylinder when removing the slave cylinder. If fluid is to be left in the master cylinder, however it is necessary to seal the vent hole in the reservoir cap, wipe the top of the reservoir and unscrew the cap. Place a piece of thick polythene over the top of the reservoir and refit the cap.

2 Wipe the hydraulic pipe union at its connection on the slave cylinder with a clean non-fluffy rag.

3 Note how the clutch lever return spring is fitted and then detach it from the slave cylinder. Undo and remove the two bolts with spring washers that secure the clutch slave cylinder to the clutch housing. Carefully withdraw the slave cylinder leaving the pushrod attached to the clutch operating lever.

4 Unscrew the slave cylinder from the end of the flexible hose and wrap the exposed end in a piece of clean non-fluffy rag to prevent dirt ingress.

5 Refitting the clutch slave cylinder is the reverse procedure to removal. It will be necessary to bleed the hydraulic system as described in Section 2.

4 Slave cylinder - dismantling, examination and re-assembly

1 Clean the exterior of the slave cylinder using a dry non-fluffy rag.

2 Carefully ease back the dust cover from the body and lift away.

3 Using a pair of circlip pliers remove the piston retaining circlip.

4 Remove the piston assembly and spring by carefully shaking out these components. Separate the piston, cup seal (noting which way round it is fitted) cup filler and spring.

5 Inspect the inside of the cylinder for score marks caused by impurities in the hydraulic fluid. If any are found a new slave cylinder will be necessary.

6 If the cylinder is sound, thoroughly clean it out with fresh hydraulic fluid.

7 The old rubber seal will probably be swollen and visibly worn. Smear the new rubber seal in hydraulic fluid and place it on the filler cup.

8 Insert the spring in the filler cup and then smear a little

hydraulic fluid on the cylinder bore. The spring, filler cup and seal may now be placed in the bore. Gently ease the edge of the seal into the bore so that it does not roll over.

9 Push the seal down the bore with the piston and retain the piston assembly in the bore with the circlip.

10 Smear the sealing areas of the new dust cover with hydraulic fluid or rubber grease and refit to the slave cylinder.

5 Clutch master cylinder - removal and refitment

1 Working from inside the car remove the spring retaining pin from the master cylinder operating fork clevis pin on the pedal.

2 Lift away the plain washer and clevis pin.

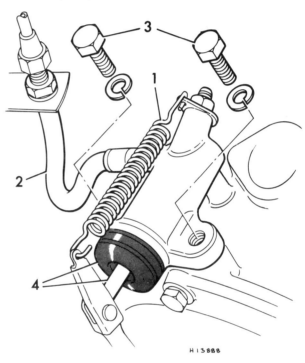

H13888

Fig. 5.1. Clutch slave cylinder removal

1 Release lever return spring
2 Hydraulic hose
3 Slave cylinder securing bolts
4 Clutch slave cylinder and pushrod

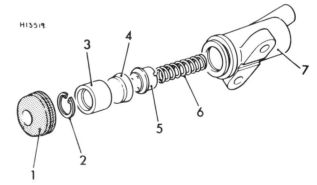

H13519

Fig. 5.2. Exploded view of clutch slave cylinder

1	Rubber dust cover	5	Cup filler
2	Circlip	6	Spring
3	Piston	7	Body
4	Cup seal		

3 It is not necessary to drain the master cylinder before removal. It will, however, be necessary to seal the vent hole in the reservoir cap. Wipe the top of the reservoir and unscrew the cap. Place a piece of thick polythene over the top of the reservoir and refit the cap.

4 Wipe the hydraulic pipe union at its connection on the master cylinder end with a clean non-fluffy rag. Unscrew the union nut with an open-ended spanner and wrap the exposed end in a piece of clean non-fluffy rag to prevent dirt ingress.

5 Undo and remove the two nuts, spring and plain washers securing the master cylinder to the bulkhead.

6 The master cylinder may now be removed from its location. Take care not to spill any hydraulic fluid as it has a detrimental effect on paintwork.

7 The master cylinder refitting procedure is the reverse sequence to removal, but care must be taken when offering up to the bulkhead that the pushrod is in line with the clutch pedal. Once connections have been made the hydraulic system must be bled as described in Section 2.

6 Clutch master cylinder - dismantling, examination and re-assembly

1 Unscrew the filler cap and drain the fluid from the reservoir.

2 Carefully ease the rubber boot from the body and slide up the pushrod.

3 Using a pair of circlip pliers remove the circlip retaining the piston assembly in the bore.

4 Withdraw the pushrod complete with dished washer from the master cylinder body.

5 Carefully withdraw the piston complete with the secondary cup, piston washer, main cup, spring retainer and spring from the body.

6 Using the fingers only remove the secondary cup from the piston by stretching it over the end of the piston. Make a note of which way round it is fitted.

7 Thoroughly wash all parts with hydraulic fluid or methylated spirits and wipe dry.

8 Carefully examine all parts, especially the piston cups for signs of distortion, swelling, splitting or other wear and check the piston and cylinder for wear or scoring. Renew any parts that are suspect. It is recommended that, whenever a master cylinder is dismantled, new rubber seals are always fitted.

9 When re-assembling the components to the master cylinder all components to be fitted must be lubricated with clean hydraulic fluid.

10 Carefully stretch the secondary cup over the piston with the lip of the cup facing the head of the piston. This is the drilled end.

11 Fit the spring retainer into the small diameter end of the piston and insert the spring into the body. The larger of the two diameters first.

12 Next fit the main cup and cup washer over the spring retainer.

13 With the cylinder bore wet, carefully insert the piston assembly fully down into the bore. Take care not to roll the lips of the piston seals when inserting into the bore.

14 Refit the pushrod assembly and retain it in position with the circlip.

15 Smear the sealing areas of the new dust cover with hydraulic fluid or rubber grease and refit to the master cylinder.

7 Hydraulic pipe (rigid) - removal and refitment

1 Remove the rubber cover from the slave cylinder bleed nipple (if fitted) and place over it one end of a piece of plastic tube at least 12 in (30 cm) long. The other end should be placed in a glass jar.

2 Refer to Section 2 and drain the hydraulic system using the procedure described for bleeding, but allowing the master cylinder to drain.

3 Using a clean non-fluffy rag wipe the areas around the two pipe unions, and then, with an open-ended spanner unscrew the two unions.

4 Detach the pipe from the hose and master cylinder.

5 Refitting the clutch hydraulic pipe is the reverse sequence to removal. It will be necessary to bleed the clutch hydraulic system as described in Section 2.

8 Hydraulic hose (flexible) - removal and refitment

1 Refer to Section 7, paragraphs 1 and 2 and drain the clutch hydraulic system.

2 Using a clean non-fluffy rag wipe the area around the two ends of the hydraulic hose and then with an open ended spanner disconnect the hydraulic pipe end from the flexible hose.

3 Unscrew and remove the hose from the clutch slave cylinder.

4 Refitting the clutch hydraulic hose is the reverse sequence to removal. It will be necessary to bleed the clutch hydraulic system as described in Section 2.

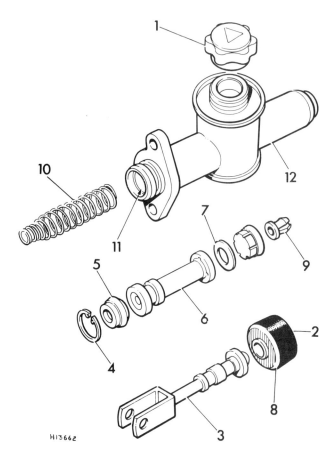

H13662

Fig. 5.3. Exploded view of clutch master cylinder

1 Cap	7 Cup washer
2 Rubber boot	8 Main cup
3 Pushrod	9 Spring retainer
4 Circlip	10 Spring
5 Secondary cup	11 Bore
6 Piston	12 Body

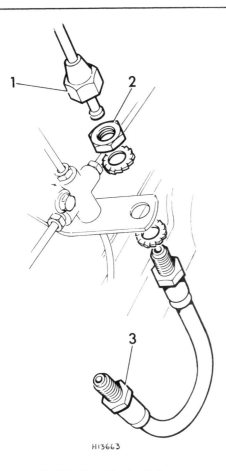

H13663

Fig. 5.4. Clutch hydraulic hose

1 *Union nut*   3 *Hydraulic hose*
2 *Nut*

9 Clutch assembly - removal and refitment

1   The clutch assembly may be removed with the power unit
in the car. Before commencing work however a word of
warning: Two special tools are necessary to enable the clutch
and flywheel assembly to be removed from the end of the
crankshaft. Without these the job is very difficult and if
improvised means are used expensive damage can result. The
tools have part numbers 18G 587, 18G 304 and 18G 304N.
2   Open the bonnet and disconnect the two battery terminals.
Unscrew the battery clamp nuts, detach the clamp and lift
away the battery.
3   Make a note of the horn cable terminal connectors and
detach the cables.
4   Detach the cooling system expansion tank hose and then
remove the tank from the battery retaining bracket.
5   Undo and remove the battery retaining bracket securing
screws and lift away the bracket complete with horn still
attached.
6   Using an overhead hoist or jack and wood packing support
the weight of the power unit.
7   Undo and remove the two set screws and spring washers
securing the right-hand engine mounting to the adaptor bracket
on the clutch housing.
8   Lift away the small engine safety brackets making a note of
how they are fitted.
9   Undo and remove the four bolts, nuts, spring and plain
washers securing the engine mounting bracket assembly to the
body.
10 Lift away the bracket assembly.

11 Undo and remove the set screws securing the engine
mounting adaptor bracket to the clutch cover. Lift away the
bracket.
12 Make a note of the cable connections to the starter motor.
Detach the cables.
13 Undo and remove the two bolts and washers securing the
starter motor to the clutch housing. Lift away the starter
motor.
14 Make a note of which way round the release lever return
spring is fitted and detach.
15 Undo and remove the eight screws, and spring washers
securing the clutch cover to the clutch housing and lift away
the cover.
16 The crankshaft must now be rotated until the slot in the
crankshaft and flywheel is exactly horizontal. If this is not
done the crankshaft primary gears 'C' shaped thrust washer
might fall out of its fitted position and cause severe damage or
make it impossible to remove the flywheel and clutch
assembly.
17 Using a pair of narrow nosed pliers remove the clutch
release bearing thrust plate circlip.
18 Lift away the thrust plate noting the word 'TOP' stamped
on the plate is facing outermost.
19 Using a small flat chisel carefully knock back the flywheel
retaining bolt lock washer tab.
20 Lock the flywheel by placing a wide bladed screwdriver
between the flywheel ring gear teeth and clutch housing and
use special tool 18G 587 to remove the retaining bolt. This is
very tight so be careful.
21 Lift away the key plate that locates the crankshaft to the
flywheel.
22 Assemble the second special tool 18G 304 and 18G 304 N
and insert the thrust button into the end of the crankshaft. Fit
the tool to the flywheel and clutch assembly.
23 Lock the flywheel again and slowly screw in the centre
bolt. This again can be tight so take care.
24 The flywheel and clutch assembly once released from the
crankshaft taper may be lifted away from the rear of the
power unit.
25 To refit the clutch assembly is basically identical to the
removal sequence but the information in the following paragraphs must be followed first.
26 Make sure that the crankshaft taper is very clean and
perfectly dry and offer up the flywheel and clutch assembly.
27 Line up the offset slot in the end of the crankshaft and
flywheel and replace the key plate.
28 Using special tool 18G 587 tighten the flywheel retaining
bolt to a torque wrench setting of 110 - 115 lb f ft (15.2 -
15.9 kg fm).
29 Undo and remove the three dowel bolts and shakeproof
washers and detach the clutch diaphragm cover. This should be
done in a progressive manner.
30 Carefully knock over the lock washer tab on the flywheel
retaining bolt. Under no circumstances may the lock washer be
levered over to the locked position as the diaphragm cover is
easily distorted or damaged causing clutch judder.
31 Refit the diaphragm cover so that the "A" mark on the
cover is fitted **opposite** the timing marks on the flywheel.
32 Replace and tighten the dowel bolts and shakeproof
washers in an even and progressive manner making sure that
they are correctly located in each pair of driving straps.
33 Replace the thrust plate with the word "TOP" facing
outwards and also adjacent to the timing marks on the
flywheel.
34 Refit the thrust plate circlip so that the ears are next to
the word "TOP" on the thrust plate.
35 Refitting the remainder of the components is a direct
reversal of the removal procedure.

10 Clutch assembly - overhaul

1   To dismantle the clutch assembly the clutch and flywheel

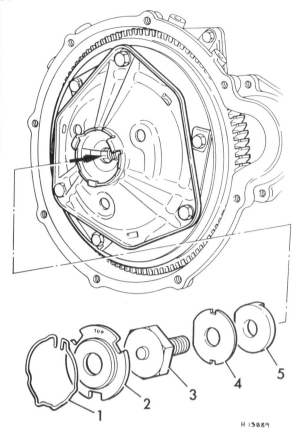

Fig. 5.5. Clutch thrust plate and flywheel securing bolt
assemblies

1 Circlip
2 Bearing thrust plate
3 Flywheel retaining bolt
4 Lockwasher
5 Key plate

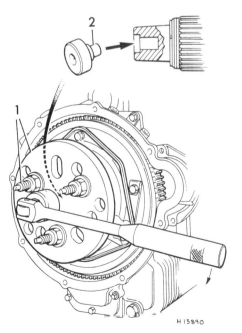

Fig. 5.6. Use of special tool to detach flywheel assembly
from end of crankshaft

1 Special puller   2 Thrust button

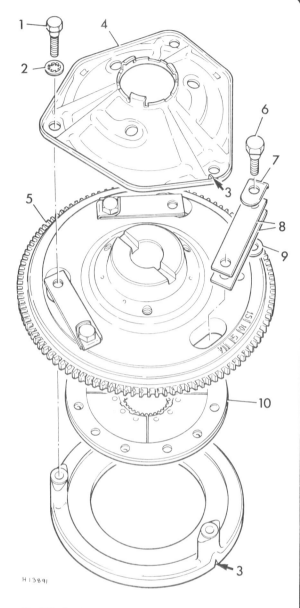

Fig. 5.7. Exploded view of clutch and flywheel assembly

1 Dowel bolt
2 Shakeproof washer
3 Alignment mark
4 Diaphragm
5 Flywheel
6 Dowel bolt
7 Tab washer
8 Straps
9 Spacer
10 Driven plate

Fig. 5.8. Centralisation of clutch driven plate

assembly must first be removed from the power unit as described in Section 9.

2 Undo and remove the three dowel bolts and shakeproof washers securing the diaphragm to the flywheel. This should be done in a progressive manner.

3 Locate the assembly marking "A" on the diaphragm cover and pressure plate and then lift off the diaphragm.

4 The flywheel should next be removed from the pressure plate.

5 Now remove the clutch driven plate making a note of which way round it is fitted.

6 Carefully knock back the lock washer tabs of the three driving strap securing bolts. Undo and remove the bolts and lock washers.

7 Lift away each pair of driving straps making a note of the spacer washer which is fitted between the straps and the flywheel.

8 With the clutch assembly dismantled wipe all parts clean ready for inspection.

9 Inspect the pressure plate for signs of scoring or damage. Also examine the diaphragm spring for signs of damage, wear and fractures. Check the driving straps for signs of elongated holes and the securing bolts for wear.

10 The driven plate should be inspected for signs of oil contamination or burning of the linings. Examine the linings for wear on their faces and finally check the centre hub splines for wear. If apparent, also inspect the crankshaft primary gear splines for wear as it may be that the gear will have to be renewed as well.

11 Obtain any new parts as necessary and then re-assembly can begin. Using feeler gauges check the primary gear end float between the backing ring and primary gear. This should be between 0.0035 - 0.0065 in (0.089 - 0.165 mm). Should adjustment be necessary full information will be found in Chapter 6.

12 Place the pressure plate on a flat surface with the securing lugs uppermost.

13 A special tool is now necessary to enable the clutch driven plate to be centralised relative to the pressure plate. It has a part number of 18G 684. If the tool is not available a wooden one may be fashioned or alternatively a little guesswork may be used. Locate the clutch driven plate with the boss facing downwards on the centraliser tool.

14 Lower the flywheel onto the pressure and driven plates and line up the "A" mark on the pressure plate with the 1/4 timing mark on the flywheel. Refit the driving straps not forgetting the spacer washer between the straps and the flywheel.

15 Replace the strap securing bolts with new lock washers and lightly tighten.

16 Fit the diaphragm so that the "A" mark is in alignment with that on the pressure plate. Do not yet fully tighten the securing bolts.

17 Tighten the driving strap securing bolts to a torque wrench setting of 18 lb f ft (2.5 kg fm). Bend up the lock washer tab.

18 Tighten the diaphragm retaining bolts to a torque wrench setting of 15 - 18 lb f ft (2.1-2.5 kg fm).

19 The centraliser tool should next be removed (if fitted).

20 The clutch/flywheel assembly is now ready for refitting to the power unit.

11 Clutch release bearing assembly - removal and refitment

1 Open the bonnet and disconnect the two battery clamp nuts; detach the clamp and lift away the battery.

2 Using an overhead hoist or jack and wood packing, support the weight of the power unit.

3 Undo and remove the two set screws and spring washers securing the right-hand engine mounting to the adaptor bracket on the clutch housing.

4 Lift away the small engine safety brackets making a note of how they are fitted.

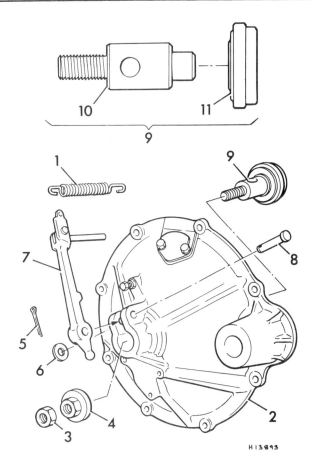

Fig. 5.9. Clutch cover and release bearing assembly

1 Release lever return spring	7 Release lever
2 Clutch cover	8 Clevis pin
3 Locknut	9 Release bearing and
4 Plunger stop	plunger assembly
5 Split pin	10 Plunger
6 Plain washer	11 Release bearing

5 Undo and remove the four bolts, nuts, spring and plain washers securing the engine mounting bracket assembly to the body.

6 Lift away the bracket assembly.

7 Undo and remove the set screws securing the engine mounting adaptor bracket to the clutch cover. Lift away the bracket.

8 Make a note of which way round the release lever return spring is fitted and detach.

9 Undo and remove the eight screws and spring washers securing the clutch cover to the clutch housing and lift away the cover.

10 Undo and remove the plunger stop bolt and locknut.

11 Withdraw the split pin, lift away the washer and remove the clevis pin which acts as the release lever fulcrum.

12 Pull the release lever out of the release bearing plunger.

13 Remove the release bearing and plunger assembly from the cover.

14 Check the clutch release bearing for wear or roughness when the inner track is held and the outer track rotated. If it is blue in colour it is an indication that it has overheated due to incorrect clutch adjustment.

15 To remove the release bearing, using a bench vice and suitable metal packing, press the old bearing from the plunger assembly.

16 Re-assembly and refitment of the release bearing is the

reverse sequence to removal. Take care that the clutch release lever is fitted the correct way round. Finally adjust the clutch clearance between the release lever and stop as described in Section 12.

12 Clutch - adjustments

Throw-out stop:
1 Screw the plunger stop and locknut out away from the housing to the limit of its travel.
2 An assistant should now fully depress the clutch pedal.
3 Screw the plunger stop up against the housing. Now release the clutch pedal and screw the stop in a further one flat of the stop. This should be approximately 0.007 - 0.010 in (0.20 - 0.25 mm).
4 Hold the plunger stop and tighten the locknut.

Return stop:
1 Pull the release lever outwards against the spring pressure until all the free movement is taken up.
2 Measure the clearance between the stop and the release lever. The correct clearance is 0.020 in (0.5 mm) see Fig. 5.10.
3 To adjust the clearance, slacken the locknut and screw the stop in or out until the correct clearance is obtained. Tighten the locknut.

13 Clutch pedal - removal and refitment

1 Refer to Chapter 12 and remove the front parcel shelf on the driver's side of the car.
2 Withdraw the retaining spring pin from the master cylinder operating fork clevis pin on the pedal.
3 Lift away the plain washer and withdraw the clevis pin.
4 Make a note of which way round the clutch and brake pedal return springs are fitted and detach the springs from the pedal bracket.
5 Undo and remove the screw and washer retaining the pedal pivot pin retaining clip to the side of the pedal bracket.
6 Withdraw the retaining spring clip from the clutch side of the pivot pin.
7 Carefully push the pivot pin through the pedal assemblies until the clutch pedal can be lifted away.
8 Refitting the pedal to the pedal bracket is the reverse sequence to removal. Lubricate the pivot pin with a little engine oil and the return spring with a little grease to ensure quiet operation.

14 Clutch faults - squeal: diagnosis and cure

1 If on taking up the drive, or when changing gear, the clutch squeals, this is a sure indication of a badly worn clutch release bearing. As well as regular wear due to normal use, wear of the clutch release bearing is much accentuated if the clutch is 'ridden', or held down for long periods with a gear selected and the engine running. To minimise wear of this component the car should always be taken out of gear at traffic lights and for similar hold ups.
2 The clutch release bearing is not an expensive item to renew. There is no other cure.

15 Clutch faults - slip: diagnosis and cure

1 Clutch slip is a self evident condition which occurs when the clutch friction plate (driven plate) is badly worn; the release arm free travel is insufficient; oil or grease has got onto the flywheel or pressure plate faces; or the pressure plate itself is faulty.
2 The reason for clutch slip is that, due to one of the faults listed above, there is either insufficient pressure from the

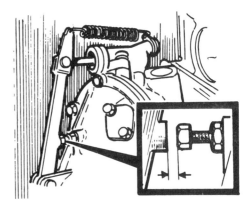

Fig. 5.10. Clutch adjustment

Inset shows clearance measurement point

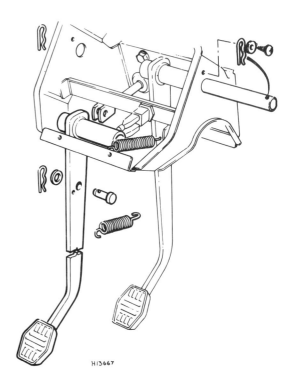

H15667

Fig. 5.11. Clutch pedal and bracket assembly

pressure plate, or insufficient friction from the friction plate, to ensure a solid drive.
3 If small amounts of oil get onto the clutch, they will be burnt off under the heat of clutch engagement, in the process gradually darkening the linings. Excessive oil on the clutch will burn off leaving a carbon deposit which can cause quite bad slip, fierceness, or spin and judder.
4 If clutch slip is suspected, and confirmation of this condition is required, there are several tests which can be made:
a) With the engine in second or third gear and pulling lightly up a moderate incline, sudden depression of the accelerator pedal may cause the engine to increase its speed without any

increase in road speed. Easing off on the accelerator will then give a definite drop in engine speed without the car slowing.

b) Drive the car at a steady speed in top gear and, braking with the left foot, try and maintain the same speed by pressing down on the accelerator. Providing the same speed is maintained, a change in the speed of the engine confirms that slip is taking place.

c) In extreme cases of clutch slip the engine will race under normal acceleration conditions.

If slip is due to oil or grease on the linings a temporary cure can sometimes be effected by squirting carbon tetrochloride into the clutch housing. The permanent cure, of course, is to renew the clutch driven plate, and to trace and rectify the oil leak.

16 Clutch faults - spin: diagnosis and cure

1 Clutch spin is a condition which occurs when there is a leak in the clutch hydraulic actuating mechanism; the release arm free travel is excessive; there is an obstruction in the clutch either on the primary gear splines, or in the unit itself; or the oil may have partially burnt off the clutch linings and have left a resinous deposit which is causing the clutch disc to stick to the pressure plate or flywheel.

2 The reason for clutch spin is that due to any, or a combination of, the faults just listed, the clutch pressure plate is not completely freeing from the centre plate even with the clutch pedal fully depressed.

3 If clutch spin is suspected, the condition can be confirmed by extreme difficulty in engaging first gear from rest, difficulty in changing gear, and very sudden take-up of the clutch drive at the fully depressed end of the clutch pedal travel as the clutch is released.

4 Check the clutch master cylinder and slave cylinder and the connecting hydraulic pipe or hose for leaks. Fluid in one of the rubber boots fitted over the end of either the master or slave cylinder is a sure sign of a leaking piston seal.

5 If these points are checked and found to be in order then the fault lies internally in the clutch, and it will be necessary to remove it for examination.

17 Clutch faults - judder: diagnosis and cure

1 Clutch judder is a self evident condition which occurs when the power unit mountings are loose or too flexible; when there is oil on the faces of the clutch friction plate; or when the clutch has been assembled incorrectly.

2 The reason for clutch judder is that due to one of the faults just listed, the clutch pressure plate is not freeing smoothly from the friction disc, and is snatching.

3 Clutch judder normally occurs when the clutch pedal is released in first or reverse gears, and the whole car shudders as it moves backwards or forwards.

Chapter 6 Gearbox and automatic transmission

For modifications, and information applicable to later models, see Supplement at end of manual

Contents

Specifications

Manual transmission:

Number of forward speeds	4
Synchromesh action	All forward speeds

Ratios:

Top	1.000 : 1
Third	1.433 : 1
Second	2.218 : 1
First	3.525 : 1
Reverse	3.544 : 1

Automatic transmission:

Application	1300 models only
Torque converter ratio range	1 : 1 to 2 : 1

Ratios:

Top	1.000 : 1
Third	1.460 : 1
Second	1.845 : 1
First	2.690 : 1
Reverse	2.690 : 1

Torque wrench settings

Manual transmission:

	lb f ft	kg fm
Case to crankcase bolts	6	0.83
First motion shaft nut	150	20.74
Third motion shaft nut	150	20.74

Automatic transmission:

	lb f ft	kg fm
Converter centre bolt	114	15.75
Converter - six central bolts	24	3.32
Converter drain plugs	20	2.77
Converter housing bolts	18	2.49
Case to crankcase nuts	12	1.66
5/16 in. UNF bolts	20	2.77
3/8 in. UNF bolts	30	4.15

1 General description

The manual transmission is of the four forward speed type with synchromesh action on all forward speeds. Gear selection is by a floor mounted remote control gear lever, connected to the transmission by two rods.

Upon initial inspection, the unit appears to be similar to that fitted to the established 1100/1300 range of cars but, there are several modifications. In the main these are confined to the laygear, mainshaft, selector control rod attachments, synchromesh and inboard drive shaft constant velocity joints.

Although the unit looks complicated it is relatively easy to dismantle and overhaul, provided, that a comprehensive tool kit is used. However, before overhaul, consideration should be given to purchasing a reconditioned unit with a guarantee, rather than spend nearly the same amount of money on a new set of gears in order to do the job yourself.

1300 models may be fitted with automatic transmission as

an optional extra. It is of the three element fluid torque convertor type, connected to a bevel gear train which is able to give a range of four forward speeds and one reverse. The system is controlled by a floor mounted selector lever within a gated quadrant marked with six positions.

The system can be used as a fully automatic four speed gearbox, with the gears changing automatically from rest to maximum speed according to the throttle position and engine load. If a lower gear ratio is required to obtain greater acceleration, an instant full throttle position (ie 'kickdown' on the accelerator) immediately produces the down change.

Complete manual control or override is possible in the "1", "2" and "3" positions. However, it is very important that downward changes are made within the speed range of the gear selected, otherwise, serious damage may result to the automatic gearbox components. The second, third and top speed positions provide engine braking whether driving in automatic or manual conditions. Manual selection allows the driver to stay in a particular gear to suit road conditions. There is no

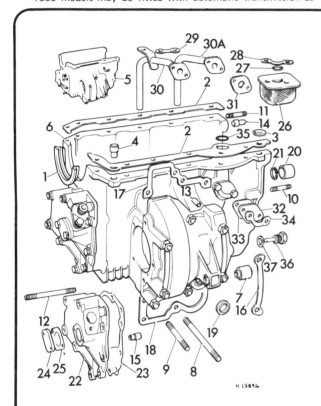

Fig. 6.1. Transmission casing

1	Oil seal	20	Bearing
2	Gasket	21	Circlip
3	Collar	22	Speedometer
4	Dowel		drive housing
5	Transmission casing	23	Gasket
6	Case assembly	24	Cover plate
7	Bush	25	Gasket
8	Stud	26	Oil strainer
9	Stud	27	Sealing ring
10	Stud	28	Lockwasher
11	Stud	29	Lockwasher
12	Stud	30	Pick up pipe
13	Dowel	31	Gasket
14	Dowel	32	Cover plate
15	Dowel	33	Gasket
16	Lockwasher	34	Lockwasher
17	Gasket	35	Sealing ring
18	Gasket	36	Drain plug
19	Oil seal	37	Washer

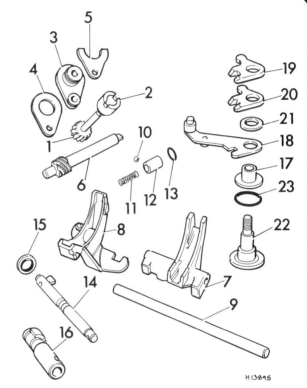

Fig. 6.2. Transmission selector mechanism

1	Speedometer pinion	13	'O' ring
2	Bush	14	Selector shaft
3	Bush	15	Oil seal
4	Gasket	16	Interlock spool
5	Retainer	17	Bush
6	Gear and spindle	18	Reverse lever
7	1st and 2nd speed fork	19	Upper bell crank lever
8	3rd and 4th speed fork	20	Centre bell crank lever
9	Selector fork shaft	21	Spacer
10	Detent ball	22	Pivot pin
11	Detent spring	23	'O' ring
12	Detent sleeve		

engine braking in first gear.

Information on the automatic transmission is confined to that which the author considers to be within the capabilities of the reader. No overhaul details are given as special tools and equipment are required. Any suspected faults should be referred to the local BLMC garage.

2 Gearbox removal

The manual or automatic gearbox is removed from the car together with the engine and differential assembly. Full information on removal and separating from the engine will be found in Chapter 1.

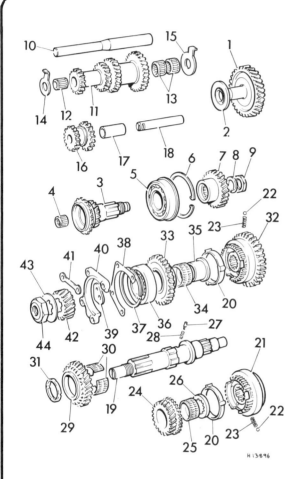

Fig. 6.3. Mainshaft assembly

1	Idler gear	25	Needle roller bearing
2	Thrust washer	26	Thrust washer
3	First motion shaft	27	Peg
4	Needle roller bearing	28	Spring
5	First motion shaft bearing	29	Second speed gear
6	Circlip	30	Needle roller bearing
7	First motion shaft drive gear	31	Thrust washer
8	Tab washer	32	Reverse mainshaft gear and 1st & 2nd gear synchroniser
9	Nut	33	First speed gear
10	Layshaft	34	Needle roller bearing
11	Lay gear	35	First speed gear journal
12	Needle roller bearing	36	Ball bearing
13	Needle roller bearing	37	Spring ring
14	Thrust washer (small)	38	Shim
15	Thrust washer (large)	39	Locating plate
16	Reverse idler assembly	40	Retainer - third motion shaft
17	Bush	41	Lockwasher
18	Reverse idler shaft	42	Final drive pinion
19	Third motion shaft	43	Lockwasher
20	Baulk ring	44	Pinion retaining nut
21	3rd & 4th speed synchronizer assembly		
22	Ball		
23	Spring		
24	Third speed gear		

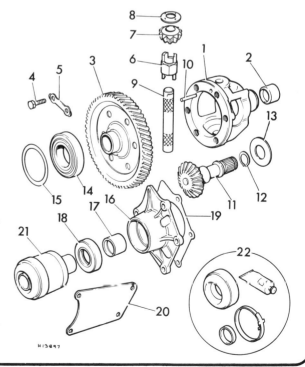

Fig. 6.4. Differential gears and end covers

1	Differential case assembly	12	Circlip
2	Bush	13	Thrust washer
3	Drive gear assembly	14	Ball bearing
4	Bolt	15	Shim
5	Lockwasher	16	End cover assembly
6	Thrust block	17	Bush
7	Differential pinion	18	Oil seal
8	Pinion thrust washer	19	Cover gasket
9	Pinion centre pin	20	Exhaust mounting bracket
10	Peg	21	Drive shaft joint
11	Differential gear	22	Boot

3 Gearbox (manual) - dismantling, overhaul and re-assembly

1 Thoroughly clean the exterior if it is dirty and wipe dry with a non-fluffy rag.

2 Undo and remove the screws and spring washers securing the final drive end covers. Carefully lift these away and recover any shims between the gasket and main casing.

3 The selector shaft detent spring, sleeve and ball bearing should next be removed.

4 Using a chisel, knock back the lockwasher tabs for the final drive housing securing nuts; undo and remove the nuts and lockwashers.

5 Wrap some pvc tape over the selector shaft to protect the oil seal, and carefully remove the final drive housing.

6 The final drive gear assembly may now be lifted away.

7 Undo and remove the screw and spring washer securing the speedometer drive pinion retainer plate to the housing. Lift away the retainer plate and pinion housing assembly.

8 The speedometer drive pinion may now be lifted away.

9 Undo and remove the bolts and washers securing the engine mounting adaptor housing. Lift away the housing.

10 Undo and remove the screws and spring washers securing the speedometer drive housing to the main casing. Lift away the housing and gasket.

11 Bend back the lock washer tabs and undo and remove the two screws securing the oil suction pipe to the main casing. Carefully pull out the pipe.

12 Using a pair of circlip pliers carefully remove the circlip that retains the first motion shaft roller bearing in position.

13 The roller bearing should now be removed. It may be either 'dismantled' and a new one fitted or carefully eased from the end of the shaft.

14 Bend back the lock washer tab on the first motion shaft securing nut.

15 Knock back the lockwasher tab from the third motion shaft final drive gear securing nut.

16 The selector shaft should now be rotated in an anti-clockwise direction to disengage the operating stub and inter-lock spool from the bell crank levers.

17 Using a screwdriver engage first and fourth gears simultaneously to lock the gear train.

18 Using a large socket undo and remove the third motion shaft final drive gear nut.

19 Withdraw the lock washer and final drive gear.

20 Again, using a large socket, undo and remove the first motion shaft gear nut.

21 Withdraw the lock washers and first motion shaft gear.

22 Return the first and fourth gears to their neutral positions.

23 Bend back the lock washer tabs on the third motion shaft bearing retainer bolts. Undo and remove the four bolts and lock washers.

24 The retainer and adjustment shims may now be lifted away.

25 Remove the reverse locking plate.

26 Using a suitable diameter drift carefully remove the lay-shaft. It can only be removed from the clutch housing end.

27 Remove the small thrust washer from the laygear; lift out the laygear and recover the larger thrust washer.

28 Using a pair of circlip pliers carefully remove the first motion shaft bearing retaining circlip.

29 The first motion shaft and bearing and third motion shaft must now be removed from the end casing. For this a slide hammer is necessary. A horse shoe shaped spacer is necessary for removal of the third motion shaft. This spacer can be made out of an old bearing outer track or weighing machine weight. A mole wrench and hammer can be used instead of the slide hammer if the latter is not available.

30 Refer to Fig. 6.11 and using a soft drift, drive the third motion shaft towards the clutch end of the gearbox. Take care not to disengage the third/fourth speed synchroniser from its hub and releasing the ball bearings and springs.

31 Insert the horse shoe shaped spacer and then drift the other end of the third motion shaft in the opposite direction to

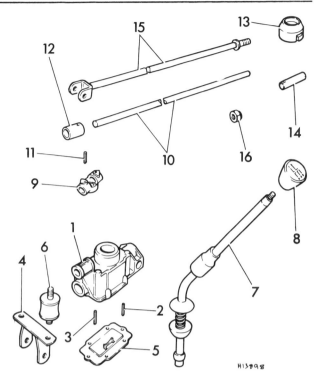

Fig. 6.5. Gear selector mechanism

1 Housing	9 Extension rod eye
2 Pin - long	10 Extension rod
3 Pin - short	11 Slotted spring pin
4 Mounting bracket	12 Coupling
5 Bottom cover	13 Spring retainer
6 Bobbin	14 Support rod eye
7 Change speed lever	15 Steady rod
8 Knob	16 Nut

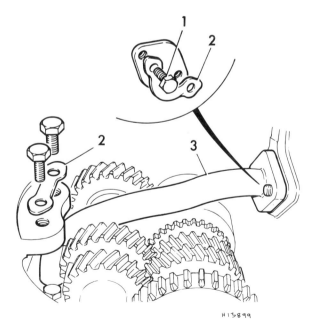

Fig. 6.6. Oil suction pipe removal

1 Bolt	3 Oil suction pipe
2 Lockwasher	

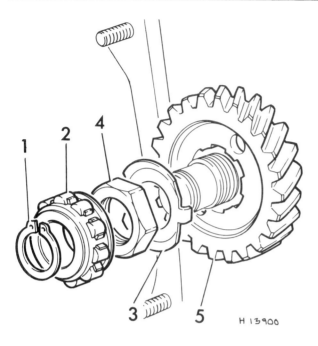

Fig. 6.7. First motion shaft gear removal

1 Circlip   4 Nut
2 Roller race   5 First motion shaft
3 Lockwasher   gear

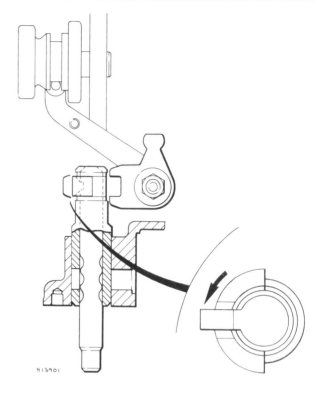

Fig. 6.8. Selector shaft movement to disengage operating stub

remove the third motion shaft bearing from the centre web of the casing.

32 Should the bearing not be completely removed from the centre web by the description in the preceding paragraphs it is permissible to lever it out using a screwdriver between the casing and bearing circlip.

33 Lift out the third motion shaft assembly.

34 The oil strainer may next be removed.

35 Carefully remove the reverse idler shaft and gear.

36 Using a suitable diameter parallel pin punch remove the roll pin that secures the third/fourth speed selector fork to its shaft.

37 Lift away the selector shaft and forks.

38 Undo and remove the bellcrank lever pivot post nut and washer.

39 Lift away the bellcrank levers, washers and pivot sleeve, Note the location and markings on the levers to ensure correct re-assembly.

40 Remove the interlock spool and selector shaft from the inside of the casing.

41 If the bellcrank lever pivot post oil seal is to be renewed drift out the pivot post and remove the old O-ring seal.

42 Remove the two circlips that retain the idler gear needle roller bearing in the gearbox casing.

43 The idler gear bearing may now be drifted out from the casing web.

44 The second idler gear bearing should now be removed from the flywheel housing. Ideally a special tool should be used (18G 581) but it is possible to warm up the flywheel housing and 'shock' or lever it out of position. Unfortunately it is located in a blind hole.

45 Extract the circlip that retains the outer race of the first motion shaft spigot bearing in the flywheel housing and remove the outer race. Again a special tool is necessary (18G 617A) but it can be removed using the principle described in paragraph 44.

46 Carefully remove the primary gear oil seal located in the flywheel housing. Note which way round it is fitted.

47 Thoroughly clean all parts and inspect all bearings and

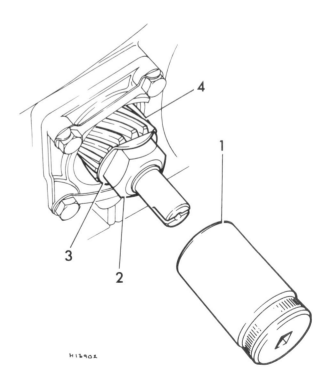

Fig. 6.9. Removal of third motion shaft final drive gear nut

1 Socket   3 Lockwasher
2 Nut   4 Final drive gear

thrust washers for wear or damage. The gear teeth should be checked for uneven wear or chipping and, if evident, the assembly should be further dismantled and new parts fitted. Always use new gaskets and O-ring oil seals.

48 To re-assemble first fit a new primary gear oil seal to the flywheel housing. Make sure it is the correct way round.

49 Carefully fit the first motion shaft spigot bearing outer race into the flywheel housing.

50 Return the bearing in position with the circlip.

51 Using a piece of tube of suitable diameter carefully fit the idler gear bearing into the housing. Do not drift it fully home.

52 Refit the inner circlip into the gearbox casing and carefully fit a new idler gear bearing. Retain with a second circlip.

53 Lubricate a new O-ring oil seal and fit onto the bellcrank lever pivot post. Drift the pivot post into position in the gearbox casing.

54 Fit the selector shaft into the interlock spool and refit the assembly into the gearbox so that the operating stub is facing away from the pivot post.

55 Refit the sleeve and bellcrank levers (in order previously noted) onto the pivot post and tighten the self locking nut.

56 It is important that the selector shaft and interlock spool are not turned into engagement with the bellcrank levers until the first and third motion shaft gear retaining nuts have been fully tightened to the correct torque wrench settings.

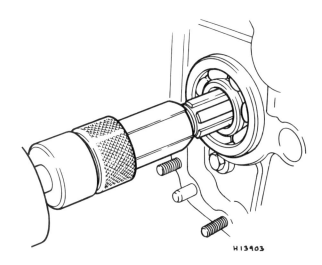

Fig. 6.10. Use of slide hammer to remove first motion shaft

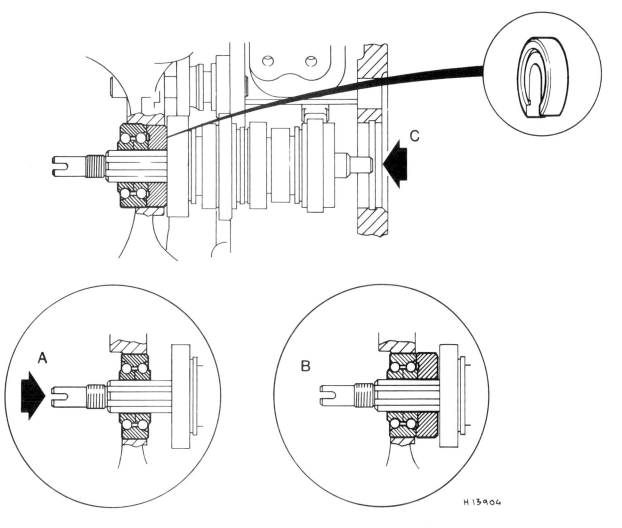

Fig. 6.11. Third motion shaft removal (see text)

| A | Drift rearward | B | Insert horse shoe shaped tool | C | Drift assembly in direction of arrow |

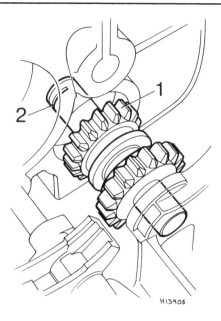

Fig. 6.12. Reverse idler gear and shaft assembly

1   Reverse idler gear
2   Shaft (Note slot rear end)

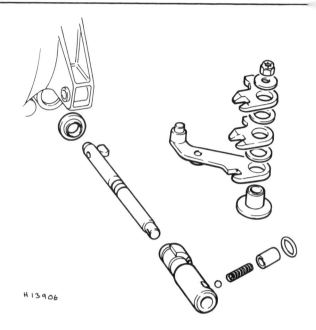

Fig. 6.13. Selector bellcrank lever
assembly

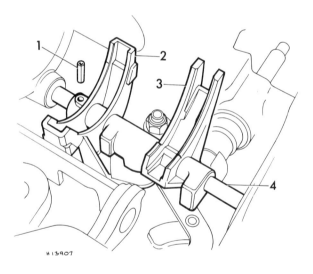

Fig. 6.14. Selector forks

1   Roll pin   3   1st & 2nd speed selector
2   3rd & 4th speed   fork
    selector fork   4   Selector shaft

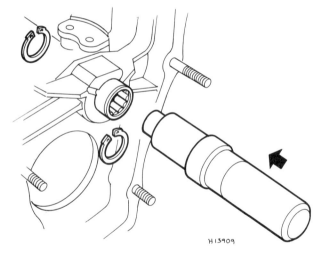

Fig. 6.15. Fitting new idler gear bearing

57 Refit the third/fourth speed selector fork.
58 Refit the first speed selector fork and drift the selector rod through the casing and forks. Line up the hole in the shaft with the hole in the third/fourth speed fork.
59 Carefully drift the roll-pin in until it is flush with the fork.
60 Position the reverse idler gear in engagement with the reverse bellcrank lever pivot and insert the shaft.
61 Position the oil strainer in the casing.
62 If the third motion shaft is to be dismantled and overhauled it should be done now as described in Section 5.

63 Likewise, if the first motion shaft is to be dismantled and overhauled it should be done now as described in Section 4.
64 Place the third motion shaft assembly into the gear casing and ensure the two selector forks are correctly located.
65 Using a suitable diameter tube drift the third motion shaft bearing into the centre web of the casing.
66 Fit the first motion shaft needle roller bearing into its location in the gear.
67 Using a suitable diameter tube, drift the first motion shaft assembly into the casing.

68 One of two size of circlips should be used to retain the bearing position. A special tool "18G 257" will facilitate the gap measurement.

Gap	Circlip number
0.096 - 0.098 in (2.43 - 2.48 mm)	2A 3710
0.098 - 0.100 in (2.48 - 2.54 mm)	2A 3711

69 Fit the needle roller bearings into the laygear and then refit the laygear and shaft together with its thrust washers.
70 Using feeler gauges measure the laygear end float which should be 0.002 - 0.006 in (0.05 - 0.15 mm). Select and fit the required thrust washer.

Washer thickness	Part number
0.123 - 0.124 in (3.12 - 3.14 mm)	22G 856
0.125 - 0.126 in (3.17 - 3.20 mm)	22G 857
0.127 - 0.128 in (3.22 - 3.25 mm)	22G 858
0.130 - 0.131 in (3.30 - 3.32 mm)	22G 859

71 Refit the layshaft and reverse shaft locking plate, turning the shafts as necessary until the slots are in their correct positions.
72 Refit the third motion shaft bearing retainer less any shims found; lightly and evenly tighten the retainer bolts.
73 Using feeler gauges measure the gap and select the necessary shims as given in the following table.

When gap is:	Use shims totalling:
0.005 - 0.006 in (0.13 - 0.15 mm)	0.005 in (0.13 mm)
0.006 - 0.008 in (0.15 - 0.20 mm)	0.007 in (0.18 mm)
0.008 - 0.010 in (0.20 - 0.25 mm)	0.009 in (0.23 mm)
0.010 - 0.012 in (0.25 - 0.30 mm)	0.011 in (0.28 mm)
0.012 - 0.014 in (0.30 - 0.35 mm)	0.013 in (0.33 mm)
0.014 - 0.015 in (0.35 - 0.38 mm)	0.015 in (0.38 mm)

74 Refit the shims under the layshaft and reverse shaft locking plate.
75 Refit the bearing retainer with new lock washers and tighten the securing screws to a torque wrench setting of 18 lb f ft (2.5 kg fm). Lock by bending over the lock washer tabs.
76 Using a screwdriver engage the first and fourth gears simultaneously so as to lock the gear train.
77 Replace the final drive pinion, a new lock washer and securing nut onto the third motion shaft. Tighten the final drive gear pinion nut to a torque wrench setting of 150 lb f ft (20.7 kg fm). Bend over the lock washer tab.
78 Replace the first motion shaft gear and new lock washer. Refit and tighten the securing nut to a torque wrench setting of 150 lb f ft (20.7 kg fm).
79 Replace the first motion shaft roller bearing and retain with the circlip.
80 Return the first and fourth gears to their neutral positions.
81 Rotate the selector shaft and interlock spool into engagement with the bellcrank levers.
82 Fit the oil suction pipe into the strainer.
83 Fit a new joint washer and locking plates, tighten the external flange securing screws first, then the pipe bracket screws. Bend over the locking plate tabs.
84 Refit the speedometer drive housing with a new joint washer to the gearbox casing. Tighten the securing nuts and screws to a torque wrench setting of 18 lb f ft (2.5 kg fm).
85 Replace the speedometer drive pinion together with a new joint washer.
86 Replace the engine mounting adaptor housing and secure with the set screws and spring washers.
87 Wrap some pvc tape around the selector shaft and then refit the final drive gear assembly and housing. It will be necessary to adjust the final drive gear assembly position as described in Chapter 8.
88 Refit the selector shaft sleeve, ball and spring followed by the final drive end covers.
89 The transmission unit is now ready for refitting to the engine.

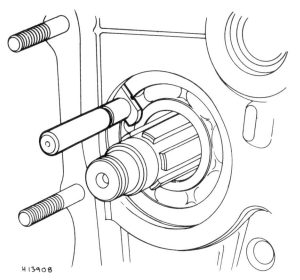

H13908

Fig. 6.16. First motion shaft bearing circlip thickness measurement tool

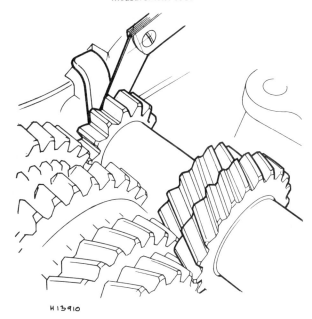

H13910

Fig. 6.17. Laygear end float measurement

4 First motion shaft (manual gearbox) - removal, overhaul and refitment

1 To gain access to the first motion shaft the engine/transmission unit must first be removed from the car. Then remove the clutch/flywheel assembly and finally the flywheel housing. All relevant information will be found in Chapter 1.
2 Using a pair of circlip pliers remove the first motion shaft roller bearing circlip.
3 Carefully ease the roller bearing from the end of the first motion shaft.
4 Bend back the lockwasher tab from the first motion shaft securing nut.
5 The idler and primary gear should next be removed.
6 Suitably lock the primary gear train and then undo and remove the first motion shaft securing nut and lock washer.

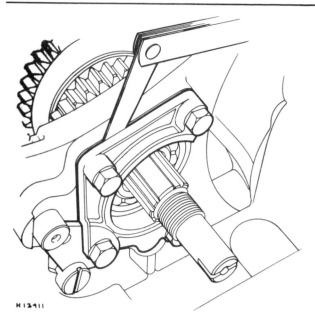

Fig. 6.18. Measurement of third motion shaft retainer to casing web gap

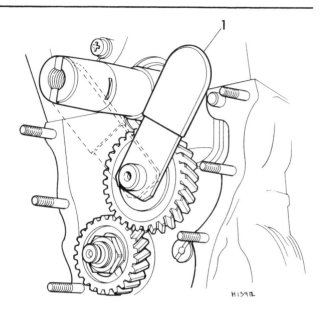

Fig. 6.19. Tool locking primary gear train

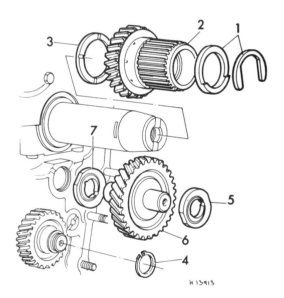

Fig. 6.20. Primary drive gear train

1	Thrust washer and backing ring	4	Circlip
2	Primary gear	5	Thrust washer
3	Thrust washer	6	Idler gear
		7	Thrust washer

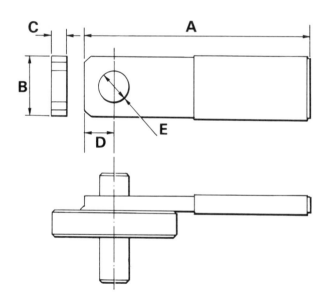

Fig. 6.21. Tool for locking primary gear train

A	5 ¼ in. (133 mm)	D	¾ in. (19.05 mm)
B	1 ½ in. (38 mm)	E	¾ in. (19.05 mm)
C	3/8 in. (9.5 mm)		

This is very tight so if possible make up the special tool shown in Figs. 6.19 and 6.21.

7 Withdraw the first motion shaft gear.

8 Using a pair of circlip pliers remove the circlip that secures the first motion shaft bearing.

9 Using a slide hammer or other suitable means remove the first motion shaft assembly from the gearbox casing.

10 Using a large bench vice and suitable packing, press the first motion shaft from the bearing.

11 Carefully examine the gear and baulk ring surfaces for wear, damage or grooving. Also check the first motion shaft

bearing and the internal needle roller bearing for wear. Obtain new parts as necessary.

12 To re-assemble first carefully press the first motion shaft into the bearing.

13 Lubricate the internal needle roller bearing and insert it into the first motion shaft.

14 Position the baulk ring into the third/fourth speed synchronizer hub.

15 Using a suitable diameter tube, drift the first motion shaft assembly into the casing.

16 One of two sizes of circlip should now be used to retain

the bearing in position. A special tool '18G 257' will facilitate the gap measurement,

Gap	Circlip number
0.096 - 0.098 in (2.43 - 2.48 mm)	2A 3710
0.098 - 0.100 in (2.48 - 2.54 mm)	2A 3711

17 Suitably lock the primary gear train and refit the first motion shaft gear with a new lock washer. Refit and tighten the nut to a torque wrench setting of 150 lb f ft (20.7 kg fm). Bend over the lock washer tab.
18 Carefully drift the roller bearing onto the first motion shaft and replace the retaining circlip.
19 If not already done, refit the idler gear - with its thrust washers to the gear train. The larger spindle of the gear locates in the gearbox.
20 Refit the crankshaft primary gear, thrust washers and backing ring. Refer to Section 9 and check the gear end float. Adjust if necessary.
21 Re-assembly of the flywheel housing and clutch/flywheel assembly is now the reverse sequence to dismantling.

5 Third motion shaft (manual gearbox) - removal, overhaul and refitment

1 Refer to Section 3 and follow the sequence described up to removal of the third motion shaft (paragraph 33).
2 Remove the third/fourth speed synchronizer and baulk ring.
3 Carefully depress the front thrust washer plunger and turn the washer until its splines register with those on the shaft.
4 Lift away the thrust washer plunger and spring.
5 Slide off the third speed gear and also its needle roller bearing.
6 Working at the other end of the shaft, remove the first speed gear and then the needle roller bearing and its journal.
7 Remove the combined reverse mainshaft gear and first/second speed synchronizer assembly together with its baulk rings.
8 Carefully press in the two plungers that secure the rear thrust washer, turn it until it is in alignment with the shaft splines and withdraw it from the shaft.
9 Recover the two plungers and spring.
10 Slide off the second speed gear.
11 Next remove the second speed gear split caged needle roller bearing.
12 Lift away the baulk rings from the synchronizer assemblies.
13 Wrap a cloth around each synchronizer assembly to collect the balls and springs and push the synchronizer hub from the sliding coupling.
14 Carefully examine all gear teeth for excessive wear or damage. Also check the third motion shaft bearing for signs of excessive wear, pitting, security of cages and the fit of the bearing in the gearbox casing.
15 Check the two thrust washers for wear and obtain new if worn. Examine the baulk rings for wear; they should be checked with their mating tapers on the gears. Should the baulk rings not engage before they contact the edge of the gear, the hub and baulk rings must be renewed.
16 Inspect the splines on the third motion shaft for wear. Finally inspect the synchronizer balls and springs, and obtain new if worn.
17 Re-assembly of the third motion shaft is a direct reversal of the dismantling procedure.

6 Speedometer drive gear - removal and refitment

1 This work may be carried out with the transmission unit either in or out of the car.
2 Drain the oil from the engine/transmission unit.
3 Suitably support the power unit and then undo and remove

the two bolts and nuts that secure the left-hand engine mounting to the housing casting.
4 Slowly lower the engine until the housing casting is clear of the engine mounting.
5 Undo and remove the nuts and spring washers, securing the housing casting, from the speedometer drive housing.
6 Undo and remove the two screws and spring washers securing the end plate. Lift away the end plate and gasket.
7 Detach the speedometer drive cable from the speedometer drive pinion housing.
8 Undo and remove the screw and spring washer securing the pinion housing retaining plate and housing. Lift away the retaining plate, housing assembly and drive pinion.
9 The speedometer drive gear may now be lifted away.
10 Refitting the drive gear is the reverse sequence to removal. Always use new gaskets.

7 Speedometer drive gear pinion - removal and refitment

1 Detach the speedometer drive cable from the speedometer drive pinion housing.
2 Undo and remove the screw and spring washer that secures the pinion housing retaining plate and housing. Lift away the retaining plate and housing assembly.
3 The speedometer drive pinion may now be lifted away.
4 Refitting the speedometer drive gear pinion is the reverse sequence to removal. Fit a new pinion housing joint washer.

8 Speedometer drive housing - removal and refitment

1 Suitably support the weight of the power unit and then remove the left-hand engine mounting.
2 Undo and remove the mounting casting securing nuts and bolt. Lift away the casting.
3 Detach the speedometer drive cable from the speedometer drive pinion housing.
4 Undo and remove the screw and spring washer that secure the pinion housing retaining plate and housing. Lift away the retaining plate and housing assembly.
5 The speedometer drive pinion may now be lifted away.
6 Undo and remove the speedometer drive housing securing screws and spring washers. Lift away the housing and recover the joint washer.
7 Refitting the speedometer drive housing is the reverse sequence to removal.

9 Primary drive gear train - removal and refitment

1 Remove the clutch/flywheel assembly and also the flywheel housing. Full information will be found in Chapter 1 and Chapter 5.
2 Remove the primary gear thrust washer and backing ring.
3 The primary gear may now be slid off the end of the crankshaft.
4 Lift away the primary gear front thrust washer.
5 Using a pair of circlip pliers remove the circlip that retains the first motion shaft roller bearing.
6 Carefully ease off the roller bearing from the first motion shaft.
7 Lift away the idler gear and thrust washers.
8 The gear train must now be locked. If possible an old idler gear and piece of steel bar should be made up as shown in Fig. 6.27.
9 Place the tool into the idler gear bearing with the handle against the crankshaft.
10 Bend back the lock washer tab securing the first motion shaft gear retaining nut.
11 Undo and remove the nut and lift off the first motion shaft gear.
12 Carefully examine all gears for signs of damage or wear. If

evident a new set must be obtained. Do not renew individual gears. Inspect the thrust washers and obtain new; if they are worn, scored or damaged.

13 To re-assemble first fit the first motion shaft gear and new lock washer.

14 Lock the gear train by placing the holding tool on the opposite side of the crankshaft.

15 Replace and tighten the first motion shaft gear retaining nut to a torque wrench setting of 150 lb f ft (20.7 kg fm).

16 Remove the holding tool.

17 The primary gear end float must now be checked and set. Refit the primary gear with its front thrust so that the chamfered side of the washer is towards the crankshaft.

18 Replace the rear backing ring and thrust washer.

19 Using feeler gauges check the primary gear end float which should be between 0.0035 - 0.0065 in. (0.089 - 0.165 mm). If necessary it may be set using a different thickness thrust washer:

    1   0.112 - 0.114 in. (2.84 - 2.89 mm)
    2   0.114 - 0.116 in. (2.89 - 2.94 mm)
    3   0.116 - 0.118 in. (2.49 - 2.99 mm)
    4   0.118 - 0.120 in. (2.99 - 3.04 mm)

20 Remove the primary gear assembly again.

21 The idler gear end float must now be adjusted. Assemble the idler gear to the transmission with the longer spindle inserted in the transmission and a thrust washer on the transmission side of the gear.

22 Obtain a little dental wax or putty and assemble between two thin washers of suitable diameter to pass over the idler gear spindle. Fit to the flywheel side of the idler gear.

23 Fit a new flywheel housing joint washer and refit the flywheel housing. Tighten the securing nuts and bolts to a torque wrench setting of 11 lb f ft (2.5 kg fm).

24 Remove the housing and joint washer and with a micrometer or vernier measure the thickness of the two washers and wax or putty assembly.

25 Subtract 0.004 - 0.007 in. (0.102 - 0.178 mm), from this figure and obtain a thrust washer of the required thickness:

    1   0.132 - 0.133 in. (3.35 - 3.37 mm)
    2   0.134 - 0.135 in. (3.40 - 3.42 mm)
    3   0.136 - 0.137 in. (3.45 - 3.47 mm)
    4   0.138 - 0.139 in. (3.50 - 3.53 mm)

26 Fit a second new flywheel housing joint washer. Do not re-use the one that was used in determining the thrust washer thickness (paragraph 23).

27 Refit the primary gear with its selected front thrust washer, backing ring and rear thrust washer.

28 The flywheel housing and clutch/flywheel assemblies may now be refitted, this being a direct reversal of the removal procedure.

10 Gear change lever - removal and refitment

1   Unscrew the gear change lever knob from the lever.

2   Remove the front compartment floor carpet.

3   Undo and remove the screws that secure the gaiter retaining ring to the floor panel. Draw the gaiter up and from the lever.

4   Depress and turn the bayonet cap fixing so releasing the gear change lever from the remote control assembly.

5   Lift away the gear change lever.

6   Refitting the gear change lever is the reverse sequence to removal.

11 Gear change remote control assembly - removal and refitment

1   Refer to Section 10 and remove the gear change lever.

2   Using a suitable diameter parallel pin punch carefully tap out the roll pin that secures the extension rod to the selector rod at the final drive housing.

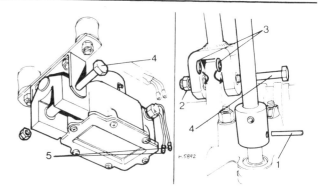

Fig. 6.22. Remote control assembly attachments (later type)

1 Roll pin	4 Bolt
2 Nut	5 Reverse light switch
3 Plain washer	

Fig. 6.23. Gear change lever components

3   Undo and remove the nut and bolt that secures the remote control steady rod to the final drive housing on the transmission unit.

4   Undo and remove the one nut and bolt that secures the remote control housing to the mounting bracket.

5   Lift away the remote control assembly.

6   Refitting the remote control is the reverse sequence to removal.

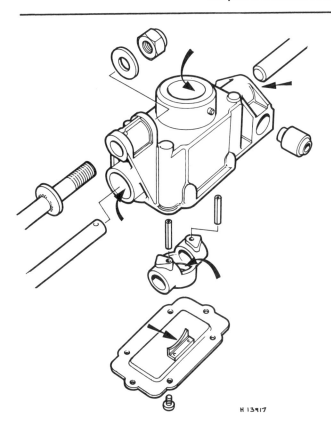

Fig. 6.24. Remote control components

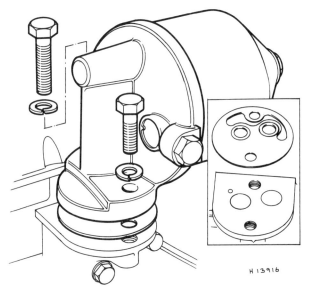

Fig. 6.25. Oil filter assembly removal
Inset shows gasket which must be fitted the correct way round

12 Gear change remote control assembly - overhaul

1 Refer to Section 11 and remove the remote control from the car.
2 Mount the assembly up-side-down in a vice and undo and remove the bottom cover plate securing screws. Lift away the cover plate.
3 Undo and remove the nut and plain washer securing the steady rod to the housing.
4 Move the extension rod edge rearwards and remove the roll pin that secures the extension rod to the rod eye.
5 Lift away the extension rod.
6 Move the extension rod eye forwards and remove the roll pin that secures the support rod to the extension rod eye.
7 The support rod may now be drifted out.
8 The extension rod eye can now be lifted away.
9 Inspect all moving parts for excessive wear and obtain new as necessary.
10 Re-assembly is the reverse sequence to removal. Apply a little 'Duckhams Laminoid 'O' Grease' with a brush to all internal parts as they are being fitted.

13 Gear change remote control mountings - removal and re-fitment

1 Remove the front compartment floor carpeting.
2 Undo and remove the nuts and spring washers that secure the remote control mountings to the tunnel panel.
3 Carefully lower the remote control assembly.
4 Undo and remove the nuts and spring washers that secure the mountings to the support bracket.
5 Lift away the mountings.
6 Refitting the mountings is the reverse sequence to removal.

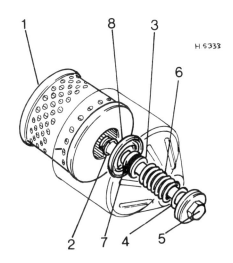

Fig. 6.26. Oil filter assembly components

1	Filter element	5	Centre bolt
2	Circlip	6	Spring
3	Steel washer	7	Sealing washer
4	Sealing ring	8	Sealing plate

14 Oil filter assembly (automatic transmission) - removal and refitment

1 Place a small container under the filter head and then undo and remove the two bolts securing the complete assembly to the adaptor.
2 Recover the joint washer.
3 To gain access to the element, unscrew the filter bowl retaining bolt and lift away the bowl and element.
4 Lift out the element and discard. No attempt should be made to clean it.
5 Thoroughly clean the filter bowl and head with petrol and wipe dry with a clean non-fluffy rag.

6 Using a small screwdriver extract the sealing ring from the filter head and fit a new one.

7 Refitting the element and filter bowl is the reverse sequence to removal. Tighten the centre bolt to a torque wrench setting of 14 lb f ft (1.94 kg fm).

8 The capacity of the oil filter is 1 pint (0.6 litres).

15 Lubrication system (automatic transmission) - draining and refilling

The system is common to both the engine and transmission units. To drain the system proceed as follows:

1 Wipe the area around the transmission unit casing and remove the drain plug.

2 Allow the oil to drain out for at least 10 minutes. It should be noted that the converter will still retain a small amount of oil.

3 Remove all metallic particles from the magnetic drain plug and fit a new sealing washer.

4 Refit the drain plug and tighten to a torque wrench setting of 25 lb f ft (3.4 kg fm).

5 With the car standing on level ground refill with 'Castrol GTX' or a similar multigrade engine oil. The refill capacity will be approximately 9 pints (5 litres).

6 Top up to the correct mark on the dipstick and then select position 'N'. Start the engine and run for 1-2 minutes. Stop it again, wait for 1 minute, take a dipstick reading and adjust the oil level as necessary.

16 Selector cable (automatic transmission) - check and adjustment

1 Chock the rear wheels, apply the handbrake, select position "N" and start the engine.

2 Move the selector to the "R" position and check that reverse has been engaged.

3 Slowly move the lever back towards the "N" position ensuring that the gear is disengaged just before or exactly when the lever locates in the "N" position.

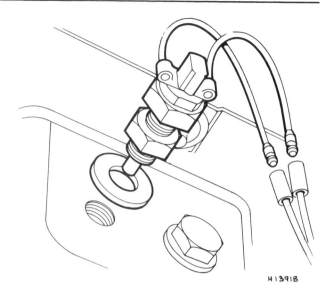

Fig. 6.27. Starter inhibitor switch

4 Repeat the instructions in paragraphs 2 and 3 but this time for the first gear "1" position.

5 Should adjustment be necessary undo and remove the two bolts and spring washers securing the bellcrank cover plate, lift away the cover plate.

6 Slacken the large nut that secures the cable into the housing mechanism.

7 Carefully push the transverse rod fully into the gearbox using the bellcrank lever.

8 Move the selector lever to the "D" position on the selector panel and hold it in this position while a second person adjusts the cable.

9 Gently push the outer cable into the selector mechanism assembly and tighten the cable securing nut.

10 Before refitting the cover plate repeat the tests described in paragraphs 1 to 4 inclusive.

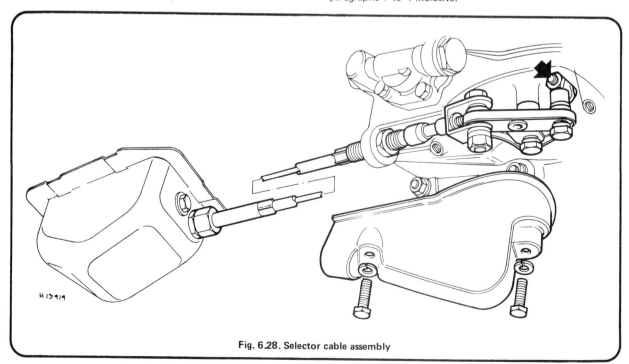

Fig. 6.28. Selector cable assembly

17 Selector cable assembly (automatic transmission) - removal and refitment

1 Undo and remove the two bolts and spring washers securing the bellcrank cover plate. Lift away the cover plate.
2 Undo and remove the bolt, nut and washers that secure the cable fork to the bellcrank lever.
3 Slacken the fork securing nut and unscrew the fork from the cable.
4 Remove the fork retaining nut and the two rubber ferrules.
5 Undo and remove the outer cable locknut and pull the cable until it is clear of the transmission unit. Lift away the second locking nut.
6 Release the outer cable securing nut at the selector mechanism assembly.
7 Suitably grip the crimped end of the cable and unscrew it out of the selector mechanism assembly.
8 To refit first fit the cable securely into its fork end located in the selector mechanism assembly.
9 Refitting is now the reverse sequence to removal. It will be necessary to set the position of the cable where it passes through the anchor boss on the converter housing so that there are equal threads showing on each side of the boss when the nuts are tight.
10 Refer to Section 16 and adjust the cable.

18 Starter inhibitor switch (automatic transmission) - removal, refitment and adjustment

1 Working under the car, disconnect the two electrical connections at the snap connectors.
2 Slacken the switch lock nut and then unscrew and remove the switch from the selector mechanism housing.
3 To refit the switch first move the selector lever to the "N" position.
4 Screw the switch into the selector mechanism housing.
5 Connect a test light and battery to the two electrical connectors. Unscrew the switch until the test light just goes out.
6 Now screw the switch into the housing mechanism until the light just comes on. Screw the switch in a further one half turn and tighten the locknut.
7 Check that the light only comes on when the selector lever is in the "N" position.
8 Remove the test light and battery, and reconnect the two electrical connectors to the snap connectors.
9 Finally ensure that the engine will only start when "N" position is selected.

19 Selector mechanism assembly (automatic transmission) - removal and refitment

1 Refer to Section 17 and disconnect the selector cable from the transmission unit.
2 Disconnect the inhibitor switch wiring at the two snap connectors on the switch.
3 Disconnect the selector indicator panel illuminating light wiring at the snap connectors.
4 Unscrew and remove the selector lever knob and then the tapered nut.
5 Carefully pull off the selector indicator panel.
6 Undo and remove the screws and plain washers securing the selector mechanism assembly to the underside of the car.
7 Lower the assembly from the underside of the car.
8 Release the outer cable securing nut and turn the cable to unscrew it from its connecting yoke.
9 Refitting the selector mechanism assembly is the reverse sequence to removal. However, the following additional points should be noted:
   a) Set the position of the cable where it passes through the

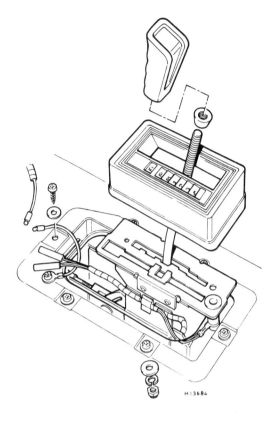

Fig. 6.29. Selector mechanism removal

anchor boss on the converter housing so that there are an equal number of threads showing on each side when the nuts are tight.
b) Adjust the selector cable as described in Section 16.

20 Selector mechanism assembly (automatic transmission) - overhaul

1 Refer to Section 19 and remove the selector mechanism assembly.
2 Slacken the locknut and unscrew the inhibitor switch.
3 Unscrew the cable securing nut and the union from the selector housing.
4 Unscrew the selector cable from the operating mechanism.
5 Undo and remove the two screws that secure the mechanism to the housing. There is one screw at each end.
6 The mechanism may now be lifted out of the housing.
7 Release the electrical wiring from the retaining clip and pull out the bulb holders.
8 Lift away the electrical wiring.
9 Carefully remove the E-clips and plain washer and withdraw the forward pin and cable fork.
10 Remove the E-clip and withdraw the actuator pivot pin.
11 Lift the actuator assembly from the frame.
12 Undo and remove the bolt and nut and detach the selector lever and spring from the actuator.

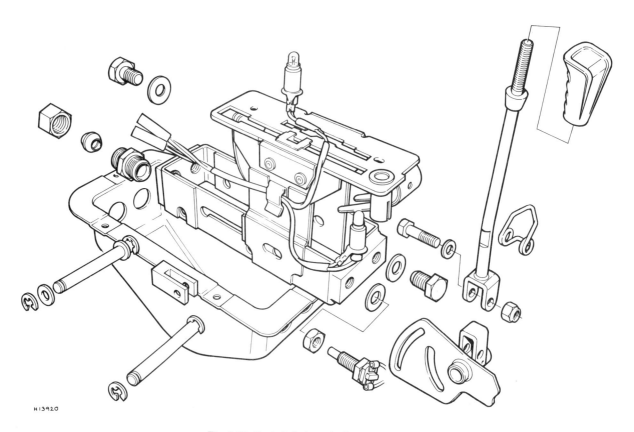

H13920

Fig. 6.30. Exploded view of selector mechanism

13 Re-assembly of the selector mechanism is the reverse sequence to dismantling. Lubricate all moving parts with 'Duckhams Laminoid 'O' Grease'. All E-clips should be renewed.

21 Fault diagnosis - manual transmission

Symptom	Reason/s	Remedy
Weak or ineffective synchromesh	Synchronising cones worn, split or damaged	Dismantle and overhaul transmission unit. Fit new gear wheels and synchronising cones.
	Synchromesh dogs worn, or damaged	Dismantle and overhaul transmission unit. Fit new synchromesh unit.
Jumps out of gear	Broken gearchange fork rod spring	Dismantle and replace spring.
	Transmission unit coupling dogs badly worn	Dismantle transmission unit. Fit new coupling dogs.
	Selector fork rod groove badly worn	Fit new selector fork rod.
	Selector fork rod securing screw and locknut loose	Tighten securing screw and locknut.
Excessive noise	Incorrect grade of oil in transmission unit or oil level too low	Drain, refill, or top up transmission unit with correct grade of oil.
	Bush or needle roller bearings worn or damaged	Dismantle and overhaul transmission unit. Renew bearings.
	Gearteeth excessively worn or damaged	Dismantle, overhaul transmission unit. Renew gear wheels.
	Laygear thrust washers worn allowing excessive end play	Dismantle and overhaul transmission unit. Renew thrust washers.
Excessive difficulty in engaging gear	Clutch pedal adjustment incorrect	Adjust clutch pedal correctly.

For 'Fault diagnosis' - automatic transmission - see next page

22 Fault diagnosis - automatic transmission

IMPORTANT: To carry out a full test to trace a malfunction of the automatic transmission an oil pressure gauge (0 - 300 psi) (0 - 21.1 kg cm^2) and a tachometer must be used. The oil pressure gauge is fitted to the filter head and the tachometer to the ignition coil and earth. For those without this equipment there are several tests that may still be carried out. Always find the cause of the trouble before removing the unit from the car. Where possible always rectify any fault found before proceeding to the next test. This is particularly important with tests 1 to 4. With tests 5 to 11 it may be possible to complete these tests, noting any faults found. However, it is possible that this could allow one fault to mask a second one.

Test	Fault	Rectification
1 Check the oil level	a Oil level incorrect	1a Correct the oil level.
2 Check the throttle with the pedal fully depressed	a Throttle not fully open	2a Adjust the throttle cable.
3 Check that the starter will operate only when 'N' is selected	a Starter will not operate in 'N' b Starter operates in all positions	3a Adjust the inhibitor switch. 3b Check the inhibitor switch and its wiring for short-circuiting.
4 Check the adjustment of the selector cable	a The cable is out of adjustment	4a Adjust the cable.
5 If possible, run the engine until it reaches its normal operating temperature. Chock the wheels, apply the brakes and run the engine at 1,000 rev/min. Select each transmission position in turn and note the pressure registered.	a In position 'N', '1', '2', '3', 'D': Less than 95 lb/in^2 (6.7 kg/cm^2) b In position 'R': Less than 162 lb/in^2 (11.4 kg/cm^2)	5a Refer to 'Pressure test diagnosis' 5b Refer to 'Pressure test diagnosis'
6 Apply the hand and foot brakes, and with the engine idling, select 'R' from 'N' and 'I' from 'N'.	a Excessive bump on engagement of 'R' or 'I' b Engine stalls on engagement of 'R' or 'I'	6a Reduce engine idle speed. 6b Increase engine idle speed.
7 Select 'I', release the brakes and check that the car drives forward but that there is no engine braking when the throttle is released	a Car does not drive forward b Engine braking can be felt	7a Remove and check the forward clutch; if satisfactory renew the free wheel. 7b Renew the free wheel.
8 Select 'I' and drive away, using the manual gear-change to select '2' and '3' progressively as the road speed increases. When the road speed is above 25 mph (40 km h) select 'D' and release the throttle pedal	a Drive in '1' but not in '2' b Drive In '1' and '2' but not in '3' c Drive in '1', '2', and '3', but no upward gear-change (to fourth gear) on selecting 'D'	8a Check the second gear brake band adjustment. If satisfactory, check the second gear servo. 8b Check the third gear brake band adjustment. If satisfactory, check the third gear servo. 8c Check the kick-down linkage adjustment. If correct, check the governor for freedom of operation. If the governor is satisfactory, remove and check the top reverse clutch.
9 Stop the car, select 'D' and accelerate up through the gears using 'kick-down'. Check that the gear-changes occur at the following road speeds: 1—2 change at 27 to 35 mph (44 to 56 km h) 2—3 change at 39 to 47 mph (64 to 76 km h) 3—4 change at 52 to 60 mph (85 to 97 km h)	a Gear-changes occur at low speeds b Gear-changes occur at high speed	9a Check the kick-down linkage adjustment. 9b Check the kick-down linkage adjustment. If correct, check the governor for freedom of operation.
10 Stop the car, select 'R' and drive the car backwards	a Car will not drive backwards	10a Check reverse gear brake band adjustment. If satisfactory, check the reverse servo.

11 Chock the wheels and apply the hand and foot brakes. Select 'R' and depress the throttle pedal fully **for not more than 10 seconds.** Note the highest rev/min obtained. Select 'D' and hold full throttle **for not more than 10 seconds.** Note the highest rev/min obtained

a A reading outside the range 1,700 to 1,800 rev/min

11a Refer to 'Stall test diagnosis'

Pressure test diagnosis

For pressure readings refer to test 5 of the previous Section. These should be considered a minimum.

Fault	Possible cause
1 Low pressure - all selector positions	a Blocked oil strainer. b Damaged valve block. c Worn or leaking pump d Wrongly fitted filter gasket.
2 Low pressure in positions 1, 2, 3 and D	Leakage from forward clutch or forward clutch supply line.
3 Low pressure in position 2	Leakage from second gear servo or second gear servo supply line.
4 Low pressure in position 3	Leakage from third gear servo or third gear servo supply line.
5 Low pressure in position R	a Leakage from reverse servo to reverse servo supply line. b Leakage from top/reverse clutch or top/reverse clutch supply line.

Stall test diagnosis

For the procedure refer to test 11 of the first test Section.

Engine speed	Indication
Below 1000 rpm	Stator slip (defective converter).
Below 1600 rpm	Engine power down.
1700 to 1800 rpm	Satisfactory.
Over 1900 rpm	Transmission slip.

Chapter 7 Drive shafts and universal joints

Contents

1 General description

Drive is transmitted from the differential unit to the front wheels by means of two drive shafts. Fitted at either end of each shaft are universal joints which allow for vertical movement of the front wheels.

The outer universal joints are of the Hardy Spicer Birfield constant velocity joint type. The drive shaft fits inside the circular outer constant velocity joint which is also on the driven shaft. Drive is transmitted from the drive shaft to the driven shaft by six steel balls. These are located in curved grooves, machined in line with the arms of the shaft on the inside of the driven shaft and outside of the drive shaft, which keeps them together. The constant velocity joint is packed with a special grease and enclosed in a rubber boot.

The inboard constant velocity joint on manual transmission models is similar to that of the outer joint but on automatic transmission models a universal joint of conventional design is used.

Removal and overhaul of the drive shafts requires special tools as well as time so before attempting any of the service operations described in this Chapter read the instructions thoroughly and decide if the job is within your capabilities as well as the contents of your tool box.

2 Drive shaft - removal and refitment (manual gearbox)

Important: Several special tools are required to carry out this work correctly. It is possible to remove and refit a drive shaft without these tools provided good workshop facilities are available. Before commencing work read the appropriate section and decide if this work is within your scope. If in doubt leave it to the local BLMC garage.

1 Remove the wheel trim and carefully ease out the front wheel hub cover with a screwdriver.

2 Straighten the drive shaft nut split pin ears and withdraw the split pin.

3 Unscrew the drive shaft nut and lift away the collar from the drive shaft.

4 Chock the rear wheels, slacken the front wheel nuts, jack up the front of the car and support on firmly based stands. Remove the road wheels.

5 Wipe the top of the hub master cylinder reservoir, unscrew the cap and place a piece of polythene over the filler neck. Refit the cap. This is to stop syphoning during subsequent operations.

6 Wipe the area around the brake hose union and then unscrew the union nut securing the brake pipe to the hose at the bracket on the front hub.

7 Unscrew the nut to release the brake hose from the bracket on the front hub.

8 Undo and remove the steering rack tie-rod ball joint to steering arm securing nut and then using a universal balljoint separator detach the balljoint from the steering arm.

9 Undo and remove the nuts and spring washers securing the swivel hub joints to the suspension arms. Again using a universal balljoint separator disconnect the swivel hub from the suspension arms.

10 The swivel hub should now be drawn from the drive shaft. It may be necessary to tap the swivel hub with a soft faced hammer.

11 Should the front hub inner bearing, inner race, remain on the drive shaft, remove the ball cage and bearings and then draw off the inner race using a universal three legged puller.

12 A special tool "18G 1243" is now required. Assemble this to the drive shaft and tighten the bolts of the tool so as to unlock the drive shaft from the inboard joint. Hold the body of the tool hard against the inner member of the inboard joint and withdraw the drive shaft from the inboard joint. If you are extremely lucky, this job can be carried out using tapered end tyre levers, and a large hammer.

13 The front hub bearing water shield should now be removed from the drive shaft.

14 Refitting the drive shaft is the reverse sequence to removal but the following additional points should be noted:

a) Fit the front hub bearing water shield so that the measurement between the bearing register on the drive shaft to the water shield hub is 0.25 ± 0.0625 in (6.3 ± 1.5 mm).

b) Use a suitable puller to draw the drive shaft through the hub. For this a large bolt, washer and nut and suitable threaded sleeve for joining the bolt to the drive shaft may be used.

c) Tighten the drive shaft nut to a torque wrench setting of 200 lb f ft (27.6 kg fm) and then align to the next split pin hole.

d) Tighten the swivel hub ball pin nuts to a torque wrench setting of 38 lb f ft (5.3 kg fm).

e) Referring to Chapter 1 check that the disc run-out does not exceed 0.007 in (0.17 mm).

f) Tighten the wheel nuts to a torque wrench setting of 46 lb f ft (6.42 kg fm).

g) Referring to Chapter 9 bleed the brake hydraulic system.

3 Drive shaft - removal and refitment (automatic transmission)

1 Refer to the introduction to Section 2 and then carry out the instructions in paragraphs 1 to 4 inclusive.

2 Mark the drive shaft inboard joint and final drive flanges to

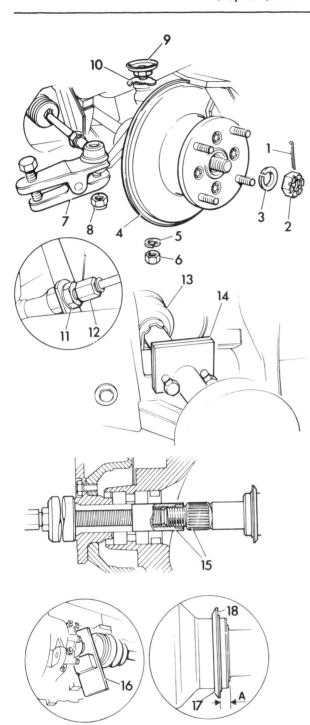

Fig. 7.1. Drive shaft removal (manual gearbox)

1	Split pin	11	Nut
2	Nut	12	Union nut
3	Collar	13	Driveshaft
4	Brake disc	14	Special tool
5	Spring washer	15	Tool assembled to drive-
6	Nut		shaft
7	Universal balljoint separator	16	Special tool (see Fig. 7.1)
8	Nut	17	Water shield
9	Nut	18	Water shield assembly
10	Lockwasher		dimension

ensure correct alignment upon re-assembly.

3 Undo and remove the four securing nuts and separate the two flanges.

4 Carefully drive the shaft out of the driving flange and swivel hub.

5 The drive shaft may now be drawn through the road wheel side of the front wing valance.

6 The front hub bearing water shield should now be removed from the drive shaft.

7 Refitting the drive shaft is the reverse sequence to removal but the several additional points should be noted. Refer to Section 2 paragraph 14 items a,b,c and e.

4 Rubber boot (drive shaft constant velocity joint) - removal and refitment

1 Remove the wheel trim, chock the rear wheels, jack up the front of the car and support on firmly based stands. Remove the road wheel.

2 Wipe the top of the brake master cylinder reservoir, unscrew the cap and place a piece of polythene over the filler neck. Refit the cap. This is to stop syphoning during subsequent operations.

3 Wipe the area around the brake hose union and then unscrew the union nut securing the brake pipe to the hose at the bracket on the front hub.

4 Unscrew the nut to release the brake hose from the bracket on the front hub.

5 **Manual gearbox:** A special tool 18G 1243 is now required. Assemble the tool to the drive shaft and tighten the bolt of the tool to unlock the drive shaft from the inboard joint. Hold the body of the tool hard against the inner member of the inboard joint and the drive shaft from the inboard joint. If

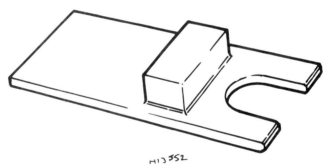

Fig. 7.2. Shaped metal lever to separate drive shaft from differential housing

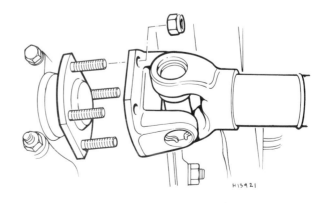

Fig. 7.3. Disconnecting drive shaft from final drive (automatic transmission)

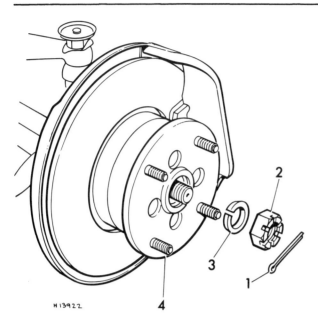

Fig. 7.4. Front hub assembly

1 Split pin
2 Nut
3 Collar
4 Hub and disc assembly

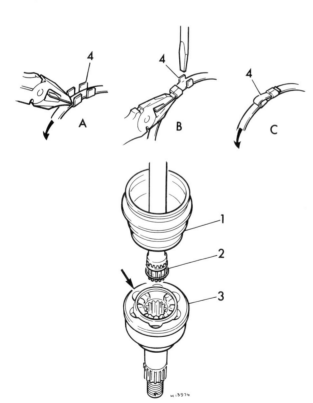

Fig. 7.5. Drive shaft constant velocity joint removal

1 Rubber boot
2 Spring ring
3 Constant velocity joint
4 Correct method of fitting rubber boot clip

you are extremely lucky this job can be carried out using tapered end tyre levers and a large hammer.

6 **Automatic transmission:** Remove the ring clamp that secures the inboard joint seal to the drive shaft.

7 Undo and remove the steering rack tie-rod balljoint to steering arm securing nut and then using a universal ball joint separator detach the ball joint from the steering arm.

8 Undo and remove the nuts and spring washers securing the swivel hub joints to the suspension arms. Again using a universal balljoint separator disconnect the swivel hub from the suspension arms.

9 **Manual gearbox:** With the special tool in position or using the levers draw the swivel hub and drive shaft assembly from the car.

10 **Automatic transmission:** Withdraw the swivel hub and drive shaft from the car.

11 Remove the two ring clamps that secure the rubber boot to the constant velocity joint and drive shaft.

12 The rubber boot may now be slid off the drive shaft.

13 Suitably hold the swivel hub and drive shaft and withdraw the drive shaft from the constant velocity joint. Ideally a slide hammer should be used but gripping the drive shaft with a wrench and tapping the wrench will achieve the same result.

14 Tilt and swivel the inner member and ball cage in the outer member of the constant velocity joint and prise the balls from the cage.

15 Now swivel the inner member and the ball cage into line with the joint axis and rotate the cage until its two large windows coincide with two of the lands in the joint outer member.

16 The inner member and cage may now be withdrawn from the outer member.

17 Swivel the inner member into line with the axis of the ball cage until the two lands of the inner member coincide with the two large windows in the ball cage.

18 The inner member may now be lifted from the chamfered bore side of the ball cage.

19 Thoroughly clean all parts and wipe with a clean non-fluffy rag.

20 Reassembly and refitting is the reverse sequence to removal but the following additional points should be noted.

21 The constant velocity joint should be packed with 1 oz (30 cm^3) of "Duckhams Bentone Grease Q 5795".

22 The inner member and cage should be fitted into the outer member of the constant velocity joint with the chamfered bore side of the cage at the blind end of the outer member and the lugs on the inner member at the open end of the outer member.

23 **1300 models (automatic transmission):** Insert 0.75 oz (23 cm^3) of "Duckhams Laminoid Grease Q 6383" into the inboard joint. Push the drive shaft into the sliding joint until it bottoms in the joint, holding the outer lip of the housing seal open to allow any air or excess grease to escape from the joint. With the drive shaft bottoming in the sliding joint check that the diameter of the housing seal does not exceed 1.75 in (44.5 mm). If necessary squeeze the grease from the seal to reduce the seal diameter.

24 Secure the rubber boot to the constant velocity joint and the drive shaft, using new clips. These must be fitted with the fold in the clip facing towards the direction of drive shaft forward rotation.

25 **1300 models (automatic transmission):** Secure the inboard joint housing to the drive shaft using a new clip.

26 Refer to Chapter 9 and bleed the air from the braking system.

---

5 Constant velocity joint - removal and refitment

1 Refer to Section 2 or 3 as applicable and remove the drive shaft assembly.

2 Remove the ring clip that secures the rubber boot to the outer member of the constant velocity joint.

3 Turn back the rubber boot to expose the joint.

4 Hold the drive shaft vertically, plunge joint uppermost, and using a soft faced hammer strike the edge of the constant velocity so as to release it from the drive shaft.

5 To refit first pack the constant velocity joint and its rubber boot with 1 oz (30 cm^3) of Duckhams Bentone Grease Q 5795".

6 Refit the drive shaft to the inner member of the constant velocity joint, using a soft faced hammer. It will be advantageous if the spring ring is helped to enter into the inner member with a screwdriver.

7 Secure the rubber boot to the outer member of the constant velocity joint with a new clip. The clip must be fitted so that its fold is facing towards the direction of drive shaft forward rotation.

6 Constant velocity joint - overhaul

There is little point in dismantling the outer constant velocity joints if they are known to be badly worn. In this case it is better to remove the old joint from the shaft and fit a new unit. To remove and then dismantle the joint proceed as follows:

1 Remove the drive shaft from the car and separate it from the front hub as described in Section 2 or 3 of this Chapter. Alternatively remove the constant velocity joint as described in Section 5. Wire the drive shaft and pot housing to stop joint separating.

2 Thoroughly clean the exterior of the drive shaft and rubber gaiter, preferably not using a liquid cleaner.

3 Mount the drive shaft vertically in between soft faces in a vice with the joint facing outwards.

Using a screwdriver, prise off the large diameter aluminium gaiter retaining ring towards the stub axle. Also prise off the small diameter aluminium ring, again using a screwdriver. Turn back the gaiter and, if it is to be renewed, it is recommended that the gaiter be cut off and thrown away.

4 Before the joint can be dismantled it must be removed from the drive shaft. This is easily done by firmly tapping the outer edge of the constant velocity joint with a hide or plastic headed hammer. Alternatively, use a copper drift located on the inner member and give the drift a sharp blow. Whichever method is used, the inner spring ring will be contracted so releasing the joint from the shaft.

5 Ease off the round section spring ring and, when re-assembling, use the new one supplied in the service kit.

6 Mark the position of the inner and outer races with a dab of paint so that upon reassembly the mated parts can be correctly replaced.

7 Refer to Fig. 7.6 and tilt the inner race until one ball bearing is released. Repeat this operation easing out each ball bearing in turn, using a small screwdriver.

8 Manipulate the cage until the special elongated slot coincides with the lands of the bell housing. Drop one of the lands into the slot and lift out the cage and race assembly (Fig. 7.7).

9 Turn the inner race at right angles to the cage and in line with the elongated slot. Drop one land into the slot and withdraw the inner race.

10 Thoroughly clean all component parts of the joint by washing in paraffin.

11 Examine each ball bearing in turn for cracks, flat spots or signs of the surface pitting. Check the inner and outer tracks for widening which will cause the ball bearings to be a loose fit. This, together with excessive wear in the ball cage, will lead to the characteristic 'knocking' on full lock. The cage, which fits between the inner and outer races, must be examined for wear in the ball cage windows and for cracks which are likely to develop across the narrower portions between the outer rims and the holes for the ball bearings. If wear is excessive then all parts must be renewed as a matched set.

12 To reassemble, first ensure that all parts are very clean and then lubricate with "Duckhams Bentone Grease, No Q5795-2"

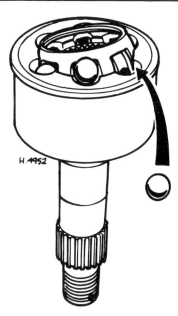

Fig. 7.6. Movement of cage and inner race to remove the ball bearings

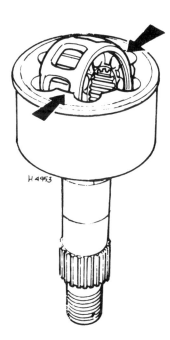

Fig. 7.7. Positioning of cage in preparation for removal

which is supplied under part number "ARF 1457". Do not, under any circumstances, use any other grease. Provided that all parts have been cleaned and well lubricated they should fit together easily without force.

13 Refit the inner race into the cage by manipulating one of the lands into the elongated slot in the cage. Insert the cage and inner race assembly into the ball joint by fitting one of the elongated slots over one of the lands in the outer race. Rotate the inner race to line up with the bell housing in its original previously marked position.

14 Taking care not to lose the position, tilt the cage until one ball bearing can be inserted into a slot. Repeat this procedure

until all six ball bearings are in their correct positions. Ensure that the inner race moves freely in the bell housing throughout its movement range, taking care that the ball bearings do not fall out.

15 Using the remainder of the special grease, pack the joint evenly. Smear the inside of a new rubber boot with the special grease (Duckhams Bentone Grease, No Q5795 supplied under part number AKF 1457) and fit the rubber boot and a new circlip to the end of the shaft.

16 Hold the shaft in a vice and locate the inner race on the splines. By pressing the constant velocity joint against the circlip, position the ring centrally and contract it in the chamber in the inner race leading edge with two screwdrivers. Using a soft faced hammer, sharply tap the end of the stub shaft to compress the ring and then tap the complete assembly onto the drive shaft. Double check that the shaft is fully engaged and the circlip fully locked against the inner race.

17 Ease the rubber boot over the constant velocity joint and ensure the moulded edges of the boot are seating correctly in the retaining groove of the shaft and bell housing. Secure in position with the large and small clips. Check that the tab of the large clip is pulled away from the direction of rotation. Do not use wire as this cuts into the rubber boot.

7 Drive shaft inboard joint - removal and refitment (manual gearbox)

1 First drain the oil from the power unit.

2 Chock the rear wheels, jack up the front of the car and support on firmly based stands. Remove the road wheel.

3 Refer to Fig. 7.2 and, uisng a metal lever as shown carefully unlock the drive shaft inboard joint from the differential unit.

4 Wipe the top of the brake master cylinder reservoir, unscrew the cap and place a piece of polythene over the filler neck. Refit the cap. This is to stop syphoning during subsequent operations.

5 Wipe the area around the brake hose union and then unscrew the union nut securing the brake pipe to the hose at the bracket on the front hub.

6 Unscrew the nut to release the brake hose from the bracket on the front hub.

7 Undo and remove the steering rack tie-rod balljoint to steering arm secuirng nut and then using a balljoint separator detach the balljoint from the steering arm.

8 Undo and remove the nuts and spring washers securing the swivel hub joints to the suspension arms. Again using a universal balljoint separator disconnect the swivel hub from the suspension arms.

9 Using the tool previously made ease the drive shaft inboard joint from the differential unit and at the same time withdraw the swivel hub and drive shaft assembly from the car. A special tool is now required. Assemble this to the drive shaft and tighten the bolts of the tool so as to unlock the drive shaft from the inboard joint. Hold the body of the tool hard against the inner member of the inboard joint and withdraw the inboard joint from the drive shaft. If the reader is extremely lucky this job can be carried out using tapered end tyre levers and a large hammer.

11 The oil flinger may now be removed from the inboard joint.

12 Refitting the drive shaft inboard joint is the reverse sequence to removal but the following additional points should be noted.

a) Push the hub and drive shaft smartly into the differential to lock the inboard joint into the final drive.

b) Tighten the swivel axle ball pin nuts to a torque wrench setting of 38 lb f ft (5.3 kg fm).

c) Tighten the road wheel nuts to a torque wrench setting of 46 lb f ft (6.42 kg fm).

d) Refer to Chapter 9 and bleed the brake hydraulic system.

8 Drive shaft inboard joint - removal and refitment (automatic transmission)

1 Chock the rear wheels, jack up the front of the car and support on firmly based stands, remove the road wheel.

2 Mark the drive shaft inboard joint and final drive flanges to ensure correct alignment upon re-assembly.

3 Undo and remove the four securing nuts and separate the two flanges.

4 Remove the ring clips that secure the seal to the inboard joint housing and the drive shaft.

5 The inboard joint may now be removed from the drive shaft.

6 Refitting the drive shaft inboard joint is the reverse sequence to removal but the following additional points should be noted.

7 Insert 0.75 oz (23 cm^3) of "Duckhams Laminoid Grease Q6383" into the inboard joint.

8 Secure the rubber boot using new clips. These must be fitted with the fold in the clip facing towards the direction of drive shaft forward rotation.

9 Push the joint assembly into the drive shaft until the drive shaft bottoms in the joint housing. Hold the housing seal lip open to allow any air or excessive grease to escape from the joint housing.

10 With the drive shaft bottoming in the joint housing check that the housing seal diameter does not exceed 1.75 in (44.5 mm). If necessary, squeeze the grease from the housing seal to reduce the seal diameter.

11 Fit a new rubber boot to drive shaft securing clip observing the method of fixing described in paragraph 8.

9 Drive shaft inboard joint - inspection and overhaul (automatic transmission)

Wear in the needle roller bearings is characterised by vibration in the transmission, 'clonks' on taking up the drive, and in extreme cases of lack of lubrication, metallic squeaking, and ultimately grating and shrieking sounds as the bearings break up.

It is easy to check if the needle roller bearings are worn with the drive shaft in position, by trying to turn the shaft with one hand, the other hand holding the differential flange. Any movement between the drive shaft and differential flange is indicative of considerable wear. If worn, the old bearings and spiders will have to be discarded and a repair kit, comprising new universal joint spiders, bearings, oil seals and retainers purchased. Check also by trying to lift the shaft and noticing any movement in the joints.

To overhaul the universal joint proceed as follows.

1 Clean away all traces of dirt and grease from the circlips located on the ends of the spiders, and remove the clips by pressing their open ends together with a pair of circlip pliers and lever them out with a screwdriver. Note: If they are difficult to remove tap the bearing face resting on top of the spider with a mallet which will ease the pressure on the circlip.

2 Hold the joint housing in one hand and remove the bearing caps and needle rollers by tapping the yoke at each bearing with a soft faced hammer. As soon as the bearings start to emerge they can be drawn out with the fingers. If the bearing cup refuses to move then place a thin bar against the inside of the bearing and tap it gently until the cup starts to emerge.

3 With the bearings removed it is relatively easy to extract the spiders from their yokes. If the bearings and spider journals are thought to be badly worn this can easily be ascertained visually with the universal joints dismantled.

4 To re-assemble ensure that the yokes and journals are clean.

5 Fit new seals and retainers on the spider journals, place the spider on the yoke and assemble the needle rollers in the bearing cups with assistance of some thin grease.

6 Partially pack the cups with grease and refit the bearing cups on the spider and tap the cups home so that they lie squarely in position.
7 Replace the circlips and ensure that the flange is free to move on the yoke.

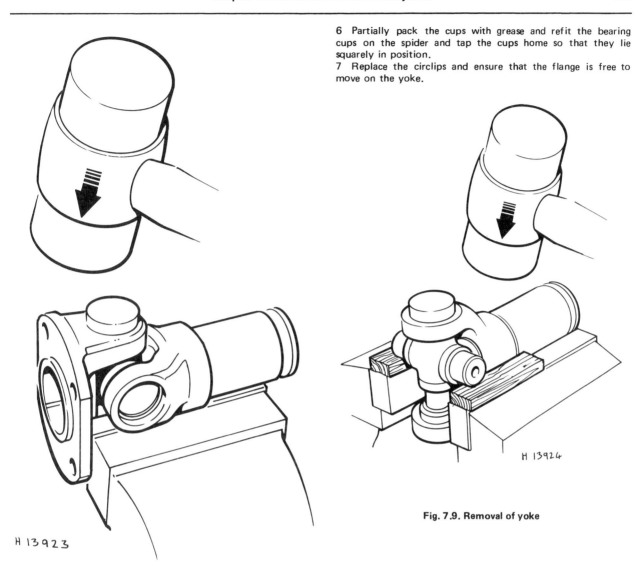

H 13923

Fig. 7.8. Bearing removal

H 13924

Fig. 7.9. Removal of yoke

For 'Fault diagnosis' see next page

10 Fault diagnosis

Symptom	Reason/s	Remedy
Vibration during medium or high speed	Worn or damaged constant velocity joint or universal joint (automatic)	Replace or overhaul.
	Unbalance due to bent drive shaft	Replace.
	Loose drive shaft installation	Tighten or replace if worn.
	Undercoating or mud on shaft causing unbalance	Clean up shaft.
	Tyre unbalance	Balance wheel and tyre assembly or replace from known good car.
	Balance weights missing	Rebalance wheel.
Knocking sound during starting or noise during coasting	Worn or damaged constant velocity joint or universal joint (automatic)	Replace or overhaul.
	Loose drive shaft installation	Tighten or replace if worn.
Knocking sound especially at full lock	Worn or damaged constant velocity joint or universal joint (automatic)	Replace or overhaul.
Whine or whistle	Worn or damaged constant velocity joint or universal joint (automatic)	Replace or overhaul.

Chapter 8 Final drive

Contents

Specifications

Type	Helical gears and differential - integral with gearbox	
Ratios:		
1100	4.333 : 1	
1300 (manual gearbox)	3.938 : 1	
1300 (automatic transmission)	3.273 : 1	
Bearing pre-load	0.004 in. (0.1 mm)	
Torque wrench settings:	lb f ft	kg fm
Driven gear to differential cage bolts	58	8.02
Differential end-cover bolts	18	2.49
Case stud nuts:		
5/16 in. UNF	18	2.49
3/8 in. UNF	25	3.46
Studs	6	0.80
Driving flange securing bolts (automatic)	40 - 45	5.5 - 6.2
Final drive gear pinion	150	20.7

1 General description

The differential unit is located on the bulkhead side of the combined engine and transmission unit. It is held in place by nuts and studs. The crownwheel, or drive gear, together with the differential gears, are mounted in the differential unit. The drive pinion is mounted on the third motion shaft.

All repairs can be carried out to the component parts of the differential unit only after the engine/transmission unit has been removed from the car. If it is wished to attend to the pinion it will be necessary to separate the transmission casing from the engine.

The differential housing and gearbox casing are machined as a matched pair when assembled so that they can only be replaced as a pair, not separately. Also the final drive gear and pinion are mated and must be changed as a pair and not as individual gears.

2 Differential, final drive gear and pinion - removal and refitment

1 Remove the engine and transmission unit as described in Chapter 1.
2 **Automatic transmission:** Using a large adjustable wrench hold each drive flange, and with a socket undo and remove the

securing bolt. The flange may now be drawn off the splined shafts.
3 Undo and remove the set screws and spring washers securing the end covers to the final drive housing.
4 Carefully lift away the end covers and gaskets. If there are

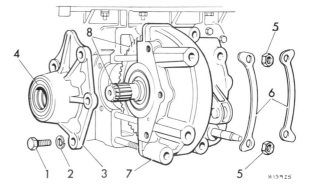

Fig. 8.1. Final drive and housing removal

1 Bolt
2 Spring washer
3 End cover
4 End cover oil seal
5 Nut
6 Lock plate
7 Final drive housing
8 Final drive/differential unit

any adjustment shims behind the crownwheel side end cover these must be kept in order and with the respective end cover.

5 Carefully remove the old oil seals from the end covers using a screwdriver or tapered drift. Note which way round the oil seals are fitted.

6 **Manual gearbox:** Remove the selector shaft detent spring, sleeve and ball bearing. Wrap some tape over the end of the selector shaft.

7 Bend back the lockwasher tabs securing the final drive housing nuts.

8 Undo and remove the final drive housing nuts and lock-washers. Carefully withdraw the final drive housing.

9 Lift away the differential assembly complete with bearings.

10 Using a universal puller and suitable thrust block withdraw the differential assembly bearings. Note which way round the bearings are fitted.

11 Mark the drive wheel and differential cage so that they may be refitted in their original positions.

12 Knock back the lockwasher tabs and then undo and remove the drive wheel securing bolts.

13 Remove the drive gear complete with the differential gear and thrust washer located in it.

14 Pull the differential gear from the crownwheel and recover the thrust washer.

15 Using a parallel pin punch carefully tap out the roll pin that retains the differential pinion pin towards the drive gear face.

16 The pinion pin may now be drifted out.

17 Lift out the differential gear thrust block.

18 The pinions and thrust washers are removed next and then the second differential gear and washer. Keep all thrust washers with their respective gears.

19 **Manual gearbox** (to paragraph 27): Unscrew the speed-ometer drive pinion retaining plate securing screw and spring washer. Lift away the retaining plate.

20 The pinion housing may now be lifted away followed by the speedometer drive pinion.

21 Undo and remove the two self locking nuts, washers and bolts which secure the left-hand mounting adaptor casting to the speedometer housing.

22 Undo and remove the speedometer housing securing screws and spring washers and lift away the housing and its gasket.

23 Knock back the lock washer tab from the final drive gear pinion nut.

24 Turn the selector shaft in an anticlockwise direction to disengage the operating stub and the interlock spool from the bellcrank levers.

25 Move the first/second speed selector fork towards the centre wheel of the gearbox casing to engage first gear.

26 Using a screwdriver drift the centre bellcrank lever inwards to select fourth gear. This will lock the gear train.

27 Knock back the final drive gear pinion nut lockwasher and using a large socket undo and remove the final drive gear pinion nut. Lift away the lockwasher and slide off the pinion.

28 **Automatic transmission:** Access to the pinion is gained by removing the forward clutch which requires the use of special

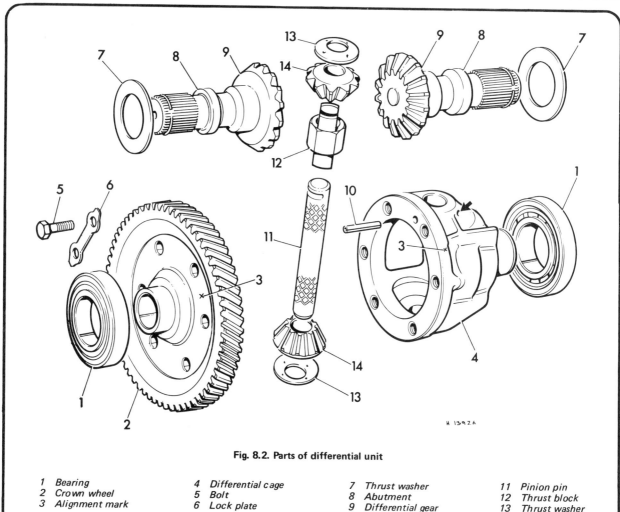

Fig. 8.2. Parts of differential unit

1 Bearing	4 Differential cage	7 Thrust washer	11 Pinion pin
2 Crown wheel	5 Bolt	8 Abutment	12 Thrust block
3 Alignment mark	6 Lock plate	9 Differential gear	13 Thrust washer
		10 Roll pin	14 Pinion

tools. Should the drive gear condition be such that the pinion gear is suspect it is best to leave any further work to the local BLMC garage.

29 Clean all parts and inspect for wear. New pinion and differential gears must be renewed as a set also using new thrust washers if they are worn. The drive gear and pinion must be renewed as a pair as they are matched during manufacture.

30 Re-assembly is the reverse sequence to dismantling, but there are several important points to be noted; these are described in the following paragraphs.

31 All traces of old gaskets and jointing compound must be removed. Always fit new gaskets, lockwashers and lockplate.

32 All attachments must be tightened to the torque wrench settings given at the beginning of this Chapter.

33 Fit new oil seals to the differential end covers using a suitable diameter tubular drift.

34 **Manual gearbox:** Move the selector bellcrank lever into the neutral position and rotate the interlock spool and selector shaft stub into engagement with the bellcrank levers.

35 Using a tubular drift drive the bearings onto the differential cage. The "Thrust" side must face outwards.

36 Refit the final drive/differential unit into the casing so that there is a slight bias towards the flywheel (or converter) end of the engine.

37 **Manual gearbox:** Wrap some tape over the end of the selector shaft before refitting the final drive housing. This will protect the oil seal.

38 Fit new lockplates and replace all securing nuts. This should be tightened sufficiently to hold the final drive firmly and yet allow it to be moved slightly from side to side.

39 Refit the flywheel (converter end) end cover and a new joint washer. Ensure that the oil holes line up.

40 Tighten the retaining screws and spring washers in a diagonal and progressive manner.

41 It is now necessary to set the pre-load adjustment. First fit the other end cover less its gasket or shims and tighten the securing screws in a diagonal and progressive manner until the end cover just nips the bearing outer race. Any further tightening will damage the end cover.

42 Using feeler gauges determine the gap between the end cover flange and the final drive housing. If there is a variation in readings the end cover securing screws have not been evenly tightened.

43 Should no gap exist between the flange and casing, remove the cover, and add a known thickness of shims between the cover and bearings to produce a clearance. This shim pack thickness must be included in the subsequent calculations.

44 The shim requirement may be calculated in the following manner (The figures are for a typical example):

Gasket (compressed thickness)	0.007 in	(0.18 mm)
minus (—) measured clearance	0.005 in	(0.13 mm)
endfloat (less shims)	0.002 in	(0.05 mm)
mean pre-load required	0.004 in	(0.10 mm)
Shim pack thickness required	0.006 in	(0.15 mm)

45 Smear a little grease onto the adjustment shims and fit them on the bearing thrust face.

46 Fit a new gasket and replace the end cover so that the oil holes are correctly aligned. Refit the securing screws and spring washers and tighten to a torque wrench setting of 18 lb f ft (2.5 kg fm)

47 **Automatic transmission:** Lubricate the end cover oil seals and refit the drive flanges. Fit new seals to each flange securing bolt, hold the flange with a wrench and tighten each bolt to a torque wrench setting of 40-45 lb f ft (5.5-6.2 kg fm).

48 When refitting the speedometer drive housing use a new joint washer with the sides smeared with a little jointing compound such as "Hylomar".

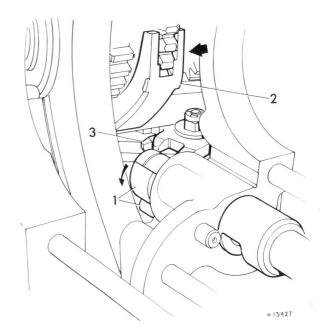

H 13927

Fig. 8.3. Positioning of selector shaft

1 Rotation of selector shaft to disengage operating stub and the interlock spool from bellcrank levers
2 First/second speed selector fork
3 Centre bellcrank lever

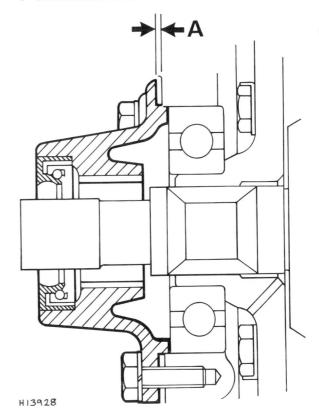

H13928

Fig. 8.4. End cover clearance (A)

---

3 Differential cage bearings - removal and refitment

For full information refer to Section 2, paragraphs 1 to 10 inclusive.

4 Differential end cover oil seal - removal and refitment

1 Drain the power unit oil into a container of suitable capacity.
2 Apply the handbrake, chock the rear wheels, jack up the front of the car and support on firmly based axle stands. Remove the road wheel.
3 It is now necessary to release the drive shaft from the final drive. For this a special tool is required. See Chapter 7, Section 2 or 3 as applicable.
4 Undo and remove the nut and spring washer securing the suspension lower arm to the swivel hub.
5 Using a universal balljoint separator detach the suspension lower arm from the swivel hub.
6 Unlock and then remove the nut that secures the suspension upper arm to the swivel hub.
7 Using a universal balljoint separator detach the suspension upper arm from the swivel hub.
8 Suitably support the swivel hub assembly so as to avoid stretching the hydraulic brake hose.
9 Carefully withdraw the drive shaft assembly, complete with the inboard joint, out of the differential assembly by a sufficient amount to enable the differential end cover to be removed.
10 Temporarily refit the swivel hub to the suspension arm so as to support the swivel hub.
11 Left-hand end cover: Undo and remove the securing screws and spring washers and withdraw the end cover complete with its joint washer. Note that the adjustment shims are fitted against the face of the differential cage bearings.
12 Right-hand end cover: Undo and remove the securing screws and spring washers and withdraw the end cover complete with its joint washer. Note that this end cover is under tension from the gearbox selector shaft detent spring which will be partly exposed when the cover is removed.
13 Remove the old oil seal from the end cover using a drift.
14 Refitting the oil seal and drive shaft assembly is the reverse sequence to removal. The following additional points should be noted:
a) Clean off all traces of the old gasket and any jointing compound on either the end cover or housing mating faces.
b) Smear a little jointing compound such as 'Hylomar' to both sides of new end cover gaskets.
c) Tighten the end cover securing screws to a torque wrench setting of 18 lb f ft (2.5 kf fm).

Chapter 9 Braking system

Contents

Specifications

Make	Girling
Footbrake	Hydraulic; operates on all four wheels. Servo unit - optional fitment
Handbrake	Mechanical; operates on rear wheels only

Type of brakes:

Front	Disc - self adjusting
Rear	Drum

Front discs:

Disc diameter	9.68 in. (2.46 mm)
Wheel cylinder diameter	2.0 in. (50.8 mm)
Pad area (total)	17.4 in.^{2} (112.2 cm^2)
Pad minimum permissible thickness	1/8 inch (3.2 mm)
Pad material	M108
Disc runout (max.)	0.007 in. (0.17 mm)

Rear drums:

Drum diameter	8.0 in. (203.2 mm)
Wheel cylinder diameter	0.5625 in. (14.2875 mm)
Shoe width	1.5 in. (38.1 mm)
Total swept area	76 sq. in. (490 sq. cm)
Hub bearing end float	0.001 - 0.005 in. (0.03 - 0.13 mm)

Servo unit type	Girling 28 'Super Vac'

Master cylinder:

Single:

Type	C.V. (centre valve) with integral reservoir
Diameter (non servo)	0.625 in. (15.88 mm)
(with servo)	0.750 in. (19.05 mm)

Tandem:
Type   ...   .   CV/TV (tipping valve) with integral reservoir
Diameter ...   .   0.75 in. (19.05 mm)

Torque wrench settings:

	lb f ft	kg fm
Braking disc to drive flange bolts	42	5.81
Braking disc shield to swivel hub bolt	21	2.96
Caliper to swivel hub bolts	66	9.18
Front hose bracket nuts	21	2.96
Rear brake backplate bolt nuts	20	2.75
Bleed screw	5	0.69
Adjuster nuts	5	0.69
Master cylinder to servo	17	2.35
Master cylinder tipping valve nut	40	5.53
Pressure differential switch	2.5	0.35
Pressure differential warning actuator adaptor	38	5.2
Drive shaft nut	150	20.7
PDWA switch	3	0.5
Wheel nuts	46	6.42

1 General description

Disc brakes are fitted to the front wheels and drum brakes to the rear. A servo unit can be fitted to all models, as an optional extra. The servo unit operates on all the brake units when the brake pedal is depressed. It is mounted between the brake pedal and master cylinder assembly.

The front brakes are of the rotating disc and semi-rigidly mounted caliper design, whilst the rear brakes are of the internal expanding single leading shoe type and can be operated by the handbrake or footbrake.

The front brake disc is secured to the driving flange of the hub, and the caliper mounted on the steering swivel. On the inner disc face of the caliper is a single hydraulic cylinder in which are placed two outward facing pistons. One piston is in contact with a friction pad, which in turn is incontact with one face of the disc, and the second piston presses in a yoke which transmits the pressure to a second pad in contact with the outer face of the disc. Hydraulic fluid is able to pass to the cavity between the two pistons.

The rear brakes have one cylinder operating two shoes for each wheel. Attached to each of the rear wheel operating cylinders is a mechanical expander, operated by the handbrake lever, via a cable which runs from the handbrake lever to the backplate brake levers. This provides an independent means of rear brake application.

Drum brakes have to be adjusted periodically to compensate for wear in the linings, whereas the front disc brakes are adjusted automatically. It is not usually necessary to adjust the handbrake system, as its efficiency is largely dependent on the condition of the brake linings and the adjustment of the brake shoes. The handbrake can, however, be adjusted separately from the footbrake operated hydraulic system.

The hydraulic brake functions in the following manner: On depression of the brake pedal, hydraulic fluid under pressure is pushed from the master cylinder to the brake operating cylinders at each wheel by means of a four way union, steel pipes and flexible hoses. On some models a tandem master cylinder is fitted so that if part of the brake hydraulic system should fail the remaining part will still be operative.

A pressure differential warning actuator, located within the engine compartment is fitted into the pipe line leading to the rear brakes and operates a warning light should the pressure in the system become unbalanced.

A mechanically operated stop light switch is secured to the pedal mounting bracket and is operated by the brake pedal lever.

Warning: Metric brake fittings are used on models covered by this manual. Always use metric spanners and ensure that when threaded replacement parts are being used they have metric threads.

2 Drum brakes - adjustment (rear wheels only)

1 Jack up the rear of the car and place on firmly based stands. Also chock the front wheels to ensure that the car cannot roll backwards or forwards.

2 Release the handbrake and, working under the car, locate the adjuster as shown in Fig. 9.1. The brakes are adjusted by turning the square headed adjuster in a clockwise or anti-clockwise direction. Always use a square headed brake adjuster spanner as the edges of the adjuster are easily burred if an adjustable wrench or open ended spanner is used.

3 Turn the adjuster in a clockwise direction, when viewed from the centre of the car, until the brake shoes lock the wheel. Turn the adjuster back until the wheel is free to rotate without the shoes rubbing.

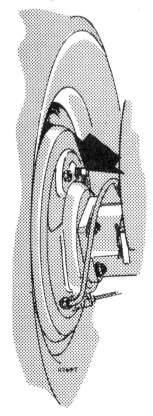

Fig. 9.1. Drum brake adjuster (arrowed)

4 Spin the wheel and apply the brakes hard to centralise the shoes. Re-check that it is not possible to turn the adjusting screw further without locking the wheel.

5 Note: A rubbing noise when the wheel is spun is usually due to dust on the brake drum and shoe lining. If there is no obvious slowing down of the wheel due to brake binding there is no need to slacken off the adjusters until the noise disappears. It is better to remove the drum and clean, taking care not to inhale any dust.

6 Repeat this process for the other brake drum. A useful tip is to paint the heads of the adjusting screws white which will facilitate future adjusting by making the adjuster heads easier to see. Also a little graphite penetrating oil on the adjuster threads will prevent the possibility of seizure by rusting.

3 Bleeding the hydraulic system

Whenever the brake hydraulic system has been overhauled, partially renewed, or the level in the reservoir becomes too low, air will have entered the system necessitating bleeding. During the operation, the level of hydraulic fluid in the reservoir should not be allowed to fall below half full, otherwise air will be drawn into the system again.

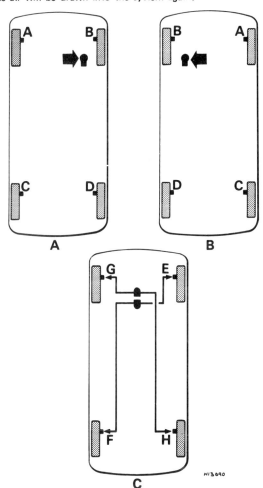

Fig. 9.2. Brake bleed sequence

Single master cylinder
A RHD models   B LHD models
Tandem master cylinder
C All models

1 Obtain a clean and dry glass jar, plastic tubing at least 15 inches (40 cm) long and of suitable diameter to fit tightly over the bleed screw, and a supply of hydraulic fluid.

2 Check that on each rear brake backplate the wheel cylinder is free to slide within its locating slot. Ensure that all connections are tight and all bleed screws closed. Check the wheels and release the handbrake.

3 Fill the master cylinder reservoir and the bottom inch of the jar with hydraulic fluid. Take extreme care that no fluid is allowed to come into contact with the paintwork as it acts as a solvent and will damage the finish.

4 **Single master cylinder type system:** Start bleeding at the front bleed screw which is furthest from the master cylinder and finish at the rear brake nearest to the master cylinder. The correct sequence is as follows: Front left, front right, rear left and rear right.

5 **Tandem master cylinder type system:** Bleed the system supplied by the secondary master cylinder chamber first. Commence bleeding at the front bleed screw and then bleed the diagonally opposite rear brake. The correct sequence is as follows: Front right, rear left, front left and rear right.

6 **All models:** Having decided the procedure open the first bleed screw about three quarters of a turn. Place one end of the bleed tube over the bleed nipple and submerge the other end of the tube in the fluid in the jar. Note: end of the tube must remain submerged, throughout the bleeding operation.

7 An assistant should now pump the brake pedal by first depressing it one full stroke followed by three short but rapid strokes and allowing the pedal to return of its own accord. Check the fluid level in the reservoir. Carefully watch the flow of fluid into the glass jar and, when air bubbles cease to emerge with the fluid during the next down stroke, tighten the bleed screw. Remove the plastic bleed tube and tighten the bleed screw to a torque wrench setting of 5 lb f ft (0.7 kg fm). Do not overtighten. Replace the rubber dust cap if fitted. Top up the fluid in the reservoir.

8 Continue bleeding the hydraulic system until all four units have been bled.

9 Sometimes it may be found that the bleed operation for one or more cylinders is taking a considerable time. The cause is probably air being drawn past the bleed screw threads when the screw is loose. To counteract this condition, it is recommended that at the end of each downward stroke the bleed screw be tightened to stop air being drawn past the threads.

10 If after the bleed operation has been completed, the brake pedal operation still feels spongy, this is an indication that there is still air in the system, or that the master cylinder is faulty.

11 **Pressure differential warning actuator valve (dual line systems only:** Should it be noticed that during the bleed operation and with the ignition switched on the warning light glows, the bleed operation must be continued until all traces of air are removed. Ascertain which brake caused the light to glow and then attach a bleed tube to the bleed screw at the opposite end of the car and open the bleed screw. Slowly depress the brake pedal and, when the light goes out, release the pedal and tighten the bleed screw.

12 Check and top up the reservoir fluid level with fresh hydraulic fluid. Never re-use old brake fluid. Finally check the drum brake adjustment.

4 Brake shoes (drum brakes only) - inspection, removal and refitment

Note: before attempting this operation, refer to the Note at the beginning of Section 16 in Chapter 11.

After high mileages, it will be necessary to fit replacement shoes with new linings. Replacement shoes can be obtained on an exchange basis.

4.1 Rear wheel removed

4.3 Lifting away hub dust cap

4.4 The split pin must next be removed

4.5 Removing nut retainer

4.6a The hub nut

4.6b Lifting away special washer. Earlier type shown — for details of later type see Chapter 11 Section 16.

4.7 Removal of brake drum

4.8 The brake assembly ready for inspection

1   Chock the front wheels, jack up the rear of the car and place on firmly based axle stands. Remove the road wheel (photo).

2   Release the handbrake and back off the brake shoe adjuster by turning in an anticlockwise direction when viewed from the centre of the car.

3   Using a wide bladed screwdriver, carefully prise off the hub dust cap (photo).

4   With a pair of pliers straighten the legs and withdraw the split pin (photo).

5   Next lift away the nut retainer from over the nut (photo).

6   Unscrew the nut and lift away followed by the washer from the stub shaft (photos).

7   The brake drum assembly may now be removed from the stub shaft. Be prepared for the left-hand hub to have a left-hand thread and the right-hand hub to have a right-hand thread. If it is tight, use a soft faced hammer and tap outwards on the circumference, rotating the drum at the same time (photo).

8   The brake linings should be renewed if they are so worn, that the rivet heads are flush with the surface of the lining. If bonded linings are fitted, they must be renewed when the lining material has worn down to 1/16 inch (1.6 mm) at its thinnest point (photo).

9   Using a pair of pliers, release the trailing brake shoe anti-rattle springs by rotating through 90°. Lift away the steady pin, spring and cup washer.

10 Disengage the tracking shoe from the wheel cylinder abutment and then the abutment in the adjuster link.

11 Repeat the operation in paragraph 9 for the leading shoe.

12 Carefully remove both brake shoes complete with springs, at the same time easing the handbrake operating lever from the leading shoe. Take care that the links in the adjuster housing do not fall out, and retain them with an elastic band around the adjuster assembly.

13 If the shoes are to be left off for awhile, do not depress the brake pedal otherwise the piston will be ejected from the cylinder causing unnecessary work.

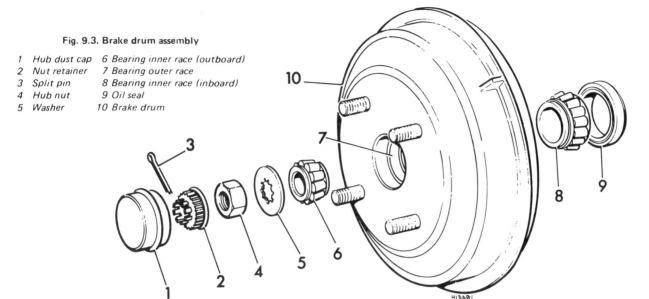

Fig. 9.3. Brake drum assembly

1 Hub dust cap	6 Bearing inner race (outboard)
2 Nut retainer	7 Bearing outer race
3 Split pin	8 Bearing inner race (inboard)
4 Hub nut	9 Oil seal
5 Washer	10 Brake drum

14 Thoroughly clean all traces of dust from the shoes, back-plate and brake drums using a stiff brush. It is recommended that compressed air is **not** used as it blows up dust, which should not be inhaled. Brake dust can cause judder or squeal on brake application and, therefore, it is important to clean out as described.

15 Check that the piston is free in its cylinder, that the rubber dust covers are undamaged and in position, and that there are no hydraulic fluid leaks. Ensure the handbrake lever assembly is free and the brake adjuster operates correctly. Lubricate the threads on the adjusting wedge with a graphite based penetrating oil.

16 Prior to re-assembly, smear a trace of "Castrol PH Brake Grease" on the steady platforms, both ends of the brake shoes and the adjuster links. Do not allow any grease to come into contact with the linings or rubber parts. Refit the shoes in the reverse sequence to removal, taking care that the adjuster links are correctly positioned in the adjuster housing with the angle of the link registering against the adjuster wedge. The two pull off springs should preferably be renewed every time new shoes are fitted and must be refitted in their original web holes. Position the upper one between the web and the backplate and the lower one between the web and brake drum (when fitted). The double section spring is the lowermost spring.

17 Back off the adjuster and replace the brake drum and hub assembly. Refit the special washer and nut.

18 Spin the brake drum and hub and while it is rotating tighten the hub nut to a torque wrench setting of 5 lb f ft (0.69 kg fm).

19 Stop the drum and hub from spinning and back off the nut.

20 Tighten the hub nut finger tight and then fit the hub nut retainer so that one arm of the retainer covers the left-hand half of the split pin hole in the stub shaft.

21 Slacken the hub nut and retainer to uncover fully the split pin hole.

22 Fit a new split pin, bending its legs circumferentially around the retainer to lock the nut and retainer.

23 Do not pack the dust cap with grease. Replace the road wheel.

24 Adjust the rear brakes as described in Section 2 and then lower the car to the ground. Check correct adjustment of the handbrake and finally road test.

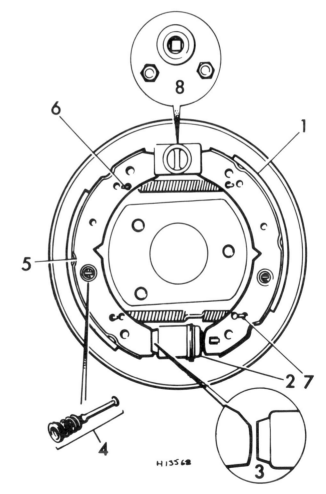

Fig. 9.4. Rear brake components (Sec 4)

1	Leading shoe	5	Trailing shoe
2	Wheel cylinder	6	Return spring (plain)
3	Abutment for trailing shoe	7	Return spring (shaped)
4	Anti-rattle spring assembly	8	Adjuster

5 Wheel cylinders (rear brakes) - removal, inspection, overhaul and refitment

If hydraulic fluid is leaking from the brake wheel cylinder, it may be necessary to dismantle it and replace the seal. Should brake fluid be found running down the side of the wheel or if it is noticed that a pool of liquid forms alongside one wheel and the level in the master cylinder has dropped, it is indicative of a failed seal.

1 Remove the brake drum/hub assembly and brake shoes as described in Section 4. Clean down the rear of the backplate using a stiff brush. Place a quantity of rag under the backplate to catch any hydraulic fluid that may issue from the open pipe or wheel cylinder.

2 Wipe the top of the brake master cylinder reservoir and unscrew the cap. Place a piece of thick polythene over the top of the reservoir and replace the cap. This is to stop hydraulic fluid syphoning out.

3 Using an open ended spanner, carefully unscrew the hydraulic pipe connection union to the rear of the wheel cylinder.

4 Extract the split pin and lift away the washer and clevis pin connecting the handbrake cable yoke to the wheel cylinder operating lever.

5 Ease off the rubber boot from the rear of the wheel cylinder.

6 Using a screwdriver, carefully draw off the retaining plate and spring plate from the rear of the wheel cylinder.

7 The wheel cylinder may now be lifted away from the brake backplate. Detach the handbrake lever from the wheel cylinder.

8 To dismantle the wheel cylinder; first, ease off the rubber dust cover retaining ring with a screwdriver, and the rubber dust cover itself. Withdraw the piston from the wheel cylinder body and, with the fingers, remove the piston seal from the piston noting which way round it is fitted, (Do not use a screwdriver as this could scratch the piston).

9 Inspect the inside of the cylinder for general wear, or scratch marks, caused by impurities in the hydraulic fluid. If wear is excessive, or scratches are present, the cylinder and piston will require renewal. **Note:** If the wheel cylinder requires renewal always ensure that the replacement is exactly similar to the one removed.

10 If the cylinder is sound, thoroughly clean it out with fresh hydraulic fluid.

11 The old rubber seal will probably be swollen and visibly worn. Smear a new rubber seal with hydraulic fluid and re-assemble into the cylinder. Fit a new dust seal and retaining clip.

12 Using "Castrol PH Brake Grease", smear the backplate where the wheel cylinder slides, and refit the handbrake lever on the wheel cylinder ensuring that it is the correct way round. The spindles of the lever must engage in the recess on the cylinder arms.

13 The handbrake lever may now be fed through the slot in the backplate until the neck of the wheel cylinder is correctly located in the slot.

14 Slide the spring plate between the wheel cylinder and backplate. The retaining plate may now be inserted between the spring plate and wheel cylinder, taking care the pips of the spring plate engage in the holes of the retaining plate.

15 Replace the rubber boot and reconnect the handbrake cable yoke to the handbrake lever. Insert the clevis pin, head upwards and plain washer. Lock with a new split pin.

16 Re-assembling the brake shoes and drum/hub assembly is the reverse sequence to dismantling. Finally, bleed the hydraulic system as described in Section 3.

6 Adjusters (drum brakes) - removal and refitment

1 Should it be necessary to remove the brake adjuster, first

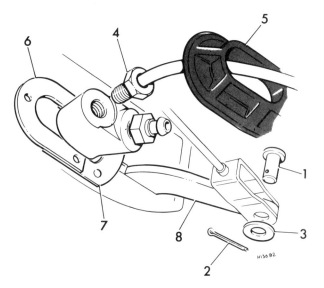

Fig. 9.5. Rear brake wheel cylinder removal

1	Clevis pin	5	Dust cover
2	Split pin	6	Spring clip
3	Washer	7	Spring plate
4	Union nut	8	Handbrake lever

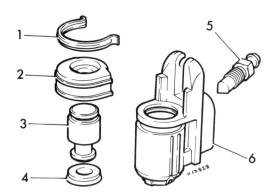

Fig. 9.6. Exploded view of wheel cylinder

1	Clip	4	Seal
2	Dust cover	5	Bleed screw
3	Piston	6	Body

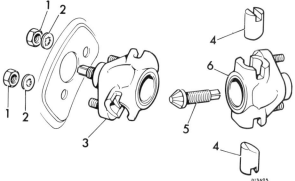

Fig. 9.7. Brake shoe adjuster

1	Securing nut	4	Adjuster link
2	Washer	5	Adjuster wedge
3	Adjuster	6	Adjuster body

remove the road wheel, brake drum/hub assembly and brake shoes as described in Section 4.

2   Undo and remove the two adjuster retaining nuts and shakeproof washers. The adjuster can now be lifted away from the backplate.

3   Check that the adjuster wedge can be screwed both in and out to its fullest extent, without showing signs of tightness.

4   Lift away the two adjuster links and thoroughly clean the adjuster assembly. Inspect the adjuster body and two links for signs of excessive wear. Fit new parts as necessary.

5   Lightly smear the adjuster links with "Castrol PH Grease" and re-assemble. Double-check correct operation by holding the two links between the fingers and rotating the adjuster wedge whereupon the two links should move together.

7   Backplate (drum brakes) - removal and refitment

1   To remove the backplate, refer to Section 4 and remove the drum/hub assembly.

2   Extract the split pin amd lift away the plain washer locking the clevis pin securing the handbrake cable yoke to the wheel cylinder handbrake lever. Lift away the clevis pin.

3   Wipe the top of the brake master cylinder reservoir and unscrew the cap. Place a piece of thick polythene over the reservoir and refit the cap. This is to stop hydraulic fluid syphoning out.

4   Using an open ended spanner, carefully unscrew the hydraulic pipe connection union to the rear of the wheel cylinder.

5   Undo and remove the nuts, bolts and spring washers securing the backplate to the radius arm. Lift away the backplate.

6   Refitting the backplate is the reverse sequence to removal. It will be necessary to bleed the brake hydraulic system as described in Section 3.

8   Handbrake - adjustment

It is usual when the rear brakes are adjusted that any excessive free movement of the handbrake will automatically be taken up. However, in time, the handbrake cables will stretch and it will be necessary to take up the free play by shortening the forward cable at the point where it is attached to the compensator.

Never try to adjust the handbrake to compensate for wear on the rear brake linings. It is usually badly worn brake linings that lead to the excessive handbrake travel. If upon inspection the rear brake linings are in good condition, or they have been renewed recently and the handbrake reaches the end of its ratchet travel before the brakes operate, adjust the cable as follows:

1   Refer to Section 2 and ensure the rear brakes are correctly adjusted.

2   Release the handbrake lever and then pull it on until the third notch position on the ratchet is reached.

3   Push against the lower edge of the rear seat, at the centre and free it from the body clips. Lift the seat to gain access to the handbrake compensator.

4   Release the locknut and with an open ended spanner hold the forward cable hexagon. Turn the adjuster until the correct tension is obtained and then tighten the locknut. It should now be possible to just turn the rear wheels.

5   Release the handbrake lever and check that the rear brakes are not binding.

9   Handbrake cables - removal and refitment

1   Chock the front wheels, jack up the rear of the car and support on firmly based axle stands.

2   Push against the lower edge of the rear seat, at the centre

and free it from the body clips. Lift away the seat to gain access to the handbrake compensator. Also remove the rear floor cover.

Front cable:

1   Remove the seat belts centre console and then undo and remove the six self tapping screws secuirng the handbrake lever cover retainer.

2   Pull the cover up the lever and move the handbrake lever to the off position.

3   Undo and remove the two bolts, spring and plain washers securing the handbrake lever base to the floor panel.

4   Withdraw the split pin and lift away the plain washer and clevis securing the front cable yoke to the underside of the lever.

5   Slacken the locknut and unscrew the front cable from the adjuster nut located at the front of the compensator.

6   The front cable may now be lifted away.

7   Refitting the front cable is the reverse sequence to removal. Make sure that the cable passes under the rear seat support and seat belt bracket. Ensure that the seat belt centre console pivots correctly. Adjust the cable as described in Section 8.

Rear cable

1   Extract the split pin and lift away the washer and clevis pin connecting the handbrake cable yoke to the wheel cylinder operating lever.

2   Detach the balance lever from the rear cable nipple.

3   Remove the rear cable retaining nut. It will probably be necessary for a second person under the car to hold the outer cable hexagon.

4   Undo and remove the nut and spring washer and detach the cable abutment from the suspension arm bracket.

5   Remove the clips securing the cable to the suspension arm and completely remove the rear handbrake cable.

6   The sequence for removing the second rear cable is identical to that just described.

7   Refitting the rear cable is the reverse sequence to removal. Make sure the cable abutment is fitted to the **inside face** on the suspension arm bracket. Apply a little grease to the exposed section of the rear cable and yoke. Also ensure the rubber bellows are correctly located to prevent dirt ingress. Adjust the handbrake cable as described in Section 8.

10   Handbrake lever - removal and refitment

1   Carefully pull back the floor covering around the handbrake lever and then undo and remove the six self tapping screws securing the handbrake lever cover retainer.

2   Pull the cover up the lever and move the lever to the off position.

3   Extract the split pin and lift away the washer and clevis pin connecting the handbrake cable yoke to the underside of the handbrake lever.

4   Undo and remove the two bolts, spring and plain washers securing the handbrake lever frame to the floor panel.

5   Lift away the handbrake lever assembly.

6   Refitting the handbrake is the reverse sequence to removal. Adjust the cable as described in Section 8.

11   Handbrake lever assembly - dismantling and re-assembly

1   Refer to Section 10 and remove the handbrake lever assembly.

2   Using either a drill or file remove the head from the lever pin. Tap out the remains of the pin and separate the lever from the ratchet and mounting bracket. Remove the ferrule.

3   Using either a drill or file remove the head from the pawl rivet. Tap out the remains of the rivet and lift away the pawl.

4   Withdraw the operating shaft assembly from the lever and then pull the button from the operating shaft. Remove the

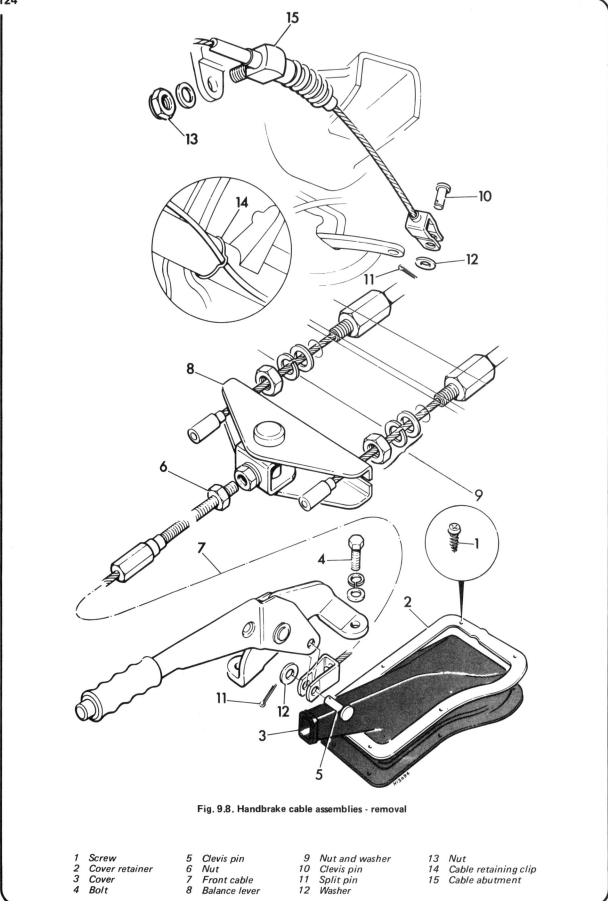

Fig. 9.8. Handbrake cable assemblies - removal

1 Screw	5 Clevis pin	9 Nut and washer	13 Nut
2 Cover retainer	6 Nut	10 Clevis pin	14 Cable retaining clip
3 Cover	7 Front cable	11 Split pin	15 Cable abutment
4 Bolt	8 Balance lever	12 Washer	

Starlock washer.

5 Inspect the pawl and ratchet for wear and obtain new parts as necessary.

6 Re-assembly of the handbrake lever assembly is the reverse sequence to removal. Lubricate all moving parts with a little engine oil.

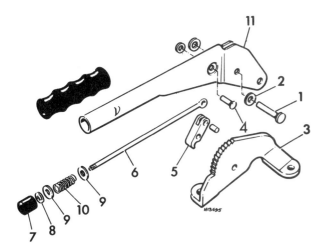

Fig. 9.9. Handbrake lever component parts

1 Pivot pin	7 Button
2 Washer	8 Starlock washer
3 Ratchet	9 Plain washer
4 Pawl retaining rivet	10 Spring
5 Pawl	11 Lever
6 Operating shaft	

12 Brake pads (disc brakes) - removal, inspection and refitment

1 Apply the handbrake, jack up the front of the car and place on firmly based axle stands. Remove the road wheel (photos).

2 Using a pair of pliers, withdraw the two pad retaining pin locking wire clips and withdraw the retaining pins. The two pads may now be lifted out of the caliper (photos).

3 Inspect the thickness of the lining material and, if it is less than 1/8 inch (3.2 mm) it is recommended that the pads be renewed. If one of the pads is slightly more worn than the other, it is permissible to change these round. (Assuming that the discs and pads are not heavily scored). Always fit new pads of the manufacturer's recommended specification.

4 To refit the pads, it is first necessary to extract a little brake fluid from the system. To do this, fit a plastic bleed tube to the bleed screw and immerse the free end in 1 inch (25 mm) of hydraulic fluid in a jar. Slacken off the bleed screw one complete turn and press back the indirect piston. Next, push the yoke towards the disc until the new indirect pad can be inserted. Press back the direct piston into the bore and then tighten the bleed screw. Fit the new 'direct' pad.

5 Insert the retaining pins with their heads furthermost from the caliper pistons and secure with wire clips.

6 Wipe the top of the hydraulic fluid reservoir and remove the cap. Top up, and depress the brake pedal several times to settle the pads, and then recheck the hydraulic fluid level.

13 Calipers (disc brakes) - removal, overhaul and refitment

1 Chock the rear wheels, apply the handbrake, remove the front wheel trim and slacken the wheel nuts. Jack up the front of the car and support on firmly based stands. Remove the road wheel.

12.1a Removing road wheel

12.1b Caliper ready for pad removal

12.2a Wire clip removal

12.2b Withdrawing pad retaining pin

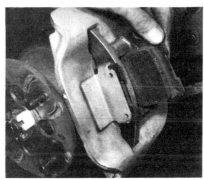

12.2c Lifting away the pads

2 Wipe the top of the brake master cylinder reservoir and unscrew the cap. Place a piece of thick polythene over the top and refit the cap. This is to prevent hydraulic fluid syphoning out.

3 Using an open ended spanner, undo the union nut securing the brake hydraulic pipe at the support bracket, on the front swivel hub.

4 Remove the nut and lockwasher to release the front hose from the bracket on the front swivel hub. Remove the lockwasher and plug the hose to prevent dirt ingress.

5 Undo and remove the two nuts and spring washers and withdraw the hose support bracket from the caliper bolts.

6 Undo and remove the two caliper securing bolts and carefully lift the caliper assembly from the brake disc.

7 Using a pair of pliers, withdraw the two pad retaining pin wire clips and remove the two retaining pins. Lift away the pads.

8 Place the yoke of the caliper between soft faces in a bench vice and tighten sufficiently to hold the caliper.

9 Using the fingers, press the indirect piston fully into its bore in the caliper and then press the cylinder body down.

10 Make a note of the position of the yoke spring relative to the yoke, and then lift away the spring.

11 Very carefully remove the retaining rings and dust covers from the cylinder, if necessary using a small screwdriver. The bore or piston must not be scratched.

12 Lift out the special bias ring from the indirect piston.

13 Using a compressed air jet, applied to the hydraulic pipe connection bore, eject the two pistons, taking suitable precautions to prevent them from flying out.

14 The seals may be removed from the cylinder using a non-metallic rod, or the fingers.

15 Finally remove the bleed nipple. It is important that the adjustment screw within the cylinder body is not disturbed.

16 Thoroughly clean the internal parts of the caliper using methylated spirits.

17 Carefully inspect the fine finish of the bore and pistons, and if signs of scoring, or corrosion are evident, a new caliper assembly must be obtained. Before commencing to re-assemble, obtain a new seal set and also a new bias spring.

18 To re-assemble the caliper, first fit the new bias spring into the indirect piston, in such a manner, that the radius end enters the piston first.

19 Apply a little clean hydraulic fluid to the pistons and seals,

but not to the cylinder grooves or sliding edges of the yoke.

20 Very carefully fit the previously wetted seals into the cylinder grooves and then fit the pistons into the cylinder. The indirect piston with the bias ring must be fitted in the opposite end of the cylinder to the pads.

21 Refit the dust cover and retaining rings, making sure that the widest retaining ring secures the dust cover furthermost from the pads.

22 The yoke spring is next refitted to the yoke, and this must be positioned as was noted during dismantling.

23 Fit the cylinder to the yoke, engaging the tongue of the yoke into the slot of the bias ring fitted into the indirect piston.

24 With a small screwdriver, locate the legs of the yoke spring into the sliding grooves on the cylinder. The angled leg of the spring must engage in the groove on the cylinder opposite to the bleed screw. Refit the bleed screw.

25 The pads may now be refitted, this being the reverse sequence to removal.

26 Refitting the caliper is the reverse sequence to removal. Make sure that a lockwasher is fitted on each side of the bracket and tighten the locknut without twisting the hose. It will be necessary to bleed the hydraulic system, full details of which may be found in Section 3.

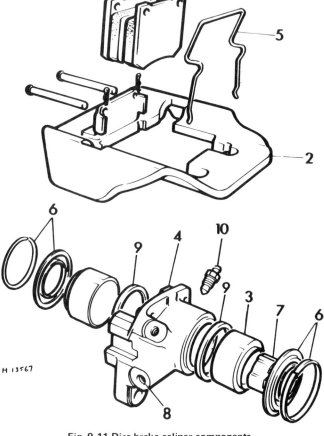

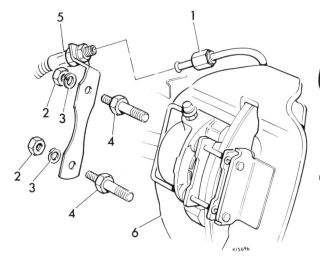

Fig. 9.10. Disc brake caliper removal

1 Union nut   4 Shaped bolt
2 Nut   5 Brake hose
3 Spring washer   6 Caliper assembly

Fig. 9.11 Disc brake caliper components

1 Brake pads   cover
2 Yoke   7 Bias spring
3 Indirect piston   8 Hydraulic fluid inlet
4 Cylinder body   9 Piston seal
5 Yoke spring   10 Bleed screw
6 Dust cover retaining ring and

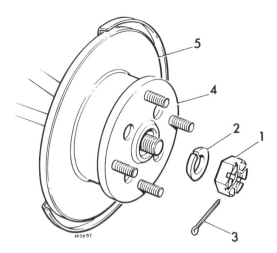

Fig. 9.12. Front brake disc and drive flange removal

1   Nut   4   Drive flange
2   Collar   5   Disc
3   Split pin

---

14 Disc (front disc brakes) - removal, inspection, renovation and refitment

1   Chock the rear wheels and apply the handbrake. Jack up the front of the car and support on firmly based axle stands. Remove the road wheel.
2   Remove the front brake caliper as described in Section 13.
3   Remove the dust cap and extract the split pin from the drive shaft nut.
4   Undo and remove the drive shaft nut and extract the split collar.
5   Using a universal three legged puller, with the feet located behind the wheel mounting flange (drive plate), and a suitable thrust pad, carefully draw the disc and drive plate assembly from the drive shaft.
6   Mark the relative positions of the disc and drive plate so that they may be refitted in their original positions, and separate the two parts.
7   Thoroughly clean the disc and inspect for signs of deep scoring or excessive corrosion. If these are evident, the disc may be re-machined but no more than a total of 0.060 inch (1.524 mm) may be removed. It is however, desirable to fit a new disc if at all possible.
8   Refitting the dsic is the reverse sequence to removal. The hub nut must be tightened to a torque wrench setting of 150 lb f ft (20.7 kg fm) and aligned to the next split pin hole. Always lock with a new split pin.
9   Measure the run-out at the outer periphery of the disc by means of feeler gauges positioned between the inside of the caliper and the disc. If the run-out of the friction faces exceeds 0.007 in (0.17 mm), remove the disc and reposition it on the drive plate. Should the run-out be really bad, the disc is probably distorted due to overheating and a new one must be fitted.

---

15 Disc dust shield - removal and refitment

1   Refer to Section 14 and remove the disc and drive flange assembly.
2   Undo and remove the bolt and spring washer securing the dust shield to the hub. Lift away the dust shield.
3   Refitting the dust shield is the reverse sequence to removal.

---

16 Master cylinder (single) - removal and refitment

1   Apply the handbrake and chock the front wheels. Drain the fluid from the master cylinder reservoir and master cylinder by attaching a plastic bleed tube to one of the brake bleed nipples, undo the screw one turn and then pump the fluid out into a clean glass container, by means of the brake pedal. Hold the brake pedal against the floor at the end of each stroke and tighten the bleed screw. When the pedal has returned to its normal position, loosen the bleed screw and repeat the process until the master cylinder is empty.
2   **Bulkhead mounted type:** Extract the spring clip and remove the clevis pin securing the pushrod yoke to the brake pedal.
3   **Both types:** Wipe the area around the hydraulic pipe union and disconnect the pipe from the master cylinder. Plug the end of the pipe to stop dirt ingress.
4   **Bulkhead mounted type:** Undo and remove the two nuts, spring washers and bolts securing the master cylinder to the bulkhead.
5   **Servo Unit mounted type:** Undo and remove the two nuts and spring washers securing the master cylinder to the servo unit.
6   **Both types:** Carefully lift away the master cylinder.
7   Refitting is the reverse sequence to removal. Always start the union nut on the end of the hydraulic pipe before finally tightening the master cylinder securing nuts and/or bolts. It will be necessary to bleed the hydraulic system as described in Section 3.

---

17 Master cylinder (single) - dismantling and re-assembly

If a replacement master cylinder is to be fitted, it will be necessary to lubricate the seals before fitting to the car as they have a protective coating when originally assembled. Remove the blanking plug from the hydraulic pipe union seating. Ease back and remove the plunger dust cover. Inject clean hydraulic fluid into the master cylinder and operate the piston several times so the fluid will spread over all the internal working surfaces.

If the existing master cylinder is to be dismantled for overhaul or inspection, after removal proceed as follows:
1   Ease back and remove the plunger dust cover.
2   Using a pair of thin-nosed pliers release the circlip from inside the bore. The pushrod and dished washer assembly may now be removed.
3   Carefully withdraw the complete plunger assembly from the bore. The assembly is separated by lifting the thimble leaf over the shouldered end of the plunger. The plunger seal may now be eased off using the fingers only.
4   Depress the plunger return spring, allowing the valve stem to slide through the keyhole in the thimble thus releasing the tension in the spring.
5   Detach the valve spacer, taking care of the spacer spring washer which will be found located under the valve head.
6   Examine the bore of the cylinder carefully for any signs of scores or ridges or excessive wear. If this is found to be smooth with only negligible wear, new seals can be fitted. If, however, there is any doubt about condition of the bore, then a new master cylinder must be fitted.
7   If examination of the seals shows them to be apparently oversize or swollen, or very loose in the plunger, suspect oil contamination of the hydraulic system. Ordinary lubricating oil will swell these rubber seals, and if one is found to be swollen, it is reasonable to assume that all seals in the braking system will need attention.
8   Thoroughly clean all parts in either fresh hydraulic fluid or methylated spirits. Ensure that the bypass ports are clear.
9   All components should be lubricated with clean brake fluid before they are assembled. Fit a new valve seal the correct way round so that the flat side is correctly seating on the valve

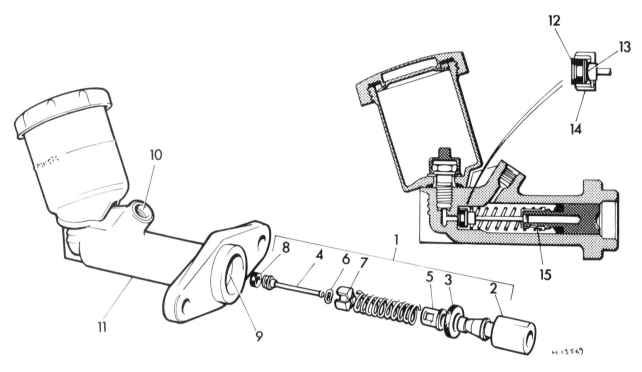

Fig. 9.13. Single master cylinder components

1	Piston assembly	6	Curved washer	10	Outlet port	13 Curved washer fitted in
2	Piston	7	Spacer	11	Master cylinder body	spacer
3	Piston seal	8	Valve seal	12	Valve seal correctly fitted on	14 Spacer
4	Valve stem	9	Master cylinder bore		valve head	15 Thimble leaf depressed
5	Thimble					

head. Place the dished washer with the dome against the underside of the valve head. Hold it in position with the valve spacers, ensuring that the legs face towards the valve seal.

10 Replace the plunger return spring centrally on the spacer, insert the thimble into the spring, and depress until the valve stem engages in the keyhole in the thimble.

11 Ensure that the spring is central on the spacer before fitting a new plunger seal onto the plunger, with the flat face against the face of the plunger.

12 Insert the reduced end of the plunger into the thimble until the thimble engages under the shoulder of the plunger, and press home the thimble leaf.

13 Check that the master cylinder bore is clean and smear with clean brake fluid. With the plunger suitably lubricated with brake fluid, carefully insert the assembly into the bore - end first. Ease the lips of the plunger seal carefully into the bore.

14 Fit the pushrod and washer in place and secure with the circlip. Smear the sealing area of the dust cover with Rubber Grease and also pack the cover with this grease to act as a dust trap. Fit the dust cover to the master cylinder body.

18 Master cylinder (tandem) - removal and refitment

1 Drain the tandem master cylinder and reservoir in a similar manner to that described for the single master cylinder. Full information will be found in Section 16, paragraph 1.

2 Using an open ended spanner disconnect the secondary and primary supply pipe from the master cylinder body. Plug the ends to prevent dirt ingress.

3 Undo and remove the two nuts and spring washers securing the master cylinder to the rear of the servo unit and lift away the master cylinder.

4 Refitting the tandem master cylinder is the reverse sequence to removal. Always start the union nuts before finally tightening the master cylinder retaining nuts. It will be necessary to bleed the hydraulic system and full details will be found in Section 3.

19 Master cylinder (tandem) - dismantling and re-assembly

1 Refer to the introduction to Section 16 with regard to replacement master cylinders.

2 Undo and remove the two screws holding the reservoir to the cylinder body. Lift away the reservoir. Using a suitable sized Allen key or wrench unscrew the tipping valve nut and lift away the seal. Using a suitable diameter rod, push the primary plunger down the bore, this operation enables the tipping valve to be withdrawn.

3 Using a compressed air jet, carefully applied to the rear outlet pipe connection, blow out all the master cylinder internal components. Alternatively, shake out the parts. Take care that adequate precautions are taken to ensure all parts are caught as they emerge.

4 Separate the primary and secondary plungers from the intermediate spring. Use the fingers to remove the gland seal from the primary plunger.

5 The secondary plunger assembly should be separated by lifting the thimble leaf over the shouldered end of the plunger. Using the fingers, remove the seal from the secondary plunger.

6 Depress the secondary spring, allowing the valve stem to slide through the keyhole in the thimble, thus releasing the tension in the spring.

7 Detach the valve spacer, taking care of the spring washer which will be found located under the valve head.

8 Examine the bore of the cylinder carefully for scores,

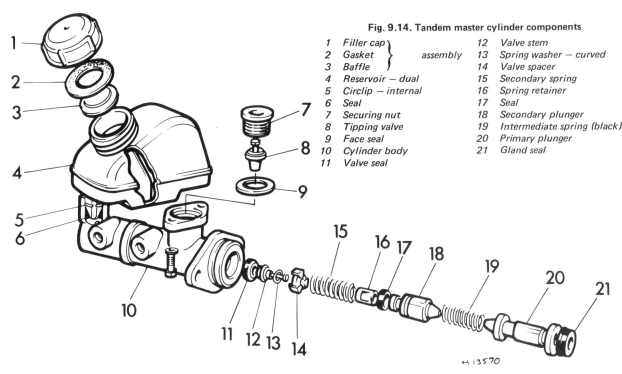

Fig. 9.14. Tandem master cylinder components

1	Filler cap	12	Valve stem
2	Gasket	13	Spring washer — curved
3	Baffle	14	Valve spacer
4	Reservoir — dual	15	Secondary spring
5	Circlip — internal	16	Spring retainer
6	Seal	17	Seal
7	Securing nut	18	Secondary plunger
8	Tipping valve	19	Intermediate spring (black)
9	Face seal	20	Primary plunger
10	Cylinder body	21	Gland seal
11	Valve seal		

(Items 1, 2, 3 bracketed as "assembly")

ridges or excessive wear. If the bore is found to be completely smooth, with only negligible wear, new seals can be fitted. If, however, there is any doubt about the condition of the bore, then a new cylinder must be fitted.

9 If examination of the seals shows them to be apparently oversize, swollen, or very loose on the plungers, suspect oil contamination in the system. Oil will swell these rubber seals, and if one is found to be swollen, it is reasonable to assume that all seals in the braking system will need attention.

10 Thoroughly clean all parts in either fresh hydraulic fluid or methylated spirits. Ensure that the bypass ports are clear.

11 All components should be assembled wet by dipping in clean brake fluid. Using fingers only, fit new seals to the primary and secondary plungers ensuring that they are the correct way round. Place the dished washer with the dome against the underside of the valve seat. Hold it in position with the valve spacers ensuring that the legs face towards the valve seal.

12 Replace the plunger return spring centrally on the spacer, insert the thimble into the spring and depress until the valve stem engages in the keyhole of the thimble.

13 Insert the reduced end of the plunger into the thimble, until the thimble engages under the shoulder of the plunger, and press home the thimble leaf. Replace the intermediate spring between the primary and secondary plungers.

14 Check that the master cylinder bore is clean and smear with clean brake fluid. With the complete assembly suitably lubricated with brake fluid, carefully insert the assembly into the bore. Ease the lips of the plunger seals carefully into the bore. Push the assembly fully home.

15 Refit the tipping valve assembly and seal, to the cylinder bore and tighten the securing nut to a torque wrench setting of 40 lb f ft (5.5 kg fm). Replace the hydraulic fluid reservoir and tighten the two retaining screws.

16 The master cylinder is now ready for refitment to the servo unit.

20 Servo unit - description

The vacuum servo unit is fitted into the brake hydraulic circuit in series with the master cylinder to provide assistance to the driver when the brake pedal is depressed. This reduces the effort required by the driver to operate the brakes under all braking conditions.

The unit operates by vacuum obtained from the induction manifold and comprises, basically, a booster diaphragm, control rod, slave cylinder and non-return valve.

The servo unit and hydraulic master cylinder are connected together so that the servo unit piston rod acts as the master cylinder pushrod. The driver's braking effort is transmitted through another pushrod to the servo unit piston and its built-in control system. The servo unit piston does not fit tightly into the cylinder, but has a strong diaphragm to keep its edges in constant contact with the cylinder wall, so assuring an air-tight seal between the two parts. The forward chamber is held under vacuum conditions created in the inlet manifold of the engine, and during periods when the brake pedal is not in use, the controls open a passage to the rear chamber so placing it under vacuum conditions as well. When the brake pedal is depressed, the vacuum passage to the rear chamber is cut off and the chamber opened to atmospheric pressure. The consequent rush of air pushes the servo piston forward in the vacuum chamber and operates the main pushrod to the master cylinder.

The controls are designed so that assistance is given under all conditions and, when the brakes are not required, vacuum in the rear chamber is established when the brake pedal is released. All air from the atmosphere entering the rear chamber is passed through a small air filter.

Under normal operating conditions the vacuum servo unit is very reliable and does not require overhaul except at very high mileage. In this case it is necessary to obtain a service exchange unit, rather than, attempt to repair the original unit.

21 Servo unit - removal and refitment

1 Refer to Section 16 or 18, as applicable, and remove the master cylinder from the servo unit.

2 Slacken the clip and disconnect the vacuum hose from the servo unit non-return valve.

3 Undo and remove the three screws securing the parcel shelf on the driver's side. Lift away the parcel shelf.

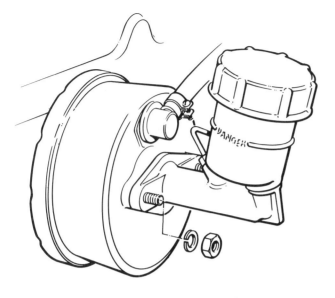

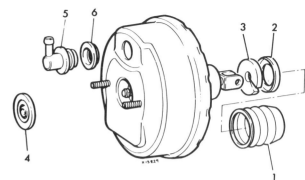

Fig. 9.16. Servo unit external components

1	Rubber dust cover	4	Grommet
2	Retainer	5	Non return valve
3	Filter	6	Grommet

4   Remove the spring clip securing the servo unit operating rod yoke to the pedal clevis. Lift away the plain washer and withdraw the clevis pin.

5   Undo and remove the four nuts and spring washers securing the servo unit to the mounting bracket and body. Lift away the servo unit.

6   Refitting the servo unit is the reverse sequence to removal. It will be necessary to bleed the hydraulic system as described in Section 3.

22 Servo unit non-return valve - removal and refitment

1   The servo unit should not be completely dismantled so if it develops an internal fault it should be renewed. Even if the unit is dismantled there would probably be extreme difficulty in obtaining spare parts. The only two service operations that may be carried out are renewing the non-return valve (this Section) and the air filter (Section 23).

2   To renew the non-return valve; first, detach the vacuum hose from the valve union.

3   Note the angle of the valve union and then insert a wide blade screwdriver between the valve and grommet. Pull on the valve whilst twisting the screwdriver to release it from the body.

4   Recover the grommet.

5   Refitting the grommet and valve is the reverse sequence to removal. Lubricate the ribs of the valve with a little Rubber Grease.

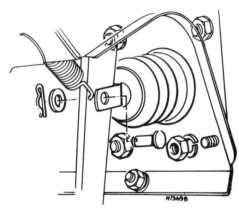

Fig. 9.15. Servo unit attachments

23 Servo unit filter - removal and refitment

1   Carefully pull back the dust cover and then ease the filter retainer from the servo neck.

2   Using a small screwdriver ease out the filter. Cut it in half and lift away.

3   Cut a new filter diagonally to the centre hole, fit it over the pushrod and carefully ease it into the housing.

4   Refit the filter retainer and dust cover.

24 Pressure differential warning actuator valve - removal, overhaul and refitment

1   Wipe the top of the brake cylinder fluid reservoir and unscrew the cap. Place a piece of polythene over the top and refit the cap. This is to prevent hydraulic fluid syphoning out. For safety reasons disconnect the battery.

2   Detach the cable connector at the top of the pressure differential warning actuator valve switch.

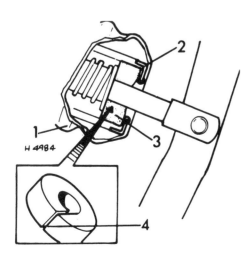

Fig. 9.17. Servo unit air filter renewal

1	Rubber dust cover	3	Air filter
2	Retainer	4	Diagonal cut

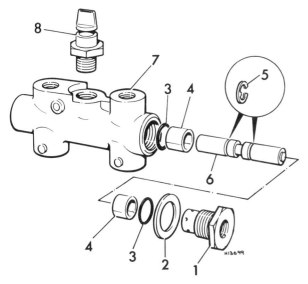

Fig. 9.18. Exploded view of pressure differential warning actuator valve

1 End adaptor	5 Circlip
2 Copper washer	6 Piston
3 'O' ring	7 Body
4 Sleeve	8 Switch

3 Wipe the area around the valve assembly and, using an open ended spanner, unscrew the six union nuts. Detach the pipes from the valve. Plug the ends of the pipes to prevent dirt ingress.

4 Undo and remove the valve securing bolt and spring washer and lift away the valve. Take care not to spill any hydraulic fluid onto the paintwork as it acts as a paint solvent.

5 Wipe down the outside of the valve and then unscrew the switch from the top of the body.

6 Unscrew the end adaptor and tap the open end of the valve against a wooden block to extract the piston assembly.

7 If the sleeve is still in the bore shake it out and extract the "O" ring.

8 Remove the second sleeve and "O" ring and carefully press the two shaped circlips from their grooves in the piston.

9 Thoroughly clean all parts - except the switch-in fresh brake fluid or methylated spirits and then examine the bore and sleeves for signs of scoring or corrosion. If evident a new valve assembly will be necessary.

10 Temporarily reconnect the electric switch to its wiring and actuate the plunger to test the action of the switch and warning light circuit.

11 All parts must be assembled wet by dipping in clean brake fluid. Fit new circlips to the piston.

12 Fit the sleeves, check that they slide freely over the piston and then fit the new 'O' rings.

13 Position the piston assembly in the entrance to the valve bore and push it fully into the bore in one even stroke.

14 Screw in the end adaptor and tighten finger tight to correctly locate the 'O' ring on the piston.

15 Remove the end adaptor and taking care use a small screwdriver to press the seal further down the bore until it abuts the sleeve.

16 Fit a new gasket and screw in the end adaptor. Tighten to a torque wrench setting of 38 lb f ft (5.2 kg fm).

17 Working through the switch port, ease the piston towards the adaptor until the two sleeves are central under the port.

18 Screw in the electrical switch and tighten to a torque wrench setting of 3 lb f ft (0.5 kg fm). Should no resistance be felt remove the switch and recheck the position of the sleeve.

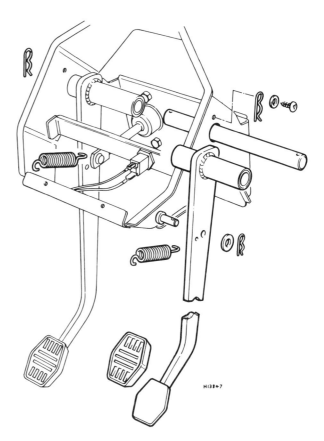

Fig. 9.19. Brake pedal assembly

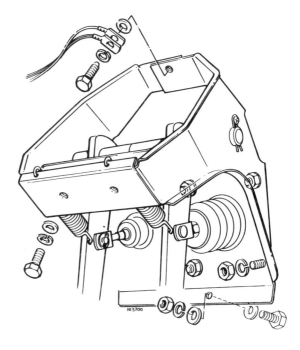

Fig. 9.20. Brake pedal support bracket and attachments

19 Refitting the valve is the reverse sequence to removal. It will be necessary to bleed the complete hydraulic system as described in Section 3.
20 The valve must now be reset. First apply the brake pedal hard and the warning light should go out, and stay out, even when the brake pedal is released.
21 Should the light not go out, the pressure in the system is unbalanced and the valve or the switch should be checked for correct operation. See also Section 3, paragraph 11.
22 If the brake failure warning light is off, check that the bulb is in order. Press the test-push and the light should glow.
23 Apply pressure to the brake pedal. The warning light will remain off if the hydraulic system is functioning satisfactorily and will come on to indicate hydraulic failure in one side of the system.

25 Brake pedal - removal and refitment

1 Undo and remove the three screws securing the parcel shelf on the driver's side. Lift away the parcel shelf.
2 Remove the spring clip securing the servo unit or master cylinder operating rod yoke to pedal clevis. Lift away the plain washer and withdraw the clevis pin.
3 Disconnect the column switch terminals. Release the steering column securing screws and support the column on the seat.
4 Disconnect the clutch and brake pedal return springs from the bracket. Note which way round the springs are fitted.
5 Undo and remove the self tapping screw and plain washer securing each spring clip to the pedal bracket.
6 Remove the spring clip on the other end of the pedal pivot pin.
7 Withdraw the pedal pivot pin as far as possible and allow the clutch pedal to hang on its pushrod.
8 The brake pedal assembly may now be lifted away.
9 Refitting the pedal to pedal bracket is the reverse sequence to removal. Lubricate the pivot pin with a little engine oil and the return springs with a little grease to ensure quiet operation.

26 Hydraulic pipes and hoses - general

1 Carefully examine all brake pipes/hoses, pipe hose connections and unions, periodically.
2 First examine for signs of leakage where the pipe unions occur. Then examine the flexible hoses for signs of chafing and fraying and, of course, leakage. This is only a preliminary part of the flexible hose inspection, as exterior condition does not necessarily indicate the interior condition, which will be considered later.
3 The steel pipes must be examined carefully and methodically. They must be cleaned off and examined for any signs of dents, corrosion or other damage and corrosion should be scraped off and, if the depth of pitting is significant, the pipes will need renewal. This is particularly likely in those areas underneath the car body where the pipes are exposed and unprotected.
4 If any section of pipe is to be taken off, first wipe and then remove the fluid reservoir cap and place a piece of polythene over the reservoir neck. Refit the cap, this will stop syphoning during subsequent operations.
5 Rigid pipe removal is usually quite straightforward. The unions at each end are undone, the pipe and union pulled out, and the centre sections of the pipe removed from the body clips. Where the pipes are exposed to full force of road and weather they can sometimes be very tight. As one can only use an open ended spanner and the unions are not large, burring of the flats is not uncommon when attempting to undo them. For this reason a self-locking grip wrench (mole) is often the only way to remove a stubborn union.
6 To remove a flexible hose, wipe the unions and bracket free from dust and undo the union nut from the metal pipe end.
7 Detach the hose from the bracket, be it either a clip or locknut.
8 The flexible hose may now be unscrewed from its attachment.
9 With the flexible hose removed, examine the internal bore. If it is blown through first, it should be possible to see through it. Any specks of rubber which come out, or signs of restriction in the bore, means that the rubber lining is breaking up and the pipe must be renewed.
10 Rigid pipes which need renewing can usually be purchased at any garage where they have the pipe, unions and special tools to make them up. All they need to know is the total length of the pipe, the type of flare at each end with the union, and the length and thread of the union.
11 Replacement of the pipe is a straightforward reversal of the removal procedure. If the rigid pipes have been made up it is best to get all the 'sets' (bends) in them before trying to install them. Also if there are any acute bends, as your supplier to put these in for you on a special tube bender, otherwise you may kink the pipe and thereby decrease the bore area and fluid flow.
12 With the pipes replaced, remove the polythene from the reservoir cap and bleed the system as described in Section 3.

27 Fault diagnosis - Braking system

Symptom	Reason/s	Remedy
PEDAL TRAVELS ALMOST TO THE FLOOR BEFORE BRAKES OPERATE		
	Brake fluid level too low	Top up master cylinder reservoir. Check for leaks.
	Wheel cylinder or caliper leaking	Dismantle wheel cylinder or caliper, clean and fit new rubbers and bleed brakes.
	Master cylinder leaking (Bubbles in master cylinder fluid)	Dismantle master cylinder, clean, and fit new rubbers. Bleed brakes.
	Brake flexible hose leaking	Examine and fit new hose if old hose leaking. Bleed brakes.
	Brake line fractured	Replace with new brake pipe. Bleed brakes.
	Brake system unions loose	Check all unions in brake system and tighten as necessary. Bleed brakes.
	Linings over 75% worn	Fit replacement shoes and brake linings.
	Drum brakes badly out of adjustment	Jack up car and adjust rear brakes.
BRAKE PEDAL FEELS SPRINGY		
	New linings not yet bedded-in	Use brakes gently until springy pedal feeling leaves.
	Brake drums or discs badly worn and weak or cracked	Fit new brake drums or discs.
	Master cylinder securing nuts loose	Tighten master cylinder securing nuts. Ensure spring washers are fitted.
BRAKE PEDAL FEELS SPONGY		
	Wheel cylinder or caliper leaking	Dismantle wheel cylinder or caliper, clean, fit new rubbers, and bleed brakes.
	Master cylinder leaking (Bubbles in master cylinder reservoir)	Dismantle master cylinder, clean, and fit new rubbers and bleed brakes. Replace cylinder if internal walls scored.
	Brake pipe line or flexible hose leaking	Fit new pipeline or hose.
	Unions in brake system loose	Examine for leaks, tighten as necessary.
BRAKES UNEVEN IN OPERATION — PULLING TO ONE SIDE		
	Linings and brake drums or discs contaminated with oil, grease, or hydraulic fluid	Ascertain and rectify source of leak, clean brake drums, fit new linings.
	Tyre pressures unequal	Check and inflate as necessary.
	Radial ply tyres fitted at one end of car only	Fit radial ply tyres of the same make to all four wheels.
	Brake backplate, caliper or disc loose	Tighten backplate, caliper or disc securing nuts and bolts.
	Brake shoes or pads fitted incorrectly	Remove and fit shoes or pads correct way round.
	Different type of linings fitted at each wheel	Fit the linings specified by the manufacturers all round.
	Anchorages for front or rear suspension loose	Tighten front and rear suspension pick-up points including spring locations.
	Brake drums or discs badly worn, cracked or distorted	Fit new brake drums or discs.
BRAKES TEND TO BIND, DRAG, OR LOCK-ON		
	Brake shoes adjusted too tightly	Slacken off rear brake shoe adjusters two clicks.
	Handbrake cable over-tightened	Slacken off handbrake cable adjustment.
	Reservoir vent hole in cap blocked with dirt	Clean and blow through hole.
	Master cylinder by-pass port restricted - brakes seize in 'on' position	Dismantle, clean, and overhaul master cylinder. Bleed brakes.
	Wheel cylinder seizes in 'on' position	Dismantle, clean and overhaul wheel cylinder. Bleed brakes.
	Rear brake shoe pull off springs broken, stretched or loose	Examine springs and replace if worn or loose.
	Rear brake shoe pull off springs fitted wrong way round, omitted, or wrong type used	Examine, and rectify as appropriate.
	Handbrake system rusted or seized in the 'on' position	Apply 'Plus Gas' to free, clean and lubricate.

Chapter 10 Electrical system

For modifications, and information applicable to later models, see Supplement at end of manual

Contents

Specifications

System	12 volt negative earth

Battery:

	A9	A11
Type	Lucas A9 or A11	
Capacity at 20 hour rate	40 amp/hr or 50 amp/hr.	
Charge rate	3.5 amps	5 amps
Maximum charge	3.6 amps	4.5 amps
Initial charge	2.5 amps	3 amps
Electrolyte to fill battery (per cell)	0.72 pint	0.91 pint

Alternator:

	Lucas 16 ACR	or 17 ACR
Type	Lucas 16 ACR	or 17 ACR
Output at 14V at 6000 rpm	34 amp	36 amp
Rotor winding resistance at 20° C (68° F)	3.3 ohm ± 5%	3.2 ohm ± 5%
Maximum permissible rotor speed	15000 rpm	15000 rpm
Brush length new	0.5 in. (12.6 mm)	0.5 in. (12.6 mm)
Brush spring tension	9 - 13 oz. f (255 - 368 gm. f)	9 - 13 oz. f (255 - 368 gm. f)

Starter motors:

Types	Lucas M35J inertia
	Lucas M35J pre-engaged
	Lucas 2M100 pre-engaged

Lucas M35J - Pre-engaged and inertia:

Brush spring tension	28 oz (0.8 kg)
Minimum brush length	3/8 in. (9.5 mm)
Minimum commutator thickness	0.08 in. (2.05 mm)
Lock torque	7 lb ft (0.97 kgm) with 350 to 375 amps
Torque at 1000 rpm	4.4 lb ft (0.61 kgm) with 260 to 275 amps
Light running current	65 amp at 8000 to 10000 rpm
Maximum armature end-float	0.010 in. (0.25 mm)
Solenoid:	
Closing (series) winding resistance	0.21 to 0.25 ohms
Hold-on (shunt) winding resistance	0.9 to 1.1 ohms

Lucas 2M100 - Pre-engaged:

Brush spring tension	36 oz (1.02 kg)
Minimum brush length	0.375 in. (9.5 mm)
Minimum commutator thickness	0.140 in. (3.5 mm)
Lock torque	14.4 lb ft (2.02 kgm) with 463 amps
Torque at 1000 rpm	7.3 lb ft (1.02 kgm) with 300 amps
Light running current	40 amp at 6000 rpm (approx)
Maximum armature end-float	0.010 in. (0.25 mm)
Solenoid:	
Closing (series) winding resistance	0.25 to 0.27 ohm
Hold on (shunt) winding resistance	0.76 to 0.80 ohm

Wiper motor:

Type	Lucas 14W two speed, self switching
Armature end-float	0.004 - 0.008 in. (0.1 - 0.2 mm)
Running current - light	1.5 amps at 13.5 volts
Resistance: armature winding	0.27 to 0.35 ohm at 16º C (60º F)
Brush length (minimum)	0.1875 in. (4.7625 mm)
Brush spring tension	5 to 7 oz. f (140 to 180 gm. f approx.)
Arm pressure on spring	11 to 13 oz. f (310 to 370 gm. f)

Horns:

Type	Lucas 9H or 6H
Maximum current consumption:	
6H	3 amps
9H	4 amps

Bulbs:

	Wattage
Headlight (UK and rhd - export) sealed beam	75/60
Headlight (lhd - except France) sealed beam	60/50
Headlight (France only) - renewable bulb	45/40
Sidelight	5
Flasher (front and rear)	21
Stop, tail light	5/21
Number plate light	5
Interior light	6
Panel and warning lights	2.2
Automatic transmission selector lever light (when fitted) ...	3
Brake warning light (tandem master cylinder)	1.5
Hazard warning light	2.2
Heated rear screen warning light	2

1 General description

The electrical system is of the 12 volt type and the major components comprise a 12 volt battery of which the negative terminal is earthed, a Lucas alternator which is fitted to the right-hand side of the engine - and is driven from the pulley on the front of the crankshaft, and a starter motor which is mounted on the front offside of the engine compartment.

The battery supplies a steady amount of current for the ignition, lighting and other electrical circuits, and provides a reserve of electricity when the current consumed by the electrical equipment exceeds that being produced by the alternator.

The battery is charged by a Lucas 16 or 17 ACR alternator (information will be found in Section 6).

When fitting electrical accessories to cars with a negative earth system it is important (if they contain silicon diodes or transistors) that they are connected correctly, otherwise serious damage to the component concerned may result. Items such as radios, tape recorders/players, electric tachometer, automatic dipping, parking lamp and anti-dazzle mirrors should be checked for correct polarity.

It is important that the battery leads are always disconnected if the battery is to be boost charged or if any body repairs are to be carried out, using electric arc welding equipment. Serious damage can be caused to the more delicate instruments, especiallly those containing semi-conductors.

Where the electrical systems of later models differ from the early ones, the information covering the later models and all Estate models will be found in Chapter 13.

2 Battery - removal and refitment

1 The battery is in a special carrier fitted on the right-hand wing valance of the engine compartment. It should be removed once every three months for cleaning and testing. Disconnect the negative (−) and then the positive (+) leads from the battery terminals by slackening the clamp retaining nuts and bolts or by unscrewing the retaining screws if terminal caps are fitted instead of clamps.
2 Unscrew the clamp bar retaining nuts, and lower the clamp bar to the side of the battery. Carefully lift the battery from its carrier. Hold the battery vertical to ensure that none of the electrolyte is spilled.
3 Replacement is a direct reversal of this procedure.
Note: Replace the positive lead before the negative and smear the terminals with petroleum jelly (Vaseline) to prevent corrosion. **Never** use ordinary grease as applied to other parts of the car.

3 Battery - maintenance and inspection

1 Normal weekly battery maintenance consists of checking the electrolyte level of each cell to ensure that the separators are covered by ¼ inch (6.3 mm) of electrolyte. If the level has fallen, top up the battery, using distilled water only. Do not overfill. If the battery is overfilled or any electrolyte spilled, immediately wipe away any excess as electrolyte attacks and corrodes any metal it comes into contact with very rapidly.
2 If the battery is of the Lucas 'Pacemaker' design a special topping up procedure is necessary as follows:
a) The electrolyte levels are visible through the translucent battery case or may be checked by fully raising the vent cover and tilting to one side. The electrolyte level in each cell must be kept such that the separator plates are just covered. To avoid flooding the battery must not be topped up within half an hour of it having been charged from any source other than from the generating system fitted to the car.
b) To top up the levels in each cell, raise the vent cover and pour distilled water into the trough until all the rectangular filling slots are full of distilled water and the bottom of the trough is just covered. Wipe the cover seating grooves dry and press firmly into position. The correct quantity of distilled water will automatically be distributed to each cell.
c) The vent must be kept closed at all times except when being topped up or taking specific gravity readings.
3 If the battery has the 'Auto-Fill' device fitted, a special sequence is required. The white balls in the 'Auto-Fill' battery are part of the automatic topping up device which ensures correct electrolyte level. The vent chamber should remain in position at all times except when topping up or taking specific gravity readings. If the electrolyte level in any of the cells is below the bottom of the filling tube top up as follows:
a) Lift off the vent chamber cover.
b) With the battery level, pour distilled water into the trough until all the filling tubes and trough are full.
c) Immediately replace the cover and allow the water in the trough and tubes to flow into the cells. Each cell will automatically receive the correct amount of water.
4 As well as keeping the terminals clean and covered with

petroleum jelly, the top of the battery, and especially the top of the cells should be kept clean and dry. This helps to prevent corrosion and ensure that the battery does not become partially discharged by leakage through dampness and dirt.
5 Inspect the battery securing nuts, battery clamp bar, tray and battery leads for corrosion (white fluffy deposits on the metal which are brittle to touch). If any corrosion is found, clean off the deposit with ammonia, and paint over the clean metal with an anti-rust, anti-acid paint.
6 At the same time inspect the battery case for cracks. If a crack is found, clean and plug it with one of the proprietary compounds marketed by such firms as Holts for this purpose. If leakage through a crack has been excessive then it will be necessary to refill the appropriate cell with fresh electrolyte as described later. Cracks are frequently caused at the top of the battery case by pouring in distilled water in the middle of winter **after** instead of **before** a run. This gives the water no chance to mix with the electrolyte and so the former freezes, expands and splits the battery case.
7 If topping up becomes excessive and the case has been inspected for cracks that could cause leakage, but none are found, the battery is being overcharged and the alternator control will have to be checked.
8 With the battery on the bench at the three monthly interval check, measure the specific gravity with a hydrometer to determine the state of charge and condition of the electrolyte. There should be very little variation between the different cells and, if a variation in excess of 0,025 is present, it will be due to either:
a) Loss of electrolyte from the battery at some time caused by spilling or a leak, resulting in a drop in the specific gravity of the electrolyte when the electrolyte was replaced with distilled water instead of fresh electrolyte.
b) An internal short circuit caused by buckling of the plates or similar malady pointing to the likelihood of total battery failure in the near future.
9 The specific gravity of the electrolyte for fully charged conditions at the electrolyte temperature indicated, is listed in table 'A'. The specific gravity of a fully discharged battery at different temperatures of the electolyte is given in table 'B'.

Table A
Specific gravity - battery fully charged
1.268 at 100°F or 38°C electrolyte temperature
1.272 at 90°F or 32°C electrolyte temperature
1.276 at 80°F or 27°C electrolyte temperature
1.280 at 70°F or 21°C electrolyte temperature
1.284 at 60°F or 16°C electrolyte temperature
1.288 at 50°F or 10°C electrolyte temperature
1.292 at 40°F or 4°C electrolyte temperature
1.296 at 30°F or -1.5°C electrolyte temperature

Table B
Specific gravity - battery fully discharged
1.098 at 100°F or 38°C electrolyte temperature
1.102 at 90°F or 32°C electrolyte temperature
1.106 at 80°F or 27°C electrolyte temperature
1.110 at 70°F or 21°C electrolyte temperature
1.114 at 60°F or 16°C electrolyte temperature
1.118 at 50°F or 10°C electrolyte temperature
1.122 at 40°F or 4°C electrolyte temperature
1.126 at 30°F or -1.5°C electrolyte temperature

4 Battery - electrolyte replenishment

1 If the battery is in a fully charged state and one of the cells maintains a specific gravity reading which is 0.025 or more lower than the others and a check of each cell has been made with a special cadmium rod type voltmeter to check for short circuits, then it is likely that electrolyte has been lost from the cell with the low reading at some time.
2 Top up the cell with a solution of 1 part sulphuric acid to

2.5 parts of water. If the cell is already fully topped up draw some electrolyte out with a pipette.

3 When mixing the sulphuric acid and water **never add water to sulphuric acid** - always pour the acid slowly onto the water in a glass container. **If water is added to sulphuric acid it will explode.**

4 Continue to top up the cell with the freshly made electrolyte and then recharge the battery and check the hydrometer readings.

5 Battery - charging

1 When heavy demand is placed upon the battery, such as when starting from cold, and much electrical equipment is continually in use, it is a good idea occasionally to have the battery fully charged from an external source at the rate of 3.5 to 4 amps.

2 Continue to charge the battery at this rate until no further rise in specific gravity is noted over a four hour period.

3 Alternatively, a trickle charger, charging at the rate of 1.5 amps can be safely used overnight.

4 Except for topping up, the vent on "Pacemaker" type batteries must be kept closed. The electrolyte will flood over if the cover is raised while the battery is being trickle or fast charged.

5 Fast charging must only be undertaken in extreme circumstances and must not exceed 40 amps for A9 batteries, or 50 amps for A11 batteries, for a maximum period of one hour.

6 When checking or testing a "Pacemaker" type battery, a single cell heavy duty discharge tester cannot be used.

7 Whilst charging a battery, the temperature of the electrolyte should never exceed 100°F.

6 Alternator - general description

The Lucas 16 or 17 ACR series alternator is fitted to models covered by this manual. The main advantage of the alternator over a dynamo lies in its ability to provide a high charge at low revolutions. Driving slowly in heavy traffic with a dynamo invariably means no charge is reaching the battery. In similar conditions even with the wipers, heater, lights and perhaps radio switched on, the alternator will ensure a charge reaches the battery.

An important feature of the alternator is a built in output control regulator, based on 'thick film' hybrid integrated micro - circuit technique, which results in the alternator being a self contained generating and control unit.

The system provides for direct connection of a charge light, and eliminates the need for a field switching relay and warning light control unit - necessary with former systems.

The alternator is of the rotating field ventilated design and comprises, principally, a laminated stator on which is wound a star connected 3 phase output winding, a twelve pole rotor carrying the field windings - each end of the rotor shaft runs in ball race bearings which are lubricated for life, natural finish diecast end brackets, incorporating the mounting lugs, a rectifier for converting the AC output of the machine to DC for battery charging, and an output control regulator.

The rotor is belt driven from the engine through a pulley to the rotor shaft, a pressed steel fan adjacent to the pulley draws cooling air through the alternator. This fan forms an integral part of the alternator specification. It has been designed to provide adequate air flow with a minimum of noise, and to withstand the high stresses associated with maximum speed. Rotation is clockwise viewed on the drive end. Maximum rectification of alternator output is achieved by six silicon diodes housed in a rectifier pack and connected as a 3 phase full wave bridge. The rectifier pack is attached to the outer face of the slip ring end bracket and contains also three 'field' diodes; at normal operating speeds, rectified current from the stator output windings flows through these diodes to

provide self excitation of the rotor field, via brushes bearing on face type slip rings.

The slip rings are carried on a small diameter moulded drum attached to the rotor shaft outboard of the rotor shaft axle, while the outer ring has a mean diameter of 0.75 inch (19.05 mm). By keeping the mean diameter of the slip rings to a minimum, relative speeds between brushes and rings, and hence wear, are also minimal. The slip rings are connected to the rotor field winding by wires carried in grooves in the rotor shaft.

The brush gear is housed in a moulding screwed to the outside of the slip ring end bracket. This moulding thus encloses the slip ring and brush gear assembly, and together with the shielded bearing, protects the assembly against entry of dust and moisture.

The regulator is set during manufacture and requires no further attention. Briefly the 'thick film' regulator comprises resistors and conductors screen printed onto a 1 inch (25.4 mm) square aluminuim substrate. Mounted on the substrate are Lucas semi-conductors consisting of three transistors, a voltage reference diode and a field rectification diode, and two capacitors. The internal connections between these components and the substrate are made by Lucas patented connectors. The whole assembly is 0.0625 inch (1.59 mm) thick and is housed in a recess in an aluminium heat sink, which is attached to the slip ring end bracket. Complete hermatic sealing is achieved by a silicon rubber encapsulent to provide environmental protection.

Electrical connections to external circuits are brought out to Lucas connector blades, these being grouped to accept a moulded connector socket which ensures correct connections.

7 Alternator - routine maintenance

1 The equipment has been designed for the minimum amount of maintenance in service, the only items subject to wear being the brushes and bearings.

2 Brushes should be examined after 60,000 miles (100, 000 km) and renewed if necessary. This is a job best left to the local BLMC garage or auto-electrical engineering works.

3 The bearings are pre-packed with grease for life, and should not require any further attention.

4 For full information on fan belt adjustment and alternator removal see Chapter 2.

8 Starter motor - general description

One of two types of starter motor is fitted to Allegro models covered by this manual depending on the date of manufacture, car specification and the destined market.

The starter motors are not interchangeable although they engage with a common flywheel starter ring gear. With the inertia type starter motor, the relay is fitted to the rear of the front grille, whereas the pre-engaged type has the solenoid on the top of the motor.

The principle of operation of the inertia type starter motor is as follows: When the ignition switch is turned, current flows from the battery to the starter motor solenoid switch which causes it to become energized. Its internal plunger moves inwards and closes an internal switch so allowing full starting current to flow from the battery to the starter motor. This causes a powerful magnetic field to be induced into the field coils which causes the armature to rotate.

Mounted on helical splines is the drive pinion which because of the sudden rotation of the armature, is thrown forwards along the armature shaft and so into engagement with the flywheel ring gear. The engine crankshaft will then be rotated until the engine starts to operate on its own and, at this point, the drive pinion is thrown out of mesh with the flywheel ring gear.

The pre-engaged starter motor operates by a slightly

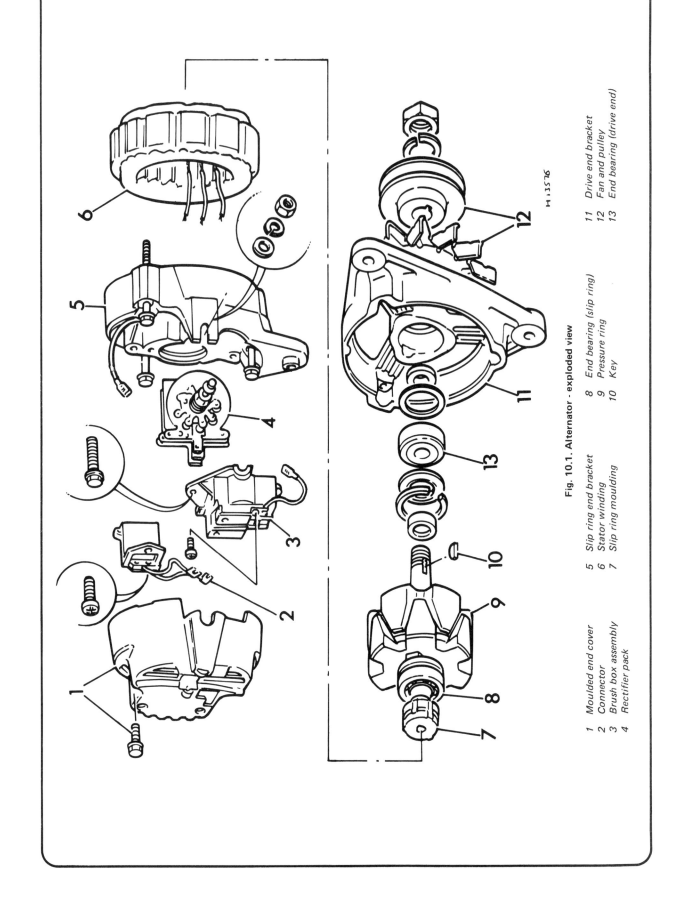

H.1576

Fig. 10.1. Alternator - exploded view

1 Moulded end cover
2 Connector
3 Brush box assembly
4 Rectifier pack

5 Slip ring end bracket
6 Stator winding
7 Slip ring moulding

8 End bearing (slip ring)
9 Pressure ring
10 Key

11 Drive end bracket
12 Fan and pulley
13 End bearing (drive end)

different method using end face commutator or brushes instead of brushes located on the side of the commutator.

The method of engagement on the pre-engaged starter differs considerably in that the drive pinion is brought into mesh with the starter ring gear before the main starter current is applied.

When the ignition is switched on, current flows from the battery to the solenoid which is mounted on the top of the starter motor body. The plunger in the solenoid moves inwards so causing a centrally pivoted engagement lever to move in such a manner that the forked end pushes the drive pinion into mesh with the starter ring gear. When the solenoid plunger reaches the end of its travel, it closes an internal contact and full starting current flows to the starter field coils. The armature is then able to rotate the crankshaft so starting the engine.

A special one way clutch is fitted to the starter drive pinion so that when the engine just fires and starts to operate on its own, it does not drive the starter motor.

9 Starter motor (M35J inertia) – testing on engine

1 If the starter motor fails to operate, then check the condition of the battery by turning on the headlamps. If they glow bright for several seconds and then gradually dim, the battery is in an uncharged condition.

2 If the headlamps continue to glow brightly and it is obvious that the battery is in good condition then check the tightness of the battery wiring connections (and in particular the earth lead from the battery terminal to its connection on the body-frame). Check the tightness of the connections at the relay switch and at the starter motor. Check the wiring with a voltmeter for breaks or shorts.

3 If the wiring is in order then check that the starter motor switch is operating. To do this, press the rubber covered button in the centre of the relay switch under the bonnet. If it is working, the starter motor will be heard to 'click' as it tries to rotate. Alternatively check it with a voltmeter.

4 If the battery is fully charged, the wiring in order, and the switch working but the starter motor fails to operate then it will have to be removed from the car for examination. Before this is done, however, ensure that the starter pinion has not jammed in mesh with the flywheel. Check by turning the square end of the armature shaft with a spanner. This will free the pinion if it is stuck in engagement with the flywheel teeth.

10 Starter motor (M35J - inertia) - removal and refitment

1 Disconnect the positive and then the negative terminals from the battery. Also disconnect the starter motor cable from the terminal on the starter motor end cover.

2 Undo and remove the two bolts which secure the starter

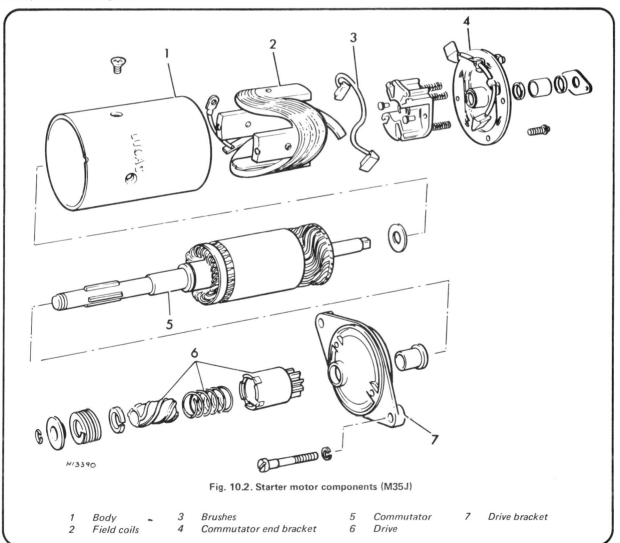

Fig. 10.2. Starter motor components (M35J)

1	Body	3	Brushes	5	Commutator	7	Drive bracket
2	Field coils	4	Commutator end bracket	6	Drive		

motor to the clutch and flywheel housing. Lift the starter motor away by manipulating the drive gear out from the ring gear area and then from the engine compartment.
3 Refitting is the reverse procedure to removal. Make sure that the starter motor cable, when secured in position by its terminal, does not touch any part of the body or power unit which could damage the insulation.

11 Starter motor (M35J - inertia) - dismantling and re-assembly

1 With the starter motor on the bench, first mark the relative positions of the starter motor body to the two end brackets.
2 Undo and remove the two screws and spring washers securing the drive end bracket to the body. The drive end bracket, complete with armature and drive, may now be drawn forwards from the starter motor body.
3 Lift away the thrust washer from the commutator end of the armature shaft.
4 Undo and remove the two screws securing the commutator end bracket to the starter motor body. The commutator end bracket may now be drawn back about an inch allowing sufficient access so as to disengage the field bushes from the bracket. Once these are free, the end bracket may now be completely removed.
5 With the motor stripped, the brushes and brush gear may be inspected. To check the brush spring tension, fit a new brush into each holder in turn and, using an accurate spring balance, push the brush on the balance tray until the brush protrudes approximately 0.0625 in (1.588 mm) from the holder. Make a note of the reading which should be approximately 28 ounces. If the spring pressures vary considerably the commutator end bracket must be renewed as a complete assembly.
6 Inspect the brushes for wear and fit a new brush which is nearing the minimum length of 0.375 in (9.525 mm). To renew the end bracket brushes, cut the brush cables from the terminal posts and, with a small file or hacksaw, slot the head of the terminal posts to a sufficient depth to accommodate the new leads. Solder the new brush leads to the posts.
7 To renew the field winding brushes, cut the brush leads approximately 0.25 in (6.35 mm) from the field winding junction and carefully solder the new brush leads to the remaining stumps, making sure that the insulation sleeves provide adequate cover.
8 If the commutator surface is dirty or blackened, clean with a petrol dampened rag. Carefully examine the commutator for signs of excessive wear, burning or pitting. If evident it may be reconditioned by having it skimmed at the local engineering works or BLMC garage, who will possess a centre lathe. The thickness of the commutator must not be less than 0.08 in (2.032 mm). For minor reconditioning, the commutator may be polished with glass paper, **Do not undercut the mica insulators between the commutator segments.**
9 With the starter motor dismantled, test the field coils for open circuit. Connect a 12 volt battery with a 12 volt bulb in one of the leads between each of the field brushes and a clean part of the body. The lamp will light if continuity is satisfactory between the brushes, windings and body connection.
10 Replacement of the field coils calls for the use of a wheel operated screwdriver, a soldering iron, caulking and riveting operations and is beyond the scope of the majority of owners. The starter motor body should be taken to an automobile electrical engineering works for new field coils to be fitted. Alternatively purchase an exchange Lucas starter motor.
11 Check the condition of the bushes and they should be renewed when they are sufficiently worn to allow visible side movement of the armature shaft.
12 To renew the commutator end bracket bush, drill out the rivets securing the brush box moulding and remove the moulding, bearing seal retaining plate and felt washer seal.
13 Screw in a ½ inch tap and withdraw the bush with the tap.
14 As the bush is of the phospher bronze type it is essential that it is allowed to stand in engine oil for at least 24 hours before fitment. Alternatively soak in oil at 100°C for 2 hours.
15 Using a suitable diameter drift, drive the new bush into position. Do not ream the bush as its self lubricating properties will be impaired.
16 To remove the drive end bracket bush it will be necessary to remove the drive gear as described in paragraphs 18 and 19.
17 Using a suitable diameter drift remove the old bush and fit a new one as described in paragraphs 14 and 15.
18 To dismantle the starter motor drive, first use a press to push the retainer clear of the circlip which can then be removed. Lift away the retainer and main spring.
19 Slide off the remaining parts with a rotary action of the armature shaft.
20 It is most important that the drive gear is completely free from oil, grease and dirt. With the drive gear removed, clean all parts thoroughly in paraffin. **Under no circumstances oil the drive components.** Lubrication of the drive components could easily cause the pinion to stick.
21 Re-assembly of the starter motor drive is the reverse sequence to dismantling. Use a press to compress the spring and retainer sufficiently to allow a new circlip to be fitted to its groove on the shaft. Remove the drive from the press.
22 Re-assembly of the starter motor is the reverse sequence to dismantling.

12 Starter motor (M35J pre-engaged) - testing on engine

The testing procedure is basically similar to the M35J inertia starter as described in Section 9. However, note the following instructions before removing the starter.

Ensure that the pinion gear has not jammed in mesh with the flywheel, due either to a broken solenoid spring, or dirty pinion gear splines. To release the pinion, engage low gear and, with the ignition switched off, rock the car backwards and forwards to release the pinion from mesh with the ring gear. If the pinion still remains jammed the starter motor must be removed for further examination.

When automatic transmission is fitted it will not be possible to rock the car to free the pinion gear.

13 Starter motor (M35J pre-engaged) - removal and refitment

1 Disconnect the positive and then the negative terminals from the battery.
2 Make a note of the electrical connections at the rear of the solenoid and disconnect the top heavy duty cable. Also release the two Lucar terminals situated below the heavy duty cable. There is no need to undo the lower heavy duty cable at the rear of the solenoid.
3 Undo and remove the two bolts which hold the starter motor in place and lift away upwards.
4 Replacement is a sttaightforward reversal of the removal sequence. Check that the electrical cable connections are clean and firmly attached to their respective terminals.

14 Starter motor (M35J pre-engaged) - dismantling and re-assembly

1 Detach the heavy duty cable, linking the solenoid "STA" terminal to the starter motor terminal, by undoing and removing the securing nuts and washers.
2 Undo and remove the two nuts and spring washers securing the solenoid to the drive end bracket.
3 Carefully withdraw the solenoid coil unit from the drive end bracket.
4 Lift off the solenoid plunger and return spring from the engagement lever.
5 Remove the rubber sealing block from the drive end bracket.

6 Remove the retaining ring (spire nut) from the engagement lever pivot pin and withdraw the pin.

7 Unscrew and remove the two drive end bracket securing nuts and spring washers and withdraw the bracket.

8 Lift away the engagement lever from the drive operating plate.

9 Extract the split pin from the end of the armature and remove the shim washers and thrust plate from the commutator end of the armature shaft.

10 Remove the armature, together with its internal thrust washer.

11 Withdraw the thrust washer from the armature.

12 Undo and remove the two screws securing the commutator end bracket to the starter motor body.

13 Carefully detach the end bracket from the yoke, at the same time disengaging the field brushes from the brush gear. Lift away the end bracket.

14 Move the thrust collar clear of the jump ring, and then remove the jump ring. Withdraw the drive assembly from the armature shaft.

15 Inspection and renovation is basically the same as for the Lucas M35J inertia starter motor and full information will be found in Section 11. The following additions necessitated by the fitting of the solenoid coil should be noted:

16 If a bush is worn, so allowing excessive side movement of the armature shaft, the bush must be renewed. Drift out the old bush with a piece of suitable diameter rod, preferably with a shoulder on it to stop the bush collapsing.

17 Soak a new bush in engine oil for 24 hours or if time does not permit, heat in an oil bath at 100°C for two hours prior to fitting.

18 As new bushes must not be reamed after fitting it must be pressed into position using a small mandrel of the same diameter as the bush and with a shoulder on it. Place the bush on the mandrel and press into position using a bench vice.

19 Use a test light and battery to test the continuity of the coil windings between terminal "STA" and a good earth point on the solenoid body. If the light fails to come on, the solenoid should be renewed.

20 To test the solenoid contacts for correct opening and closing, connect a 12 volt battery and a 60 watt test light between the main unmarked Lucar terminal and the "STA" terminal. The light should not come on.

21 Energise the solenoid with a separate 12 volt supply connected to the small unmarked Lucar terminal and good earth on the solenoid body.

22 As the coil is energised the solenoid should be heard to operate and the test lamp should light with full brilliance.

24 To fit a new set of contacts, first undo and remove the moulded cover securing screws.

25 Unsolder the coil connections from the cover terminals.

26 Lift away the cover and moving contact assembly.

27 Fit a new cover and moving contact assembly, soldering the connections to the cover terminals.

28 Refit the moulded cover securing screws.

29 Whilst the motor is apart, check the operation of the drive clutch. It must provide instantaneous take up of the drive in one direction and rotate easily and smoothly in the opposite direction.

30 Make sure that the drive moves smoothly on the armature shaft splines without binding or sticking.

31 Reassembly of the starter motor is the reverse sequence to dismantling. The following additional points should be noted:

32 When assembling the drive, always use a new retaining ring (spire nut) to secure the engagement lever pivot pin.

33 Make sure that the internal thrust washer is fitted to the commutator end of the armature shaft before the armature is fitted.

34 Make sure that the thrust washers and plate are assembled in the correct order and are prevented from rotating separately by engaging the collar pin with the locking piece on the thrust plate.

15 Starter motor (2M 100 pre-engaged) - testing on engine

The test procedure for this type of starter motor is basically identical to that for the Lucas M35J pre-engaged starter motor. Full information will be found in Section 12.

16 Starter motor (2M100 pre-engaged) - removal and refitment

The removal and refitting sequence for the type of starter motor is basically identical to that for the Lucas M35J pre-

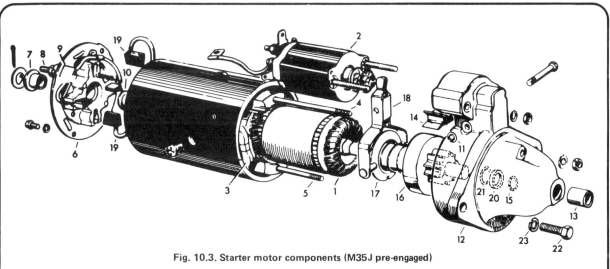

Fig. 10.3. Starter motor components (M35J pre-engaged)

1	Armature	7	Commutator end bracket bush	12	Drive end bracket
2	Solenoid			13	End bracket bush
3	Field coil	8	Field terminal	14	Grommet
4	Pole piece and long stud	9	Terminal insulating bush	15	Jump ring
5	Pole piece and short stud	10	Thrustplate	16	Roller clutch drive
6	Commutator end bracket	11	Pivot pin retaining clip	17	Bearing bush

18	Lever and pivot assembly
19	Brush
20	Thrust collar
21	Shim
22	Fixing bolt
23	Lockwasher

engaged starter motor. Full information will be found in Section 13.

17 Starter motor (2M100 pre-engaged) - dismantling and re-assembly

1 Undo and remove the nut and spring washer that secures the connecting link between the solenoid and starter motor at the solenoid "STA" terminal. Carefully ease the connecting link out of engagement of the terminal post on the solenoid.
2 Undo and remove the two nuts and spring washers that secure the solenoid to the drive end bracket.
3 Carefully ease the solenoid back from the drive end bracket, lift the solenoid plunger and return spring from the engagement lever, and completely remove the solenoid.
4 Recover the shaped rubber block that is placed between the solenoid and starter motor body.
5 Carefully remove the end cap seal from the commutator end cover.
6 Ease the armature shaft retaining ring (spire nut) from the armature shaft. **Note:** The retaining ring must not be re-used, but a new one obtained ready for fitting.
7 Undo and remove the two long through bolts and spring washers.
8 Detach the commutator end cover from the yoke, at the same time disengaging the field brushes from the brush box moulding.
9 Lift away the thrust washer from the armature shaft.

10 The starter motor body may now be lifted from the armature and drive end assembly.
11 Ease the retaining ring (spire nut) from the engagement lever pivot pin. **Note:** The retaining ring must not be re-used, but a new one obtained ready for fitting.
12 Using a parallel pin punch of suitable size, remove the pivot pin from the engagement lever and drive end bracket.
13 Carefully move the thrust collar clear of the jump ring, and slide the jump ring from the armature shaft.
14 Slide off the thrust collar, and finally remove the roller clutch drive and engagement lever assembly from the armature shaft.
15 For inspection and servicing information of the brush gear, commutator, and armature refer to Section 11, paragraphs 5 to 8 inclusive.
16 To test the field coils refer to Section 11, paragraphs 9 and 10.
17 Check the condition of the bushes and if they show signs of wear remove the old ones and fit new as described in Section 11, paragraphs 11 to 17. Disregard the reference in paragraph 16 to the removal of the drive gear as this will have already been done.
18 Whilst the motor is apart, check the operation of the drive clutch. It must provide instantaneous take up of the drive in one direction and rotate easily and smoothly in the opposite direction.
19 Make sure that the drive moves smoothly on the armature shaft splines without binding or sticking.
20 Reassembling the starter motor is the reverse sequence to

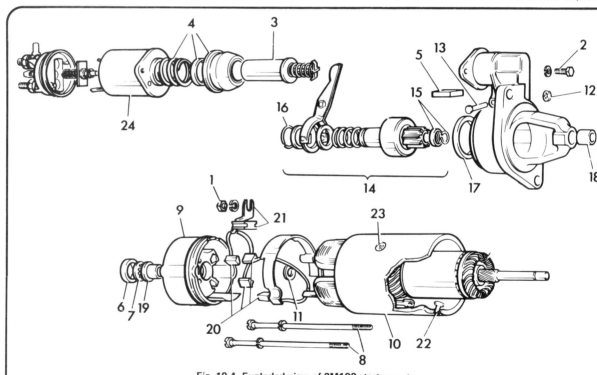

Fig. 10.4. Exploded view of 2M100 starter motor

1 Connecting link securing nut	8 Through bolts	18 Drive end bracket armature shaft brush
2 Solenoid to drive end bracket securing set-screw	9 Commutator end cover	19 Commutator end cover armature shaft bush
3 Solenoid plunger	10 Yoke	20 Field coil brushes
4 Solenoid plunger return spring, spring seat and dust excluder	11 Thrustwasher	21 Terminal and rubber grommet
5 Rubber grommet	12 Retaining ring (spire nut)	22 Rivet
6 Armature end cap seal	13 Engagement lever pivot pin	23 Pole shoe retaining screw
7 Armature shaft retaining ring (spire nut)	14 Armature and roller clutch drive assembly	24 Solenoid
	15 Thrust collar and jump ring	
	16 Spring ring	
	17 Dirt seal	

dismantling. The following additional points should be noted:

21 When assembling the drive end bracket always use a new retaining ring (spire nut) to secure the engagement lever pivot pin.

22 Make sure that the internal washer is fitted to the commutator end of the armature shaft before the armature end cover is fitted.

23 Always use a new retaining ring (spire nut) onto the armature shaft to a maximum clearance of 0.10 in (0.254 mm) between the retaining ring and the bearing brush shoulder. This will be the armature end float.

24 Tighten the through bolts to a torque wrench setting of 8 lb f ft (1.0 kg fm) and the nuts securing the solenoid to the drive bracket to 4.5 lb f ft (0.61 kg fm).

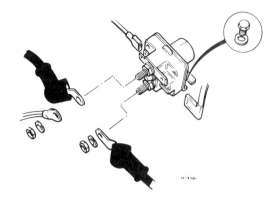

Fig. 10.5. Starter motor solenoid (Inèrtia)

18 Starter motor solenoid - removal and refitment

Inertia starter motor

1 For safety reasons, disconnect the battery.

2 Pull back the rubber covers and unscrew the terminal nuts. Detach the cables from the main terminals.

3 Disconnect the cables from the terminal blades on the solenoid.

4 Undo and remove the two screws securing the solenoid to the mounting bracket. Lift away the solenoid.

5 Refitting the solenoid is the reverse sequence to removal.

Pre-engaged starter motor

1 For safety reasons, disconnect the battery.

2 Undo and remove the terminal nut and detach the cables from the terminal post on the solenoid.

3 Disconnect the cables from the terminal blades on the solenoid.

4 Undo and remove the nut that secures the connecting link to the terminal "STA" on the solenoid.

5 Undo and remove the two nuts and bolts or set screws securing the solenoid to the drive end bracket. Lift away the solenoid.

6 Refitting the solenoid is the reverse sequence to removal.

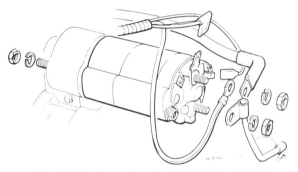

Fig. 10.6. Starter motor solenoid M35J pre-engaged

19 Starter solenoid relay - removal and refitment

1 For safety reasons, disconnect the battery.

2 Make a note of the location of the four cables and then disconnect from the solenoid relay.

3 Undo and remove the two screws securing the relay to the wing valance. Note that the earth cable is retained by one of the screws.

4 Lift away the solenoid relay.

5 Refitting the starter solenoid is the reverse sequence to removal.

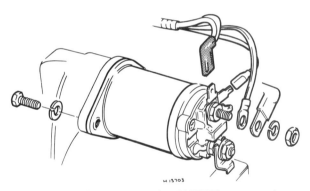

Fig. 10.7. Starter motor solenoid 2M100 pre-engaged

20 Flasher unit and circuit - fault tracing and rectification

The flasher unit is enclosed in a small metal container and is operated when the ignition is on by the composite switch mounted on the steering column.

If the flasher unit fails to operate, or works either very slowly or very rapidly, check out the flasher indicator circuit as described below, before assuming there is a fault in the unit itself.

1 Examine the direction indicator bulbs front and rear for broken filaments.

2 If the external flashers are working, but the internal flasher warning lights on one or both sides have ceased to function, check the filaments and replace as necessary (Section 37).

3 With the aid of the wiring diagram check all the flasher circuit if a flasher bulb is sound but does not work.

4 In the event of total indicator failure, check the "4-4 U" fuse.

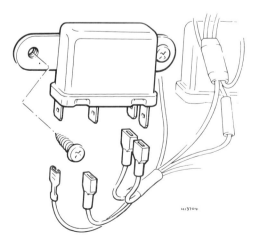

Fig. 10.8. Starter solenoid relay

5 With the ignition switched on, check that current is reaching the flasher unit by connecting a voltmeter between the "plus" or "B" terminal and the "L" terminal and operate the flasher switch. If the flasher bulb lights up the flasher unit itself is defective and must be replaced as it is not possible to dismantle and repair it. The flasher unit is located under the dashboard adjacent to the steering column (Rhd models).

21 Windscreen wiper arms - removal and refitment

1 Before removing a wiper arm, turn the windscreen wiper switch on and off to ensure the arms are in their normal parked position parallel with the bottom of the windscreen.
2 To remove the arm, pivot the arm bracket and pull the wiper arm head off the splined drive, at the same time easing back the clip with a screwdriver.
3 When replacing an arm, place it so it is in the correct relative parked position and then press the arm head onto the splined drive till the retaining clip clicks into place.

22 Windscreen wiper mechanism - fault diagnosis and rectification

Should the windscreen wiper fail, or work very slowly then check the terminals for loose connections, and make sure the insulation of the external wiring is not broken or damaged. If this is in order then check the current the motor is taking by connecting up a 0-20 ammeter in the circuit and turning on the wiper switch. Consumption should be 1.5 amp (low speed) and 2.5 amp (high speed).

If no current is passing check fuse "4-4U". If the fuse has blown, replace it after having checked the wiring of the motor and other electrical circuits serviced by this fuse for short circuits. If the fuse is in good condition, check the wiper switch.

If the wiper takes a very high current, check the wiper blades for freedom of movement. If this is satisfactory, check the gearbox cover and gear assembly for damage and measure the end float which should be between 0.002 to 0.008 in (0.05 to 0.2 mm). The end float is set by the thrust screw. Check that excessive friction in the cable connecting tubes, caused by too small a curvature, is not the cause of the high current consumption.

If the motor takes a very low current, ensure that the battery is fully charged. Check the brush gear, after removing the commutator end bracket, and ensure that the brushes are free to move. If necessary, renew the tension spring. If the brushes are very worn they should be replaced with new ones. The armature may be checked by substitution.

23 Windscreen wiper blades - changing wipers arc

If it is wished to change the area through which the wiper blades move, this is simply done by removing each arm in turn from each splined drive, and then replacing it on the drive in a slightly different position.

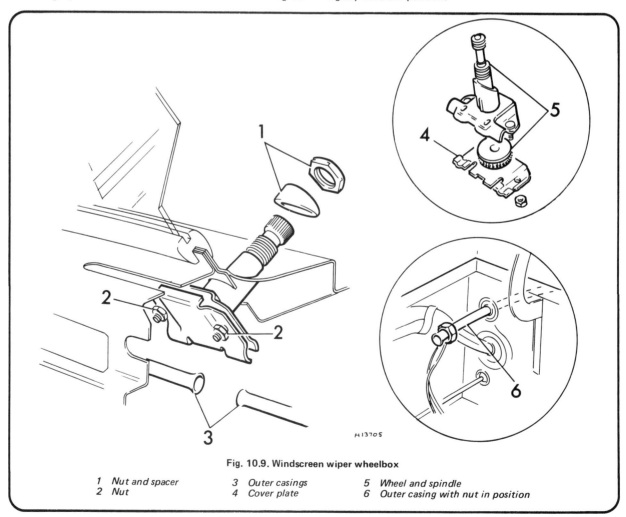

H13705

Fig. 10.9. Windscreen wiper wheelbox

1	Nut and spacer	3	Outer casings	5	Wheel and spindle
2	Nut	4	Cover plate	6	Outer casing with nut in position

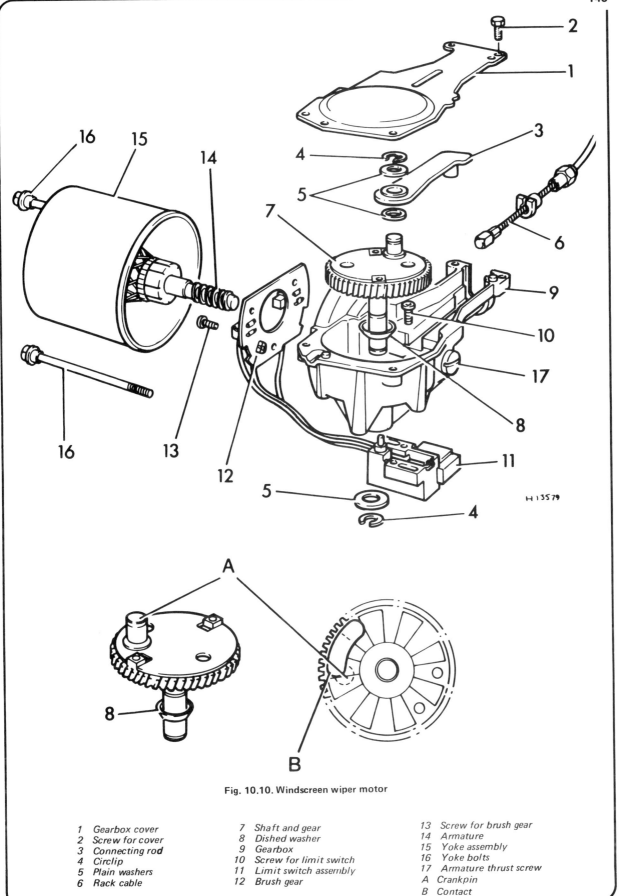

H 13579

Fig. 10.10. Windscreen wiper motor

1   Gearbox cover
2   Screw for cover
3   Connecting rod
4   Circlip
5   Plain washers
6   Rack cable

7   Shaft and gear
8   Dished washer
9   Gearbox
10   Screw for limit switch
11   Limit switch assembly
12   Brush gear

13   Screw for brush gear
14   Armature
15   Yoke assembly
16   Yoke bolts
17   Armature thrust screw
A   Crankpin
B   Contact

24 Windscreen wiper motor and drive - removal and refitment

1 For safety reasons, disconnect the battery.
2 Refer to Section 21 and remove the wiper arms.
3 Disconnect the multi-pin terminal connector from the windscreen wiper motor body.
4 Unscrew the outer casing retaining nut from the motor ferrule. Slide the nut down the cable tube.
5 Undo and remove the motor strap securing screws and plain washers. Lift away the strap and mounting pad.
6 The motor assembly complete with rack cable may now be drawn from the engine compartment.
7 Refitting the wiper motor and rack cable is the reverse sequence to removal but the following additional points should be noted:
a) Smear the cable rack with a little Ragosine Listate Grease.
b) Carefully push the cable rack into the outer casing ensuring the rack engages with the wheelbox gear teeth. The rack must not be buckled or kinked.

25 Windscreen wiper motor, drive and wheelboxes - removal and replacement

1 Refer to Section 24 and remove the windscreen wiper motor and drive rack.
2 Refer to Chapter 12 and remove the facia panel.
3 Disconnect the demister hoses and remove the demister ducts.
4 Undo and remove the screw that secures each demister duct and carefully withdraw the demister ducts.
5 Undo and remove the retaining nut and remove the spacer from each wheelbox.
6 Unscrew but do not completely remove the nuts clamping the wheelbox halves (plates) together.
7 The rack outer casing may now be removed from the wheelboxes.
8 The two wheelbox assemblies may now be removed from their locations into the top panel.
9 If necessary remove the cover plate.
10 Wash the wheelbox components in paraffin and wipe dry.
11 Inspect the condition of the wheel teeth and cable rack. If signs of wear are evident new parts should be obtained.
12 To refit first grease the wheels and spindles with a little Ragosine Listate Grease and then refit the wheelboxes to the top panel.
13 Carefully align the outer casings and tighten the wheelbox covers.
14 It is important that the motor to wheelbase rack outer casing is positioned correctly and is not kinked or flattened. To ensure free rack movement the radius of the outer casing must not be less than 9 in (23 cm).
15 Should excessive friction be suspected remove the rack cable from the motor and insert into the outer casing. Using a pull type spring scale test the pull required to draw the cable rack from the casing and wheelbase. This must not exceed 6 lb f (2.7 kg f).
16 Refitting is now the reverse sequence to removal.

26 Windscreen wiper motor - dismantling, inspection and re-assembly

1 Refer to Fig. 10.10 and remove the four gearbox cover retaining screws and lift away the cover. Release the circlip and flat washer securing the connecting rod to the crankpin on the shaft and gear. Lift away the connecting rod followed by the second flat washer.
2 Release the circlip and washer securing the shaft and gear to the gearbox body.

3 De-burr the gear shaft and lift away the gear making a careful note of the location of the dished washer.
4 Scribe a mark on the yoke assembly and gearbox to ensure correct reassembly and unscrew the two yoke bolts from the motor yoke assembly. Part the yoke assembly including armature from the gearbox body. As the yoke assembly has residual magnetism ensure that the yoke is kept well away from metallic dust.
5 Unscrew the two screws securing the brush gear and the terminal and switch assembly and remove both the assemblies.
6 Inspect the brushes for signs of excessive wear. If the main brushes are worn to a limit of 0.1875 in (4.763 mm) or the narrow section of the third brush is worn to the full width of the brush fit a new brush gear assembly. Ensure that the three brushes move freely in their boxes. If a push type spring gauge is available, check the spring rate which should be between 5 to 7 oz. f (140-200 g.f) when the bottom of the brush is level with the bottom of the slot in the brush box. Again, if the spring rate is incorrect, fit a new brush gear assembly.
7 If the armature is suspect take it to an automobile electrician to test for open or short circuiting.
8 Inspect the gear wheel for signs of excessive wear or damage and fit a new one if necessary.
9 Reassembly is the reverse procedure to dismantling but there are several points that require special attention.
10 Use only Ragosine Listate grease to lubricate the gear wheel teeth and cam, the armature shaft worm gear, connecting rod and its connecting pin, the cross head slide and cable rack and wheelbox gear wheels.
11 Use only ''Shell Turbo 41'' oil to lubricate the bearing bushes, the armature shaft bearing journals (sparingly), the gear wheel shaft and crankpin, the felt washer in the yoke bearing (thoroughly soak) and the wheelbox spindles.
12 The yoke assembly fixing bolts should be tightened using a torque wrench set to 14 lb f ft (0.16 kg fm).
13 When a replacement armature is to be fitted, slacken the thrust screw so as to provide end float for fitting the yoke.
14 The thrust disc inside the yoke bearing should be fitted with the concave side towards the end face of the bearing. The dished washer fitted beneath the gear wheel should have its concave side towards the gear wheels as shown in Fig. 10.10.
15 The larger of the two flat washers is fitted underneath the connecting rod and the smaller one on top, under the retaining circlip.
16 To adjust the armature end float, tighten the thrust screw and then turn back one quarter of a turn so giving an end float of between 0.004 and 0.008 in (0.05 - 0.2 mm). The gap should be measured under the head of the thrust screw. Fit a shim of suitable size beneath the head, and tighten the screw.

27 Windscreen washer jet and pump - removal and refitment

Washer jet
1 Using a knife carefully lift the lip of the jet and prise the jet out of the body.
2 Disconnect the tube from the jet. Take care not to break the jet union.
3 Refitting the washer jet is the reverse sequence to removal.

Washer pump
1 For safety reasons disconnect the battery.
2 Make a note of the electrical connections to the pump and detach the two terminal connectors.
3 Disconnect the two plastic tubes from the pump.
4 Undo and remove the two screws that secure the pump to the bulkhead. Lift away the pump.
5 If the pump should prove to be faulty, it will have to be renewed as it is a sealed unit and individual parts are not available.
6 Refitting the washer pump is the reverse sequence to removal.

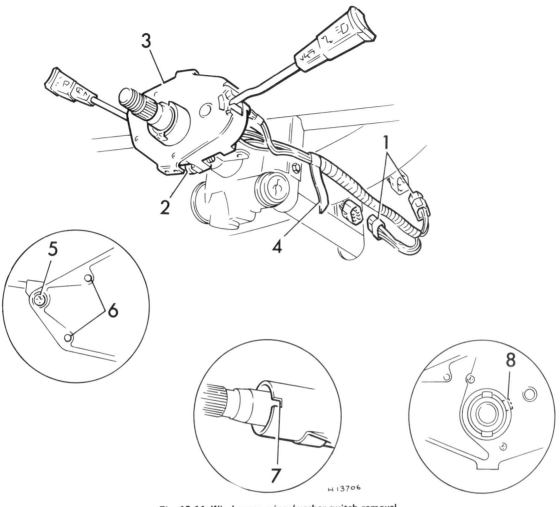

Fig. 10.11. Windscreen wiper/washer switch removal

1 Multi pin connectors	4 Electrical tape	7 Outer column slot
2 Switch clamp screw	5 Screw	8 Alignment of striker dog
3 Switch assembly	6 Rivets	

28 Windscreen wiper/washer switch - removal and refitment

1 For safety reasons disconnect the battery.
2 Refer to Chapter 11 and remove the steering wheel.
3 Locate the two multi-pin connectors under the facia adjacent to the steering column and disconnect the two multi-pin connectors.
4 Undo but do not remove the switch clamp screw located under the mounting plate.
5 The switch assembly may now be lifted from the end of the steering column.
6 Remove the plastic harness tape and separate the electric leads for the two switches.
7 Carefully drill out the two rivets securing the windscreen wiper/washer switch to the mounting plate.
8 Undo and remove the screw securing the windscreen wiper/washer switch to the mounting plate.
9 Refitting the windscreen wiper/washer switch is the reverse sequence to removal. Care must be taken to ensure that the lug on the inner diameter of the switch locates in the slot in the steering outer column. Also the striker dog on the nylon switch centre must be in line with and towards the direction indicator switch stalk.

29 Horn - fault tracing and rectification

1 If a horn works badly or fails completely, first check the wiring leading to it for short circuits and loose connections. Also check that the horn is firmly secured and that there is nothing lying on the horn body.
2 The horn should never be dismantled, but it is possible to adjust it. This adjustment is to compensate for wear of the moving parts only and will not affect the tone. To adjust the horn proceed as follows:
a) On either the Lucas 9H or 6H models there is a small adjustment screw on the broad rim of the horn nearly opposite the two terminals. Do not confuse this with the large screw in the centre.
b) Turn the adjustment screw anticlockwise until the horns just fail to sound. Then turn the screw a quarter of a turn clockwise which is the optimum setting.
c) It is recommended that if the horn has to be reset in the car, the fuse 1-1U should be removed and replaced with a piece of wire, otherwise the fuse will continually blow due to the continuous high current required for the horn in continual operation.
d) With twin horns, the horn which is not being adjusted

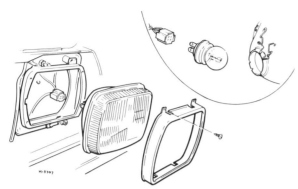

Fig. 10.12. Headlight assembly
*Inset shows alternative pre-focus bulb used for
export models*

should be disconnected while adjustment of the other takes
place.

30 Headlight unit - removal and refitment

1 For safety reasons disconnect the battery.
2 Refer to Chapter 12 and remove the radiator grille .
3 Locate and disconnect the cable adaptor from the terminal
blades at the rear of the sealed beam light unit.
4 Undo and remove the three screws securing the light unit
rim to the backplate.
5 Lift away the rim and sealed beam light unit.
6 Should it be necessary to remove the backplate drill out
the four 'pop' rivets. Lift away the backplate.
7 Reassembly and refitting the headlight unit is the reverse
sequence to removal. It is permissible to use self tapping
screws instead of rivets to secure the backplate to the front
panel. Reset the headlight alignment as described in Section
31.

Headlight bulb

On some models a pre-focus bulb is used instead of a sealed
beam unit. To renew the bulb and reflector proceed as
follows:
1 For safety reasons, disconnect the battery.
2 Refer to Chapter 12 and remove the radiator grille.
3 Locate and disconnect the cable adaptor from the terminal
blades at the rear of the bulb.
4 To remove the bulb release the spring clip and withdraw
the bulb.
5 Undo and remove the three screws securing the reflector
rim to the backplate.
6 The combined reflector and lens may now be lifted away.
Check that the fan anti-rattle rubbers are correctly located in
the backplate.
7 Should it be necessary to remove the backplate drill out
the fan 'pop' rivets. Lift away the backplate.
8 Re-assembly and refitting the headlight reflector and lens
and bulb is the reverse sequence to removal. It is permissible
to use self-tapping screws instead of rivets to secure the
backplate to the front panel. Reset the headlight alignment as
described in Section 31.

31 Headlight beam - adjustment

The headlights may be adjusted for both vertical and
horizontal beam position by the two screws located as shown
in Fig. 10.13.
They should be set so that on full or high beam, the beams
are set slightly below parallel with a level road surface. Do not

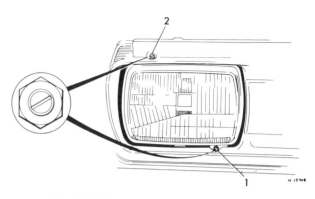

Fig. 10.13. Headlight beam adjustment points

1   Vertical adjustment   2   Horizontal adjustment

forget that the beam position is affected by how the car is
normally loaded for night driving and set the beams loaded to
this condition. Before adjustment is commenced check that the
tyre pressures are correct.
Although this adjustment can be approximately set at home
using a vertical wall it is recommended that this be left to the
local garage who will have the necessary optical equipment to
do the job more accurately.

32 Front, side and flasher light bulb - removal and refitment

1 Undo and remove the three screws and sealing washers
securing the lens to the light body. Lift away the lens.
2 To remove either bulb push the bulb in and turn anti-
clockwise to release the bayonet fitting.
3 Should it be necessary to remove the light body disconnect
the light cables from the wiring harness snap connectors inside
the front wings. Note the connections to ensure correct refitment.
4 Undo and remove the four nuts and distance pieces
securing the light body to the front wing.
5 Lift away the light body and gasket.
6 Refitting the light body and bulb is the reverse sequence to
removal.

33 Rear stop, tail and flasher light bulbs - removal and re-fitment

1 Working inside the luggage compartment pull the bulb
holder from the rear of the light body.
2 To remove the bulb push the bulb in and turn anti-
clockwise to release the bayonet fitting.
3 Should it be necessary to remove the complete assembly
make a note of the terminal blade connectors to the bulb
holders and detach.
4 Undo and remove the four nuts securing the light body to
the rear wing.
5 Lift away the light body and gasket.
6 If the lenses are to be renewed it is necessary to remove
the light body and then working from the rear undo and
remove the four screws securing the two lenses to the body.
7 Re-assembly and refitting is the reverse sequence to
removal. Note that the lugs in the bulb holder apertures in the
light body prevent the bulb holder from being fitted incorrectly.

34 Number plate light bulb - removal and refitment

1 Push in and turn the light lens 90° in either direction to
release it from the light body.

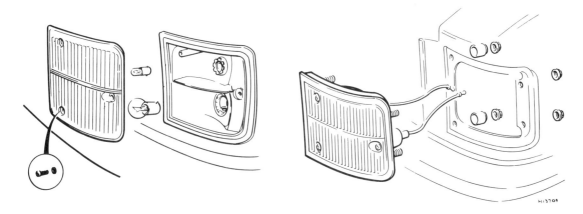

Fig. 10.14. Front, side and flasher light assembly

(left)   Bulb renewal   (right)   Light assembly removal

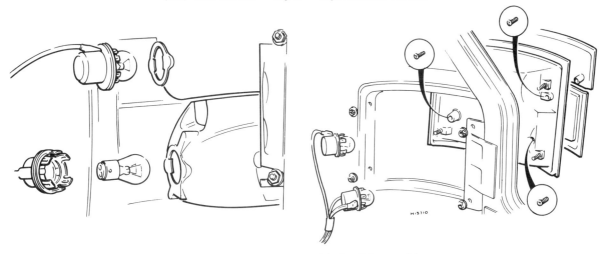

Fig. 10.15. Rear stop, tail and flasher light assembly

(left)   Bulb renewal   (right)   Light assembly removal

2   The capless bulb may now be pulled from the light body.
3   Should it be necessary to remove the light assembly first detach the cable at the snap connector located inside the luggage compartment.
4   Undo and remove the two screws and plain washers securing the light body to its mounting bracket.
5   Lift away the light assembly.
6   Refitting the light assembly and bulb is the reverse sequence to removal.

35 Reverse light bulb - removal and refitment

1   Undo and remove the two screws, clips and rubber pads securing the lens to the body. Lift away the lens.
2   The festoon bulb may now be unclipped from the spring contacts.
3   Should it be necessary to remove the reverse light assembly first detach the cable from the wiring harness located in the luggage compartment.
4   Undo and remove the two nuts securing the light assembly to the body.
5   The light assembly may now be detached from the body.
6   Refitting the light assembly and bulb is the reverse sequence to removal.

36 Interior light and luggage compartment light bulb - removal and refitment

Interior light

1   Carefully, and lightly, press together the upper and lower surface of the lens to release it from the light body. Lift away the lens.
2   The festoon bulb may now be unclipped from the spring contacts.
3   Should it be necessary to remove the interior light assembly disconnect the battery for safety reasons and then undo and remove the two screws securing the light body to the roof.
4   Make a note of the two cable connections and detach from the light body.
5   Refitting the light body and lens is the reverse sequence to removal.

Luggage compartment light

1   Undo and remove the two screws securing the light assembly to the boot interior.
2   The festoon bulb may now be unclipped from the spring contacts.
3   Should it be necessary to remove the light assembly disconnect the battery for safety reasons.

4 Make a note of the two cable connections and detach from the light assembly.

5 Refitting the bulb and light assembly is the reverse sequence to removal.

---

37 Warning and illumination bulb - removal and refitment

Panel light

1 For safety reasons, disconnect the battery.

2 Carefully pull off the instrument panel front casing from the four retaining clips in the instrument rear casing.

3 Undo and remove the four screws securing the instrument pack to the instrument rear casing. Pull the instrument pack from the facia.

4 Press the release lever on the speedometer cable connector and disconnect the speedometer cable from the rear of the instrument.

5 Pull out the relevant bulb holder from the rear of the instrument panel.

6 The capless bulb may now be pulled out from the bulb holder.

7 Refitting the bulb and instrument pack is the reverse sequence to removal.

Automatic transmission selector light

1 For safety reasons, disconnect the battery.

2 Remove the selector lever knob and locknut.

3 The nacelle may next be pulled from the selector mechanism.

4 Partially raise the light body located in the rear end of the change speed gate and withdraw the bulb holder from the light body.

5 Move the selector lever rearwards and withdraw the bulb holder from the slide light body.

6 The bulb may now be lifted away from the bulb holder.

7 Refitting the bulb and holder is the reverse sequence to removal.

Hazard warning light

1 Working behind the heater cover carefully press out the hazard warning light.

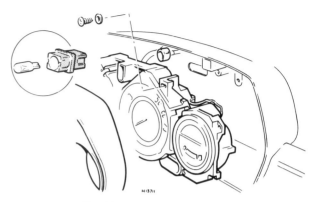

Fig. 10.16. Panel light bulb renewal
Inset shows bulb and holder

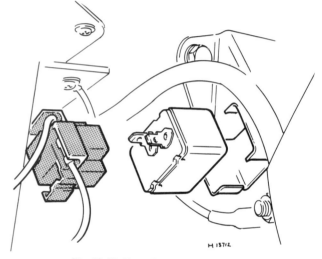

Fig. 10.17. Hazard warning flasher unit

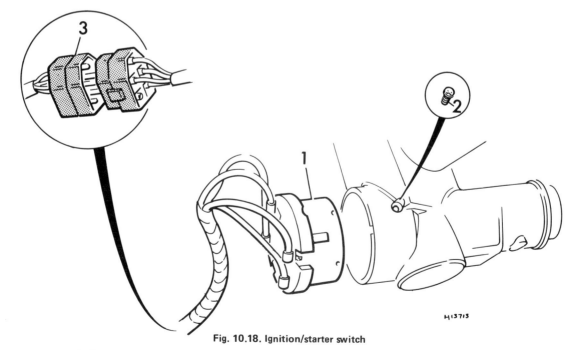

Fig. 10.18. Ignition/starter switch

1 Switch assembly   *2 Switch securing screw*   *3 Multi pin connector*

2 The bulb holder may now be removed from the warning light.
3 Lift away the bulb from the holder.
4 Refitting the bulb and holder is the reverse sequence to removal.

38 Flasher unit (hazard warning) - removal and refitment

1 For safety reasons, disconnect the battery.
2 Pull the flasher unit from its holder which is mounted on the left-hand side of the steering column mounting bracket.
3 Note the two electrical cable connections and detach from the flasher unit.
4 Refitting the flasher unit is the reverse sequence to removal.

39 Switches (general) - removal and refitment

Ignition/starter switch
1 For safety reasons, disconnect the battery.
2 Refer to Chapter 11, and remove the steering column cowl.
3 Locate the multi-pin connector for the switch cables and detach at the harness.
4 Undo and remove the screw that retains the switch in the lock housing.
5 The switch assembly may now be detached.
6 Refitting the ignition/starter switch is the reverse sequence to removal. Ensure that the locating peg on the switch registers in the groove in the lock housing.

Lighting switch
1 For safety reasons disconnect the battery.
2 Undo and remove the four screws and washers that secure the heater cover. Lift away the heater cover.
3 Note the electrical cable connections at the rear of the switch and detach the cables.
4 Depress the two 'catches' on the switch body inwards and remove from the heater cover.

5 Refitting the lighting switch is the reverse sequence to removal.

Door pillar switch
1 Undo and remove the two screws that secure the switch to the door pillar.
2 Draw the switch from the door pillar and detach the cable from the rear of the switch.
3 Take care that the cable does not 'disappear' into the switch aperture.

Luggage compartment switch
1 Detach the cable at the rear of the switch.
2 Undo and remove the screw, plain and spring washers securing the switch mounting bracket to the body.
3 To detach the switch from its mounting bracket drill out the 'pop' rivet.
4 Refitting the luggage compartment switch is the reverse sequence to removal. If a 'pop' rivet is not available use a small nut and bolt.

Heated rear screen switch
1 For safety reasons disconnect the battery.
2 Undo and remove the two screws securing the heater cover to the facia.
3 Detach the bulb holder from the rear of the switch.
4 Make a note of the electric cable connections at the rear of the switch and detach.
5 Depress the two 'catches' on the switch body inwards and remove from the heater cover.
6 Refitting the heated rear screen switch is the reverse sequence to removal.

Hazard warning switch
1 For safety reasons disconnect the battery.
2 Carefully reach behind the heater cover and press out the hazard warning switch.
3 Make a note of the electric cable connections at the rear of the switch and detach.
4 Refitting the hazard warning switch is the reverse sequence to removal.

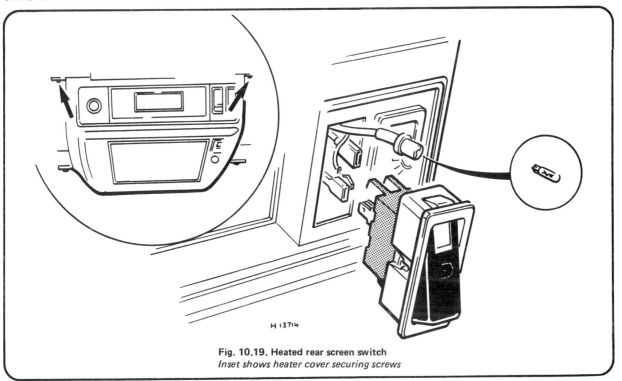

H 13714

Fig. 10.19. Heated rear screen switch
Inset shows heater cover securing screws

Stop light switch

1   For safety reasons disconnect the battery.
2   Undo and remove the screws and spring washers securing the driver's side parcel tray. Lift away the parcel tray.
3   Make a note of the electric cable connections at the rear of the switch and detach.
4   Undo and remove the outer locknut and withdraw the switch from its mounting bracket.
5   Refitting the stop light switch is the reverse sequence to removal. It must however be adjusted as described in the following paragraphs.
6   Refit the switch to its mounting bracket until the contacts are just open. Tighten the locknut. This position is best obtained using a test light and battery between the switch terminal blades.
7   Now slacken the inner locknut half a turn and tighten the outer locknut.

Headlight dip/flasher and horn switch

Full information will be found in Section 28.

---

40 Fuses - general

The main fuses are mounted in block form and located on the right-hand side of the bulkhead in the engine compartment. If any of the fuses blow due to a short circuit or similar trouble, trace the source of trouble and rectify before fitting a new fuse. The layout is shown in Fig. 10.20.
1 - 1U (Fuse rating 35 amp) The units protected by this fuse are:
  Interior light
  Horn
  Cigar lighter (if fitted)
  Split brake test switch and warning light (if fitted)
  Cooling fan motor and relay.
2 - 2U (Fuse rating 15 amp) rhd models:
  All side, tail, panel and number plate lights.
  Lhd models only:
  All side, tail, panel and number plate lights fitted to the right-hand side of the car.
3 - 3U (Fuse rating 15 amp) lhd models only
  All side, tail, panel and number plate lights fitted to the left-hand side of the car. It is not used on rhd models.
4 - 4U (Fuse rating 35 amp) The following units protected by this fuse operate only when the ignition is switched on. Fit all accessories to this fuse.
  Windscreen wiper/washer switch
  Windscreen wiper motor
  Windscreen washer motor
  Flasher unit and flasher lights
  Stop lights
  Cooling fan relay and thermostat
  Automatic transmission gear quadrant light (if fitted)
  Heated rear screen and switch
5 - 5U (Fuse rating 15 amp) Heater motor and switch
Spare fuses:
  Two spare fuses are fitted to the centre of the fuse block.
Line fuses:
  A line fuse is often fitted to protect individual units such as radio sets. Access to the fuse is gained by holding one end of the cylindrical tube, pushing in and twisting the other end. The fuse may be lifted out.

---

41 Instrument testing

The bi-metallic resistance equipment for the fuel and thermal type temperature gauges comprises an indicator head and transmitter with the unit connected to a common voltage stabilizer. This item is fitted because the method of operation of the equipment is voltage sensitive, and a voltage stabilizer is necessary to ensure a constant voltage supply at all times.

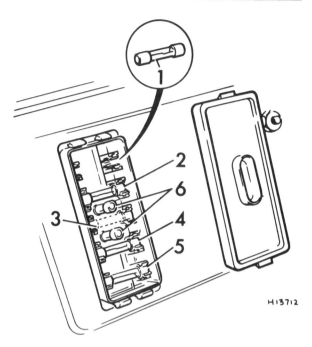

Fig. 10.20. Fuse box layout
(See text for fuse identification)

Special test equipment is necessary when checking correct operation of the voltage stabilizer, fuel gauge and temperature gauge so, if a fault is suspected, the car must be taken to the local BLMC garage who will have this equipment.

There are, however, several initial checks that can be carried out without this equipment and these are described in Chapter 2 and 3.

---

42 Printed circuit - removal and refitment

1   For safety reasons disconnect the battery.
2   Rhd models only. Release the clip that secures the speedometer cable to the bulkhead.
3   Carefully pull off the instrument panel front casing. It is held in position by four clips.
4   Undo and remove the four self tapping screws and plain washers that secure the instrument pack to the instrument rear casing. Pull the instrument pack from the facia.
5   Press the release lever on the speedometer cable connector and disconnect the speedometer cable from the rear of the instrument.
6   Depress the retainer and withdraw the cable multi-pin connector. The instrument pack may now be removed from the car.
7   Pull out the voltage stabilizer.
8   Undo and remove the self tapping screws and lift away the voltage stabilizer connectors.
9   Next remove the panel and warning light bulb holders.
10 Undo and remove the four dowel nuts and wave washers that secure the temperature and fuel gauges to the rear of the pack.
11 Carefully withdraw the printed circuit plastic retaining pegs and carefully lift away the printed circuit.
12 Refitting the printed circuit is the reverse sequence to removal.

---

43 Voltage stabilizer - removal and refitment

1   The voltage stabilizer is a push fit into the rear of the instrument panel printed circuit.

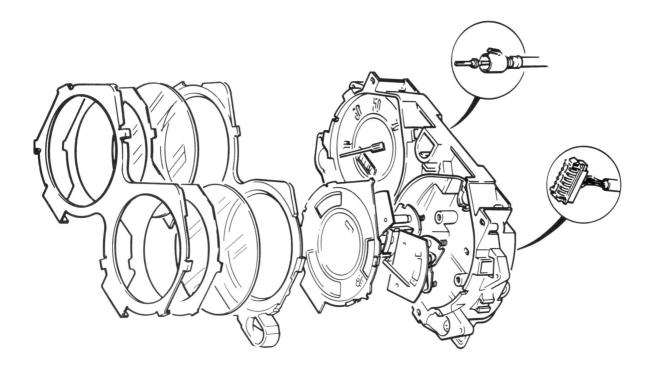

Fig. 10.21. Exploded view of twin pack gauges

2 To remove the unit refer to Section 42 and follow the instructions given in paragraphs 1 to 7 inclusive.
3 Refitting the voltage stabilizer and instrument pack is the reverse sequence to removal.

44 Temperature and fuel gauges - removal and refitment

Temperature gauge
1 Refer to Section 42 and follow the instructions given in paragraphs 1 to 6 inclusive.
2 Carefully prise back the tabs and lift away the instrument bezel and joint washer.
3 Lift away the glasses and instrument cover.
4 Undo and remove the two dowel nuts and wave washers securing the temperature gauge to the pack.
5 Lift away the temperature gauge.
6 Refitting the temperature gauge and instrument pack is the reverse sequence to removal.
   The sequence for removal of the fuel gauge is basically identical to that for the temperature gauge.

45 Speedometer head - removal and refitment

1 Refer to Section 42 and follow the instructions given in paragraphs 1 to 6 inclusive.
2 Carefully prise the tabs and lift away the instrument bezel and joint washer.
3 Lift away the glasses and instrument cover.
4 Undo and remove the two screws that secure the speedometer to the instrument pack.
5 Lift away the speedometer head noting the location of the grommet and ferrules.

6 Refitting the speedometer head is the reverse sequence to removal.

46 Speedometer cable - removal and refitment

1 For safety reasons disconnect the battery.
2 Rhd models. Release the clip that secures the speedometer cable to the bulkhead.
3 Carefully pull off the instrument panel front casing. It is held in position by four clips.
4 Undo and remove the four self tapping screws and plain washers that secure the instrument pack to the instrument rear casing. Pull the instrument pack from the facia.
5 Press the release lever on the speedometer cable connector and disconnect the speedometer cable from the rear of the instrument.
6 Depress the retainer and withdraw the cable multi-pin connector. The instrument pack may now be removed from the car.
7 The inner cable may now be withdrawn from the outer cable.
8 If it is necessary to remove the outer cable, first unscrew the speedometer cable from the pinion housing on the side of the gearbox (or automatic transmission unit).
9 Withdraw the speedometer cable complete with the grommet and clip from the engine compartment.
10 Finally remove the grommet and clip from the outer cable.
11 Refitting the speedometer inner and outer cables is the reverse sequence to removal. Lightly grease the inner cable and insert into the outer cable. Withdraw it by about 8 inches (200 mm) and wipe off surplus grease. Do not use oil, as it will find its way into the instrument head.

47 Fault diagnosis - Electrical system

Symptom	Reason/s	Remedy
	Battery discharged	Charge battery.
	Battery defective internally	Fit new battery.
	Battery terminal leads loose or earth lead not securely attached to body	Check and tighten leads.
	Loose or broken connections in starter motor circuit	Check all connections and check any that are loose.
	Starter motor switch or solenoid faulty	Test and replace faulty components with new.
	Starter motor pinion jammed in mesh with ring gear	Disengage pinion by turning squared end of armature shaft.
	Starter brushes badly worn, sticking or brush wires loose	Examine brushes, replace as necessary, tighten down brush wires.
	Commutator dirty, worn, or burnt	Clean commutator, recut if badly burnt.
	Starter motor armature faulty	Overhaul starter motor, fit new armature.
	Field coils earthed	Overhaul starter motor.
STARTER MOTOR TURNS ENGINE VERY SLOWLY		
	Battery in discharged condition	Charge battery.
	Starter brushes badly worn, sticking, or brush wires loose	Examine brushes, replace as necessary, tighten down brush wires.
	Loose wires in starter motor circuit	Check wiring and tighten as necessary.
STARTER MOTOR OPERATES WITHOUT TURNING ENGINE		
	Starter motor pinion sticking on the screwed sleeve	Remove starter motor, clean starter motor drive.
	Pinion or ring gear teeth broken or worn	Fit new gear ring, and new pinion to starter motor drive.
STARTER MOTOR NOISY OR EXCESSIVELY ROUGH ENGAGEMENT		
	Pinion or ring gear teeth broken or worn	Fit new ring gear, or new pinion to starter motor drive.
	Starter drive main spring broken	Dismantle and fit new main spring.
	Starter motor retaining bolts loose	Tighten starter motor securing bolts. Fit new spring washer if necessary.
BATTERY WILL NOT HOLD CHARGE FOR MORE THAN A FEW DAYS		
	Battery defective internally	Remove and fit new battery.
	Electrolyte level too low or electrolyte too weak due to leakage	Top up electrolyte level to just above plates.
	Plate separators no longer fully effective	Remove and fit new battery.
	Battery plates severely sulphated	Remove and fit new battery.
	Fan belt slipping	Check belt for wear, replace if necessary, and tighten.
	Battery terminal connections loose or corroded	Check terminals for tightness, and remove all corrosion.
	Alternator not charging properly	Remove and overhaul alternator.
	Short in lighting circuit causing continual battery drain	Trace and rectify.
IGNITION LIGHT FAILS TO GO OUT, BATTERY RUNS FLAT IN A FEW DAYS		
	Fan belt loose and slipping, or broken	Check, replace, and tighten as necessary.
	Alternator not charging correctly	Seek specialist advice if all electrical connections are satisfactory.

Failure of individual electrical equipment to function correctly is dealt with alphabetically, item by item, under the headings listed below:

Fuel gauge		
Fuel gauge gives no reading	Fuel tank empty!	Fill fuel tank.
	Electric cable between tank sender unit and gauge earthed or loose	Check cable for earthing and joints for tightness.
	Fuel gauge case not earthed	Ensure case is well earthed.
	Fuel gauge supply cable interrupted	Check and replace cable if necessary.
	Fuel gauge unit broken	Replace fuel gauge.
Fuel gauge registers full all the time	Electric cable between tank unit and gauge broken or disconnected	Check over cable and repair as necessary.
Horn		
Horn operates all the time	Horn-push either earthed or stuck down	Disconnect battery earth. Check and rectify source of trouble
	Horn cable to horn push earthed	Disconnect battery earth. Check and rectify source of trouble.

Symptom	Reason/s	Remedy
Horn fails to operate	Blown fuse	Check and renew if broken. Ascertain cause.
	Cable or cable connection loose, broken or disconnected	Check all connections for tightness and cables for breaks.
	Horn has an internal fault	Remove and overhaul horn.
Horn emits intermittent or unsatisfactory noise	Cable connections loose	Check and tighten all connections.
	Horn incorrectly adjusted	Adjust horn until best note obtained.
Lights		
Lights do not come on	If engine not running, battery discharged	Push-start car, charge battery.
	Light bulb filament burnt out or bulbs broken	Test bulbs in live bulb holder.
	Wire connections loose, disconnected or broken	Check all connections for tightness and wire cable for breaks.
	Light switch shorting or otherwise faulty	By-pass light switch to ascertain if fault is in switch and fit new switch as appropriate.
Lights come on but fade out	If engine not running battery discharged	Push-start car, and charge battery.
Lights give very poor illumination	Lamp glasses dirty	Clean glasses.
	Reflector tarnished or dirty	Fit new reflectors.
	Lamps badly out of adjustment	Adjust lamps correctly.
	Incorrect bulb with too low wattage fitted	Remove bulb and replace with correct grade.
	Existing bulbs old and badly discoloured	Renew bulb units.
	Electrical wiring too thin not allowing full current to pass	Rewire lighting system.
Lights work erratically - flashing on and off, especially over bumps	Battery terminals or earth connection loose	Tighten battery terminals and earth connection.
	Lights not earthing properly	Examine and rectify.
Windscreen wipers		
Wiper motor fails to work	Contacts in light switch faulty	By-pass light switch to ascertain if fault is in switch and fit new switch as appropriate.
	Blown fuse	Check and replace fuse if necessary.
	Wire connections loose, disconnected or broken	Check wiper wiring. Tighten loose connections.
	Brushes badly worn	Remove and fit new brushes.
	Armature worn or faulty	If electricity at wiper motor remove and overhaul and fit replacement armature.
	Field coils faulty	Purchase reconditioned wiper motor.
Wiper motor works very slowly and takes excessive current	Commutator dirty, greasy or burnt	Clean commutator thoroughly.
	Drive to wheelboxes too bent or unlubricated	Examine drive and straighten out severe curvature. Lubricate.
	Wheelbox spindle binding or damaged	Remove, overhaul, or fit replacement.
	Armature bearings dry or unaligned	Replace with new bearings correctly aligned.
	Armature badly worn or faulty	Remove, overhaul, or fit replacement armature.
Wiper motor works slowly and takes little current	Brushes badly worn	Remove and fit new brushes.
	Commutator dirty, greasy, or burnt	Clean commutator thoroughly.
	Armature badly worn or faulty	Remove and overhaul armature or fit replacement.
Wiper motor works but wiper blades remain static	Driving cable rack disengaged or faulty	Examine and if faulty, replace.
	Wheelbox gear and spindle damaged or worn	Examine and if faulty, replace.
	Wiper motor gearbox parts badly worn	Overhaul or fit new gearbox.

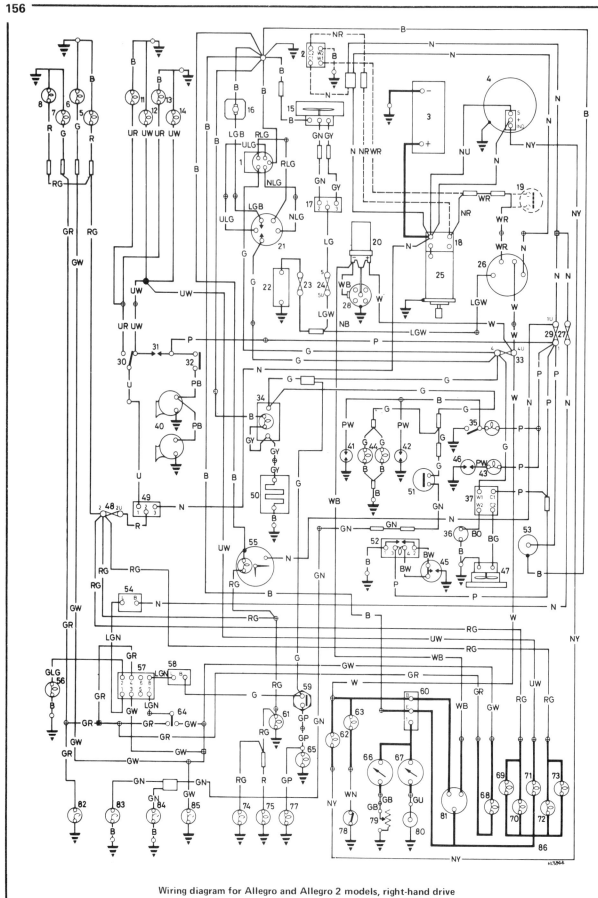

Wiring diagram for Allegro and Allegro 2 models, right-hand drive

Key to wiring diagram for right-hand drive cars. Not all items are fitted to all models

1   Wiper motor
2   Starter solenoid relay (if fitted)
3   Battery
4   Alternator
5   RH side lamp
6   RH front flasher lamp
7   LH front flasher lamp
8   LH side lamp
9   RH repeater flasher (if fitted)
10 LH repeater flasher (if fitted)
11 RH dip headlamp
12 RH main headlamp
13 LH dip headlamp
14 LH main headlamp
15 Heater motor
16 Electric windscreen washer
17 Heater switch
18 Starter solenoid
19 Automatic transmission inhibitor (if fitted)
20 Ignition coil
21 Combined wiper and washer switch
22 Radio (if fitted)
23 Line fuse for radio
24 Fuse unit (No. 5 fuse)
25 Starter motor
26 Ignition/starter switch
27 Line fuse (if fitted)
28 Distributor
29 Fuse unit (No. 1 fuse)
30 Dip switch
31 Headlamp flasher switch
32 Horn push
33 Fuse unit (No. 4 fuse)
34 Heated back light switch (if fitted)
35 Interior light
36 Radiator cooling fan thermostat
37 Radiator cooling fan relay
38 Induction heater and thermostat (if fitted)
39 Suction chamber heater (if fitted)
40 Horn(s)
41 RH door switch
42 LH door switch
44 Automatic gear quadrant illumination (if fitted)

45 Split brake differential switch (if fitted)
47 Radiator cooling fan motor
48 Fuse unit (No. 2 and No. 3 fuse)
49 Lighting switch
50 Heated back light (if fitted)
51 Reverse light switch (if fitted)
52 Split brake test switch and warning light (if fitted)
53 Cigar lighter (if fitted)
54 Hazard warning flasher unit
55 Clock (if fitted)
56 Hazard warning lamp
57 Hazard warning switch
58 Flasher unit
59 Stop lamp switch
60 Instrument voltage stabilizer
61 RH tail lamp
62 No charge warning lamp
63 Oil pressure warning lamp
64 Direction indicator switch
65 RH stop lamp
66 Fuel gauge
67 Water temperature gauge
68 Direction indicator warning lamp
69 Panel lamp (if fitted)
70 Panel lamp
71 Main beam warning lamp
72 Panel lamp
73 Panel lamp (if fitted)
74 LH tail lamp
75 Number plate illumination lamp
76 Number plate illumination lamp
77 LH stop lamp
78 Oil pressure switch
79 Fuel gauge tank unit
80 Water temperature transmitter
81 Tachometer (if fitted)
82 LH rear flasher lamp
83 LH reverse lamp (if fitted)
84 RH reverse lamp (if fitted)
85 RH rear flasher lamp
86 Printed circuit instrument panel

Cable colour code

N	Brown	LG	Light green
U	Blue	O	Orange
R	Red	W	White
K	Pink	Y	Yellow
P	Purple	B	Black
G	Green	S	Slate

When a cable has two colour code letters the first denotes the main
colour and the second denotes the tracer colour

158

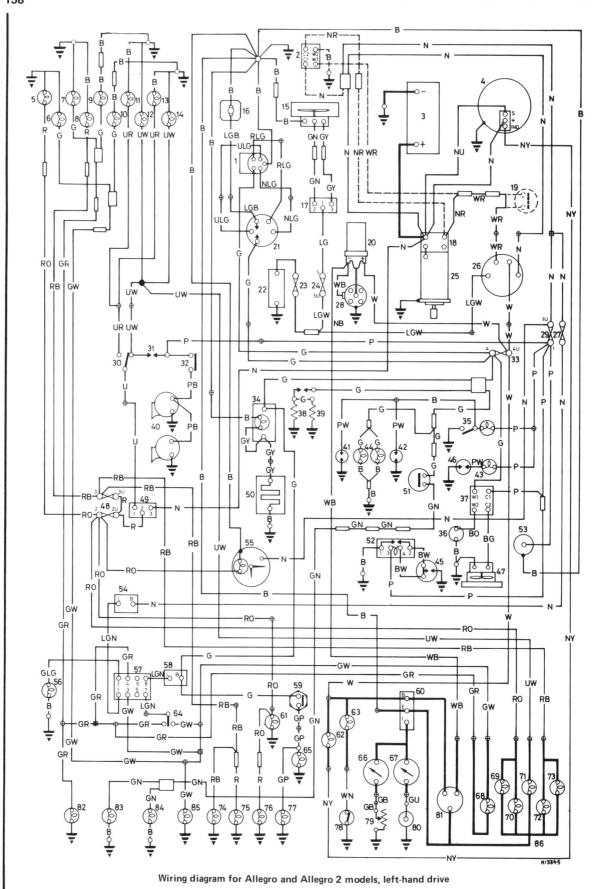

Wiring diagram for Allegro and Allegro 2 models, left-hand drive

M13845

Key to wiring diagram for left-hand drive cars. Not all items are fitted to all models

1 Wiper motor
2 Starter solenoid relay (if fitted)
3 Battery
4 Alternator
5 RH side lamp
6 RH front flasher lamp
7 LH front flasher lamp
8 LH side lamp
9 RH repeater flasher (if fitted)
10 LH repeater flasher (if fitted)
11 RH dip headlamp
12 RH main headlamp
13 LH dip headlamp
14 LH main headlamp
15 Heater motor
16 Electric windscreen washer
17 Heater switch
18 Starter solenoid
19 Automatic transmission inhibitor (if fitted)
20 Ignition coil
21 Combined wiper and washer switch
22 Radio (if fitted)
23 Line fuse for radio
24 Fuse unit (No. 5 fuse)
25 Starter motor
26 Ignition/starter switch
27 Line fuse (if fitted)
28 Distributor
29 Fuse unit (No. 1 fuse)
30 Dip switch
31 Headlamp flasher switch
32 Horn push
33 Fuse unit (No. 4 fuse)
34 Heated back light switch (if fitted)
35 Interior light
36 Radiator cooling fan thermostat
37 Radiator cooling fan relay
38 Induction heater and thermostat (if fitted)
39 Suction chamber heater (if fitted)
40 Horn(s)
41 RH door switch
42 LH door switch
44 Automatic gear quadrant illumination (if fitted)

45 Split brake differential switch (if fitted)
47 Radiator cooling fan motor
48 Fuse unit (No. 2 and No. 3 fuse)
49 Lighting switch
50 Heated back light (if fitted)
51 Reverse light switch (if fitted)
52 Split brake test switch and warning light (if fitted)
53 Cigar lighter (if fitted)
54 Hazard warning flasher unit
55 Clock (if fitted)
56 Hazard warning lamp
57 Hazard warning switch
58 Flasher unit
59 Stop lamp switch
60 Instrument voltage stabilizer
61 RH tail lamp
62 No charge warning lamp
63 Oil pressure warning lamp
64 Direction indicator switch
65 RH stop lamp
66 Fuel gauge
67 Water temperature gauge
68 Direction indicator warning lamp
69 Panel lamp (if fitted)
70 Panel lamp
71 Main beam warning lamp
72 Panel lamp
73 Panel lamp (if fitted)
74 LH tail lamp
75 Number plate illumination lamp
76 Number plate illumination lamp
77 LH stop lamp
78 Oil pressure switch
79 Fuel gauge tank unit
80 Water temperature transmitter
81 Tachometer (if fitted)
82 LH rear flasher lamp
83 LH reverse lamp (if fitted)
84 RH reverse lamp (if fitted)
85 RH rear flasher lamp
86 Printed circuit instrument panel

Cable colour code

N	Brown	LG	Light green
U	Blue	O	Orange
R	Red	W	White
K	Pink	Y	Yellow
P	Purple	B	Black
G	Green	S	Slate

When a cable has two colour code letters the first denotes the main
colour and the second denotes the tracer colour

Chapter 11 Suspension and steering

For modifications, and information applicable to later models, see Supplement at end of manual

Contents

Specifications

Front suspension:

Type	Independent with arms of unequal length, trailing tie-rods and hydragas displacers which are interconnected front to rear
Front hub ball pin end float	0.000 - 0.003 in. (0.000 - 0.076 mm)
Swivel hub inclination	9⁰ 30'
Camber angle	1⁰ 20' positive
Caster angle	4⁰ positive

Rear suspension:

Type	Independent with trailing arms and hydrogas displacers
Radius arm assembly dimension, (vertical from rear hub centre to body wheel arch)	
Saloon models	10.12 in (257 mm)
Estate models with commission numbers prior to the following:	
D67 A2S 16500 N67 H4S 9300	
D67 A4S 21500 V67 H4S 4000	
S67 A2S 22000 N67 H4D 4000	
S67 A4S 57000 S67 A3W 4000	
S67 H4S 24000 S67 H3W 1600	11.7 in (298 mm)
Estate models with commission numbers commencing at those above	14.5 in (368 mm)
Wheel bearing end float	0.001 - 0.005 in. (0.025 - 0.127 mm)

Steering:

Type	Rack and pinion
Rack travel either side of centre	2.64 in. (67 mm)
Pinion turns, lock to lock	3.5
Pinion bearing pre-load	0.001 - 0.003 in. (0.25 - 0.76 mm)
Joint washer thickness	0.010 in. (0.25 mm)
Shim gap	0.011 - 0.013 in. (0.28 - 0.33 mm)
Rack support yoke to cover plate clearance	0.002 - 0.005 in. (0.05 - 0.13 mm)
Joint washer thickness	0.010 in. (0.25 mm)
Ball pin centre dimension	47.30 in. (1201.6 mm)
Front wheel alignment	0.1563 ± 0.0313 in. (4 mm ± 1 mm) or 0⁰ 30' ± 0⁰ 7'30'' included angle (toe-out)
Turning circle	33.25 ft (10.13 m) approx

Note: *See Chapter 13 for front wheel alignment specifications and turning circle data for Series 3 models*

	lb f/in.^{2}	
Hydragas suspension pressure	340 lb f/in.^{2} (23.9 kg f/cm^2) - nominal	
Car trim height	14.68 $\pm$ 0.24 in. (373 $\pm$ 6 mm) - see text	

Torque wrench settings:	lb f ft	kg f m
Front suspension		
Hub ball pin retainer	70	9.69
Hub ball pin nut	38	5.30
Hub nut (drive shaft)	200	27.6
	and then align to next split pin hole	
Upper arm pivot bolt	105	14.58
Lower arm pivot bolt	52	7.14
Drive flange bolt	42	5.81
Rear suspension		
Cross tube rubber mounting bolts to body	37	5.09
Cross tube rubber mounting bolts to cross tube	18	2.55
Radius arm pivot shaft nut	105	14.58
Check strap bracket bolt nut	44	6.12
Steering		
Steering wheel nut	35	4.84
Column universal joint clamp bolt	20	2.77
Balljoint to steering arm nut	35	4.84
Balljoint lock nut	35	4.84
Rack clamp screws	20	2.77
Arm bolts	35	4.84
Rack/pinion end cover bolts	15	2.07
Road wheels		
Wheel nuts	46	6.42
Rear hub retaining nut - bedding in	5	0.69

1 General description

The suspension fitted to Allegros is of the independent type with the Hydragas suspension units interconnected front and rear.

The 'Hydragas' suspension is essentially simple, comprising an integral spring and damper unit at each wheel. The units use an inert gas as a springing medium. The weight of the car is carried by a water based fluid under pressure and the units are interconnected front to rear, the whole system being hermetically sealed. The units are designed to last the life of the car and the spring - damper unit requires no maintenance and its unique arrangement of using a rolling diaphragm eliminates the friction and wear of sliding seals.

The 'Hydragas' system operates with a leverage of between 4 and 5 to 1 so reducing the size of the units. The cross tube rear suspension has been designed to contain these 'levered loads' so that only forces of wheel load magnitude are fed on to the body structure. It is rubber mounted at its ends, to a compliant sub-frame of extreme simplicity.

The load from the unit passes through the shroud and into a pin which acts as the pivot about which the trailing arm turns. The opposing load from the piston, via the knuckled joint on the arm, is fed through two dual concentric bushes and thence to the pivot pin. The reaction on the unit, of a similar magnitude to wheel load, is taken on to the body by a rubber pad acting directly on the spherical chamber.

The extent of softening the wheel rate in the pitch mode is constrained by consideration of trim change with load. Limitation of trim changes is mainly achieved by torsioned rate of the dual concentric bonded rubber bushes in the rear arms. On Allegro models these rubber bushes are free when the wheel is in the bump position. In the unladen position they provide a 'false load' at each wheel of 81 lb f (40.5 kg f) pulling the body down. This false load reduces the precentage increase of load at the rear when the car is laden with luggage and passengers and has the effect of reducing the attitude change.

The windup torque from the dual concentric bushes is transmitted through serrations on their inner sleeve to the shroud. These bushes also provide the location of the rear wheel, demand no maintenance and take the place of the taper roller bearings and torsion bar of the established Austin 1100/1300 models.

At the front the unit is mounted vertically with the piston acting on the upper support arm through the knuckle joint. The upper support arm is pivoted on two 0.75 in (19.05 mm) bore dual concentric bushes which take the unit load, provide the required parasitic rate and allow fore and aft flexibility for compliance as at the rear. These bushes also require no maintenance.

The steering system is of the rack and pinion type. Positioned at each end of the rack is a ball joint which is attached to the inner end of the tie-rod. The balljoint, and part of the tie-rod, is enclosed in a rubber gaiter which is held in position by a clip at each end. It protects the balljoint and rack preventing road dust and dirt entering and causing premature wear.

The outer end of the tie-rod is threaded for adjustment, and is adjusted by shims between the end cover and pinion housing, whilst backlash between the pinion and rack is controlled by shims between the cover plate yoke and the pinion housing.

2 Front hub bearings - removal and refitment

1 Remove the wheel trim and hub cover. Undo and remove the drive shaft nut and recover the collar from the drive shaft.
2 Chock the rear wheels, apply the handbrake, jack up the front of the car and support on firmly based axle stands. Remove the road wheel.
3 Wipe the top of the brake master cylinder reservoir, unscrew the cap and place a piece of polythene over the filler neck. Refit the cap. This is to prevent syphoning of hydraulic fluid during subsequent operations.
4 Wipe the area around the pipe to hose union at the rear of the front hub and then unscrew the union nut. Part the pipe from the hose and tape the open ends to stop dirt ingress.

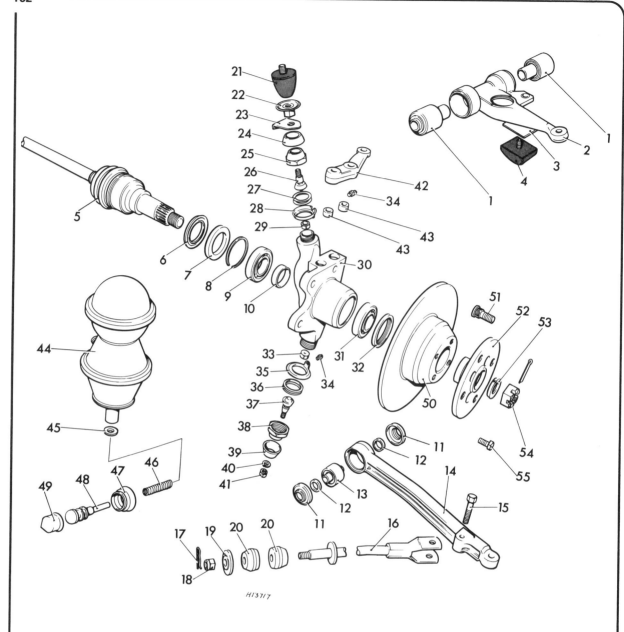

Fig. 11.1. Front suspension assembly

1	Upper arm pivot bush	20	Tie-rod pad	39	Dust cover
2	Suspension upper arm	21	Bump rubber	40	Spring washer
3	Locating plate	22	Ball pin nut and	41	Ball pin nut
4	Rebound rubber		reaction pad	42	Steering arm
5	Drive shaft	23	Lockwasher	43	Hollow dowel
6	Bearing water shield	24	Dust cover	44	Hydragas displacer unit
7	Oil seal	25	Ball pin retainer	45	Spacer (1300 2 door
8	Oil seal spacer	26	Ball pin		auto. transmission only)
9	Hub inner bearing	27	Shim	46	Knuckle joint spring
10	Bearing spacer	28	Retainer lockwasher	47	Knuckle joint dust cover
11	Balljoint water shield	29	Ball seat	48	Knuckle joint ball pin
	(early models only)	30	Swivel hub	49	Ball pin socket
12	Balljoint seal (early models only)	31	Hub outer bearing	50	Braking disc
13	Lower arm balljoint	32	Oil seal	51	Wheel stud
14	Suspension lower arm	33	Ball seat	52	Drive flange
15	Tie-rod bolt	34	Grease nipple	53	Drive shaft collar
16	Suspension tie-rod	35	Retainer lockwasher	54	Drive shaft nut
17	Spring clip	36	Shim	55	Drive flange set-bolt
18	Nut	37	Ball pin		
19	Washer	38	Ball pin retainer		

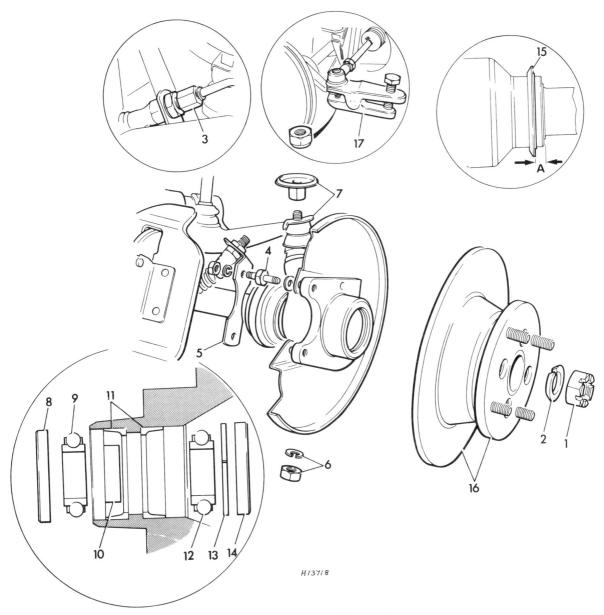

H 137/8

Fig. 11.2. Front hub assembly removal

1	Hub nut	7	Nut and tab washer	13	Spacer
2	Collar	8	Oil seal	14	Oil seal
3	Union nut	9	Inner race	15	Dust shield
4	Brake hose bracket set bolts	10	Bearing spacer	16	Drive flange and brake disc assembly
5	Brake hose bracket	11	Bearing outer race	17	Use of universal balljoint separator
6	Nut and spring washer	12	Inner race		

A 0.25 ± 0.0625 in. $(6.3 \pm 1.5$ mm$)$

5   Undo and remove the two nuts and set bolts securing the brake hose bracket and caliper to the swivel hub.

6   The driving flange and braking disc may now be lifted from the swivel hub.

7   Undo and remove the nut and washer securing the steering rack tie-rod balljoint to the steering arm and separate the balljoint from the steering arm using a universal balljoint separator.

8   The swivel hub must next be disconnected from the suspension arms. Undo and remove the upper and lower securing nuts and washers and then using a universal balljoint separator disconnect the swivel hub from the upper and lower suspension arms.

9   Separate the drive shaft from the swivel hub and lift the swivel hub away. Should the front hub inner bearing race remain on the drive shaft remove the ball cage and balls and withdraw the bearing inner race using a universal puller and suitable thrust block.

10 Using a tapered drift remove the inner and outer oil seals from the front hub. Each bearing inner race may now be drifted out and the bearing spacer recovered.

11 The bearing outer race and oil seal spacer may now be removed from the front hub.

12 Re-assembly and refitting the front hub is the reverse sequence to removal, but the points described in the following

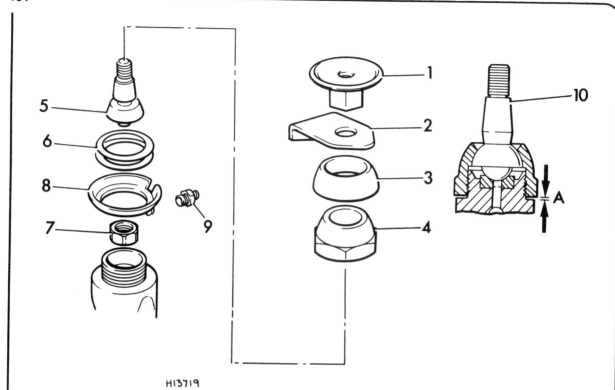

H13719

Fig. 11.3. Front hub upper balljoint assembly

1	Nut	4	Ball pin retainer	7	Seat	10	Cross sectional view through balljoint assembly
2	Lockwasher	5	Ball pin	8	Lockwasher	A	See text
3	Dust cover	6	Shims	9	Grease nipple		

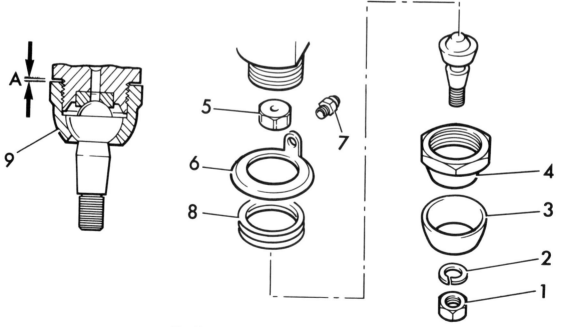

Fig. 11.4. Front hub lower balljoint assembly

1	Nut	3	Dust cover	6	Lockwasher	9	Cross sectional view through balljoint assembly
2	Spring washer	4	Ball pin retainer	7	Grease nipple	A	See text
		5	Ball seat	8	Shims		

paragraphs should be noted.

13 Pack the bearings with grease and drift the bearings into the front hub. The sides marked "THRUST" must face towards each other.

14 Fit the oil seals, using a suitable diameter drift, so that their sealing lips face towards the bearings. Smear a little grease onto the sealing lip.

15 The hub bearing water shield must be fitted onto the drive shaft 0.25 ± 0.0625 in (6.3 ± 1.5 mm) when measured from the bearing register on the drive shaft to the water shield hub.

16 All attachments must be tightened to the recommended torque wrench settings as given at the beginning of this Chapter.

17 Measure the brake disc runout at the outer circumference. This must not exceed 0.007 in (0.17 mm).

18 Bleed the brake hydraulic system as described in Chapter 9.

3 Front hub assembly - overhaul

1 Refer to Section 2 and remove the front hub bearings.

2 Undo and remove the set screw and spring washer securing the brake disc dust cover to the front hub.

3 Bend back the lock washer tabs then undo and remove the two set bolts securing the steering arm to the swivel hub. Recover the two hollow dowels from the top of the swivel hub.

4 Remove the dust cover from the upper balljoint, unlock and then unscrew the ball pin retainer.

5 Withdraw the ballpin, ballseat, ball pin retainer and shims.

6 Unscrew the grease nipple to release the lockwasher.

7 Repeat procedure in paragraphs 4-6 inclusive for the lower balljoint.

8 Re-assembly is the reverse sequence to removal. Refer to Section 4 or 5 as applicable for information on re-assembling the upper and lower balljoints.

4 Front hub upper balljoint - removal and refitment

1 Chock the rear wheels, apply the handbrake, jack up the front of the car and support on firmly based stands. Remove the road wheel.

2 Bend back the lock washer tab and unscrew the upper balljoint securing nut from the top of the suspension upper arm.

3 Using a universal balljoint separator disconnect the balljoint from the suspension arm.

4 Remove the dust cover from the balljoint and then unlock and unscrew the ballpin retainer.

5 Withdraw the ball pin, ball seating, ball pin retainer and shims.

6 Unscrew the grease nipple and lift away the lockwasher.

7 To re-assemble: first, fit the ball seat, ball pin, and ball pin retainer - less the lock washer and shims to the front hub. Tighten the ball pin retainer until the ball pin is just nipped.

8 Using feeler gauges measure the gap between the front hub and ball pin retainer.

9 Dismantle the balljoint assembly again and then grease and re-assemble. This time replace the lock washer, grease nipple and shims. The combined thickness of the lock washer and shims must be equal to the gap measured in paragraph 8 plus a maximum of 0.003 in (0.076 mm) to produce a ball pin end float equal to 0.000 - 0.003 in (0 - .076 mm). The nominal thickness of the lock washer is 0.03 in (0.91 mm).

10 Tighten the ball pin retainer to a torque wrench setting of 70 lb f ft (9.69 kg fm).

11 The nut must be locked using three flats of the ball pin retainer.

12 Replace the ball pin dust cover and inject a little grease into the balljoint.

13 Re-assembly is the reverse sequence to removal. Tighten the ball pin nut to a torque wrench setting of 38 lb f ft (5.3 kg fm).

Note: *Balljoint lapping-in is covered in Chapter 13.*

5 Front hub lower balljoint - removal and refitment

1 Chock the rear wheels, apply the handbrake, jack up the front of the car and support on firmly based axle stands. Remove the road wheel.

2 Undo and remove the nut and spring washer securing the balljoint to the suspension lower arm.

3 Using a universal balljoint separator disconnect the balljoint from the suspension arm.

4 Remove the dust cover from the balljoint and then unlock and unscrew the ball pin retainer.

5 Withdraw the ball pin, ball seating, ball pin retainer and shims.

6 Unscrew the grease nipple and lift away the lock washer.

7 Re-assembly is identical to that for the upper balljoint. For full information refer to Section 4 paragraphs 7 to 13 inclusive.

6 Front suspension lower arm - removal and refitment

1 Apply the handbrake, chock the rear wheels, jack up the front of the car and support on firmly based axle stands. Remove the road wheel.

2 Undo and remove the nut and spring washer securing the balljoint to the suspension lower arm.

3 Using a universal balljoint separator disconnect the balljoint from the suspension arm.

4 Undo and remove the nut, spring washer and bolt securing the tie-rod to the suspension lower arm.

5 Undo and remove the nut, spring washer and bolt securing the suspension lower arm to the body.

6 Lift away the two water shields and seals from the lower arm balljoint.

7 Should it be necessary to remove the bush it may be pressed out using a bench vice and suitable diameter sockets. Before doing so however note the exact position of the bush.

8 When fitting a new bush only press it in as far as was noted before removal of the old bush.

9 Refitting the front suspension lower arm is the reverse sequence to removal but the following additional points should be noted:

a) Pack a little grease into the water shields to prevent moisture pentration.

b) The lower arm pivot bolt should be tightened to a torque wrench setting of 52 lb f ft (7.14 kg fm).

c) Tighten the swivel hub ball pin retaining nut to a torque wrench setting of 38 lb f ft (5.3 kg fm).

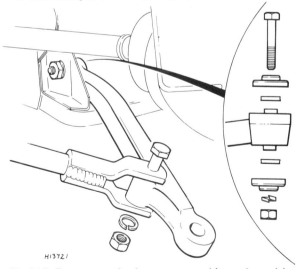

H13721

Fig. 11.5. Front suspension lower arm assembly - early models
Later models do not have watershields and seals

7   Front suspension upper arm - removal and refitment

1   This operation will not normally be possible to carry out at home because the 'Hydragas' system must be depressurised. If the equipment is available full instructions for operation are given on the machine.

2   Apply the handbrake, chock the rear wheels, jack up the front of the car and support on firmly based axle stands. Remove the road wheel.

3   Depressurise the Hydragas system.

4   Undo and remove the nut and spring washer securing the rebound rubber to the suspension upper arm. Lift away the rebound rubber.

5   Bend back the lock washer tab and unscrew the upper ball-joint securing nut from the top of the suspension upper arm.

6   Using a universal balljoint separator disconnect the balljoint from the suspension arm.

7   Undo and remove the nut, bolt and washer securing the upper arm to the body.

8   Remove the upper arm complete with displacer unit knuckle joint and spacer (if fitted). Remove the spring from the displacer unit.

9   The knuckle joint may now be withdrawn from the upper arm.

10 Make up a spigoted mandrel with the spigot 1 in (25.4 mm) long x 0.75 in (19.05 mm) diameter and the shaft 8 in (203.2 mm) long x 1.0625 in (27 mm) diameter.

11 Now press the inner sleeve of one bush through the suspension upper arm.

12 Should the opposing bush be pressed out of the suspension upper arm during the operation in paragraph II, continue until the inner sleeve of the first bush is sheared from its rubber bonding.

13 If the opposing bush remains in position in the suspension upper arm, continue pressing until the inner sleeve of each bush is sheared from its rubber bonding.

14 Obtain a 4 in (101.6 mm) x 1.5 in (38.10 mm) diameter steel tube with a wall thickness of 0.25 in (6.35 mm).

15 Using the tube press the bush intermediate sleeve into the suspension upper arm to collapse the sleeve and shear the rubber bonding from the bush outer sleeve. Release the press or vice and withdraw the intermediate sleeve complete with rubber bonding from the suspension upper arm.

16 Using a chisel split the bush outer sleeve and withdraw the sleeve from the suspension upper arm.

17 To refit the bushes, ideally they should be pulled into position using a high tensile steel bolt, nut and washers. When the bush outer sleeves meet, the bush outer sleeve should be 0.068 - 0.078 in (1.72 - 1.97 mm) as measured from the outer face of the bore in the suspension upper arm to the outer face of the bush outer sleeve.

18 Refitting the upper suspension arm is the reverse sequence to removal but the points in the following paragraphs should be noted.

19 Pack the displacer knuckle joint with "Dextragrease Super GP".

20 Tighten the swivel hub ball pin nut to a torque wrench setting of 38 lb f ft (5.3 kg fm).

21 The pivot bolt washer must be fitted under the head of the bolt.

22 A special tool is now required. It is a front suspension setting gauge and has a part number of 18G 1245.

23 Position the upper arm in its assembly position and using tool 18G 1245 adjusted so that dimension "A" (Fig. 11.7 is 0.09375 in (2.38 mm) when measured from the upper face of the tool body to the top of the parallel portion of the tool adjusting screw flange.

24 With a torque wrench mounted on the upper arm pivot bolt head tighten the bolt to a torque wrench setting of 105 lb f ft (14.58 kg fm).

25 Repressurise the Hydragas system.

8   Front suspension tie-rod - removal and refitment

1   Apply the handbrake, chock the rear wheels, jack up the front of the car and support on firmly based axle stands. Remove the road wheel.

2   Undo and remove the nut and spring washer securing the lower balljoint to the lower suspension arm.

3   Using a universal balljoint separator disconnect the balljoint from the suspension arm.

4   Withdraw the spring clip at the end of the tie-rod and undo and remove the nut securing the tie-rod to the body mounted bracket.

5   Undo and remove the nut, spring washer and bolt securing the tie-rod to the lower suspension arm. Lift away the tie-rod.

6   Refitting the tie-rod is the reverse sequence to removal. However the following additional points should be noted:

a) Ensure that the rubber pads are fitted with the short tapered end next to the body mounted bracket.

b) Tighten the swivel hub ball pin nut to a torque wrench setting of 38 lb f ft (5.3 kg fm).

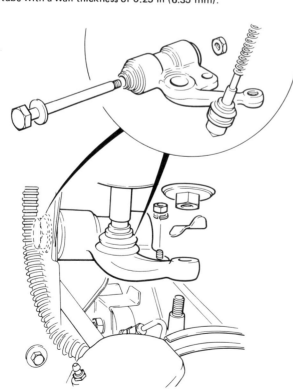

Fig. 11.6. **Front suspension upper arm assembly**

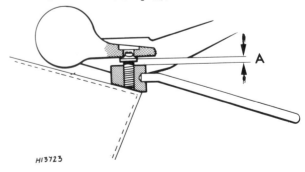

HI3723

Fig. 11.7. **Front suspension upper arm assembly - setting**

A   See text

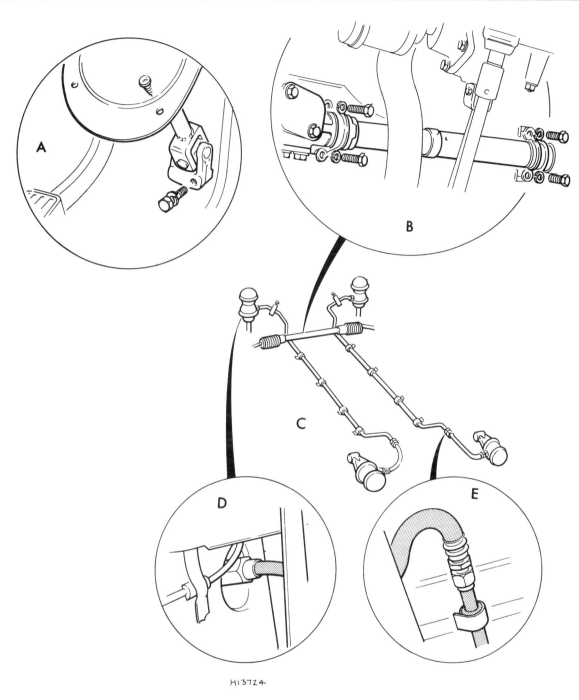

H13724

Fig. 11.8. Displacer connecting pipe removal

A *Lower coupling*   D *Front union*
B *Rack clamp attachments*   E *Rear union*
C *Connecting pipes*

9 Displacer connecting pipe - removal and refitment

1 This operation will not normally be possible to carry out at home because the 'Hydragas' system must be depressurised. If the equipment is available full instructions for operation are given on the machine.
2 Raise the car at least 4 ft (1.2 mm) clear of the ground preferably on a garage type lift.
3 Depressurise the 'Hydragas' system.

4 Undo and slide back the union nuts securing the displacer connecting pipe to the front displacer unit and the rear displacer connecting pipe hose.
5 Undo and remove the four bolts and spring washers securing the steering rack assembly to the underside of the car.
6 If the pipe on the driver's side of the car is to be removed, fold back the front carpet. Undo and remove the four screws securing the steering column cover to the toe-board.
7 Undo and remove the clamp bolt securing the steering column to the steering rack pinion.

8   Move the road wheel to the full lock outwards position to give clearance between the steering rack assembly and underside of the body.

9   Release the connecting pipe to the body clips.

10 The displacer connecting pipe may now be lifted away from the underside of the car.

11 Refitting the connecting pipe is the reverse sequence to removal, but the following additional points should be noted:

a) Carefully slide the sealing band on the steering rack housing to one side and insert a 0.25 in (6.35 mm) diameter rod into the steering rack to set and hold the road wheels in the straight ahead position.

b) Reconnect the steering rack pinion to the steering column making sure the steering wheel spokes are in the horizontal plane.

c) Remove the rod and reposition the sealing bond.

d) Tighten the steering column clamp bolt to a torque wrench setting of 28 lb f ft (3.87 kg fm).

e) Repressurise the 'Hydragas' system.

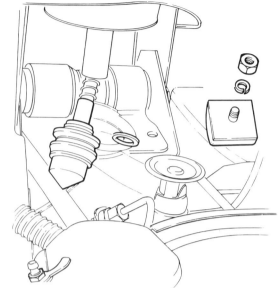

---

10 Displacer connecting pipe hose - removal and refitment

---

1   This operation will not normally be possible to carry out at home because the 'Hydragas' system must be depressurised. If the equipment is available full instructions for operation are given on the machine.

2   Chock the front wheels, jack up the rear of the car, support on firmly based axle stands and remove the road wheel.

3   Depressurise the 'Hydragas' system.

4   Undo and remove the union nuts securing the hose to the displacer unit and connecting pipe. Lift away the hose.

5   Refitting the displacer connecting pipe hose is the reverse sequence to removal but, the following additional points should be noted:

a) Ensure the rear displacer unit knuckle joint ball pin remains located in its socket in the radius arm.

b) Repressurise the 'Hydragas' system.

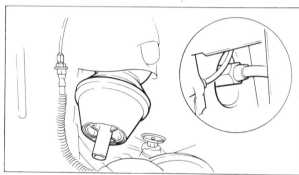

H13725

Fig. 11.9. Front displacer unit removal

---

11 Front displacer unit - removal and refitment

---

1   This operation will not normally be possible to carry out at home because the 'Hydragas' system must be depressurised. If the equipment is available full instructions for operation are given on the machine.

2   Chock the rear wheels, apply the handbrake, jack up the front of the car and support on firmly based axle stands. Remove the road wheel.

3   Depressurise the 'Hydragas' system.

4   Undo and remove the nut and spring washer securing the rebound rubber to the suspension upper arm. Lift away the rebound rubber.

5   Undo and remove the union nut securing the connecting pipe to the front displacer unit.

6   The knuckle joint and spacer (when fitted) and spring may now be lifted away from the suspension upper arm and displacer unit.

7   Lift away the displacer unit.

8   Refitting the displacer unit is the reverse sequence to removal but, the following additional points should be noted:

a) Pack the displacer unit knuckle joint with a little "Dextra-grease Super GP".

b) Ensure the knuckle joint ball pin remains located in its socket.

c) Repressurise the 'Hydragas' system.

---

12 Front displacer unit knuckle joint - removal and refitment

---

For full details refer to Section 11, and follow the instructions given in paragraphs 1 to 4, 6 and 8.

---

13 Rear displacer unit - removal and refitment

---

1   This operation will not normally be possible to carry out at home because the 'Hydragas' system must be depressurised. If the equipment is available full instructions for operation are given on the machine.

2   Chock the front wheels, jack up the rear of the car and support on firmly based axle stands. Remove the road wheel.

3   Depressurise the 'Hydragas' system.

4   Back off the radius arm pivot shaft inner nut.

5   Unscrew the union nut securing the connecting pipe hose to the rear displacer unit.

6   Using a small jack or other suitable means support the weight of the front end of the radius arm assembly.

7   Undo and remove the two bolts and spring washers securing the rear suspension cross tube rubber mounting to the body.

8   Undo and remove the four bolts and spring washers securing the rear suspension cross tube rubber mounting to the cross tube.

9   Undo and remove the nut and washer located at the inner end of the radius arm pivot shaft.

10 The cross tube rubber mounting and pivot shaft may now be withdrawn from the assembly so releasing the displacer from the radius arm.

11 Lift away the knuckle joint spring from inside the displacer unit strut.

12 Refitting the rear displacer unit is the reverse sequence to

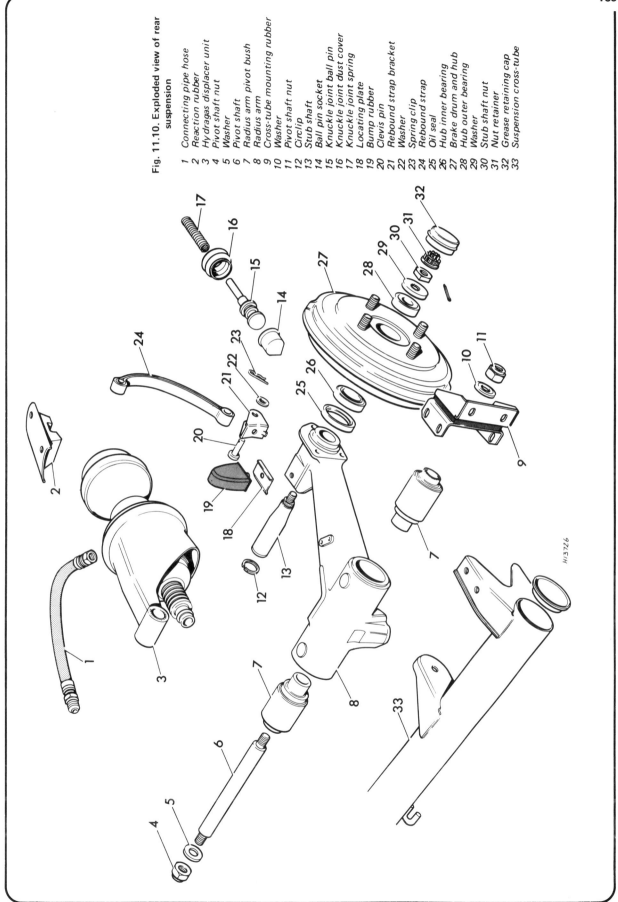

Fig. 11.10. Exploded view of rear suspension

1 Connecting pipe hose
2 Reaction rubber
3 Hydragas displacer unit
4 Pivot shaft nut
5 Washer
6 Pivot shaft
7 Radius arm pivot bush
8 Radius arm
9 Cross-tube mounting rubber
10 Washer
11 Pivot shaft nut
12 Circlip
13 Stub shaft
14 Ball pin socket
15 Knuckle joint ball pin
16 Knuckle joint dust cover
17 Knuckle joint spring
18 Locating plate
19 Bump rubber
20 Clevis pin
21 Rebound strap bracket
22 Washer
23 Spring clip
24 Rebound strap
25 Oil seal
26 Hub inner bearing
27 Brake drum and hub
28 Hub outer bearing
29 Washer
30 Stub shaft nut
31 Nut retainer
32 Grease retaining cap
33 Suspension cross-tube

HI3726

removal. The points in the following paragraphs should be noted.

13 Fit the cross tube rubber mounting to body and rubber mounting to cross tube bolts and spring washers and tighten finger tight. Leave in this condition until the radius arm has been refitted (paragraph 17).

14 Tighten the cross tube mounting rubber to cross tube set bolts to a torque wrench setting of 18 lbf ft (2.55 kg. fm).

15 Tighten the cross tube rubber mounting to body bolts to a torque wrench setting of 37 lb f ft (5.09 kg fm).

16 Locate the radius arm so that the vertical measurement between the centre of the rear hub and the wheel arch (Fig. 11.14) is within the dimensions given in the Specifications, and retain it in this position.

17 Hold the displacer unit hard against its reaction rubber and tighten the radius arm pivot nut to a torque wrench setting of 105 lb f ft (14.58 kg fm).

18 Ensure that the displacer unit knuckle joint ball pin remains positioned in its socket in the radius arm.

19 Repressurise the 'Hydragas' system.

---

14 Rear displacer unit knuckle joint - removal and refitment

1 This operation will not normally be possible to carry out at home because the 'Hydragas' system must be depressurised. If the equipment is available full instructions for operation are given on the machine.

2 Chock the front wheels, jack up the rear of the car and support on firmly based axle stands. Remove the road wheel.

3 Place a piece of hard wood between the radius arm and the bump rubber bracket on the body so as to hold the suspension in the full rebound position.

4 Depressurise the 'Hydragas' system.

5 Lift away the knuckle joint and spring from the radius arm and displacer unit.

6 Refitting the knuckle joint is the reverse sequence to removal but the following additional points should be noted:

a) Ensure that the knuckle joint ball pin remains located in its socket in the radius arm.

b) Repressurise the 'Hydragas' system.

---

15 Rear displacer unit rubber boot - removal and refitment

1 Refer to Section 14, and follow the instructions given in paragraph 1,2, 4 and 5.

2 Remove the boot from the displacer unit.

3 Remove the strut ensuring that the piston is not pulled out of the displacer diaphragm. The strut is bonded to the displacer piston with Loctite so this joint must be broken first.

4 To refit the rubber boot first place on the lower half of the displacer body, stretching the head of the boot when fitting it between the displacer body and the displacer carrier.

5 Working through the hole in the boot push the head over the upper half of the displacer body.

6 Apply a little "Loctite - Studlock" onto the strut spigot and refit the strut through the hole in the boot and into the displacer piston.

7 Re-assembly is now the reverse sequence to removal.

---

16 Rear hub bearings - removal and refitment

Note: *With effect from chassis number 140705, a modified washer is used on the rear hub assembly as a safety feature (see item 29 in Fig. 11.10). This washer is 1.475 in (37.5 mm) in*

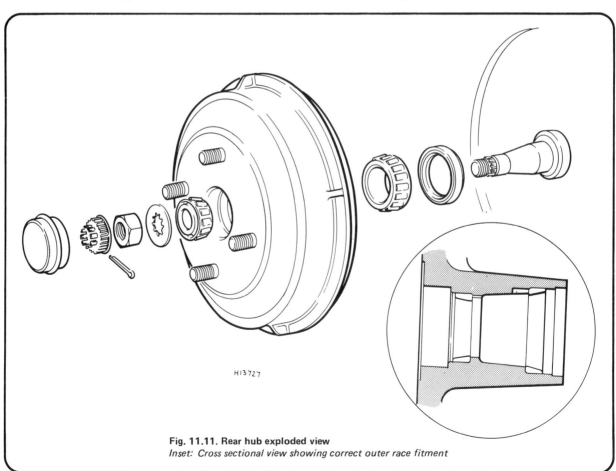

H13727

Fig. 11.11. Rear hub exploded view
Inset: Cross sectional view showing correct outer race fitment

outside diameter, compared with the earlier type which was approximately 1.2 in (30.5 mm) in outside diameter. It is important that the modified washer (part number FAM 387) is fitted in place of the original type (part number 21H 5127) on all hub assemblies regardless of whether any problems have been experienced in service.

1 Chock the front wheels, jack up the rear of the car and support on firmly based axle stands. Remove the road wheel.
2 Using a screwdriver remove the grease retainer from the centre of the rear hub.
3 Bend back the split pin ears and withdraw the split pin.
4 Lift away the nut retainer and unscrew the nut from the radius arm stub shaft. Recover the washer.
5 The rear hub and brake drum assembly may now be lifted from the stub shaft.
6 Using a screwdriver remove the oil seal from the brake drum and hub assembly.
7 Lift away the bearing inner races from the brake drum and hub assembly.
8 To remove the outer races it is best to drift them out using a soft metal tapered drift. Note which way round they are fitted.
9 Refitting the hub bearings and oil seal is the reverse sequence to removal but the points in the following paragraphs should be noted.
10 Pack the bearings and the space between the oil seal and the inner bearing with a little general purpose grease.
11 The oil seal must be refitted with its lip facing towards the bearings.
12 To set the bearing end float: spin the brake drum/hub assembly and whilst it is rotating tighten the hub nut to a torque wrench setting of 5 lb f ft (0.69 kg fm). Do not feel tempted to tighten up the retaining nut because the hub feels that it has too much play in it.
13 Stop the brake drum/hub assembly rotating and slacken the hub nut. Now tighten the hub nut finger tight.
14 Replace the hub nut retainer so that one arm of the retainer covers the left-hand half of the split pin hole in the strut shaft.
15 Back off the hub nut and retainer until the split pin hole is fully exposed.
16 Fit a new split pin and bend its ears circumferentially around the nut retainer thereby locking the nut and retainer.

---

17 Rear suspension cross tube - removal and refitment

1 This operation will not normally be possible to carry out at home because the 'Hydragas' system must be depressurised. If the equipment is available full instructions for operation are given on the machine.
2 Chock the front wheels, jack up the rear of the car and support on firmly based axle stands. Remove the road wheel.
3 Depressurise the 'Hydragas' system.
4 Wipe the top of the brake master cylinder reservoir and unscrew the cap. Place a piece of polythene over the reservoir neck and refit the cap.
5 Wipe the area around the rear brake hose to pipe unions and then unscrew the union nuts. Tape the pipe ends to prevent dirt ingress.
6 Undo and remove the nuts securing the brake hoses to the radius arm mounted brackets.
7 Undo and remove the nuts and spring washers securing the handbrake outer cables to the lugs on the radius arms.
8 Remove the split pins and remove the clevis pins attaching the handbrake inner cable to the levers at the rear of the brake backplate.
9 Withdraw the spring clips and remove the clevis pins attaching the rebound straps to the radius arms.
10 Unscrew the union nuts securing the connecting pipe hoses to the displacer units.
11 Release the clips holding the rear brake handbrake cables on to the rear suspension cross tube.
12 The exhaust system must next be removed. This is a straightforward operation and will present no problems.

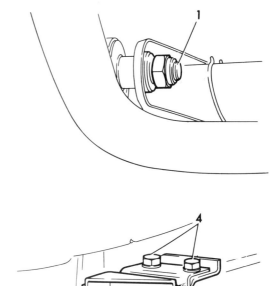

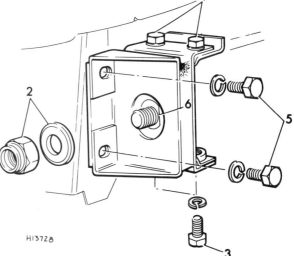

Fig. 11.12. Rear suspension cross tube mounting

1 Nut	4 Set bolts	
2 Nut and washer	5 Set bolts	
3 Set bolts	6 Flat (for reassembly - see text)	

13 Using small jacks or suitable packing support the centre of the cross tube and the rear end of each radius arm.
14 Undo and remove the four bolts and spring washers securing the cross tube rubber mountings to the body.
15 The cross tube and radius arm assembly may now be lifted away from the underside of the car.
16 Undo and remove the nut and washer located at the inner end of each radius arm pivot shaft.
17 Undo and remove the eight bolts and spring washers securing the rear suspension cross tube rubber mountings to the cross tube.
18 The radius arm assemblies may now be separated from the cross tube.
19 Refitting the cross tube and radius arm assembly is the reverse sequence to removal but the points in the following paragraphs should be noted.
20 Fit the cross tube rubber mounting to the body and rubber mounting to the cross tube bolts and spring washers and tighten finger tight and leave in this condition until the radius arm has been refitted (paragraph 24).
21 Tighten the cross tube rubber mounting to cross tube set bolts to a torque wrench setting of 18 lb f ft (2.55 kg fm).
22 Tighten the cross tube rubber mounting to body bolts to a torque wrench setting of 37 lb f ft (5.09 kg fm).

23 Locate the radius arm so that the vertical measurement between the rear hub centre to the body wheel arch is 10.12 in (257 mm) and hold in this position.

24 Hold the displacer unit hard against its reaction rubber and tighten the radius arm pivot nut to a torque wrench setting of 105 lb f ft (14.58 kg fm).

25 Ensure that the displacer unit knuckle joint ball pin remains positioned in its socket in the radius arm.

26 Repressurise the 'Hydragas' system.

18 Rear suspension cross tube rubber mounting - removal and refitment

1 It is possible to carry out this operation without depressurising the Hydragas system. However, care must be taken to ensure that the radius arm is adequately supported at both the forward and rear ends during this operation. If, when the job has been completed and the car has been lowered to the ground, the rear suspension appears to be lop-sided, then this is due to the incorrect location of the flat face on the outer end of the pivot shaft in the mounting. To create a level rear suspension system, the Hydragas unit will have to be depressurised and then re-pressurised. However, it is unusual to have to do this.

2 Chock the front wheels, jack up the rear of the car and support on firmly based axle stands. Remove the road wheel.

3 Place a jack or packing blocks under the trailing end of the arm to support it.

4 Back off the radius arm pivot shaft inner nut until it is flush with the end of the pivot shaft.

5 Undo and remove the nut and washer located at the outer end of the radius arm pivot shaft.

6 Using a small jack or suitable packing support the front end of the radius arm and then undo and remove the four bolts and spring washers securing the rubber mounting to the cross tube.

7 Undo and remove the two bolts and spring washers securing the rubber mounting to the body.

8 Refitting the cross tube rubber mounting is the reverse sequence to removal but the following additional points should be noted.

a) Make sure that the flat on the outer end of the pivot shaft engages the flat in the cross tube rubber mounting.

b) Refer to Section 17 and follow the instructions given in paragraphs 20 to 26 inclusive.

19 Rear suspension radius arm - removal and refitment

1 This operation will not normally be possible to carry out at home because the 'Hydragas' system must be depressurised. If the equipment is available full instructions for operation are given on the machine.

2 Chock the front wheels, jack up the rear of the car and support on firmly based axle stands. Remove the road wheel.

3 Using a screwdriver remove the grease retainer from the centre of the rear hub.

4 Bend back the split pin ears and withdraw the split pin.

5 Lift away the nut retainer and unscrew the nut from the radius arm stub shaft. Recover the washer.

6 The rear hub and brake drum assembly may now be lifted from the stub shaft.

7 Depressurise the 'Hydragas' system.

8 Unscrew the union nut securing the connecting pipe hose to the rear suspension displacer unit.

9 Remove the split pins and remove the clevis pins attaching the handbrake inner cable to the levers at the rear of the brake backplate.

10 Undo and remove the nut and spring washer securing the handbrake outer cable to the lug on the radius arm.

11 Wipe the top of the brake master cylinder reservoir and unscrew the cap. Place a piece of polythene over the reservoir neck and refit the cap.

12 Wipe the area around the rear brake hose to pipe unions and

then unscrew the union nut. Tape the pipe ends to prevent dirt ingress.

13 Undo and remove the nut securing the brake hose to the radius arm mounted bracket.

14 Withdraw the spring clip and lift away the clevis pin attaching the rebound strap to the radius arm bracket.

15 Slacken the radius arm pivot shaft inner nut.

16 Undo and remove the two bolts and spring washers securing the rear suspension cross tube rubber mounting to the body.

17 Undo and remove the four bolts and spring washers securing the rubber mounting to the cross tube.

18 Undo and remove the nut and washer located at the inner end of the radius arm pivot shaft.

19 The radius arm complete with cross tube rubber mounting and pivot shaft may now be lifted away.

20 Separate the rear displacer unit and its knuckle joint from the radius arm.

21 Wipe the rear wheel cylinder and backplate area free of dirt and then unscrew the brake pipe to wheel cylinder union nut.

22 Undo and remove the three nuts, bolts and spring washers securing the brake backplate assembly to the radius arm.

23 Undo and remove the nut and bolt securing the rebound check strap bracket to the radius arm.

24 Undo and remove the nut and spring washer securing the bump rubber to the radius arm.

25 Refitting the rear suspension radius arm is the reverse sequence to removal. The points in the following paragraphs should be noted.

26 Refer to Section 13 and follow the instructions in paragraphs 13 to 18 inclusive.

27 Tighten the brake back plate nuts to a torque wrench setting of 20 lb f ft (2.7 kg fm).

28 Tighten the check strap bracket nut to a torque wrench setting of 44 lb f ft (6.12 kg fm).

29 Pack the displacer knuckle joint with a little "Dextragrease Super GP".

30 Reset the rear hub bearing end float as described in Section 16, paragraphs 12 to 16 inclusive.

31 Repressurise the 'Hydragas' system.

32 Bleed the brake hydraulic system as described in Chapter 9.

20 Rear suspension radius arm bushes - removal and refitment

1 Refer to Section 19 and remove the radius arm assembly.

2 Ideally the bushes should be pressed out but if these facilities are not available note the bush locations and draw out using a high tension steel nut, bolt and suitable diameter washers.

3 Fitting the new bushes is the reverse sequence to removal. The outer sleeve of each bush must be flush with the face of its housing in the radius arm.

Note: *These rubber bushes are prone to breaking-up. The symptoms are much thumping and rattling and also tyre wear problems. The tyre wear will be the first symptom before the noise becomes really audible. Check the rear suspension at least every two years.*

21 Rear suspension radius arm stub shaft - removal and refitment

1 Refer to Section 19 and remove the radius arm assembly.

2 Using a press push the stub shaft, circlip end leading from the radius arm. If a press is not available it can be driven out providing the radius arm is well supported.

3 Using a pair of circlip pliers remove the circlip.

4 Refitting the stub shaft is the reverse sequence to removal. The fit of the stub shaft in the radius arm should be an inter-ference fit of 0.0005 - 0.0025 in (0.01 - 0.06 mm). If the stub shaft is an easy fit in the radius arm measurements should be taken and if excessive the radius arm bore should be suspect.

22 Rear suspension reaction rubber - removal and refitment

1 This operation will not normally be possible to carry out at home because the 'Hydragas' system must be depressurised. If the equipment is available full instructions for operation are given on the machine.
2 Chock the front wheels, jack up the rear of the car and support on firmly based axle stands. Remove the road wheel.
3 Depressurise the 'Hydragas' system.
4 Undo and remove the two bolts and spring washers securing the reaction rubber to the underside of the body.
5 Lift away the reaction mounting.

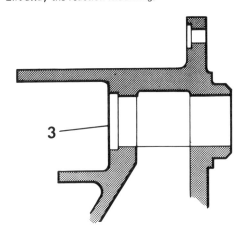

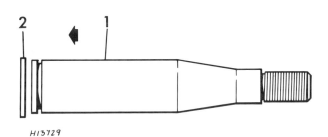

H13729

Fig. 11.13. Rear suspension radius arm stub shaft

1 *Stub shaft*   3 *Circlip register*
2 *Circlip*

6 Refitting the reaction rubber is the reverse sequence to removal. Ensure that the rear displacer unit knuckle joint ball pin remains located in its socket in the radius arm.

23 Rear suspension rebound strap - removal and refitment

1 Chock the front wheels, jack up the rear of the car and support on firmly based axle stands. Remove the road wheel.
2 Support the radius arm so that the strap is not under tension.
3 Withdraw the spring clips and remove the two clevis pins attaching the rebound strap ends to the body and radius arm.
4 Refitting the rebound strap is the reverse sequence to removal. Note that one side of the strap is marked "REAR FACE" and it must be fitted the correct way round.

24 Suspension trim height - checking

1 The information given in this section is relative to the trim height at the front of the vehicle. If adjustment is necessary, this should be left to the local BLMC garage who will have the equipment to carry out satisfactory pressure checks.
2 Should the special machine be available full instructions will be found attached to it.
3 The car must be in the unladen condition but have a full complement of petrol, oil and water.
4 Check the tyre pressures and adjust as necessary.
5 With the car on level ground rock it sideways several times to settle the suspension.
6 Check the suspension trim height by taking measurements between the centre of the front hub and underside of the wheel arch at its outer edge. The correct reading is:

14.68 ± 0.24 in (373 ± 6 mm) (up to 1976)
14.41 ± 0.40 in (366 ± 10 mm) (1976 onwards)

The trim height variation between each side of the car must not exceed 0.39 in (10 mm).

25 Rack and pinion assembly - removal and refitment

1 Chock the rear wheels, apply the handbrake, jack up the front of the car and support on firmly based axle stands. Remove the road wheels.
2 Remove the floor covering from around the intermediate shaft so as to gain access to the toe-board.
3 Undo and remove the four self tapping screws securing the cover plate to the toe-board. Lift away the cover plate.

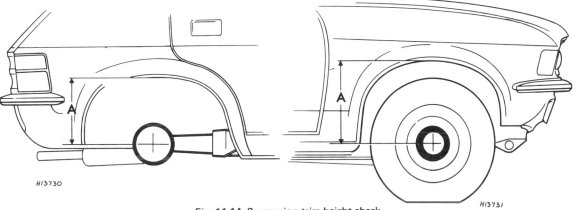

Fig. 11.14. Suspension trim height check

Rear radius arm installation (dimension A)   *Suspension trim height* (dimension A)

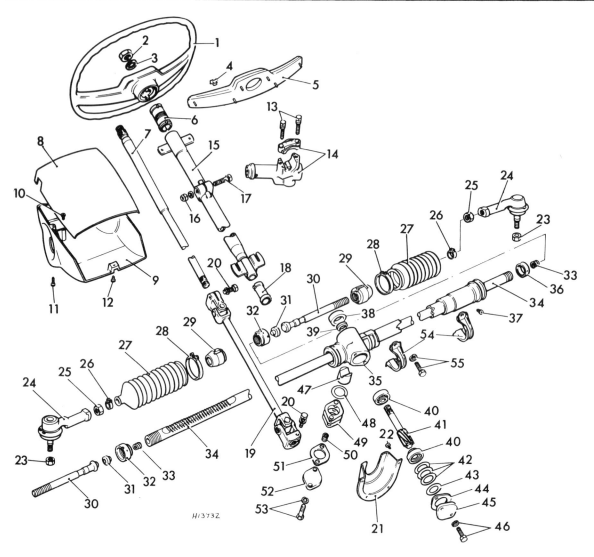

Fig. 11.15. Steering rack and pinion assembly

1 Steering wheel	16 Locknut	29 Ball housing	43 Shim - 0.060 in.
2 Nut	17 Bolt - column to upper	30 Tie-rod	(1.52 mm)
3 Lock washer	support bracket	31 Ball seat	44 Shim gasket - 0.010 in.
4 Clip - pad to wheel	18 Column lower bush	32 Locknut	(0.25 mm)
5 Steering wheel pad	19 Intermediate shaft	33 Thrust spring	45 End cover
6 Column upper bush	20 Pinch bolt and spring	34 Rack	46 Bolt and spring washer
7 Inner column	washer	35 Rack housing	47 Rack support yoke
8 Cowl - upper half	21 Cover plate	36 Rack bearing	48 'O' ring seal
9 Cowl - lower half	22 Screw - plate to body	37 Bearing retaining screw	49 Shims
10 Screw - cowl to column	23 Locknut	38 Seal washer - rack to	50 Thrust spring
bracket	24 Balljoint	body	51 Joint washer
11 Screw - lower to upper cowl	25 Locknut	39 Pinion oil seal	52 Cover plate
12 Screw - cowl to column	26 Clip - small	40 Pinion bearing	53 Bolt and spring washer
13 Shear bolt - lock	27 Rack housing seal	41 Pinion	54 Clamps - rack to body
14 Steering lock	28 Clip - large	42 Shims	55 Screw and spring washer
15 Outer column			

4 Undo and remove the bottom universal joint pinch bolt and spring washer.

5 Undo and remove the locknut that secures the tie-rod ball-joint pins to the steering arms.

6 Using a universal balljoint separator detach the ball pins from the steering arms.

7 Suitably support the rack and pinion assembly. Undo and remove the four bolts and spring washers securing the clamps to the body. Lift away the two clamps.

8 The steering rack and pinion assembly may now be lifted away from the car through the wheel arch aperture on the driver's side.

9 Recover the sealing washer from around the pinion.

10 Refitting the steering rack and pinion assembly is the reverse sequence to removal but the following additional points should be noted.

11 It is necessary to centralise the rack. Slide the rack tube seal to one side and insert a 0.25 in (6 mm) diameter dowel rod (or

drill shank) through the rack casing and engage the mating hole in the rack.

12 Move the rack so that the grooves in the rack housing engage the projections on the body brackets; at the same time a second person should hold the steering wheel with its spokes in the horizontal plane. Now engage the pinion splines.

13 Remove the dowel and replace the rack seal over the tube hole.

14 Tighten all attachments to the recommended torque wrench settings as given at the beginning of this Chapter.

15 Refer to Section 37, for information on checking the front wheel alignment.

26 Steering rack and pinion housing oil seals - removal and refitment

1 Chock the rear wheels, apply the handbrake, jack up the front of the car and support on firmly based axle stands. Remove the road wheel.

2 Slacken the balljoint locknut on the tie-rod.

3 Undo and remove the ball pin locknut and then using a universal balljoint separator detach the ball joint from the steering arm.

4 Unscrew the balljoint from the tie-rod.

5 Slacken the small diameter clip at the tie-rod end and slide from the oil seal.

6 Slacken the large diameter clip and detach the oil seal from the rack housing. Slide the oil seal from the end of the rack and pinion housing.

7 To refit the seal first position the clip on the end of the rack housing in such a manner that the clip can be tightened from below and at the front.

8 Lubricate the contact diameters of the seals and fit onto the rack housing and tie-rod. Tighten the large clip.

9 Inject 0.33 pint (0.19 litre) of "Castrol Hypoy" between the seal and tie-rod.

10 Refit the small clip and tighten.

11 Refit the balljoint and tighten the locknut to a torque wrench setting of 35 lb f ft (4.8 kg fm).

12 Refer to Section 37 for information on checking the front wheel alignment.

27 Steering wheel - removal and refitment

1 Using a knife carefully prise the pad from the steering wheel spokes.

2 Undo and remove the two screws securing the bottom cowl to the top cowl and the two screws securing the bottom cowl to the column bracket. Also remove the self-tapping screw securing the bottom cowl to the outer column.

3 Lift away the top cowl and move the bottom cowl away from the steering column.

4 Using a suitable size socket undo and remove the nut and shakeproof washer from the steering wheel hub.

5 Mark the steering wheel hub and inner column to assist correct refitment.

6 Using the palms of the hands thump the back of the spokes as near to the hub as possible to release the steering wheel from the inner column. Should it be very tight a large universal puller will be required.

7 To refit the steering wheel, move the road wheels to the straight ahead position and then align the slots in the switch bush with the steering wheel hub. Make sure that the trip dog is in line with the direction indicator switch. Refit the steering wheel, lining up the previously made marks. Check that the spokes are in the horizontal plane.

8 Replace the shakeproof washer and nut and tighten to a torque wrench setting of 35 lb f ft (4.8 kg fm).

9 Re-assembly is now the reverse sequence to removal.

28 Steering column assembly - removal and refitment

1 For safety reasons, disconnect the battery.

2 Undo and remove the two screws securing the bottom cowl to the top cowl, and the two screws securing the bottom cowl to the column bracket. Also, remove the self-tapping screw securing the bottom cowl to the outer column.

3 Lift away the top cowl and move the bottom cowl away from the steering column.

4 Locate and disconnect the ignition/starter switch multi-pin plug at the connector below the panel.

5 Locate and disconnect the direction indicator/wiper/washer switch multi-pin plugs at the connectors below the panel.

6 Undo and remove the pinch bolt and spring washer securing the intermediate shaft to the inner column.

7 Undo and remove the screw, spring washer and earthing terminal and slacken the other screw that secures the bottom of the column to the pedal bracket.

8 Undo and remove the through - bolt that secures the steering column bracket to the upper support bracket.

9 The steering column assembly may now be lifted away from inside the car.

10 To refit the steering column assembly, first slide the rack tube seal to one side and insert a 0.25 in (6 mm) diameter dowel rod (or drill shank) through the rack casing and engage the mating hole in the rack. It may be necessary to adjust the position of the front wheels to obtain the true straight ahead position.

11 Push the inner column into the intermediate shaft, fit the upper support bracket through bolt and the screws at the bottom of the column. Do not tighten yet.

12 Line up the inner column groove and fit the pinch bolt. Tighten this to a torque wrench setting of 25-30 lb f ft (3.4-4.1 kg fm).

13 Check the clearance between the steering wheel hub and the cowl. If necessary move the outer column to obtain a clearance of approximately 0.125 in (3 mm).

14 Fully tighten the column securing screws and upper support bracket through bolt.

15 Remove the rack centralisation dowel and reposition the seal over the tube seal.

16 Refitting is now the reverse sequence to removal. Check that the choke control has 0.0625 in (1.59 mm) free movement before the carburettor cam lever begins to move. Adjust it necessary as described in Chapter 3.

29 Steering column assembly - overhaul

1 Refer to Section 28 and remove the steering column assembly.

2 Mount the outer column between soft faces in a bench vice.

3 If the steering cowl is still in position it should be removed. Further information will be found in Section 32.

4 Back off the retaining screw and lift the combined direction indicator/wiper/washer switch from over the end of the column.

5 The inner column should now be pulled upwards and out from the top of the outer column. It should be noted that the serrations at the bottom of the column will damage the bottom bush so it will have to be renewed on re-assembly.

6 Using a screwdriver or other suitable means remove the top bush from the outer column.

7 Ease up the retaining tag and remove the bottom bush from the outer column.

8 Using a knife carefully prise the pad from the steering wheel spokes.

9 Using a suitable size socket undo and remove the nut and shakeproof washer from the steering wheel hub.

10 Mark the steering wheel hub and inner column to assist correct refitting.

11 Using a large universal puller draw the steering wheel from the inner column.

12 Refer to Section 33 and remove the steering column lock.
13 To re-assemble the steering column assembly, first smear the inside surface of the top and bottom bushes, also fill the grooves, with graphite grease.
14 Carefully enter the inner column into the outer column and slide down until it protrudes approximately 3 in (76 mm) from the bottom end.
15 Open the split bottom bush sufficiently to pass the bush, chamferred end first, over the splines and onto the undercut section of the column.
16 Carefully drive the bush into the outer column making sure that one of the slots in the top edge engages with the detent in the outer column.
17 Bend the retaining tag down but take care that it does not touch the inner column.
18 Using a suitable diameter tube drive the top bush, chamfered end first, into the outer column making sure that one of the slots in the lower edge engages with the detent in the outer column.
19 Move the top of the inner column until it is 3.25 in (82.6 mm) above the outer column.
20 Reassembly is now the reverse sequence to removal.

30 Steering column top bush - removal and refitment

1 For safety reasons disconnect the battery.
2 Refer to Section 27 and remove the steering wheel and cowl.
3 Back off the retaining screw and lift the combined direction indicator/wiper/washer switch from over the end of the inner column.
4 It will now be necessary to remove the top bush. It may either be eased out with a screwdriver or a hook shaped tool.
5 To refit the top bush first smear the inside of the bush with a little graphite grease. Also fill the grooves with the grease.
6 Using a suitable diameter tube drive the bush, chamfered end first into the outer column making sure that one of the slots at the lower edge engages with the detent in the outer column.
7 Re-assembly is now the reverse sequence to removal.

31 Steering column intermediate shaft - removal and refitment

1 For safety reasons, disconnect the battery.
2 Refer to Section 28 and remove the steering column assembly.
3 Remove the floor covering from around the intermediate shaft so as to gain access to the toe-board.
4 Undo and remove the four self-tapping screws securing the cover plate to the toe-board. Lift away the cover plate.
5 Undo and remove the bottom universal joint pinch bolt and spring washer.
6 The intermediate shaft may now be detached from the pinion and lifted away from inside the car.
7 Refitting the steering column intermediate shaft is the reverse sequence to removal. When pushing the universal joint onto the pinion align the groove and then fit the pinch bolt. This should be tightened to a torque wrench setting of 25 lb f ft (3.9 kg f m).

32 Steering column cowl - removal and refitment

1 Undo and remove the two securing screws and then press on the front of the top cowl until it is clear of the steering wheel hub boss. Lift away the top cowl.
2 Should the top cowl prove difficult to depress slacken the column mounting bolts and move the outer column assembly downwards.
3 Refer to Chapter 3 and disconnect the choke control cable from the carburettor.
4 Undo and remove the self-tapping screws securing the bottom cowl to the outer column.

5 Undo and remove the two screws that secure the bottom cowl to the column bracket.
6 The bottom cowl and choke control assembly may now be lifted away. It will be necessary to pull the choke cable through the body grommet.
7 Undo and remove the nut and lock washer that secures the choke control cable to the bottom cowl and remove the cable.
8 Re-assembly and refitting is the reverse sequence to removal. the following additional points should be noted:
a) When refitting the choke control cable make sure that knob symbol is the correct way up.
b) The clearance between the steering wheel hub and cowl should be approximately 0.125 in (3 mm). If necessary move the outer column assembly as necessary to obtain this clearance.
c) The control knob should have 0.0625 in (1.59 mm) free movement before the carburettor cam lever begins to move. Adjust if necessary as described in Chapter 3.

33 Steering column lock and ignition/starter switch - removal and refitment

1 For safety reasons, disconnect the battery.
2 Refer to Section 32 and remove the steering column cowl.
3 Refer to Section 28 and remove the steering column assembly.
4 Mount the outer column between soft faces in a bench vice.
5 Using a drill remove the heads of the shear bolts or use an 'easy out' and unscrew the shear bolts.
6 The lock assembly and clamp plate may now be removed from the column.
7 Refitting the switch is the reverse sequence to removal but the following additional points should be noted:
8 The lock body should be centralised over the slot in the outer column and fit the clamp plate. Do not shear the bolt heads yet.
9 Reconnect the multi-pin connectors, temporarily reconnect the battery and check that the lock operates correctly.
10 Disconnect the battery again and tighten the shear bolts until the heads break off.

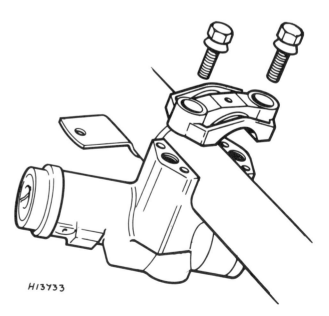

H13733

Fig. 11.16. Steering column lock and ignition/starter switch attachment

34 Steering arm - removal and refitment

1 Chock the rear wheels, apply the handbrake, jack up the front of the car and remove the road wheel.
2 Undo and remove the nut securing the tie-rod balljoint pin to the steering arm.
3 Using a universal balljoint separator detach the balljoint from the steering arm.
4 Bend back the lock washer tabs and then undo and remove the two securing bolts.
5 Lift away the steering arm and recover the two hollow dowels.
6 Refitting the steering arm is the reverse sequence to removal. Tighten all attachments to the recommended torque wrench setting as given in the Specifications at the beginning of this Chapter.
7 Refer to Section 37 and check the front wheel alignment.

35 Steering tie-rod balljoint - removal and refitment

1 Chock the rear wheels, apply the handbrake, jack up the front of the car and support on firmly based axle stands. Remove the road wheels.
2 Slacken the balljoint locknut on the tie-rod.
3 Undo and remove the ball pin locknut on the tie-rod.
4 Undo and remove the ball pin locknut and then using a universal balljoint separator detach the balljoint from the steering rim.
5 Unscrew the balljoint from the tie-rod.
6 Refitting the balljoint is the reverse sequence to removal. It will be necessary to check the front wheel alignment. Further information will be found in Section 37.

36 Rack and pinion assembly - overhaul

1 Refer to Section 25 and remove the rack and pinion assembly from the car.
2 Release the balljoint locknuts and remove the balljoints and the locknuts from the steering tie-rods.
3 Slacken the large and small seal clips and remove the seals and clips from each end of the rack housing.
4 Drain the oil from the rack housing.
5 Carefully prise up the detent in each locknut from the ball housings.
6 Using a 'C'-spanner or soft metal drift unlock and unscrew each ball housing. Detach each tie-rod from the rack ends.
7 Remove the tie-rod ball seat and thrust spring from each end of the rack.
8 Carefully prise up the detent in each locknut from the rack housing and remove the locknut.
9 Undo and remove the two bolts and spring washers securing the rack damper cover plate to the rack housing. Lift away the cover plate, gasket and shims.
10 Lift away the damper thrust spring, support yoke and 'O' ring seal from the rack housing.
11 Undo and remove the two bolts and spring washers securing the pinion end cover to the rack housing. Lift away the end cover, gasket and shims.
12 The pinion and lower bearing may now be pushed out from its housing.
13 Carefully withdraw the rack from the pinion end of the rack housing. Should the rack be drawn out from the other end the teeth will damage the rack bush.
14 Remove the pinion upper bearing from the rack housing.
15 Using a screwdriver remove the pinion oil seal from the rack housing.
16 Undo and remove the rack bush securing screw and remove the rack bush from the rack housing.
17 Thoroughly clean all parts with paraffin. Carefully inspect the teeth on the rack and also the pinion for chipping, rough-

ness, uneven wear, hollows or fractures.
18 Carefully inspect the component parts of the inner ball joints for wear or ridging and renew as necessary.
19 The outer trackrod joints cannot be dismantled and, if worn must be renewed as a complete assembly. Examine the component parts of the damper and renew any parts that show signs of wear. Pay particular attention to the oil seals and as a precautionary measure it is always best to renew them.
20 As it is difficult to refill the rack and pinion assembly with oil once it is fitted to the car, make sure that the rubber gaiters are sound before refitting them. If they are in the least bit torn or perished complete loss of oil could occur later and they would then have to be renewed.
21 To re-assemble, first fit a new rack bearing into the rack housing and against its register.
22 Using a 0.1094 in (2.7781 mm) diameter drill, cut a blind hole into the rack bush through the retaining screw hole, to a depth of 0.142 in (10.5 mm) when measured from the spot facing of the screw hole.
23 Apply a little non-hardening sealer to the bush retaining screw and fit to the rack housing. Ensure that the bush bore is not damaged.
24 Fit the upper bearing to the pinion and push the upper bearing fully into the rack housing. Remove the pinion again.
25 Carefully insert the rack into the housing from the pinion end.
26 Centralise the rack and insert a 0.25 in (6 mm) diameter rod through the rack housing and engage the mating hole in the rack.
27 Refit the pinion and then the lower bearing.
28 It is now necessary to set the pinion and bearing pre-load. First fit bearing shims until the pack stands proud of the pinion housing. Now fit the pinion end cover and tighten the bolts lightly.
29 Using feeler gauges measure the gap between the end cover and rack housing.
30 Remove the end cover and make up a shim pack to give a gap of 0.001 - 0.003 in (0.025 - 0.076 mm). The standard shim must be adjacent to the end cover. To enable an accurate setting shims are available in the following thicknesses:

Standard shims
0.060 in (1.52 mm)
0.002 in (0.06 mm)
0.005 in (0.13 mm)
0.010 in (0.25 mm)

31 Fit a new gasket and apply a little sealing compound to the threads of the bolt which is adjacent to the damper cover. Tighten the end cover bolts to a torque wrench setting of 24 lb f ft (20 kg fm).
32 Fit a new pinion oil seal flush with the end of the housing and with its sealing lips towards the pinion bearing.
33 The cover plate and rack support yoke must next be refitted. Tighten the cover plate bolts evenly until the rack is lightly clamped by the support yoke.
34 Remove the rack centralising rod previously fitted and turn the pinion through 180° in each direction and if necessary tighten or slacken the cover plate bolts until free movement without binding is obtained.
35 Using feeler gauges measure the gap between the cover plate and housing.
36 Remove the cover plate again and re-assemble fitting a new 'O' ring seal to the support yoke, a new gasket and shims to the value of the feeler gauge measurement plus support yoke to cover plate clearance of 0.002 - 0.005 in (0.05 - 0.13 mm).
37 To enable an accurate setting shims are available in the following thicknesses:

0.002 in (0.06 mm)
0.005 in (0.13 mm)
0.010 in (0.25 mm)
Gasket thickness 0.010 in (0.25 mm)

38 Refit the assembly and tighten the cover plate bolts to a torque wrench setting of 15 lb f ft (2.0 kg fm).
39 Turn the pinion through 180° in each direction from the

centre position to ensure there are no signs of tightness or binding.

40 Centralise the rack and insert the metal rod again.

41 The tie-rods are now refitted. Screw a new ball housing locknut onto each end of the rack to the limits of the thread.

42 Place the thrust spring and ball seat in the end of the rack. Insert the tie-rod in its ball housing, well lubricate the ball and tighten the ball housing until the tie-rod ball is just nipped.

43 Screw the locknut up to the ball housing. Slacken the ball housing one eighth of a turn and tighen the locknut. The housing must not turn when the locknut is being tightened. Ideally the locknut should be tightened to a torque wrench setting of 35 lb f ft (4.5 kg fm).

44 Check that there is full movement of the tie-rod.

45 Using a punch lock the locknut ring edge into the slots in the ball housing and rack.

46 Refit one of the rack seals and secure with the two clips.

47 Inject 0.33 pint (0.19 litre) of Castrol Hypoy into the housing and then refit the second seal.

48 Screw the balljoint locknut onto the tie-rods and screw on each balljoint an equal amount until the ball pin centre dimension is 47.30 in (1201.6 mm). Tighten the locknut.

49 The steering rack and pinion assembly is now ready for refitting to the car.

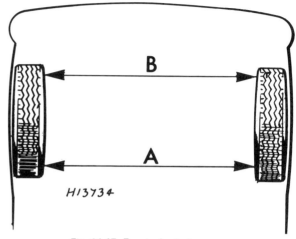

Fig. 11.17. Front wheel alignment

Dimension 'A' must be 0.156 in. (3.969 mm) less than dimension 'B' or as detailed in Chapter 13 for later models

37 Front wheel alignment

1 The front wheels are correctly aligned when they are turning out at the front 0.156 in (3.969 mm) as shown in Fig. 11.17. It is important that this measurement is taken on a centre line drawn horizontally and parallel to the ground through the centre line of the hub. The exact point should be in the centre of the sidewall of the tyre and not on the wheel rim which could be distorted and give inaccurate readings.

2 The adjustment is effected by loosening the locknut on each tie-rod balljoint and also slackening the rubber oil seal clip holding it to the tie-rod, and turning both tie-rods equally until adjustment is correct.

3 This is a job best left to your local BL garage as accurate alignment requires the use of special equipment. If the wheels are not in alignment, tyre wear will be heavy and uneven and the steering will be stiff and unresponsive.

38 Fault diagnosis - Suspension and steering

Symptom	Reason/s	Remedy
STEERING FEELS VAGUE, CAR WANDERS AND FLOATS AT SPEED		
	Tyre pressures uneven	Check pressures and adjust as necessary.
	Steering gear ball joints badly worn	Fit new balljoints.
	Suspension geometry incorrect	Check and rectify.
	Steering mechanism free play excessive	Adjust or overhaul steering mechanism.
	Front suspension and rear suspension pick-up points out of alignment	Normally caused by poor repair work after a serious accident. Extensive rebuilding necessary.
STIFF AND HEAVY STEERING	Tyre pressures too low	Check pressures and inflate tyres.
	No oil in steering gear	Top up steering gear.
	No grease in steering and suspension ball-joints	Clean nipples and grease thoroughly.
	Front wheel toe-out incorrect	Check and reset toe-out
	Suspension geometry incorrect	Check and rectify.
	Steering gear incorrectly adjusted too tightly	Check and readjust steering gear.
	Steering column badly misaligned	Determine cause and rectify (usually due to bad repair after severe accident damage and difficult to correct)
WHEEL WOBBLE AND VIBRATION	Wheel nuts loose	Check and tighten as necessary.
	Front wheels and tyres out of balance	Balance wheels and tyres and add weights as necessary.
	Steering ball joints badly worn	Replace steering gear ball joints.
	Hub bearings badly worn	Remove and fit new hub bearings.
	Steering gear free play excessive	Adjust and overhaul steering gear.

Chapter 12 Bodywork and fittings

For modifications, and information applicable to later models, see Supplement at end of manual

Contents

1 General description

The combined body and underframe is of all steel construction. This makes a very strong and torsionally rigid shell.

Following the principle of one wheel at each corner and based on improvements made to other transverse engine models the Allegro has been designed to give a high proportion of passenger space relative to the overall length. (It is just 6 inches (152.4 mm) longer, 3 inches (76.2 mm) wider and less than 1 inch (25.4 mm) higher than the Austin 1100/1300). There is more room around the engine; and the luggage compartment has a 15 cubic ft (0.42 cubic M) capacity. The latest techniques of electrophoretic painting are employed plus underbody treatment of the main floor panels, bonnet floor and all wheel arches. In addition a wax spray protection is used in the body sills and all box members of the under structure. The body design is such that there is minimum, if any, intrusion of the power unit into the passenger space in frontal collisions. Because of fire risks in rear end collisions the fuel tank has been located between the rear wheels.

The instrument cluster located in front of the 'quartic' steering wheel houses two dials, and a range of easily accessible controls. A heater and ventilation system is fitted incorporating a full flow system with outlet ducts at instrument panel level.

Although the basic design has remained the same throughout the production run of the Allegro range, the trim and interior fittings of the Series 2 and 3 models differ considerably. These are covered in Chapter 13.

2 Maintenance - exterior

1 The general condition of a car's bodywork is the one thing that significantly affects its value. Maintenance is easy but needs to be regular and particular. Neglect - particularly after minor damage can quickly lead to further deterioration and costly repair bills. It is important to keep watch on those parts of the bodywork not immediately visible, for example the underside, inside all wheel arches and the lower part of the engine compartment.

2 The basic maintenance routine for the bodywork is washing, preferably with a lot of water from a hose. This will remove all the loose solids which may have stuck to the car. It is important to flush these off in such a way as to prevent grit from scratching the finish. The wheel arches and underbody need washing in the same way to remove any accumulated mud which will retain moisture and tend to encourage rust. Paradoxically enough, the best time to clean the underbody and wheel arches is in wet weather when the mud is thoroughly wet and soft. In very wet weather the underbody is usually cleaned of large accumulations automatically and this is a good time for inspection.

3 Periodically it is a good idea to have the whole of the underside of the car steam cleaned, engine compartment included, for removal of accumulation of oily grime which sometimes collects thickly in areas near the engine and gearbox, so that a thorough inspection can be carried out to see what minor repairs and renovations are necessary. If steam facilities are not available there are one or two excellent grease solvents available which can be brush applied. The dirt can then be simply hosed off. Any signs of rust on the underside panels and chassis members must be attended to immediately. Thorough wire brushing followed by treatment with an anti-rust compound, primer and underbody sealer will prevent continued deterioration. If not dealt with the car could eventually become structurally unsound, and therefore, unsafe.

4 After washing the paintwork wipe it off with a chamois leather to give a clear unspotted finish. A coat of clear wax polish will give added protection against chemical pollutants in the air and will survive several subsequent washings. If the paintwork sheen has dulled or oxidised use a cleaner/polisher combination to restore the brilliance of the shine. This requires a little more effort but it usually is because regular washing has been neglected. Always check that door and drain holes and pipes are completely clear so that water can drain out. Brightwork should be treated the same way as paintwork. Windscreens and windows can be kept clear of smeary film which often appears, if a little ammonia is added to the water. If glass work is scratched, a good rub with a proprietary metal

polish will often clean it. Never use any form of wax or other paint/chromium polish on glass.

3 Maintenance - interior

The flooring cover, usually carpet, should be brushed or vacuum cleaned regularly to keep it free from grit. If badly stained, remove it from the car for scrubbing and sponging and make quite sure that it is dry before refitting. Seat and interior trim panels can be kept clean with a wipe over with a damp cloth. If they do become stained (which can be more apparent on light coloured upholstery) use a little liquid detergent and a soft nailbrush to scour the grime out of the grain of the material. Do not forget to keep the headlining clean in the same way as the upholstery. When using liquid cleaners inside the car do not over-wet the surfaces being cleaned. Excessive damp could get into the upholstery seams and padded interior causing stains, offensive odours or even rot. If the inside of the car gets wet accidentally it is worthwhile taking some trouble to dry it out properly. **Do not** use oil or electric heaters inside the car for this purpose. If, when removing mats for cleaning, there are signs of damp underneath, all the interior of the car floor should be uncovered and the point of water entry found. It may be only a missing grommet, but it could be a rusted through floor panel and this demands immediate attention as described in the previous Section. More often than not both sides of the panel will require treatment.

4 Maintenance - PVC external roof covering

Under no circumstances try to clean any external PVC roof covering with detergents, caustic soaps or spirit cleaners. Plain soap and water is all that is required with a soft brush to clean dirt that may be ingrained. Wash the covering as frequently as the rest of the car.

5 Minor body damage - repair

See photo sequences on pages 182 and 183.

Repair of minor scratches in the car's bodywork

If the scratch is very superficial, and does not penetrate to the metal of the bodywork - repair is very simple. Lightly rub the area of the scratch with a paintwork renovator (eg T-cut) or a very fine cutting paste, to remove loose paint from the scratch and to clear the surrounding bodywork of wax polish. Rinse the area with clean water.

Apply touch-up paint to the scratch using a thin paint brush; continue to apply thin layers of paint until the surface of the paint in the scratch is level with the surrounding paintwork. Allow the new paint at least two weeks to harden, then, blend it into the surrounding paintwork by rubbing the paintwork in the scratch area with a paint-work renovator (eg T-cut), or a very fine cutting paste. Finally apply wax polish.

An alternative to painting over the scratch is to use a paint transfer. Use the same preparation for the affected area; then simply pick a transfer of a suitable size to cover the scratch completely. Hold the transfer against the scratch and burnish its backing paper; the transfer will adhere to the paintwork, freeing itself from the backing paper at the same time. Polish the affected area to blend the transfer into the surrounding paintwork.

When a scratch has penetrated right through to the metal of the bodywork, causing the metal to rust, a different repair technique is required. Remove any loose rust from the bottom of the scratch with a penknife; then apply rust inhibiting paint (eg Kurust) to prevent the formation of rust in the future. Using a rubber or nylon applicator fill the scratch with bodystopper paste. If required, this paste can be mixed with cellulose thinners to provide a very thin paste which is ideal for filling narrow scratches. Before the stopper paste in the scratch hardens, wrap a piece of smooth cotton rag around the tip of a finger. Dip the finger in cellolose thinners and then quickly sweep it across the surface of the stopper paste in the scratch; this will ensure that the surface of the stopper paste is slightly hollowed. The scratch can now be painted over as described earlier in the Section.

Repair of dents in the car's bodywork

When deep denting of the car's bodywork has taken place, the first task is to pull the dent out, until the affected bodywork almost attains its original shape. There is little point in trying to restore the original shape completely, as the metal in the damaged area will have stretched on impact and cannot be reshaped fully to its original contour. It is better to bring the level of the dent up to a point which is about 1/8 inch (3 mm) below the level of the surrounding bodywork. In cases where the dent is very shallow anyway, it is not worth trying to pull it out at all.

If the underside of the dent is accessible, it can be hammered out gently from behind, using a mallet with a wooden or plastic head. Whilst doing this, hold a suitable block of wood firmly against the outside of the dent. This block will absorb the impact from the hammer blows and thus prevent a large area of bodywork from being 'belled-out'.

Should the dent be in a section of the bodywork which has double skin or some other factor making it inaccessible from behind, a different technique is called for. Drill several small holes through the metal inside the dent area - particularly in the deeper sections. Then screw long self-tapping screws into the holes just sufficiently for them to gain a good purchase in the metal. Now the dent can be pulled out by pulling on the protruding heads of the screws with a pair of pliers.

The next stage of repair is the removal of the paint from the damaged area, and from an inch or so of the surrounding 'sound' bodywork. This is accomplished most easily by using a wire brush or abrasive pad on a power drill, although it can be done just as effectively by hand using sheets of abrasive paper. To complete the preparations for filling, score the surface of the bare metal with a screwdriver or the tang of a file, or alternatively drill small holes in the affected area. This will provide a really good 'key' for the filler paste.

To complete the repair see the Section on filling and respraying.

Repair of rust holes or gashes in the car's bodywork.

Remove all paint from the affected area and from an inch or so of the surrounding 'sound' bodywork, using an abrasive pad or a wire brush on a power drill. If these are not available a few sheets of abrasive paper will do the job just as effectively. With the paint removed you will be able to gauge the severity of the corrosion and therefore decide whether to renew the whole panel (if this is possible) or to repair the affected area. Replacement body panels are not as expensive as most people think and it is often quicker and more satisfactory to fit a new panel than to attempt to repair large areas of corrosion.

Remove all fittings from the affected area except those which will act as a guide to the original shape of the damaged bodywork (eg. headlamp shells etc). Then, using tin snips or a hacksaw blade, remove all loose metal and any other metal badly affected by corrosion. Hammer the edges of the hole inwards in order to create a slight depression for the filler paste.

Wire brush the affected area to remove the powdery rust from the surface of the remaining metal. Paint the affected area with rust inhibiting paint; if the back of the rusted area is accessible treat this also.

Before filling can take place it will be necessary to block the hole in some way. This can be achieved by the use of one of the following materials: Zinc gauze, Aluminium tape or Polyurethane foam.

Zinc gauze is probably the best material to use for a large

hole. Cut a piece to the approximate size and shape of the hole to be filled, then position it in the hole so that its edges are below the level of the surrounding bodywork. It can be retained in position by several blobs of filler paste around its periphery.

Aluminium tape should be used for small or very narrow holes. Pull a piece off the roll and trim it to the approximate size and shape required, then pull off the backing paper (if used) and stick the tape over the hole; it can be overlapped if the thickness of one piece is insufficient. Burnish down the edges of the tape with the handle of a screwdriver or similar, to ensure that the tape is securely attached to the metal underneath.

Polyurethane foam is best used where the hole is situated in a section of bodywork of complex shape, backed by a small box section (eg. where the sill panel meets the rear wheel arch - most cars). The usual mixing procedure for this foam is as follows: Put equal amounts of fluid from each of the two cans provided in the kits, into one container. Stir until the mixture begins to thicken, then quickly pour the mixture into the hole, and hold a piece of cardboard over the larger apertures. Almost immediately the polyurethane will begin to expand, gushing out of any small holes left unblocked. When the foam hardens it can be cut back to just below the level of the surrounding bodywork with a hacksaw blade.

Having blocked off the hole the affected area must now be filled and sprayed - see Section on bodywork filling and respraying.

Bodywork repairs - filling and respraying.

Before using this Section, see the Sections on dent, deep scratch, rust holes and gash repairs.

Many types of bodyfiller are available, but generally speaking those proprietary kits which contain a tin of filler paste and a tube of resin hardener (eg. Holts Cataloy) are best for this type of repair. A wide flexible plastic or nylon applicator will be found invaluable for imparting a smooth and well contoured finish to the surface of the filler.

Mix up a little filler on a clean piece of card or board - use the hardener sparingly (follow the maker's instructions on the pack), otherwise the filler will set very rapidly.

Using the applicator, apply the filler paste to the prepared area; draw the applicator across the surface of the filler to achieve the correct contour and to level the filler surface. As soon as a contour that approximates the correct one is achieved, stop working the paste - if you carry on too long the paste will become sticky and begin to 'pick up' on the applicator.

Continue to add thin layers of filler paste at twenty-minute intervals until the level of the filler is just 'proud' of the surrounding bodywork.

Once the filler has hardened, excess can be removed using a Surform plane or Dreadnought file. From then on, progressively finer grades of abrasive paper should be used, starting with a 40 grade 'wet and dry' paper. Always wrap the abrasive paper around the flat rubber, cork or wooden block - otherwise the surface of the filler will not be completely flat. During the smoothing of the surface the 'wet and dry' paper should be periodically rinsed in water - this will ensure that a very smooth finish is imparted to the filler at the final stage.

At this stage the 'dent' should be surrounded by a ring of bare metal, which in turn should be encircled by the finely 'feathered' edge of the good paintwork. Rinse the repair area with clean water, until all of the dust produced by the rubbing down operation is gone.

Spray the whole repair area with a light coat of grey primer - this will show up any imperfections in the surface of the filler. Repair these imperfections with fresh filler paste or bodystopper, and once more smooth the surface with abrasive paper. If bodystopper is used, it can be mixed with cellulose thinners to form a really thin paste which is ideal for filling small holes. Repeat this spray and repair procedure until you are satisfied that the surface of the filler, and the feathered

edge of the paintwork are perfect. Clean the repair area with clean water and allow to dry fully.

The repair area is now ready for spraying. Paint spraying must be carried out in a warm, dry, windless and dust free atmosphere. This condition can be created artificially if you have access to a large indoor working area, but if you are forced to work in the open, you will have to pick your day very carefully. If you are working indoors, dousing the floor in the work area with water will 'lay' the dust which would otherwise be in the atmosphere; If the repair area is confined to one body panel, mask off the surrounding panels; this will help to minimise the effects of a slight mis-match in paint colours. Bodywork fittings (eg. chrome strips, door handles etc) will also need to be masked off. Use genuine masking tape and several thicknesses of newspaper for the masking operation.

Before commencing to spray, agitate the aerosol can thoroughly, then spray a test area (an old tin, or similar) until the technique is mastered. Cover the repair area with a thick coat of primer; the thickness should be built up using several thin layers of paint rather than one thick one. Using a 400 grade 'wet-and-dry' paper, rub down the surface of the primer until it is really smooth. While doing this, the work area should be thoroughly doused with water, and the wet-and dry paper periodically rinsed in water. Allow to dry before spraying on more paint.

Spray on the top coat, again building up the thickness by using several thin layers of paint. Start spraying in the centre of the repair area and then using a circular motion, work outwards until the whole repair area and about 2 inches of the surrounding original paintwork is covered. Remove all masking material 10 or 15 minutes after spraying on the final coat of paint. Allow the new paint at least 2 weeks to harden fully, then, using a paintwork renovator (eg. T-Cut), or a very fine cutting paste, blend the edges of the new paint into the existing paintwork. Finally, apply wax polish.

6 Major body damage - repair

1 Because the body is built on the monocoque principle, major damage must be repaired by a competent body repairer with the necessary jigs and equipment.
2 In the event of a crash that resulted in buckling of body panels, or damage to the roadwheels the car must be taken to a BLMC dealer or body repairer where the bodyshell and suspension alignment may be checked.
3 Bodyshell and/or suspension mis-alignment will cause excessive wear of the tyres, steering system and possibly transmission. The handling of the car will also be affected adversely.

7 Maintenance - locks and hinges

Once every 6,000 miles (10,000 km) or 6 months, the door, bonnet and boot locks and hinges should be oiled with a few drops of engine oil from an oil can. The door striker plates can be given a thin smear of grease to reduce wear and ensure free movement.

8 Door rattles - tracing and rectification

The most common cause of door rattles is a misaligned, loose or worn striker plate but other causes may be:
1 Loose door handles, window winder handles or door hinges.
2 Loose, worn or misaligned door lock components.
3 Loose or worn remote control mechanism, or a combination of these. If the striker catch is worn as a result of door rattles

This sequence of photographs deals with the repair of the dent and scratch (above rear lamp) shown in this photo. The procedure will be similar for the repair of a hole. It should be noted that the procedures given here are simplified - more explicit instructions will be found in the text

In the case of a dent the first job - after removing surrounding trim - is to hammer out the dent where access is possible. This will minimise filling. Here, the large dent having been hammered out, the damaged area is being made slightly concave

Now all paint must be removed from the damaged area, by rubbing with coarse abrasive paper. Alternatively, a wire brush or abrasive pad can be used in a power drill. Where the repair area meets good paintwork, the edge pf the paintwork should be 'feathered', using a finer grade of abrasive paper

In the case of a hole caused by rusting, all damaged sheet-metal should be cut away before proceeding to this stage. Here, the damaged area is being treated with rust remover and inhibitor before being filled

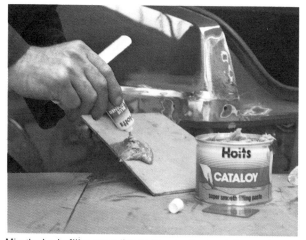

Mix the body filler according to its manufacturer's instructions. In the case of corrosion damage, it will be necessary to block off any large holes before filling - this can be done with zinc gauze or aluminium tape. Make sure the area is absolutely clean before ...

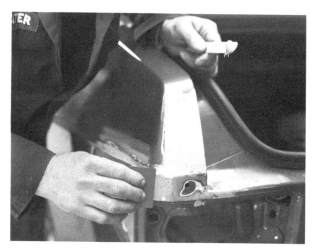

... applying the filler. Filler should be applied with a flexible applicator, as shown, for best results: the wooden spatula being used for confined areas. Apply thin layers of filler at 20-minute intervals, until the surface of the filler is slightly proud of the surrounding bodywork

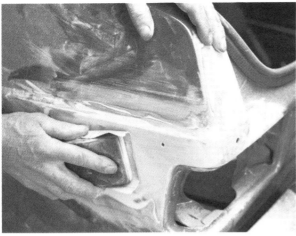

Initial shaping can be done with a Surform plane or Dreadnought file. Then, using progressively finer grades of wet-and-dry paper, wrapped around a sanding block, and copious amounts of clean water, rub-down the filler until really smooth and flat. Again, feather the edges of adjoining paintwork

The whole repair area can now be sprayed or brush-painted with primer. If spraying, ensure adjoining areas are protected from over-spray. Note that at least one-inch of the surrounding sound paintwork should be coated with primer. Primer has a 'thick' consistency, so will fill small imperfections

Again, using plenty of water, rub down the primer with a fine grade of wet-and-dry paper (400 grade is probably best) until it is really smooth and well blended into the surrounding paint-work. Any remaining imperfections can now be filled by carefully applied knifing stopper paste

When the stopper has hardened, rub-down the repair area again before applying the final coat of primer. Before rubbing-down this last coat of primer, ensure the repair area is blemish-free - use more stopper if necessary. To ensure that the surface of the primer is really smooth use some finishing compound

The top coat can now be applied. When working out of doors, pick a dry, warm and wind-free day. Ensure surrounding areas are protected from over-spray. Agitate the aerosol thoroughly, then spray the centre of the repair area, working outwards with a circular motion. Apply the paint as several thin coats.

After a period of about two-weeks, which the paint needs to harden fully, the surface of the repaired area can be 'cut' with a mild cutting compound prior to wax polishing. When carrying out bodywork repairs, remember that the quality of the finished job is proportional to the time and effort expended renew it and adjust as described later in this Chapter. Should the hinges be badly worn then they must be renewed.

9 Front door - removal and refitment

1 Refer to Section 10 and remove the door trim panel and waterproof covering.

2 Working inside the door panels, mark the washer plate at each hinge position with a pencil.

3 Undo and remove the screw that secures the window front channel to the door casing.

4 An assistant should now support the weight of the door.

5 Undo and remove the locknuts and plain washers securing the door assembly to the top and bottom hinges.

6 Lift away the two washer plates.

7 The door may now be lifted away from the aperture.

8 Recover the shim plate from the top hinge. This shim plate is not always fitted.

9 Refitting the front door is the reverse sequence to removal. It will probably be necessary to adjust the door lock and/or striker plate. Further information will be found in Section 24.

10 Front door trim panel - removal and refitment

1 With the window fully raised note the position of the regulator handle.

2 Undo and remove the regulator handle securing screw and distance piece and then slide off the handle.

3 Using a screwdriver, carefully prise off the two door pull handle end covers. Undo and remove the two securing screws and lift away the pull handle. Where an arm rest is fitted instead of the pull handle undo and remove the two securing screws and lift away the arm rest.

4 Unscrew and remove the locking button.

5 The trim panel may now be detached by carefully levering away from the door panel using a wide bladed screwdriver. Take care not to chip the paintwork.

6 If necessary remove the waterproof coverings from the door inner panel.

7 Refitting the front door trim panel is the reverse sequence to removal. If the inner panel waterproof covering has been removed make sure it is refitted correctly to ensure that no moisture can reach the trim panel.

11 Front door lock - removal and refitment

1 Raise the door glass and then referring to Section 10 remove the door trim and waterproof covering.

2 Undo and remove the screws that secure the door lock remote control to the door inner panel.

3 Carefully slide the remote control rearwards so as to release it from the door panel.

4 **Two door models only.** Detach the operating link from the clip on the door panel.

5 Unscrew and remove the locking button and then depress the locking button operating link to disengage it from the door.

6 Undo and remove the screw that secures the door glass rear channel to the inner panel.

7 Undo and remove the two nuts, shakeproof washers and plain washers that secure the door exterior handle to the outer panel. Lift away the 'U' shaped fixing bracket.

8 Use a pencil to mark the relative position of the disc latch body to the door. Then undo and remove the four screws securing the mechanism to the door.

9 Withdraw the exterior handle, disc latch mechanism and remote control as a complete assembly from the door through the exterior handle aperture in the door outer panel.

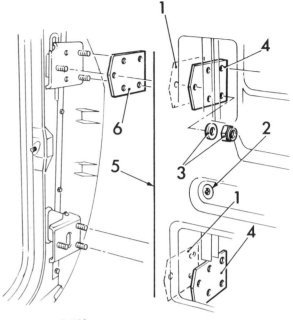

HI3735

Fig.12.1. Front door hinge assemblies

1 Washer plate location mark	4 Washer plate
2 Screw	5 Door leading edge
3 Nut and plain washer	6 Shim plate

HI3736

Fig. 12.2 Front door trim panel - removal

1 Screw	7 Arm rest (alternative)
2 Distance piece	8 Screw
3 Handle	9 Bezel
4 End cover	10 Locking button (if fitted)
5 Screw	11 Trim panel
6 Door handle	12 Clip

10 Unclip the retainers and disconnect the operating links from the disc latch mechanism.

11 Refitting the front door lock assembly is the reverse sequence to removal. Lubricate all moving parts with a little engine oil.

12 Should adjustment be necessary, refer to Section 24 for further information.

12 Front door lock remote control - removal and refitment

1 Raise the door glass and then referring to Section 10 remove the door trim panel and waterproof covering.

2 Undo and remove the screws securing the door lock remote control to the door inner panel.

3 Carefully slide the remote control rearwards so as to release it from the door panel.

4 **Two door models only.** Detach the operating link from the clip on the door panel.

5 Compress the operating link return spring and detach the link bush from the remote control frame.

6 Disconnect the linkage from the remote control handle.

7 Refitting the front door lock remote control is the reverse sequence to removal. Lubricate all moving parts with a little engine oil.

13 Front door private lock - removal and refitment

1 Raise the door glass and then referring to Section 10 remove the door trim panel and waterproof covering.

2 Carefully remove the circlip from the end of the private lock assembly. Lift away the plain washer and wave washer.

3 The operating lever may now be detached from the lock travel assembly.

4 Fit the key into the lock and withdraw the lock barrels.

5 Refitting the lock barrel is the reverse sequence to removal.

14 Front door striker plate - removal and refitment

1 Using a pencil mark the fitted position of the striker plate to act as a datum for refitment.

2 Undo and remove the two screws securing the striker plate to the door pillar. Lift away the striker plate.

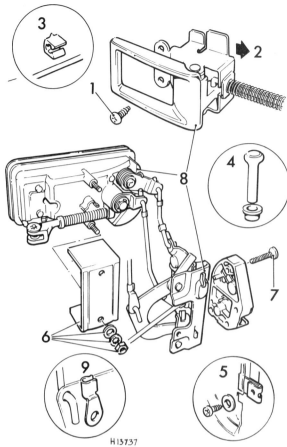

Fig. 12.3. Front door lock - removal

1 Screw - remote control securing	channel
	6 Nut, plain and spring washer
2 Slide in direction of arrow	7 Screw - latch body
3 Operation link clip	8 Exterior handle, disc latch
4 Locking button (if fitted)	and remote control
5 Screw - door glass rear	9 Retainer - operating link

Fig. 12.4. Front door private lock assembly

1 Circlip	4 Operating lever
2 Plain washer	5 Lock barrel
3 Spring washer (special)	6 Key

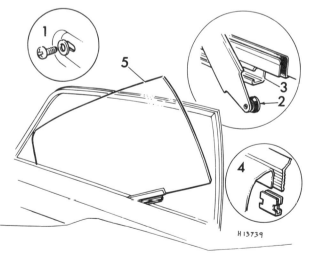

Fig. 12.5. Front door glass removal

1 Screw - window channel to door casing	3 Door glass channel
	4 Waist seal (when fitted)
2 Regulator	5 Door glass

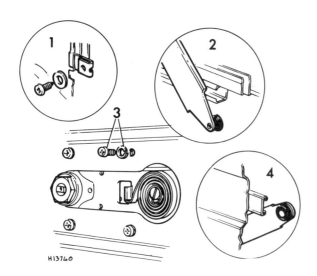

Fig. 12.6. Front door glass regulator removal

1 Screw - window channel to   3 Screw - regulator to door
   door casing   casing
2 Regulator and door glass   4 Regulator and channel
   channel   on door casing

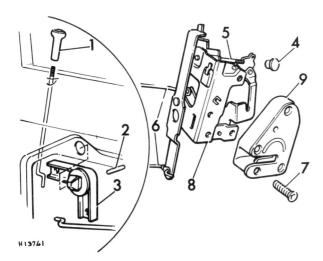

Fig. 12.7. Rear door lock removal

1 Lock button   6 Operating link
2 Locking pin   7 Screw
3 Bell crank lever   8 Disc latch mechanism
4 Knob   9 Disc latch body
5 Operating link

3 Refitting the striker plate is the reverse sequence to removal. Should it be necessary to adjust its position refer to Section 24 for further information.

15 Front door glass - removal and refitment

1 Raise the door glass and then referring to Section 10 remove the door trim and waterproof covering.
2 Locate and then undo and remove the screw that secures each window channel to the door inner panel.
3 Lower the glass fully and disengage the regulator arms from the door glass channels.

4 Carefully lower the glass until it is at the bottom of the door.
5 When a waist seal is fitted remove it from the inside edge of the door glass aperture.
6 Turn the glass to an angle of approximately 30° and lift it from the door.
7 Refitting the front door glass is the reverse sequence to removal but the following additional points should be noted:
a) Make sure that the glass is correctly located in the vertical channels.
b) Ensure that the regulator arms are correctly engaged in the channels on the bottom of the glass.
c) Lubricate all moving parts with a little engine grade oil. Make sure that the regulator controls the glass correctly and easily before refitting the door trim panel.

16 Front door glass regulator - removal and refitment

1 Raise the door glass and then referring to Section 10 remove the door trim and waterproof covering.
2 Undo and remove the screw that secures each window channel to the door casing.
3 Lower the glass fully and disengage the regulator arms from the door glass channels.
4 Carefully lower the glass until it is at the bottom of the door.
5 Undo and remove the four screws securing the regulator to the door inner panel.
6 Disengage the regulator from the door glass channel and lift away from the door.
7 Refitting the front door regulator is the reverse sequence to removal. The following additional points should be noted.
a) Ensure that the regulator arms are correctly engaged in the channels on the bottom of the glass.
b) Lubricate all moving parts with a little engine grade oil. Make sure that the regulator controls the glass correctly and easily before refitting the door trim panel.

17 Rear door - removal and refitment

1 Refer to Section 18 and remove trim panel.
2 Working inside the door panels, mark the washer plate at each hinge position with a pencil.
3 An assistant should now support the weight of the door.
4 Undo and remove the locknuts and plain washers securing the door assembly to the top and bottom hinges.
5 Lift away the two washer plates.
6 The door may now be lifted away from the aperture.
7 Refitting the door is the reverse sequence to removal. It will probably be necessary to adjust the door lock and/or striker plate. Further information will be found in Section 24.

18 Rear door trim panel - removal and refitment

The sequence for removal of the rear door trim panels is basically identical to that for the front door as described in Section 10. Should it be necessary to remove the ash tray, remove the spring clip and ease it from the panel.

19 Rear door lock - removal and refitment

1 Raise the door glass and then referring to Sections 18 and 10 remove the door trim panel and waterproof covering.
2 Undo and remove the screw that secures the remote control to the door panel.
3 Carefully slide the remote control rearwards so as to release it from the door panel.
4 Unscrew and remove the locking button.

5 The locking pin should now be pressed out from the centre of the bellcrank lever assembly. Remove the bellcrank lever assembly from the door panel and detach the assembly from the operating links.

6 Remove the bellcrank lever assembly from the door panel and detach the assembly from the operating links.

7 Unscrew and remove the knob from the end of the child safety lock operating link.

8 Use a pencil to mark the relative position of the disc latch body to the door.

9 Undo and remove the four screws securing the mechanism to the door.

10 Withdraw the disc latch mechanism, remote control and operating links as a complete assembly from the door.

11 Unclip the retainers and disconnect the operating links from the disc latch mechanism.

12 Refitting the front door lock assembly is the reverse sequence to removal. Lubricate all moving parts with a little engine oil.

20 Rear door lock remote control - removal and refitment

The sequence for removal of the rear door lock remote control is identical to that for the front door. Refer to Sections 18 and 10 for full information.

21 Rear door striker plate - removal and refitment

The sequence for removal of the rear door striker plate is identical to that for the front door. Refer to Section 14 for full information.

22 Rear door glass - removal and refitment

1 Raise the door glass and then referring to Section 18 and 10 remove the door trim and waterproof covering.

2 Undo and remove the screw securing the window channel to the door top frame.

3 Undo and remove the screw securing the window channel to the door inner panel.

4 Lower the door glass fully and then tilt the window channel forwards so as to clear the quarter light.

5 The quarter light may now be lifted away complete with sealing rubber.

6 Carefully pull the sealing rubber from the window channel and lower the channel to the bottom of the door.

7 The door glass should now be raised, using the regulator; turn the glass to an angle and lift it from the door. While this is being done the regulator arm should be detached.

8 Refitting the rear door glass is the reverse sequence to removal but the following additional points should be noted:

a) Make sure that the door glass is correctly located in the vertical channels.

b) Ensure that the regulator arms are correctly engaged in the channels on the bottom of the glass.

c) Lubricate all moving parts with a little engine oil. Make sure that the regulator controls the glass correctly and easily before refitting the door trim panel.

23 Rear door glass regulator - removal and refitment

1 Raise the door glass and then referring to Sections 18 and 10 remove the door trim and waterproof covering.

2 Raise the door glass to its uppermost position and wedge the glass in this position.

3 Undo and remove the four screws that secure the regulator to the inner panel.

4 Disengage the regulator from the door glass channel and lift away from the door.

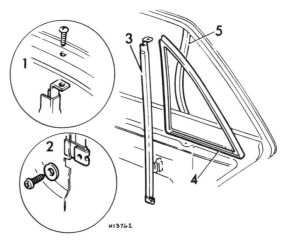

Fig. 12.8. Rear door quarterlight removal

1 Screw - window channel to door top frame	3 Window channel
	4 Quarterlight assembly
2 Screw - window channel to door casing	5 Sealing rubber

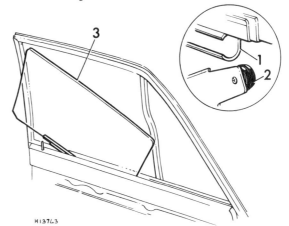

Fig. 12.9. Rear door glass removal

1 Window glass channel	2 Regulator
	3 Window glass

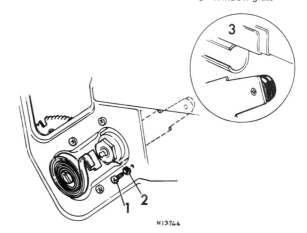

Fig. 12.10. Rear door glass regulator removal

1 Regulator securing screw	3 Window glass channel
2 Spring washer	and regulator

5   Refitting the rear door regulator is the reverse sequence to removal. The following additional points should be noted:
a) Ensure that the regulator arms are correctly engaged in the channels on the bottom of the glass.
b) Lubricate all moving parts with a little engine grade oil. Make sure that the regulator controls the glass correctly and easily before refitting the door trim panel.

24 Door locks - adjustment

Should the door not close properly or if difficulty is experienced in operating the lock it may be adjusted as follows:
1   Check that the latch disc is in the open position. It is important that the door is not slammed whilst making adjustments.
2   Slightly slacken the striker screws and with the door closed press the door inwards or pull it outwards without operating the release lever until it lines up with the body line.
3   Carefully open the door and draw a line round the striker with a pencil.
4   The striker may now be positioned by trial and error until the door closes easily without rattling, lifting or dropping.
5   Close the door and check by pressing on the door that the striker is not set in too far. It should be just possible to obtain movement at this stage as the seals are compressed.
6   Tighten the striker retaining screws securely.

25 Bonnet and hinge - removal and refitment

1   With the bonnet open, use a soft pencil and mark the outline position of both the hinges at the bonnet to act as a datum for refitment.
2   With the help of an assistant take the weight of the bonnet, and then undo and remove the hinge to bonnet securing nuts, bolts, spring and plain washers. There are two bolts to each hinge.
3   Detach the support stay and lift away the bonnet. Put in a safe place so that it will not be scratched.
4   Should it be necessary to remove the hinges, remove the hinge pin so as to release the hinge from its bracket.
5   The hinge may be lifted away through the aperture in the bulkhead.
6   Refitting the hinges and bonnet is the reverse sequence to removal. If necessary re-align the bonnet at the hinges so that the rear edge is level with the scuttle and the gaps are even.

26 Bonnet lock and safety catch - removal and refitment

Bonnet lock
1   With the bonnet open remove the radiator grille as described in Section 31.
2   Detach the locking lever return spring from the bonnet locking platform.
3   Undo and remove the two screws and spring washers securing the lock assembly to the platform.
4   The locating cup and locking plate may now be lifted away from the platform.
5   If necessary the lock pin may be removed from the bonnet by slackening the locknut and unscrewing the lock pin with a screwdriver.
6   Refitting the locating cup and locking plate, is the reverse sequence to removal. Lubricate the moving parts with a little engine grade oil.
7   When the locking pin is being refitted it will have to be adjusted so that the leading edge of the bonnet is correctly located relative to the wings.

Safety catch
1   To remove the safety catch, open the bonnet and then mark the outline of the catch mounting plate on the bonnet.
2   Undo and remove the two securing screws and spring washers and lift away the safety catch.

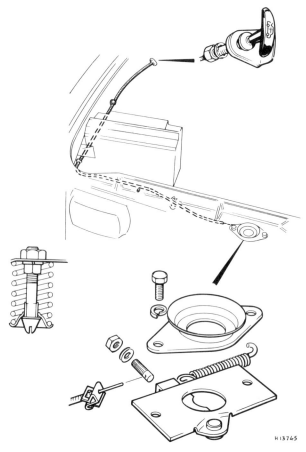

Fig. 12.11 Typical cable-operated bonnet lock assembly

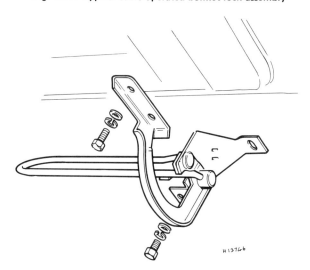

Fig. 12.12. Boot lid hinge assembly

3   Refitting the safety catch is the reverse sequence to removal. Lubricate the pivot pin with a little engine oil.

27 Boot lid and hinge - removal and refitment

Boot lid
1   With the boot lid open mark the fitted position of the hinge relative to the boot lid.

2   An assistant should now support the weight of the boot lid and then undo and remove the four bolts, spring and plain washers securing the boot lid to the hinges.
3   Lift away the boot lid.
4   Refitting the boot lid is the reverse sequence to removal. If necessary adjust its position relative to the aperture at the hinges and striker plate.

Boot lid hinge
1   To remove the hinges undo and remove the two screws, spring and plain washers securing each hinge assembly to its mounting bracket inside the boot.
2   The hinge may now be lifted away.
3   Refitting the hinges is the reverse sequence to removal. Lubricate the pivot point with a little engine oil.

---

28 Boot lid handle and lock assembly - removal and refitment

1   With the boot lid open, undo and remove the screw, shake-proof washer, plain washer and spring securing the twin-button handle assembly to the pivot plate.
2   Recover the two spring washers located between the spring and pivot plate assembly. Sometimes these washers are not fitted.
3   The twin-button handle assembly may now be lifted away from the boot lid.
4   Undo and remove the six screws, plain and spring washers securing the pivot plate and lock assemblies to the boot lid.
5   The pivot plate assembly link and lock assembly may now be lifted away from the boot lid.
6   Withdraw the safety clip to release the link and shaped washer from the pivot plate assembly.
7   The link may be unhooked from the lock assembly.
8   Refitting the assembly is the reverse sequence to removal, Lubricate all moving parts with a little engine oil.

---

29 Boot lid lock barrel and striker - removal and refitment

Lock barrel
1   Refer to Section 28 and follow the instructions given in paragraphs 1 to 3 inclusive.
2   Remove the locking sleeve and sealing washer from the turn button handle assembly.
3   Using a suitable diameter parallel pin punch carefully drive out the barrel locking pin.
4   Fit the key to the lock and withdraw the lock barrel. Recover the little plunger.
5   Refitting the lock barrel is the reverse sequence to removal.

Lock striker
1   With the boot lid open mark the outline of the striker mounting plate relative to its mounting platform.
2   Undo and remove the two bolts, spring and plain washers securing the striker mounting plate and lift it away from the platform.
3   Refitting the lock striker is the reverse sequence to removal. If necessary adjust the striker plate using the slotted holes in the striker mounting plate.

---

30 Bumper - removal and refitment

Front
1   Undo and remove the bolt, spring and plain washer and rubber distance piece securing the two ends of the bumper to the wing panels.
2   Undo and remove the two bolts, spring and plain washers securing the bumper blade to the body.
3   Carefully lift away the bumper blade.
4   Refitting the bumper blade is the reverse sequence to removal.

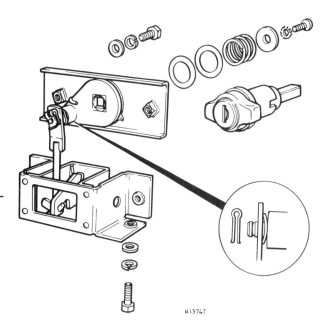

Fig. 12.13. Boot lid handle and lock assembly

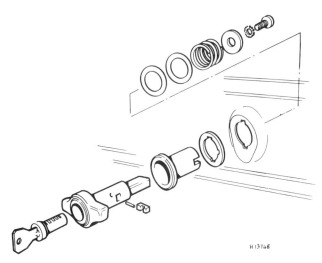

Fig. 12.14. Boot lid lock barrel assembly

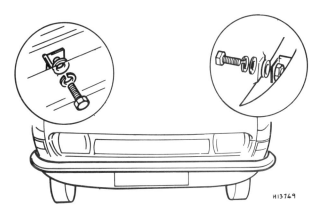

Fig. 12.15. Front bumper and attachments

Rear

1   Working inside the boot disconnect the wire from the rear number plate light terminal connector.
2   Follow the sequence as described for the front bumper.

31 Radiator grille - removal and refitment

1   Open the bonnet and locate the six screws securing the radiator grille to the front panel.
2   Undo and remove the six screws and plain washers securing the radiator grille to the front panel. Lift away the radiator grille.
3   Refitting the radiator grille is the reverse sequence to removal.

32 Windscreen - removal and refitment

1   Windscreen replacement is no light task. Leave this to the specialist if possible. Instructions are given below for the more ambitious.
2   Remove the windscreen wiper arms and blades and also the interior mirror.
3   The assistance of a second person should now be enlisted, ready to catch the glass when it is released from its aperture.
4   Working from inside the car, commencing at one top corner, press the glass and ease it and the rubber moulding from the aperture lip.
5   Remove the rubber moulding from the glass and then ease the finisher strip from the moulding.
6   Now is the time to remove all pieces of glass if the screen has shattered. Use a vacuum cleaner to extract as much as possible. Switch on the heater boost motor and adjust the controls to 'Screen Defrost' but watch out for flying pieces of glass which might be blown out of the ducting.
7   Carefully inspect the rubber moulding for signs of splitting or deterioration. Clean all traces of sealing compound from the rubber moulding and windscreen aperture flange.
8   To refit the glass first place the rubber seal onto the aperture flange.
9   Inject a little sealer (Sealastik SR51) between the rubber moulding and the glass at the outside face.
10 Lubricate the finisher channel in the seal with a concentrated soap and water solution, or with washing up liquid.
11 Fit the metal finisher and joint covers to the rubber moulding. This is only applicable where a metal finisher is fitted.
12 Apply a little sealer to the outside face of the windscreen aperture in the body.
13 Place a piece of cord into the body flange groove of the rubber moulding and cross the ends at the top centre of the moulding.
14 Apply a little sealer to the middle groove around the outside edge of the rubber moulding.
15 Offer up the glass and rubber moulding to the aperture and using the cord pull the rubber lip over the body flange. Whilst this is being done a person outside the car must apply firm pressure to the glass to ensure that the rubber moulding seats correctly onto the body flange.
16 When a plastic finisher strip is fitted a special tool is required. An illustration of the tool is shown in Fig. 12.17 and a handyman should be able to make up an equivalent using a welding or netting wire and a wooden file handle.
17 Fit the eye of the tool into the groove and feed in the finisher strip.
18 Push the tool around the complete length of the moulding feeding the finisher into the channel as the eyelet opens it. The back half beds the finisher into the moulding.
19 Remove traces of sealer using a paraffin moistened rag.
20 Refit the interior mirror and windscreen wiper arms.

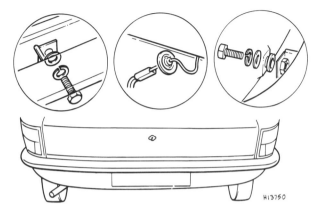

Fig. 12.16. Rear bumper and attachments

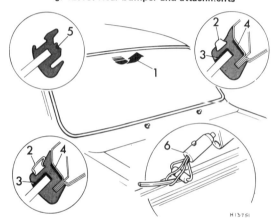

Fig. 12.17. Windscreen detail

1   Push glass outwards   5   Sealer
2   Finisher strip   6   Special tool used to fit
3   Sealer   plastic finisher strip
4   Sealer

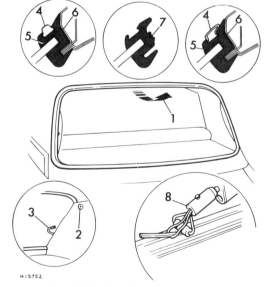

Fig. 12.18. Heated rear screen detail

1   Push glass outwards   5   Sealer
2   Trim pad clips   6   Sealer
3   Electric cable   7   Sealer
4   Finisher strip   8   Special tool used to fit
                                    plastic finisher strip

33 Heated rear screen - removal and refitment

The procedure is basically identical to that for the front windscreen, but, the following additional points should be noted:

1 On saloon car models, release the rear top corner of each upper rear quarter trim pad by carefully levering the pad away from the body panel. If working on the estate car model, remove the wiper arm and blade as described in Chapter 13.

2 Disconnect the heated rear screen feed and earth return cables from their respective connections on each end of the glass.

3 Place a piece of card over the element to protect against damage. This is extremely important.

4 Removal and refitting is now basically similar to that described in Section 32.

34 Quarter light - removal and refitment

1 This is applicable to two door models only.

2 Carefully push out the glass, rubber moulding and finisher strip from the body apertures as a complete assembly. **Note:** On some models a finisher strip is not fitted.

3 When the finisher strip is fitted next remove this from the rubber moulding and finally remove the rubber moulding from the glass.

4 Clean off all traces of sealer and inspect the rubber moulding for signs of splitting or other deterioration.

5 To refit the glass: first, refit the rubber moulding to the glass.

6 Apply a little sealer (Seelastik SR51) between the rubber moulding and the glass on the outside face.

7 Where a finisher strip is to be fitted, lubricate the channel with a concentrated soap and water solution or with washing up liquid.

8 Apply a little sealer to the outside face of the quarter light aperture in the body.

9 Place a piece of cord into the body flange groove of the rubber moulding and cross the ends at the top centre of the moulding.

10 Offer up the glass and rubber moulding to the aperture and using the cord pull the rubber lip over the body flange. Whilst this is being done a person outside the car must apply firm pressure to the glass to ensure that the rubber moulding seats correctly onto the body flange.

11 Remove traces of sealer using a paraffin moistened rag.

12 Check that the top edge of the rear quarter trim pad lies behind the outer lip of the sealing rubber.

35 Parcel tray - removal and refitment

Front
1 Undo and remove the screw and plain washer securing the parcel tray to the heater cover.

2 Undo and remove the two screws and plain washers securing the parcel tray to the dash panel.

3 Lift away the parcel tray.

4 Refitting the parcel tray is the reverse sequence to removal.

Rear
1 Open the boot lid and working inside press out the seven drive fasteners that secure the parcel tray to the parcel shelf.

2 Carefully push the parcel tray rearwards to allow the front edge to be raised clear of the seat squab.

3 Lift away the parcel tray.

4 Refitting the rear parcel tray is the reverse sequence to removal.

36 Glove box and lid assembly - removal and refitment

1 Undo and remove the two screws to release the glovebox lid

H13753

Fig. 12.19. Quarterlight assembly removal

1 Push glass assembly outwards	3 Sealer
2 Finisher strip	4 Sealer
	5 Sealing rubber outer lip

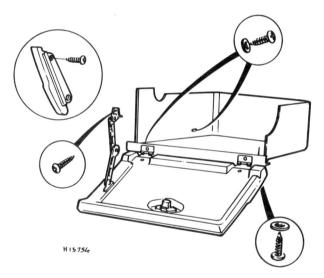

H13754

Fig. 12.20. Glove box and lid assembly attachments

stay, from the steering column mounting rail.

2 Undo and remove the two screws securing the glovebox closing panel to the dash.

3 Undo and remove the screw and plain washer that secures the glovebox to the heater cover.

4 Undo and remove the two screws and plain washers securing the glovebox to the dash panel.

5 The glovebox and lid assembly may now be lifted away.

6 Should it be necessary to remove the lock it will be necessary to drill out the two rivets securing the lock mounting plate to the glovebox lid.

7 Unscrew the bezel from the front of the lock. The lock and mounting plate may now be lifted away from the glovebox lid.

8 Refitting the lock or glovebox and lid assembly is the reverse sequence to removal.

37 Rear quarter trim - removal and refitment

1 Remove the rear seat cushion from the inside of the car.

2 Undo and remove the screws securing the squab to the body panel.

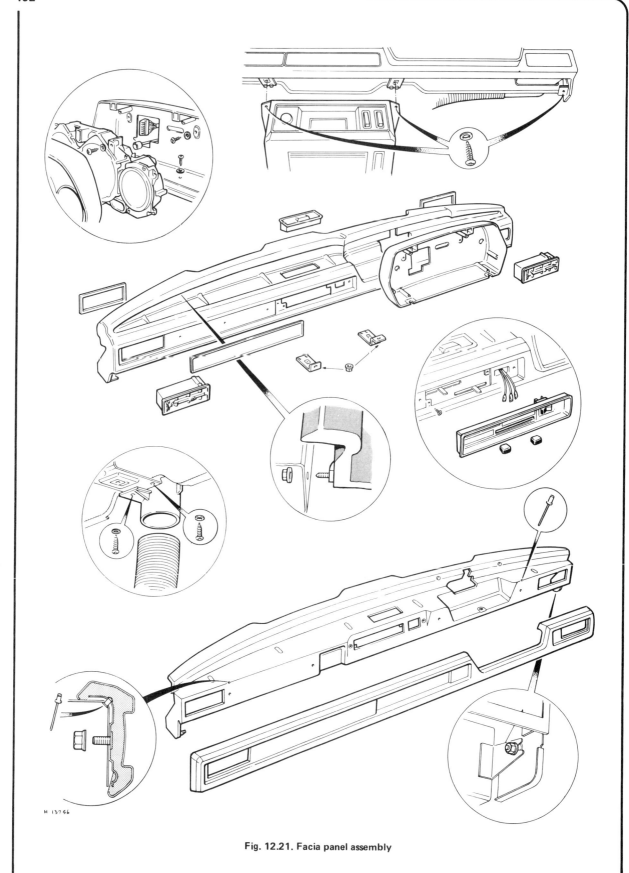

H 13756

Fig. 12.21. Facia panel assembly

3 Lift the squab upwards to release the back of the squab from the three retaining clips.

4 Lift the squab away from the inside of the car.

5 Undo and remove the bolt and spring washer securing the reel assembly to the body.

6 Lift away the reel assembly together with its locating plate and plain distance piece.

7 Carefully pull off the door seal from the register on the rear of the door aperture.

8 Undo and remove the two screws that secure the trim panel to the rear wheel arch.

9 Using a wide bladed screwdriver carefully ease the trim panel clips from the body panels. Lift away the trim panel from inside the car.

10 Should it be necessary to remove the ashtray release the spring clip from the rear and withdraw the ashtray.

11 Refitting the rear quarter trim panel is the reverse sequence to removal. It is important that the top face of the reel assembly is horizontal in both planes and also the locating plate is fitted between the trim panel and the reel assembly.

---

38 Facia assembly - removal and refitment

---

1 For safety reasons, disconnect the battery.

2 Push in each heater control knob retaining tongue and pull off the two heater control knobs.

3 Undo and remove the two screws securing the heater cover to the facia lower inner brackets.

4 The heater control bezel may now be pressed out.

5 Make a note of, and then disconnect, the three cables from the terminal blades on the heater blower switch.

6 Undo and remove the two screws securing the heater control quadrant to the facia panel.

7 Very carefully pull off the instrument front casing.

8 Undo and remove the four screws securing the instrument cluster and ease it away from the rear casing.

9 Press the release lever on the speedometer cable connector. Disconnect the speedometer cable from the rear of the instrument.

10 Disconnect the multi-pin terminal connector from the rear of the instrument cluster and lift away the complete instrument cluster assembly.

11 Undo and remove the screw that secures each demister duct to the steering column rail. On some models it will be observed that the right-hand screw also secures an earth wire eyelet.

12 Move the demister ducts to one side and then undo and remove the screws which secure the facia lower inner brackets to the steering column mounting rail.

13 Undo the two screws that secure the facia lower outer bracket to the facia end support brackets on the steering column mounting rail. On some models it will be found that studs or bolts and nuts were used instead of the screws.

14 Disconnect the air duct hoses from the face level vent ducts.

15 Undo and remove the two nuts that secure the facia to the facia top rail.

16 The facia assembly may now be lifted away from the inside of the car.

17 The instrument cluster rear casing may be removed from the facia once the three (on some models four) screws are removed.

18 If necessary remove the ashtray, using a screwdriver to ease it out of its location.

19 The face level air vents may be pushed out from the ends of the facia. Recover the face vent seals from the rear of the facia.

20 Undo and remove the two nuts to release the facia lower inner brackets from the facia. On some models this may not be applicable.

21 To release the facia lower assembly from the facia panel assembly undo and remove the four nuts and also drill out the two 'pop' rivets.

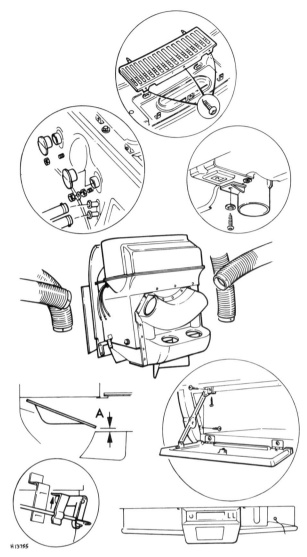

Fig. 12.22. Heater unit attachments

22 Refitting the facia assembly is the reverse sequence to removal.

---

39 Heater unit - removal and refitment

---

1 Refer to Chapter 2 and drain the cooling system.

2 Slacken the clips and disconnect the two water hoses from the heater unit matrix pipes.

3 Carefully twist and detach the end capping from the two heater air intake drain tubes.

4 Undo and remove the three nuts that secure the heater unit and also the speedometer cable clip to the dash panel. Do not lose the clip.

5 Undo and remove the three screws securing the heater air intake grille to the windscreen panel. Lift away the grille.

6 Undo and remove the four screws securing the heater cover to the facia and parcel trays.

7 Undo and remove the four screws securing the two parcel trays to the dash panel. Lift away the parcel trays.

8 Disconnect the air hoses from the heater unit, face level vent ducts and the demister ducts. Lift away the air hoses.

9 Press the retaining end of each remote control outer cable

spring clip away from the cable so as to release each clip from the bracket mounted on the heater unit.

10 Disconnect the heater control inner cables from the lever trunnions on the heater unit.

11 Make a note of the connections and disconnect the wiring harness cables from the fan motor. These are located on the left-hand side of the heater unit.

12 Undo and remove the one set screw securing the heater unit to the windscreen panel.

13 The heater unit may now be lifted away from inside the car. Take suitable precautions not to allow any water still in the heater matrix to drain out onto the remaining carpeting or upholstery - it may contain rust sediment and cause stains.

14 Finally, disconnect the seal pad and also the insulation pad from the front of the heater unit.

15 Refitting the heater unit is the reverse sequence to removal but the following additional points should be noted:

    a) The temperature control outer cable spring clip should be fitted to the heater bracket when the temperature remote control lever is set to maximum heat position. The temperature control lever on the heater unit must be up against its built in stop.

    b) The air distribution control outer cable spring clip should be fitted to the heater bracket when the air distribution remote control lever is positioned so that air flow is to the windscreen. The air distribution flap in the heater should be set to a dimension of approximately 0.25 in (6 mm) between the lower face of the flap at the rear edge and the heater casing.

40 Heater matrix - removal and refitment

1 Refer to section 39 and remove the heater unit.

2 Undo and remove the eight screws securing the matrix retaining panel to the heater control body.

3 Lift away the matrix retaining panel.

4 The matrix may now be withdrawn from the heater body. Note the location of the foam end packing pieces.

5 Refitting the heater matrix is the reverse sequence to removal.

41 Heater fan motor - removal and refitment

1 Refer to Section 39 and remove the heater unit.

2 Undo and remove the fourteen screws that secure the plenum chamber and fan motor assembly to the top half of the heater body.

3 Undo and remove the three nuts securing the motor assembly to the underside of the plenum chamber.

4 Lift away the motor assembly.

5 Carefully ease the clip from the end of the fan hub and drift the motor spindle from the fan.

6 Re-assembling the fan motor and fan and refitting is the reverse sequence to removal.

42 Face vent and duct - removal and refitment

Face vent

1 Carefully ease the face vent out from the facia assembly.

2 If necessary detach the spring clips from the face vent.

3 Refitting the face vent is the reverse sequence to removal.

Face vent duct

1 Disconnect the air hose from the face vent duct.

2 A small right-angled cross head screwdriver will now be required. If an old screwdriver is available bend the shank 1 inch (25.4 mm) from the working end using heat or cut the shank and weld it to a piece if metal bar.

3 With the tool described in paragraph 2 undo and remove the two screws securing the face vent duct to the steering column mounting rail.

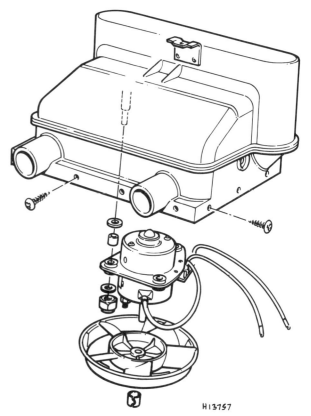

Fig. 12.23. Heater fan motor assembly

4 Push the duct forward through the steering column mounting rail and withdraw the duct from beneath the facia panel.

5 Remove the two spring nuts from the face vent duct.

6 Refitting the face vent duct is the reverse sequence to removal.

43 Heater demist duct - removal and refitment

1 For safety reasons, disconnect the battery.

2 Undo and remove the four screws securing the heater cover to the facia and parcel trays.

3 Disconnect the air hoses from the demister duct.

4 Undo and remove the screw so as to release the demister duct from the steering column mounting rail.

5 The demister duct may now be lifted away from beneath the facia.

6 Detach the two clips to release the gasket and its stiffening plate from the mouth of the demister duct.

7 Refitting the demister duct is the reverse sequence to removal.

44 Heater control cables - removal and refitment

1 For safety reasons, disconnect the battery.

2 Working through the hole in the underside of each heater control knob, press the control knob retaining tongue upwards and pull off the control knob from the control lever.

3 Undo and remove the four screws securing the heater cover to the facia panel and parcel trays.

4 Undo and remove the two screws securing each parcel tray from the dash panel.

5 Carefully ease the heater remote control bezel complete with the heater fan switch from the facia panel.

6 Undo and remove the two screws that secure the heater remote control to the facia.

7 Ease the retaining end of each remote control outer cable spring clip away from its cable to release the clip and cable from the remote control base plate.

8 Disconnect each inner cable from its lever on the remote control base plate.

9 Refitting the heater control cables is the reverse sequence to removal. It will, however, be necessary to adjust these cables as described in the following paragraphs.

10 Lubricate the moving parts of the remote control with a little Castrol LM Grease.

11 The top surface of the remote control base plate is marked with a letter "T" for identification.

12 Fit the outer cable to the remote control so that the measurement between the cable end and its spring clip on the remote control is 0.125 in (3.0 mm).

13 Refer to Section 9, paragraph 15, sub paragraphs a and b for final fitment instructions.

Chapter 13 Supplement:
Revisions and information on later models

Contents

1 Introduction

The Supplementary Chapter has been provided to cover the various modifications made to the Allegro models between the years 1973 and 1980. The subjects covered in Chapters 1 to 12 are basically applicable to all models, since only minor changes have been made during the production run of the Allegro, and most of these have been cosmetic rather than mechanical.

However, since the Allegro is now into its third series, there are numerous items to be covered which are not included elsewhere in this book. This includes all Estate models, which were not introduced until 1975.

The specifications have changed from time to time and these are detailed by model.

The main modification mechanically has been the adoption of different distributors in later models; the Lucas 45D4 and Ducellier types are covered in full in this Chapter.

2 Specifications

The specifications listed here are revised or supplementary to those given at the beginning of each of the twelve Chapters of this manual. The original specifications apply unless alternative figures are quoted here.

Engine

1100 and 1.1 models (1976 onwards)

Idle speed ...	750 rpm
Fast idle speed	
1100 models	1050 rpm
1.1 models	1200 rpm
Torque (DIN)	55 lbf ft (7.60 kgf m) at 2900 rpm
Piston ring clearance in groove - compression rings ...	0.002 to 0.004 in (0.05 to 0.10 mm)
Crankshaft endfloat	0.001 to 0.005 in (0.03 to 0.13 mm)
Oil filter ...	Disposable full flow cartridge type or renewable paper element
Valve rocker clearance - timing	0.021 in (0.53 mm)
Valve springs	
Free length - inlet and exhaust ...	1.96 in (49.78 mm)
Fitted length	1.34 in (34.04 mm)
Valve spring pressure:	
Valves open ...	106 lbf (48.31 kgf)
Valves closed ...	70 lbf (31.75 kgf)
Valve operation ...	Overhead by pushrod

1300 and 1.3 models (1976 onwards)

Idle speed	
1300 and 1.3 models	750 rpm
1300 models with emission control	850 rpm
Fast idle speed	
1300 models	1050 rpm
1300 models with emission control and 1.3 models ...	1300 rpm
Piston clearance - bottom of skirt	0.0012 to 0.0022 in (0.03 to 0.06 mm)
Piston rings	
Oil control ring ...	Apex type
Fitted gap - rails and side spring	0.010 to 0.040 in (0.25 to 1.02 mm)
Oil filter ...	Disposable cartridge type or renewable paper element (automatic transmission models)
Oil pump relief valve pressure ...	60 lbf/in^2 (4.21 kgf/cm^2)
Water pump drivebelt tension ...	0.25 in (6 mm) total deflection on longest belt run under 8 lb (3.50 kg) load
Coolant expansion tank cap blow-off pressure ...	15 lbf/in^2 (1.05 kgf/cm^2)

Carburettors
1100 and 1.1 models
Type ... ...   SU HS4, horizontal

Specification

	AUD 608 and FZX 1022	FZX 1067, FZX 1170 and FZX 1171
1100 models		
Piston spring colour	Red	Red
Jet size	0.090 in (2.29 mm)	0.090 in (2.29 mm)
Needle...	ABP	ABP
Capstat colour	—	Natural
1.1 models	FZX 1170 only	

1300 models
Type ... ...   SU HS4, horizontal

Specification
Manual gearbox models ... ...   AUD 594, AUD 595, FZX 1023, FZX 1068, FZX 1172 and FZX 1173
Automatic transmission models ... ...   AUD 567, AUD 451, FZX 1086, FZX 1174 and FZX 1175

1.3 models
Type ... ...   SU HS4, horizontal

Specification
Manual gearbox models ... ...   FZX 1172
Automatic transmission models ... ...   FZX 1174

Carburettor data

Specification	AUD 549, AUD 595 and FZX 1023	FZX 1068, FZX 1172 and FZX 1173	AUD 567 and AUD 451	FZX 1086, FZX 1174 and FZX 1175
Piston spring colour	Red	Red	Red	Red
Jet size	0.090 in (2.29 mm)	0.090 in (2.29 mm)	0.090 in (2.29 mm)	0.090 in (2.29 mm)
Needle type	ABB	AAT	AAB and AAR respectively	AAT
Capstat colour	—	Natural	—	Natural

Air intake system ... ...   Into air cleaner via thermostatically operated air valve

Heat chamber location ... ...   Attached to exhaust manifold right-hand branch

Ignition system
Spark plugs
Allegro 3 models
Type ... ...   Unipart GSP 161 or Champion N9Y
Gap ... ...   0.026 in (0.65 mm)

Coil
Allegro 3 models
Type ... ...   Lucas 16C6 or AC Delco 9977230 ballasted type
Primary resistance ... ...   1.2 to 1.5 ohms (Lucas 16C6 type)
Ballast resistance... ... ...   1.3 to 1.5 ohms (both types)

Distributors
1100 and 1300 models (1976 to 1979)
Type ... ...   Lucas 25D4, Lucas 45D4 or Ducellier

Serial numbers:	**1100 models**	**1300 models**
Lucas 25D4	41246	41257
Lucas 45D4	41418	41419

1300 models with emission control (1976 to 1979)
Type ... ...   Lucas 45D4 or Ducellier
Serial number ... ...   Lucas 41619

Allegro 3 1.1 and 1.3 models (1979 onwards)
Type ... ...   Lucas 45D4 or Ducellier

Serial numbers:	**1.1 models**	**1.3 models**
Lucas	41418 and 41793	41419 and 41768
Ducellier	525042	525048 and 525238

Distributor data

	Lucas 45D4	Ducellier
Type	Lucas 45D4	Ducellier
Rotation	Anti-clockwise	Anti-clockwise
Dwell angle:		
1100 and 1300 models	$51° \pm 5°$	$57° \pm 2° 30'$
1.1 and 1.3 models	$57° \pm 5°$	$57° \pm 5°$
Contact breaker points gap	0.014 to 0.016 in (0.35 to 0.40 mm)	0.015 in (0.38 mm) (preliminary setting only)

Condenser capacity ... 0.18 to 0.25 microfarad

Centrifugal advance

1300 models with emission control (1976 to 1979):
- No advance below ... 300 rpm
- Maximum vacuum advance ... $10°$ at 15 in Hg (380 mm Hg)
- Vacuum advance starts ... 10 in Hg (250 mm Hg)

Allegro 3 1.1 models (1979 onwards):
Crankshaft degrees and rpm. Vacuum disconnected - deceleration, with ignition set to TDC ...
- $14°$ to $18°$ at 4000 rpm
- $9°$ to $13°$ at 2400 rpm
- $6°$ to $10°$ at 1500 rpm
- $0°$ to $1°$ at 900 rpm
- No advance below ... 800 rpm
- Maximum vacuum advance ... $18°$ at 16 in Hg (356 mm Hg)
- Vacuum advance starts ... 6 in Hg (152 mm Hg)

Allegro 3 1.3 models:
Crankshaft degrees and rpm. Vacuum disconnected ...
- $18°$ to $22°$ at 5000 rpm
- $11°$ to $15°$ at 2800 rpm
- $4°$ to $8°$ at 1600 rpm
- No advance below ... 600 rpm
- Maximum vacuum advance ... $22°$ at 10 in Hg (250 mm Hg)
- Vacuum advance starts ... 2 in Hg (80 mm Hg)

Ignition timing

	1100 models	1300 models	1.1 models	1.3 models
Static	$9°$ BTDC	$8°$ BTDC	$9°$ BTDC	$8°$ BTDC
Stroboscopic, at 1000 rpm	$12°$ BTDC	$13°$ BTDC	$12°$ BTDC	$13°$ BTDC
Advance check:				
At 2400 rpm	$21°$ to $25°$ BTDC	—	$21°$ to $25°$ BTDC	—
At 2800 rpm	—	$22°$ to $26°$ BTDC	—	$19°$ to $23°$ BTDC

Note: *Timing marks are located on the flywheel and crankshaft pulley or on the pointer bracket attached to the timing cover, dependent upon model.*

Braking system
All models (1976 onwards)

Type ... Girling Supervac or Lockheed 28
Disc brake pad minimum thickness ... 0.0625 in (1.60 mm)

Electrical system
Allegro 3 models (1979 onwards)

Bulb	Wattage
Headlight:	
Rectangular type	45/40
Circular type	45/40
Sidelight	4
Side repeater flasher	4
Reversing lamp	21
Rear fog lamp	21
Front fog lamp	55
Heater control illumination	1.20
Heater blower switch lamp	1.20
Luggage compartment lamp	6
Interior lamp	6
Glovebox lamp	6
Instrument panel:	
Warning lamps	1.20
Illumination lamps	1.20
Switch illumination	2
Automatic transmission quadrant illumination	2
Number plate lamps	4
Clock	2.20

Suspension and steering
All models (1976 onwards)
Trim height (see text for details) ... ... 14.41 in ± 0.40 in (366 mm ± 10 mm)

Wheel alignment:
Front ... ... Parallel to 0.125 in (or 0^0 30' included angle) toe-out
Rear ... ... 0^0 30' toe-in at each wheel

Rear wheel camber angle ... ... 1^0 negative

Turning circle ... ... 35 ft (10.70 m) approx

Track
1976 to 1979 models (except HL):
    Front ... ... 54.937 in (1395 mm)
    Rear ... ... 55.437 in (1408 mm)
1976 to 1979 HL models only:
    Front ... ... 53.625 in (1362 mm)
    Rear ... ... 53.750 in (1365 mm)
1979 onwards models:
    Front ... ... 53.625 in (1362 mm)
    Rear ... ... 53.703 in (1364 mm)

Wheels and tyres
Allegro Mk 1 and 2 models (1973 to 1979)
Wheel size
Up to car No 226629 ... ... 4.50c x 13
From car No 226630 ... ... 4J x 13

Tyre size and type ... ... 145 - 13 radial

Tyre pressures
Saloon models:
    Front ... ... 26 lbf/in^2 (1.8 kgf/cm^2)
    Rear:
        Up to car No 226629 ... ... 30 lbf/in^2 (2.1 kgf/cm^2)
        From car No 226630 ... ... 24 lbf/in^2 (1.69 kgf/cm^2)
Estate models:
    Up to a load of 704 lb (320 kg) ... ... 24 lbf/in^2 (1.69 kgf/cm^2)
    Up to a maximum load of 875 lb (397 kg) ... ... 28 lbf/in^2 (1.97 kgf/cm^2)

Allegro 3 models (1979 onwards)
Wheel size and type ... ... 4.50J x 13 vented steel wheels

Tyre size and type
1.1, 1.3 and 1.3L Saloon models ... ... 145 - 13 radial
1.3 HL and Estate models ... ... 155 - 13 radial

Tyre pressures:
Saloon and Estate models, carrying driver, three passengers and
110 lb (50 kg) luggage:
    Front ... ... 26 lbf/in^2 (1.8 kgf/cm^2)
    Rear ... ... 24 lbf/in^2 (1.7 kgf/cm^2)
    Rear; Estate models only:
        Driver, four passengers and 125 lb (57 kg) luggage ... ... 28 lbf/in^2 (2.0 kgf/cm^2)
        Driver and luggage equivalent to maximum 875 lb (397 kg) 32 lbf/in^2 (2.3 kgf/cm^2)

Kerb weights

Allegro Mk 2 models	lb	kg
1100 2-door De-Luxe	1784	809
1100 4-door De-Luxe	1828	830
1300 2-door De-Luxe*	1803	820
1300 4-door De-Luxe*	1847	838
1300 2-door Super*	1852	840
1300 4-door Super*	1901	862
1300 Estate*	1920	873

*Add 46 lbs (21 kg) if fitted with automatic transmission

Allegro 3 models									lb	kg
1.1 2-door (manual)	...	...	...	...	...	...	...	...	1794	814
1.1 4-door (manual)	...	...	...	...	...	...	...	...	1838	834
1.1 HL 4-door (manual)	...	...	...	...	...	...	...	...	1917	870
1.3 2-door (manual)	...	...	...	...	...	...	...	...	1813	823
1.3 2-door (automatic)	...	...	...	...	...	...	...	...	1859	844
1.3 4-door (manual)	...	...	...	...	...	...	...	...	1857	843
1.3 4-door (automatic)	...	...	...	...	...	...	...	...	1903	863
1.3 L 2-door (manual)	...	...	...	...	...	...	...	...	1869	848
1.3 L 2-door (automatic)	...	...	...	...	...	...	...	...	1915	869
1.3 L 4-door (manual)	...	...	...	...	...	...	...	...	1918	870
1.3 L 4-door (automatic)	...	...	...	...	...	...	...	...	1964	891
1.3 H L 4-door (manual)	...	...	...	...	...	...	...	...	1936	878
1.3 H L 4-door (automatic)	...	...	...	...	...	...	...	...	1982	899
1.3 Estate (manual)	...	...	...	...	...	...	...	...	1876	851
1.3 Estate (automatic)	...	...	...	...	...	...	...	...	1922	872
1.3 L Estate (manual)	...	...	...	...	...	...	...	...	1984	900
1.3 L Estate (automatic)	...	...	...	...	...	...	...	...	2030	921

Dimensions

Allegro Mk 2 models

							Saloon model	Estate model
Overall length	...	...	...	...	...	...	151.65 in (3852 mm)	155.20 in (3942 mm)
Overall width	...	...				...	63.50 in (1613 mm)	
Overall height (unladen)	...	...	...	...	...	...	55 in (1397 mm)	55.30 in (1404 mm)
Wheelbase	...	...	...		...	...	96.15 in (2442 mm)	
Ground clearance	...	...	...	...	...	...	7.20 in (183 mm)	7.20 in (183 mm)

Allegro Mk 3 models

							Saloon model	Estate model
Overall length	...	...	...	...	...	...	154 in (3908 mm)	157 in (3993 mm)
Overall width (including door mirror)	...	...	...	...	...		66 in (1687 mm)	
Overall height (at kerb weight)	...	...	...	...	...		55 in (1397 mm)	55.50 in (1404 mm)
Ground clearance (at kerb weight)	...	...	...	...			7.50 in (187 mm)	

Towing and loading weights

								lb	kg
Maximum towing weight	...	...	...	...	...	...	...	1680	762
Maximum roof rack load	...	...	...	...	...	...	...	112	50
Maximum all-up weight:									
Saloon	...	...	...	...	...	...	...	710	322
Estate	...	...	...	...	...	...	...	875	397
Maximum downward load on towing hitch	...	...	...	...			110	50

Note: *If using an Allegro 3 vehicle for towing a caravan or similar load, it is recommended that a gearbox oil cooler be fitted.*

---

3 Engine

Oil filter - (renewable element type) - removal and refitting

1 Some models, especially those fitted with automatic transmission, are equipped with the older type of oil filter with a renewable element. This is mounted horizontally onto the side of the engine (at the front).

2 To remove the assembly, first place a bowl beneath it to catch any engine oil which is released.

3 Undo the centre bolt so that the filter assembly can be lifted away as a complete unit.

4 Empty any excess oil into the bowl or container, then withdraw the old element from the canister.

5 Remove the sealing ring from the filter base attached to the engine.

6 Dismantle the filter container, bolt, spring and seals, and clean them all in a paraffin bath. Then dry them thoroughly.

7 Reassemble the bolt, spring and seals into the container in the correct order; ensure that the seals are in good condition and that they fit snugly on the bolt.

8 Fit a new sealing ring to the filter base.

9 Fit a new element into the container and refit the assembly to the engine.

10 Rotate the container whilst the centre bolt is being tightened, to ensure that the sealing ring and container are correctly

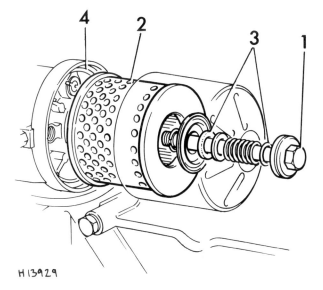

H13929

Fig. 13.1 Renewable element type oil filter — exploded view (Sec 3)

1	Bolt	3	Rubber seals
2	Renewable element	4	Sealing ring in filter base

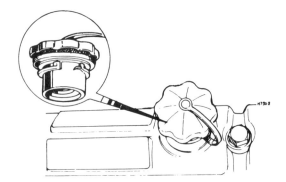

Fig. 13.2 Oil filler cap and engine breather filter (Sec 3)

located. **Note:** *Do not overtighten the centre bolt;* the specified torque is 12 to 16 lbf ft (1.7 to 2.2 kgf m).
11 Start the engine when refilled with oil, and check that there is no leakage.

Oil filler cap/engine breather filter - renewal
12 On 1100 and 1300 (1.1 and 1.3) engines, the oil filler cap (which incorporates the engine breather filter) has to be renewed as an assembly every 12 000 miles, as per the servicing schedule.
13 Undo the cap as normal and release the retaining strap from the rocker cover filler neck.
14 Discard the old cap and fit a new one in the reverse order to the removal sequence.

Checking the engine oil level - automatic transmission models
15 To check the engine oil level in 1300 or 1.3 models fitted with automatic transmission, proceed as follows.
16 Start the engine and run it for one or two minutes. Then switch off the ignition and wait for one minute.
17 Remove the dipstick and check the oil level. Top-up to the MAX mark, using the recommended type of oil as given in the front of the manual.

Engine and gearbox assembly (cars fitted with servo braking systems) - removal and refitting
18 Carry out the procedures as detailed in Chapter 1, Section 4, for removing the engine and gearbox, but in addition, the hose from the brake servo unit to the inlet manifold must be disconnected before the engine is lifted out.
19 Remove the banjo bolt, in the centre top of the inlet manifold, which secures the servo pipe in position. Do not forget to recover the two copper washers.
20 Lift the pipe and hose out of the way; tuck them in a position where they will not foul the engine as it is removed.
21 Refit the hose and pipe in the reverse order to removal. Do not forget the two copper washers on either side of the banjo union.

Timing cover - removal and refitting
22 On later 1100 and 1300 models (also all 1.1 and 1.3 models), there is a crankcase breather pipe fitted to the timing cover. The metal tubular section (attached to the timing cover itself) is, in fact, an oil separator and flame trap. This is connected by a hose to the carburettor flange.
23 Before removing the cover, undo the hose clip at the top of the separator/flame trap and pull off the hose.
24 Do not forget to refit the hose when the cover is refitted.

---

4 Cooling system

Expansion tank
1 In later Mk 2 models and all Allegro 3 models, the expansion

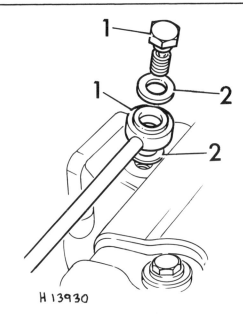

H 13930

Fig. 13.3 Brake servo vacuum pipe connection at inlet manifold (Sec 3)

   1 Banjo union and banjo bolt   *2 Copper washers*

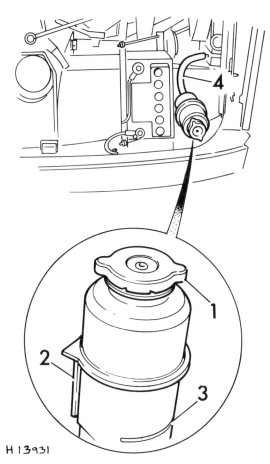

H 13931

Fig. 13.4 Later type expansion tank (Sec 4)

1 Pressure cap	*3 Coolant level mark*
2 Mounting lug	*4 Expansion tank hose*

tank is of the cylindrical type, as opposed to that shown in Section 8 of Chapter 2. It is still mounted in the front right-hand corner of the engine compartment, ahead of the battery.

2   To remove it, first undo the hose clip on the expansion hose at the radiator end. Then simply lift it out. The mounting bracket is retained to the inner wing by two self-tapping screws.

5   Fuel, carburation and exhaust systems

Air cleaner assembly (Mk 2 and 3 models) - removal and refitting

1   Mk 2 and 3 models are fitted with a thermostatic air intake temperature control valve, attached to the intake end of the air cleaner housing. From beneath this valve, a flexible hose runs to the heat chamber on the exhaust manifold.

2   When the air cleaner assembly is removed from the car, the flexible hose must be slipped off the lower intake flange of the control valve. Or it can be removed with the hose in position, in which case the hose must be pulled off the heat chamber outlet pipe.

3   When the air cleaner is refitted, the flexible hose must be reconnected to either the lower valve flange or the heat chamber, depending on how it was removed.

Air intake temperature control system (Mk 2 and 3 models) - description

4   In all Allegro Mk 2 and 3 models, air is fed into the air cleaner via the air temperature control valve, mounted between the air cleaner and the air intake.

5   The temperature of the incoming air to the air cleaner is maintained to approximately 100°F (38°C) by this system. The air temperature control unit consists basically of a canister with two inlet connections and a sponge rubber flap valve connected to a bi-metallic strip (see Fig. 13.5). One inlet pipe feeds air to the air temperature control unit from the atmosphere, whilst the other inlet is connected by a length of trunking to a heat chamber mounted over the exhaust manifold.

6   The heat chamber is mounted over the right-hand branch of the exhaust manifold, and is held in place by the manifold flange retaining nuts. One nut can be reached from the outside, but to reach the other one, the trunking must first be removed from the heat chamber so that a spanner can be inserted through the opening (see Fig. 13.6).

7   The system works basically as follows: When the engine is cold, the flap valve closes the cold air intake, and the air supplied to the carburettors is heated, being drawn from the exhaust manifold region. As the engine warms up, the bi-metallic strip expands and in so doing lifts the flap valve away from the cold air intake; a controlled mixture of both heated and cool air is thus drawn into the carburettors. Further warming-up of the engine will cause the bi-metallic strip to expand even further, until eventually the hot air intake is closed and the incoming air is drawn only from the atmosphere via the top cold air intake.

8   The air temperature control system helps to establish low emission levels and reduces the amount of choke usage, thus bringing about a fuel saving. A general improvement in cold engine performance is a further benefit of employing such a system.

Throttle damper (Mk 2 and 3 models) - removal and refitting

9   The throttle damper is mounted beneath the carburettor; to remove it, first remove the air cleaner assembly as instructed in Chapter 3 and this Section.

10   Slacken off the bolt and nut which secure the throttle damper operating lever to the throttle spindle in the carburettor.

11   Undo the retaining nut and washer which secure the damper unit to its mounting bracket; withdraw the unit from the car.

12   Refitting is basically the reverse operation to removal.

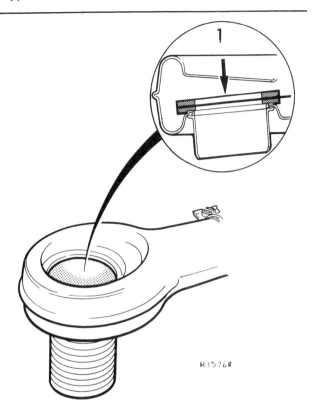

Fig. 13.5 Air intake temperature control valve (Sec 5)

1   *Insert — Engine hot: Valve closes hot air inlet and air is only drawn from atmosphere*

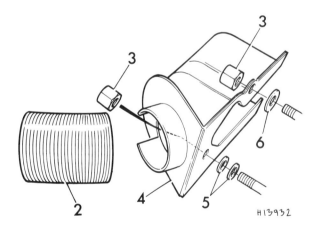

Fig. 13.6 Heat chamber (Sec 5)

2   *Flexible trunking*
3   *Manifold and heat chamber retaining nuts*
4   *Heat chamber*
5 and 6 *Washers*

However, once the damper has been refitted, the damper operating lever must be re-set.

13   Place a feeler gauge of 0.12 to 0.14 in (3.0 to 3.5 mm) between the operating lever and damper plunger.

14   Compress the damper fully by pushing the operating lever downwards as far as it will go. Then hold the lever in this position and tighten up the lever nut and bolt.

15   The lever can then be released and the feeler gauge can be removed.

Crankcase emission control systems (Mk 2 and 3 models) - description

16 Mk 2 and 3 models have much more sophisticated emission control systems than the earlier models. Two crankcase breather systems are fitted, one at the front of the engine in the timing cover, the other at the rear of the engine above the flywheel housing. Both breather systems have an oil separator and flame trap incorporated in them. Those are the small metal canisters (somewhat like miniature exhaust silencers) fitted above the breather outlets. The breathers are connected (by rubber hoses) to the controlled depression chamber of the carburettor. Engine crankcase fumes are thus drawn into the carburettor via the hoses and mix with the fuel/air mixture, where they are re-fed into the engine for combustion in the normal way. The oil filler/air filter cap, covered in Section 3, has also to be included in the emission control system as this is the way in which the air is drawn into the engine.

Inlet and exhaust manifold - removal and refitting

17 Disconnect the battery as a safety precaution.
18 Remove the air cleaner from the carburettor, as described in this Section and Chapter 3.
19 Remove the carburettor from the manifold, as described in this Section and Chapter 3.
20 Refer to Section 3, paragraph 18, and remove the brake servo vacuum pipe from the manifold.
21 Remove the carburettor gaskets, mounting block and heat shield from the manifold studs.
22 Undo the two bolts and nuts, then release the exhaust pipe-to-manifold clamp.
23 Remove the six nuts and washers which retain the exhaust and inlet manifold to the cylinder head.
24 The inlet and exhaust manifold and the heat chamber can now be withdrawn from the studs.
25 Lift the manifold gasket off the studs.
26 Fit a new manifold gasket carefully over the cylinder head studs, then refit the manifold. Refit the nuts, and do not forget to refit the heat chamber to the right-hand side flange.
27 Tighten up the nuts and refit the remainder of the components in the reverse order to removal.

---

6 Ignition system

General description (later models)

1 The Allegro range of vehicles was originally fitted with the Lucas 25D4 distributor, which is fully described in Chapter 4. From 1976 onwards, both 1100 and 1300 (1.1 and 1.3) models may have a Lucas 45D4 or a Ducellier distributor fitted as an alternative (see Specifications Section).
2 The best way to determine which distributor is used on your particular vehicle, regardless of the date of manufacture, is to observe whether or not the distributor has a micrometer adjustment facility; neither the later 45D4 nor the Ducellier have the knurled screw adjuster. This can make ignition timing slightly more difficult, but the procedures described in Section 10 of Chapter 4 still apply, bearing in mind that any fine adjustment required will necessitate that the actual distributor body be very slightly rotated.
3 Checking and adjusting the contact breaker points gap in the later 45D4 Lucas distributor is the identical procedure to that described for the 25D4 distributor, but renewal of the points and distributor overhaul operations are slightly different, and are described in the following paragraphs.
4 In the case of the Ducellier distributor, contact breaker, dwell angle and vacuum advance adjustments can only be carried out correctly using electronic test equipment, although the points can be set up approximately before any final adjustment is made. Overhaul operations are covered later in this Section.
5 Removal and refitting of the distributors is also covered in this Section.

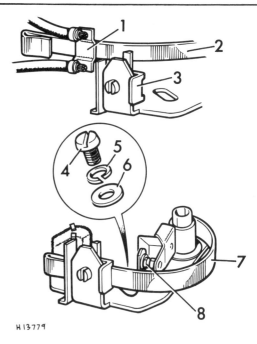

Fig. 13.7 The contact points assembly fitted to Lucas 45D4 distributors (Sec 6)

1 Terminal plate	5 Spring washer
2 Contact breaker spring arm	6 Plain washer
3 Insulated post	7 Contact assembly
4 Screw	8 Contact breaker points

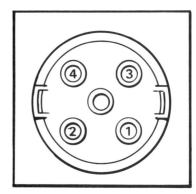

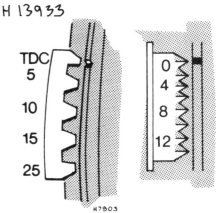

Fig. 13.8 Crankshaft pulley timing marks (later models) and distributor cap HT lead connections (Sec 6)

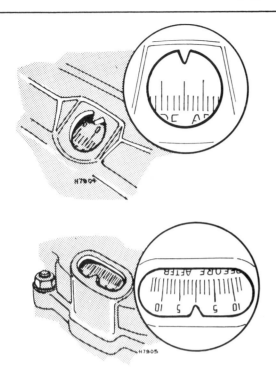

Fig. 13.9 Flywheel timing marks (Sec 6)

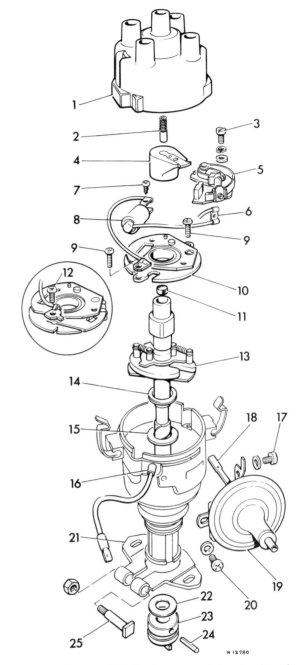

Fig. 13.10 Lucas **45D4** distributor — exploded view (Sec 6)

Contact breaker points (Lucas 45D4 distributor) removal and refitting

6 Spring back the distributor retaining clips and lift away the cap. Pull off the rotor arm and keep it in a safe place.

7 Loosen and remove the contact plate securing screws, taking great care not to drop either the screws or washers into the distributor.

8 Press the contact breaker spring arm inwards from the insulated post and release the terminal plate (with the two attached wires). The terminal plate is only clipped under the folded back portion of the spring arm.

9 The entire contact assembly can now be lifted out of the distributor.

10 When refitting the contact assembly, first clean the protective lubricant from the assembly with a fuel-moistened cloth. Clip the terminal plate to the spring arm.

11 Position the contact assembly on the distributor baseplate and fit the retaining screw and washers. Position the spring arm to the insulated post, fitting it between the two locating shoulders. The contact breaker points gap should now be checked as described in Chapter 4. Refit the rotor arm and the distributor cap.

Distributor (Lucas 45D4 and Ducellier) - removal and refitting

12 Before removing the distributor from the engine and to aid refitting, it is necessary to align the timing marks at the flywheel housing (manual transmission) or the converter housing (automatic transmission) inspection aperture. In later models (and all Allegro 3 models), which have timing marks on the crankshaft pulley, it is simpler to do this using those marks (see Fig. 13.8). To do this, proceed as described in the following paragraphs.

13 *Manual transmission*: Loosen and remove the screws securing the inspection plate to the flywheel housing (see Fig. 13.9). Remove the inspection plate to reveal the timing marks on the edge of the flywheel. If they cannot be observed, rotate the crankshaft until they appear in the aperture. Continue rotating the crankshaft until the 1/4 mark passes the pointer in the aperture. Now rotate the crankshaft in the reverse direction,

1	Distributor cap
2	Carbon brush and spring
3	Contact points screw
4	Rotor arm
5	Contact assembly
6	Terminal plate
7	Earth screw
8	Condenser
9	Baseplate retaining screws
10	Baseplate assembly
11	Felt pad
12	Baseplate retaining screw (alternative type)
13	Automatic advance mechanism
14	Steel washer
15	Spacer
16	Low tension lead and grommet
17	Vacuum unit retaining screw
18	Vacuum unit operating arm
19	Vacuum unit
20	Vacuum unit retaining screw
21	Distributor clamp plate
22	Thrust washer
23	Drive dog
24	Parallel pin
25	Clamp plate bolt

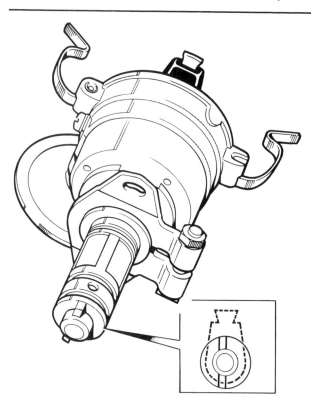

Fig. 13.11 The correct position of the driving dog on the 45D4 distributor (Sec 6)

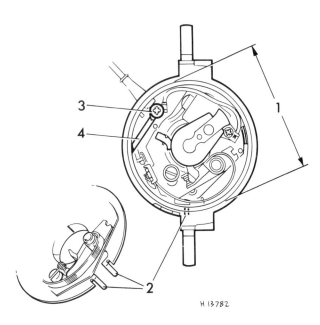

H 13782

Fig. 13.12 Fitting the alternative type baseplate on the Lucas 45D4 distributor (Sec 6)

1 Dimension across distributor cap register
2 Downward pointing prongs on baseplate
3 Earth lead
4 Slot in baseplate

until the timing marks just disappear. At this point, remove the distributor cap and observe the position of the metal portion of the rotor arm, which should be just coming up to the No 1 spark plug lead segment in the distributor cap. If it is not in this position, the crankshaft must be rotated another 180°. With the rotor arm adjacent or near the No 1 spark plug lead segment, carefully rotate the crankshaft to bring the '10' mark on the edge of the flywheel directly in alignment with the pointer in the aperture. The '10' mark on the flywheel is the correct static timing point, and when in this position the distributor points should just be opening.

14 *Automatic transmission:* The procedure described in the last paragraph should be followed, after removing the inspection plug from the converter housing. It will be noted that the 1/4 timing mark is replaced by an 'O'.

15 Where the car has timing marks on the crankshaft pulley, rotate the crankshaft until No 1 piston is at the static timing position, which is given in the Specifications Section at the beginning of this Chapter. To do this, remove the distributor cap and rotate the engine until the rotor arm is pointing to the No 1 spark plug lead segment in the distributor cap. Then turn the engine back, until the timing mark on the pulley is in line with the appropriate mark on the scale on the timing cover.

16 The engine is now correctly set up for the removal of the distributor, but first disconnect the LT cable and the vacuum advance pipe from the distributor.

17 Since the distributor cap has been removed already to check the rotor arm alignment, it is easier to remove it, if absolutely necessary, by disconnecting the four spark plug leads. Then remove it completely with the leads attached. The leads can be removed later, if required.

18 Loosen one of the bolts securing the distributor clamp plate to the cylinder block. Loosen the bolt that passes through the clamp bracket, and withdraw the distributor from the engine.

19 Provided that the timing marks were correctly set as described earlier, there is no need to identify the relative relationship of the rotor arm and the distributor body, as the slots in the driving gear and the lugs on the driving dog are offset, and can only engage in one position.

20 Refitting of the distributor is a reversal of removal and, provided that the timing marks are correctly aligned, very little fine adjustment will be required.

21 The ignition timing, however, should be checked as described in Chapter 4, Section 10. In the case of the Ducellier distributor, refer also to the Section on adjusting the contact breaker dwell angle in this Chapter.

Distributor (Lucas 45D4) - dismantling

22 Spring back the cap retaining clips and remove the cap.

23 Pull off the rotor arm and extract the felt pad from the cam.

24 Remove the two vacuum unit retaining screws, tilt the unit to disengage the link from the plate, then remove the unit.

25 Push the lower tension lead and its grommet into the distributor body.

26 Loosen and remove the two baseplate securing screws and lift out the baseplate assembly. **Note:** *An alternative type of baseplate may be used; to remove this, first loosen and remove the single securing screw. Carefully, lever the slotted segment of the baseplate from its retaining groove, then lift out the baseplate assembly.*

27 Using a suitable pin punch, drive out the drive dog parallel retaining pin, then remove the dog and thrust washer.

28 Draw out the distributor shaft complete with automatic advance mechanism, steel washer and spacer.

29 Push the moving contact spring inwards and detach the electrical terminal plate from the spring loop.

30 Remove the screw to release the earth lead and the condenser.

31 Remove the single screw and lift out the contact assembly.

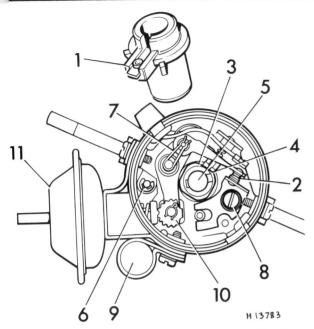

Fig. 13.13 Ducellier distributor with cap removed (Sec 6)

1　Rotor arm
2　Contact breaker points
3　Cam
4　Heel
5　Felt pad
6　Centrifugal weights pivot
7　Contact breaker arm retaining clip
8　Locking screw
9　Condenser
10　Serrated cam
11　Vacuum control unit

Distributor (Lucas 45D4) - inspection and repair

32 Thoroughly wash all the mechanical parts in petrol and wipe them dry, using a lint-free cloth.

33 Check the contact breaker points, as described in Chapter 4, Section 3. Check the distributor cap for signs of tracking, indicated by a thin black line between the segments. Renew the cap if evident.

34 If the metal portion of the rotor arm is badly burned or loose, renew the arm. If slightly burnt, clean the arm with a fine file. Check that the carbon brush moves freely in the centre of the distributor cap.

35 Do not dismantle the advance mechanism beyond removal of the control springs. If any of the moving parts, or the cam, are worn or damaged, a replacement shaft assembly must be obtained.

36 Check the fit of the shaft in its bearing. If excessive play exists, a replacement distributor must be obtained.

37 Check the baseplate assembly. If the spring between the plates is damaged, or the plates do not move freely, a replacement assembly must be obtained.

Distributor (Lucas 45D4) - reassembly

38 The reassembly procedure is essentially the reverse of the removal procedure. However, the following points must be noted:

(a) A trace of a general purpose grease or petroleum jelly should be applied to the contact breaker pivot post

(b) Lubricate the spacer and steel washer with a molybdenum disulphide dry lubricant before fitting them on the shaft

(c) Fit the thrust washer with the pips towards the drive dog

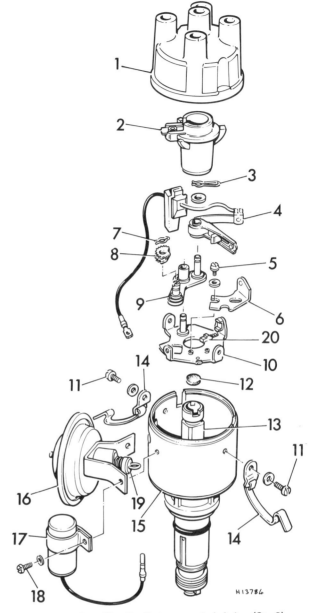

Fig. 13.14 Ducellier distributor — exploded view (Sec 6)

1　Distributor cap
2　Rotor arm
3　Long spring clip
4　Contact breaker arm
5　Locking screw
6　Contact breaker set — fixed part
7　Retaining clip
8　Serrated cam
9　Pivot posts plate
10　Baseplate
11　Spring clip and baseplate retaining screw
12　Felt pad
13　Cam
14　Spring clip
15　Distributor body
16　Vacuum control unit
17　Condenser
18　Condenser/vacuum unit retaining screw
19　Vacuum link
20　Nylon pressure pad and spring

(d)   Fit the drive dog so that the driving tongues are parallel
with the rotor arm electrode and to the left of its
centreline (see Fig. 13.11). If a new shaft has been used,
it must be drilled through the hole in the drive dog.
Whilst drilling, push the shaft from the cam end, pressing the dog and washer against the body shank

(e)   Secure the pin in the drive dog by means of a centre
punch. If the shaft is new, tap the drive end to flatten
the washer pips to ensure correct endfloat

(f)   Alternative type baseplate assembly: Position the baseplate assembly so that the two downward pointing
prongs can straddle the screw hole below the cap clip.
Press the plate into the body to engage it in the undercut

(g)   Accurately measure the dimension across the distributor
cap register on the body at right angles to the slot in the
baseplate. Position the earth lead then fit and tighten
the baseplate securing screw. Remeasure the dimension
across the cap register; if this is not at least 0.06 in
(1.50 mm) greater than that first measured, the baseplate assembly must be renewed

(h)   Check that the baseplate prongs still straddle the screw
hole. Refit the vacuum unit, engaging the operating arm
with the pin of the moving plate

(j)   Set the contact points gap to that specified

Distributor (Ducellier) - contact breaker points removal, refitting and adjustment

39 Undo the distributor cap retaining clips and lift the cap
away.
40 Remove the rotor arm and put it in a safe place.
41 Before removing the contact breaker set, remember that it
is not possible to adjust the points correctly, except with special
electronic equipment. They may be set initially to the gap given
in the Specifications Section at the beginning of this Chapter,
but this is only an approximate setting from which to work with
the proper equipment.
42 If it is absolutely necessary to change the contact breaker
points, due to total failure, then proceed as follows.
43 Remove the long spring clip from the contact breaker arm
pivot post and centre post.
44 Remove the locking screw which retains the other half of the
contact breaker set.
45 Lift out both halves of the contact breaker set and disconnect the LT lead at the spade connector in the fly lead.
46 Refit the new contact breaker set in the reverse order to
removal. Lightly smear the cam and pivot post with a general
purpose grease or petroleum jelly.
47 Set the contact breaker points gap to an initial setting of
0.015 in (0.38 mm).
48 Although the engine should run reasonably with this setting,
the final adjustments already mentioned must be carried out
using test equipment to set the dwell angle correctly. This can
be done either by a competent garage or, if the equipment is
available, by the competent home mechanic. To do this, proceed
as follows.
49 To check the dwell angle, start by connecting up the test
equipment. The dwell angle must be checked at idling speed
with the vacuum pipe disconnected. The idling speed should be
750 rpm for all 1100 and 1300 (1.1 and 1.3) models, except
the 1300 which has emission control equipment fitted. The
idling speed for that model is 850 rpm. The dwell angle should
be 57° with a variation of 2° 30' either way, for the 1100 and
1300 models or 5° either way for the 1.1 and 1.3 models.
50 If the dwell angle is incorrect, slacken the contact breaker
set locking screw and increase or decrease the points gap as
required. Lock the screw and re-check the dwell angle. Repeat
the operation, if necessary until the dwell angle is correct.
51 Check that the dwell variation is within the 2° 30' or 5°
as the engine speed is increased. Run the engine at 2000 rpm
and note the dwell angle, again with the vacuum pipe disconnected. If the variation is greater than that given in the

Specifications Section, there is a mechanical fault in the distributor itself.
52 Assuming that all is well, connect the vacuum pipe, run the
engine up to 2000 rpm, then release the accelerator. Check
the dwell variation as the engine decelerates against the data
given in the Specifications Section. This may be adjusted as
necessary by rotating the serrated cam on the eccentric pivot
in the distributor.
53 If, however, the serrated cam is altered, this will probably
alter in turn the dwell angle at idling speed. Recheck the basic
dwell angle as before.

Distributor (Ducellier) - dismantling

54 Release the distributor cap retaining clips and remove the
cap.
55 Remove the rotor arm and the felt pad from the top of
the cam.
56 Remove the contact breaker set as described in paragraphs
43 to 45 of this Section.
57 Remove the two retaining screws for the vacuum control
unit and condenser, then place the condenser to one side,
having disconnected the lead from it.
58 Remove the spring clip from the post with the serrated
cam and mark the relationship of the cam to the vacuum control
spring seat.
59 Lift off the serrated cam and unhook the spring from the
post. The vacuum control unit can then be removed and placed
to one side.
60 Remove the one remaining spring clip and the baseplate
retaining screw and lift out the baseplate, taking care that the
nylon pressure pad and spring do not fly out.

Distributor (Ducellier) - inspection and repair

61 Thoroughly wash all the mechanical parts in petrol and
wipe them dry using a lint-free cloth.
62 Inspect the contact breaker points. If they are badly worn,
burnt or pitted, renew them.
63 To reface the points, rub the faces on a fine carborundum
stone, or on fine emery paper. It is important that the faces
are rubbed flat and parallel to each other so that there will be
complete face-to-face contact when the points are closed. One
of the points will be pitted and the other will have deposits on
it. It is necessary to remove completely the built up deposits,
but unnecessary to rub the pitted point right to the stage where
all the pitting has disappeared, though obviously if this is done
it will prolong the time before the operation of refacing the
points has to be repeated.
64 Check the driveshaft for excessive wear or play. Note that
the distributor drive dog should have a certain amount of 'float'
to allow for any misalignment. It is only loosely retained to the
driveshaft.
65 Examine the distributor advance mechanism for wear. If
either the advance mechanism or the shaft have noticeable
wear or play, renew the distributor as a complete unit.
66 Check all the other minor components and renew them, if
worn.
67 Check the distributor cap for signs of cracks or tracking.
Check also that the carbon brush in the centre of the cap moves
freely against its spring.
68 Check the rotor arm and clean off any deposits with fine
emery paper. Make sure that the body is not cracked or damaged.

Distributor (Ducellier) - reassembly

69 The reassembly of the distributor is basically the reverse
procedure to dismantling. However, the following parts must
be lubricated as the distributor is reassembled.

(a)   Lubricate the centrifugal weight pivot post sparingly
with light general purpose grease or petroleum jelly

(b)   Smear the cam, the nylon pressure pad and contact
breaker pivot post with light general purpose grease

(c) Apply a few drops of engine oil to the felt pad in the top of the cam

(d) Wipe away any surplus oil or grease

70 Adjust the contact breaker points gap and dwell angle settings as described earlier in this Section.

71 If and when the distributor has been dismantled or the vacuum unit renewed, the vacuum advance setting must be checked, and re-set if necessary. This will normally have to be done by a garage.

72 To do this, run the engine idle speed with a vacuum pump connected to the unit. Use a strobe light and slowly increase the vacuum; note at which point the vacuum advance starts. In the 1100 and 1.1 models, there should be no vacuum advance below 800 rpm, and in the 1300 and 1.3 models no advance below 600 rpm, except the 1300 model with emission control system, where the figure is 300 rpm.

73 To adjust this setting, move the serrated cam in the distributor one notch at a time, until the correct setting is obtained. As mentioned in the earlier Sections, when the vacuum advance is altered, this in turn will alter the dwell angle which will have to be re-checked and re-set as necessary.

7 Electrical system (1976 models onwards)

1300 and 1.3 Estate models (1976 onwards)

Tailgate washer jet - removal and refitting

1 Remove the two screws that secure the jet to the tailgate and detach the tube from the jet.

2 Refitting is a simple reversal of the removal procedure.

Tailgate washer pump - removal and refitting

3 Raise the rear floor after undoing the two fasteners, and disconnect the two wires from the now exposed washer pump after first labelling them for correct refitting.

4 Detach the mounting rubber from the car body by removal of the two securing screws.

5 Detach the two tubes from the pump, noting the attachment points for correct refitting.

6 Remove the two rivets and washers securing the pump to the mounting rubber, and remove the pump.

7 Refitting is a reversal of the removal procedure. Ensure that the wires and tubes are connected the right way round.

Tailgate wiper motor and rack - removal and refitting

8 For safety reasons, disconnect the battery.

9 Remove the wiper arm assembly.

10 Undo the securing clips and remove the tailgate trim. Disconnect the wiring multi-plug from the wiper motor.

11 Undo the rack casing nut from the motor ferrule and remove the three bolts securing the motor to the tailgate. The motor and rack can now be removed from the rack casing.

12 Remove the gear cover from the motor after undoing the securing screws.

13 Remove the C-clip, detach the connecting link from the crank pin and rack, and remove the rack from the motor ferrule.

14 Refitting is a reversal of the removal procedure. Lubricate the rack with Ragosine Listate grease as necessary.

Tailgate wiper wheelbox - removal and refitting

15 For safety reasons, disconnect the battery.

16 Remove the wiper arm assembly.

17 Remove the nut and spacer from the wheelbox spindle.

18 Carry out the instructions given in paragraphs 10 and 11.

19 Remove the wheelbox and rack casing from the tailgate, and the inner spacer from the wheelbox.

20 The rack casing can be removed from the wheelbox after slackening the two retaining plate nuts on the wheelbox.

21 Refitting is a reversal of the removal procedure. Lubricate the drivewheel of the wheelbox and the wiper rack with Ragosine Listate grease, if necessary.

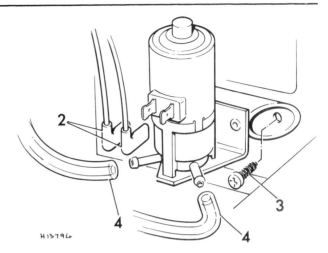

H13794

Fig. 13.15 Tailgate washer pump (Sec 7)

2 Terminal connection
3 Mounting securing screw
4 Washer pump tubes

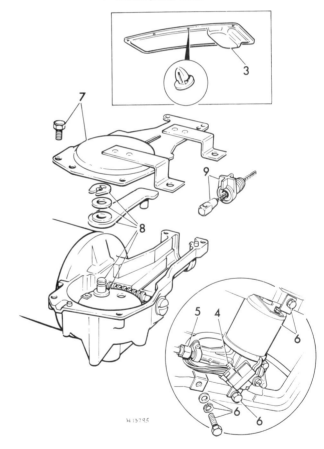

H13795

Fig. 13.16 Tailgate wiper motor and rack assembly (Sec 7)

3 Tailgate trim
4 Multi-plug
5 Rack casing nut
6 Motor securing screw
7 Gear cover and securing screw
8 E-clip, connecting link, crank pin and washers
9 Rack

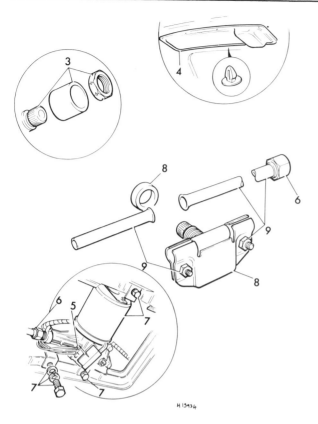

Fig. 13.17 Tailgate wiper wheelbox (Sec 7)

3 Nut, spacer and spindle   7 Motor securing screws
4 Tailgate trim   8 Inner spacer
5 Multi-plug   9 Retaining plate nuts and
6 Rack casing nut   rack casing

Tailgate wiper/washer switch - removal and refitting

22 For safety reasons, disconnect the battery.
23 Push the switch out of the heater cover from behind, and disconnect the wiring plug.
24 Refitting is a reversal of the removal procedure.

Tail, stop and flasher lamp assembly and bulbs (Estate) - removal and refitting

25 Unlock and push the rear seat squab forwards.
26 Undo the securing clips and detach the luggage compartment side trim, starting at the front end.
27 To renew the bulbs, pull the two bulb holders from the lamp assembly. Press the bulbs in and turn anti-clockwise to release them. Refitting is a reversal of the removal procedure, but align the bulb holders correctly with the lugs in the lamp assembly apertures.
28 To remove the lamp assembly, remove the two rubber plugs from the bottom of the tailgate opening inner side panel.
29 Pull the two bulb holders from the lamp assembly, remove the four nuts and remove the lamp assembly from the body of the vehicle.
30 Removal of the four screws enables the two lenses to be removed from the lamp assembly.
31 Refitting is a reversal of the removal procedure.
32 Refit the luggage compartment side trim panel.

Saloon and Estate models (1976 onwards)

Brake failure warning lamp - removal and refitting

33 Disconnect the battery as a safety precaution.
34 Disconnect the wiring from the lamp from behind the heater

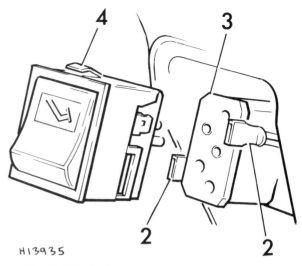

H13935

Fig. 13.18 Brake failure warning lamp removal (Sec 7)

2 Spade connectors   4 Retaining spring clip
3 Block connector

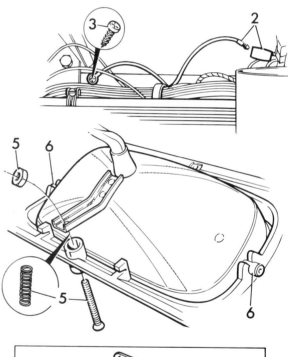

H13796

Fig. 13.19 Fog lamp removal (Sec 7)

2 Feed wire connection
3 Earthing screw
4 Fog lamp surround screw
5 Beam setting screw, spring and nut
6 Pivots

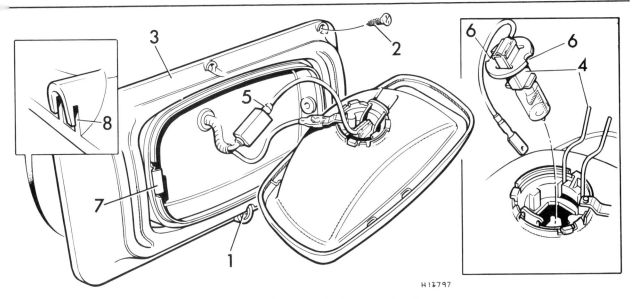

Fig. 13.20 Fog lamp — bulb renewal (Sec 7)

1 Beam setting screw	3 Fog lamp surround	5 Connector	7 Light unit clips
2 Fog lamp surround retaining screw	4 Bulb	6 Notches	8 Lug

cover. There are two spade connectors (one at each side) and a block connector.

35 Press the switch out of the heater cover to remove it.

36 Refitting is the reverse procedure to the above.

Fog lamp - removal, refitting and setting the beam

37 Disconnect the battery as a safety precaution.

38 Disconnect the feed wire to the fog lamp from the push-in connector by the front crossmember.

39 Remove the earth wire retaining screw from the front crossmember.

40 Remove the three screws along the top of the fog lamp surround then withdraw the lamp and surround complete. Lift it upwards and forwards, so that the lugs on the lower edge of the surround are freed from the front valance.

41 With the assembly removed from the car, undo and remove the beam setting screw, spring and nut which are located in the lower edge of the surround.

42 The fog lamp pivot pins on either side can now be released from the lugs on the surround and the lamp unit can be separated from the surround.

43 Refitting is the reverse procedure to the above.

44 To set the fog lamp beam, either screw the adjusting screw in to raise the beam, or out (anti-clockwise) to lower it.

Fog lamp - bulb renewal

45 Disconnect the battery as a safety precaution. Fully slacken the beam setting screw, and insert a screwdriver between the right-hand side of the lamp rim and the body to remove the light unit.

46 Undo the bulb retaining spring clip and lift it up. Then withdraw the bulb.

47 Refit the bulb to the lamp unit. Note that it can only fit one way as the bulb has notches in the flange. One is square and the other rounded. These must correspond to the lugs in the lamp holder.

48 Do not touch the bulb glass or it will cause discoloration during use. If the glass is inadvertently touched, clean it off using methylated spirit and a lint-free piece of rag.

49 Refit the lamp unit and re-set the beam as described in paragraph 44.

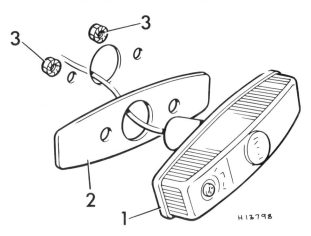

Fig. 13.21 Flasher side repeater lamp assembly (Sec 7)

1 Lamp unit	2 Gasket	3 Retaining nuts

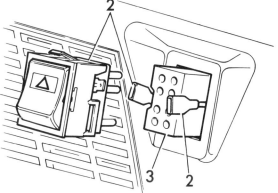

Fig. 13.22 Later type illuminated hazard flasher switch (Sec 7)

2 Spade connectors	3 Multi-pin connector

Key to Fig. 13.23 Wiring diagram — Mk 2 1100 and 1300 models, RH drive (Sec 7)

1	LH sidelamp	36	Heated backlight
2	LH front direction indicator lamp	37	Reverse lamp switch
3	RH front direction indicator lamp	38	Fuse (No 2)
4	RH sidelamp	39	Light switch
5	LH headlamp dipped beam	40	Radiator cooling fan relay
6	LH headlamp main beam	41	Radiator cooling fan thermostatic switch
7	RH headlamp dipped beam	42	Cigar lighter
8	RH headlamp main beam	43	Radiator cooling fan
9	Windscreen washer motor	44	Hazard warning flasher unit
10	Heater blower motor	45	Hazard warning lamp
11	Battery	46	Hazard warning switch
12	Alternator	47	Direction indicator flasher unit
13	Windscreen wiper motor	48	Stoplamp switch
14	Windscreen wiper/washer switch	49	Voltage stabilizer
15	Heater blower motor switch	50	Direction indicator switch
16	Ignition coil	51	RH tail lamp
17	Starter motor solenoid	52	Oil pressure warning light
18	Radio (if fitted)	53	LH stop lamp
19	Distributor	54	No charge warning light
20	Starter motor	55	Fuel gauge
21	Ignition/starter switch	56	Coolant temperature gauge
22	Line fuse (radio — if fitted)	57	Direction indicator warning lamp
23	Fuse (No 5)	58	Reverse lamps
24	Fuse (No 1)	59	RH rear direction indicator lamp
25	Fuse (No 3)	60	Number plate illumination lamp
26	Headlamp dipswitch	61	LH tail lamp
27	Headlamp flasher switch	62	RH stop lamp
28	Horn push	63	Oil pressure switch
29	Fuse (No 4)	64	Fuel gauge tank unit
30	Horn	65	Coolant temperature transmitter
31	Heated backlight switch	66	Direction indicator warning lamp
32	Interior lamp	67	Instrument panel lamp
33	Interior lamp LH door switch	68	Headlamp main beam warning lamp
34	Interior lamp RH door switch	69	Instrument panel lamp
35	Rear interior lamp (if fitted)	70	Instrument panel printed circuit

Cable colour code

B	Black
U	Blue
N	Brown
K	Pink
P	Purple
R	Red
G	Green
LG	Light Green
O	Orange
S	Slate
W	White
Y	Yellow

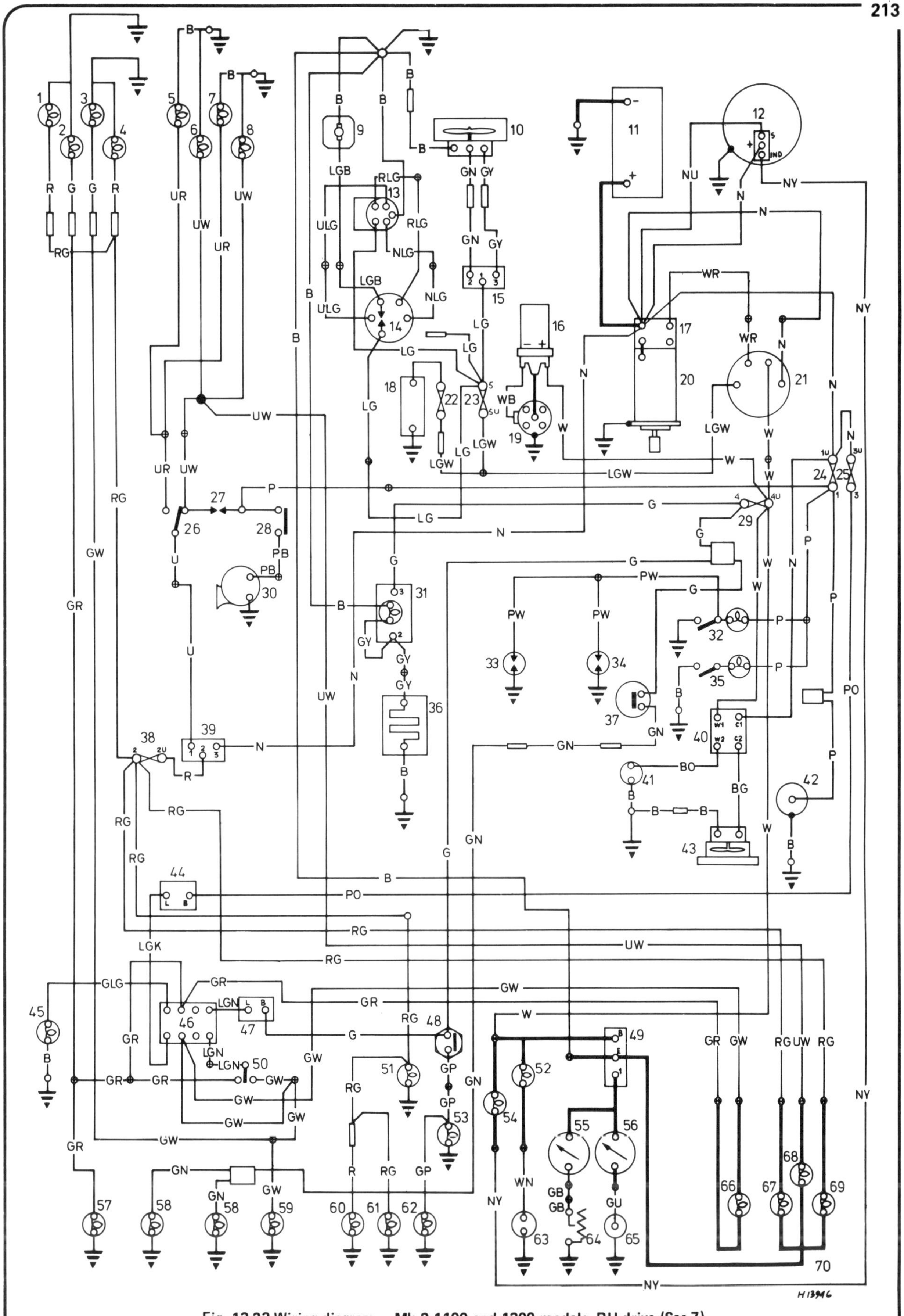

Fig. 13.23 Wiring diagram — Mk 2 1100 and 1300 models, RH drive (Sec 7)

H13946

Key to Fig. 13.24 Wiring diagram — Mk 2 1300 models, RH drive with automatic transmission (Sec 7)

1	Starter motor solenoid relay	38	Rear interior lamp (if fitted)
2	LH sidelamp	39	Heated backlight
3	LH front direction indicator lamp	40	Reverse lamp switch
4	RH front direction indicator lamp	41	Fuse (No 2)
5	RH sidelamp	42	Light switch
6	LH headlamp dipped beam	43	Radiator cooling fan relay
7	LH headlamp main beam	44	Radiator cooling fan thermostatic switch
8	RH headlamp dipped beam	45	Cigar lighter
9	RH headlamp main beam	46	Radiator cooling fan
10	Windscreen washer motor	47	Hazard warning flasher unit
11	Heater blower motor	48	Hazard warning lamp
12	Battery	49	Hazard warning switch
13	Alternator	50	Direction indicator flasher unit
14	Windscreen wiper motor	51	Stoplight switch
15	Windscreen wiper/washer switch	52	Voltage stabilizer
16	Heater blower motor switch	53	Direction indicator switch
17	Ignition coil	54	RH tail lamp
18	Starter motor solenoid	55	Oil pressure warning light
19	Automatic transmission inhibitor switch	56	LH stop lamp
20	Radio (if fitted)	57	No charge warning light
21	Distributor	58	Fuel gauge
22	Starter motor	59	Coolant temperature gauge
23	Ignition/starter switch	60	Direction indicator warning lamp
24	Line fuse (radio — if fitted)	61	Reverse lamps
25	Fuse (No 5)	62	RH rear direction indicator lamps
26	Fuse (No 1)	63	Number plate lamp
27	Fuse (No 3)	64	LH tail lamp
28	Headlamp dipswitch	65	RH stop lamp
29	Headlamp flasher switch	66	Oil pressure switch
30	Horn push	67	Fuel gauge tank unit
31	Fuse (No 4)	68	Coolant temperature transmitter
32	Horn	69	Direction indicator warning lamp
33	Heated backlight switch	70	Instrument panel lamp
34	Interior lamp	71	Instrument panel lamp
35	Interior lamp LH door switch	72	Headlamp main beam warning lamp
36	Automatic transmission selector lever	73	Instrument panel lamp
37	Interior lamp RH door switch	74	Instrument panel printed circuit

Cable colour code

B	Black
U	Blue
N	Brown
K	Pink
P	Purple
R	Red
G	Green
LG	Light Green
O	Orange
S	Slate
W	White
Y	Yellow

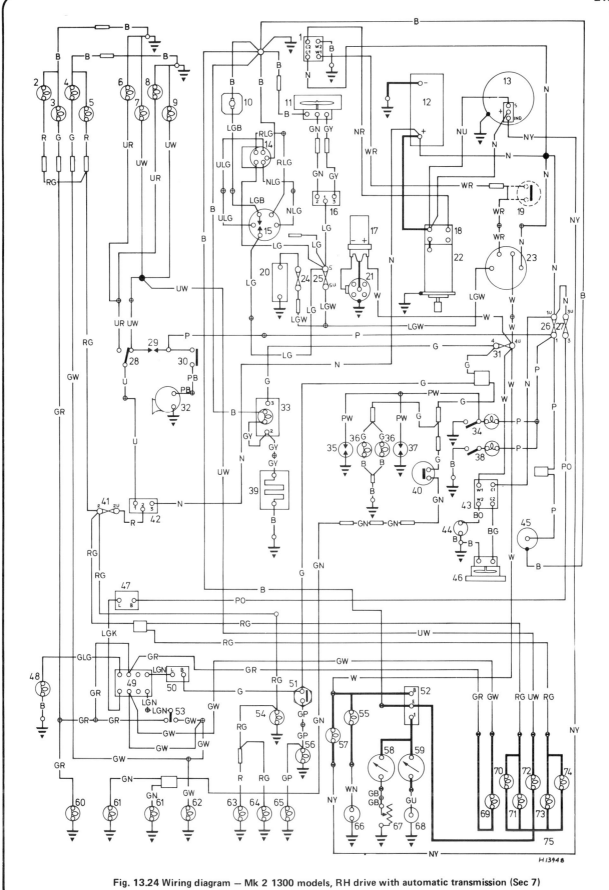

Fig. 13.24 Wiring diagram — Mk 2 1300 models, RH drive with automatic transmission (Sec 7)

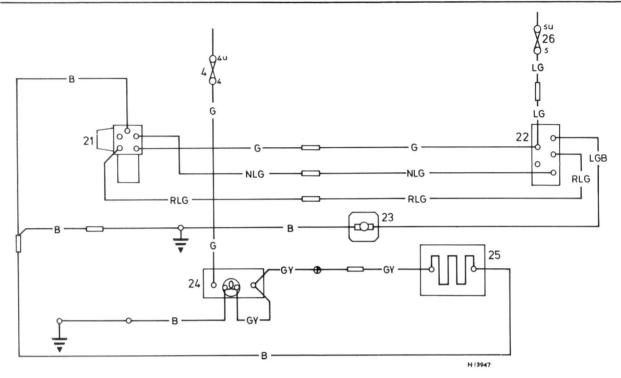

Fig. 13.25 Wiring diagram for tailgate wiper/washer and heated rear screen — Estate models (Sec 7)

4	Fuse unit (No 4 fuse)	24	Heated rear screen switch
21	Tailgate wiper motor	25	Heated rear screen
22	Tailgate wiper and washer switch	26	Fuse unit (No 5 fuse)
23	Tailgate washer motor		

Cable colour code

B	Black	K	Pink
U	Blue	R	Red
N	Brown	W	White
G	Green	Y	Yellow
LG	Light Green		

When a cable has two colour code letters the first denotes
the main colour and the second denotes the tracer colour.

Flasher side repeater lamp - removal
50 Disconnect the battery as a safety precaution.
51 Disconnect the wiring to the lamp unit at the push-in connector in the engine compartment.
52 Undo the two nuts which retain the lamp unit to the front wing. These are reached from up inside the wing above the front wheel.
53 Withdraw the lamp and feed wire through the hole in the wing. The gasket can be removed as well.
54 Refitting is the reverse procedure to removal.

Flasher side repeater lamp - bulb renewal
55 Remove the single lens retaining screw and remove the lens.
56 Remove the bayonet type bulb and renew it.
57 Refit the lens and retaining screw.

Hazard warning light switch (Mk 2 models)
58 Later models are fitted with an illuminated hazard flasher switch, unlike the earlier type where the switch and warning light were separate items.
59 To remove the switch, which is mounted on the right-hand side of the heater cover, proceed as follows.
60 Disconnect the two wiring spade connectors, one on either

side of the switch, from behind the heater cover. Then push the switch out of the heater cover and separate it from the multi-pin connector into which it is fitted.
61 Should the warning bulb require renewal, insert an electrician's screwdriver under the notch at each side of the lens and lever the lens from the rocker switch itself. The bulb is simply unscrewed.

8 Electrical system - Allegro 3 models (1979 onwards)

General
1 In the electrical system, there have been numerous alterations and additions to the Allegro 3 range of vehicles.
2 A completely new instrument panel (of the printed circuit type) has been fitted and all the indicator and warning lights are now incorporated in one vertical section in the centre of this panel. In the basic model, the panel consists of just the two major dials, the right-hand one incorporating the fuel and temperature gauge, in addition to the warning lights section. All L models have a large clock in the main right-hand section and two smaller gauges on either side for the fuel and coolant. HL models have a tachometer as the major right-hand instru-

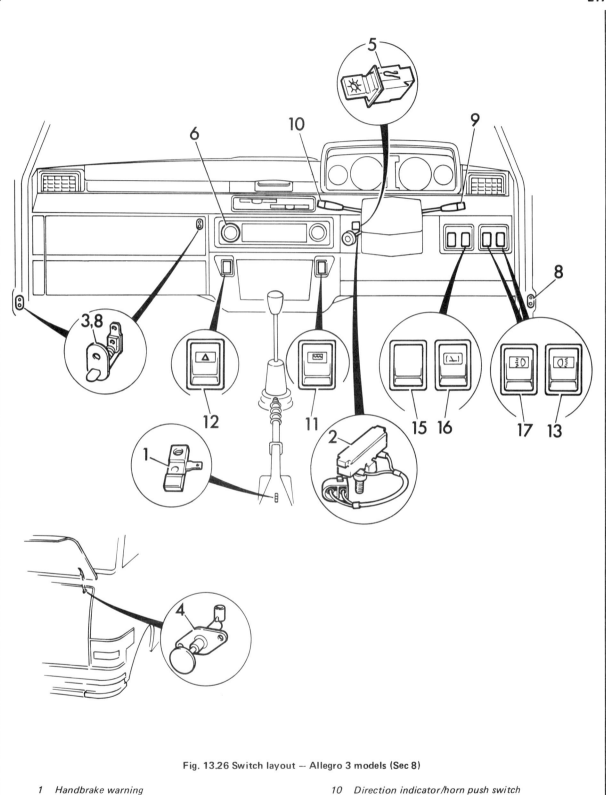

Fig. 13.26 Switch layout — Allegro 3 models (Sec 8)

1	Handbrake warning	10	Direction indicator/horn push switch
2	Choke warning light	11	Heated rear window switch
3 and 8	Glovebox and door-operated courtesy light switch	12	Hazard flasher switch
4	Boot light switch	13	Fog rear guard lamp switch
5	Main lighting switch	15	Spare
6	Heater blower switch	16	Tailgate wash/wipe switch (Estate models only)
9	Washer/wiper switch	17	Front fog lamps switch (where fitted)

ment, with the fuel and coolant gauges on either side. A smaller clock (of a similar type, as fitted to the Vanden Plas models) is fitted to the HL models and is mounted in the centre console. All L and HL models now have an illuminated cigar lighter fitted as standard equipment.

3   In lighting, all HL vehicles are now equipped with four round headlamps, whilst the other models are still fitted with twin rectangular headlamps.

4   All models now feature circular side repeater flashers, a rear fog guard lamp and reversing lights as standard equipment.

5   The bulb fittings have been considerably revised and these are covered in the Specifications Section at the beginning of this Chapter.

6   The main lighting switch has also been changed and is now located on the left-hand side of the steering column shroud.

7   In the new range, all HL models are also fitted with a push-button LW/MW radio as standard with two speakers, one either side below the facia panel.

Main lighting switch - removal and refitting

8   The main lighting switch in Allegro 3 models is located in the left-hand side of the steering column shroud, in front of and below the column dipswitch/horn control switch.

9   To remove the switch, first disconnect the battery as a safety precaution.

10 Remove the three screws which hold the two half casings of the steering column shroud together. There are two on the left and one on the right.

11 Carefully, ease the right-hand half casing away from the steering column. It is quite a tight fit, but it can be done! Take care not to damage the stalk switch.

12 Disconnect the multi-plug connector from the lighting switch in the left-hand half casing.

13 Now ease the left-hand half casing away from the steering column. As with the right-hand part, this is a tight fit.

14 Depress the spring clip on the inside of the left-hand half casing to remove the lighting switch.

15 Refitting is the reverse procedure to removal.

Round headlamp unit (HL models) - removal and refitting

16 Disconnect the battery as a safety precaution.

17 Remove the two screws (one at the top and one at the bottom) of the headlamp trim surround.

18 Remove the three screws which secure the headlamp re-taining ring then lift the ring and sealed beam unit away from the body.

19 Place the retaining ring to one side and disconnect the multi-plug connector from the rear of the headlamp sealed beam unit.

Round headlamps (twin) assembly - removal and refitting

20 The complete twin headlamp assembly can be removed in one piece, if required.

21 Disconnect the battery as a safety precaution.

22 Remove the two screws which secure the top of the head-lamp mounting plate to the front panel.

23 Remove the other two screws, from inside the engine compartment, which retain the bottom of the headlamp mounting plate.

24 Disconnect the multi-plug connectors from the rear of each headlamp unit and withdraw the complete headlamp assembly from the car.

25 Refitting the sealed beam unit or the complete assembly is the reverse procedure to removal.

Side repeater flasher lamps - removal and refitting

26 The round side repeater flasher lamps fitted to the Series 3 models are different from those fitted to earlier models, which were elongated units bolted to the front wing panel.

27 The new units are of the circular 'press-in - push-out' type and are easily removed by inserting the hand up inside the

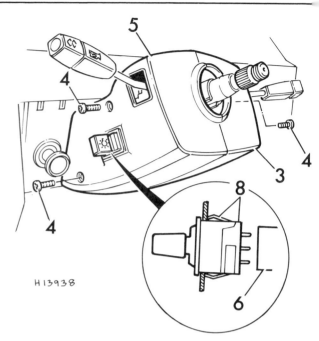

Fig. 13.27 Main lighting switch removal (Sec 8)

3   *Steering column shroud — right half*
4   *Shroud retaining screws*
5   *Steering column shroud — left half*
6   *Multi-plug socket*
8   *Switch and spring clip*

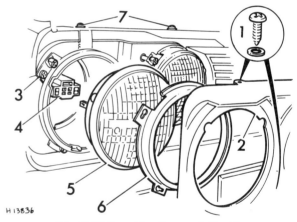

Fig. 13.28 Round headlamp unit (Sec 8)

1   *Trim retaining screws*
2   *Trim surround*
3   *Sealed beam unit and retaining ring screws*
4   *Multi-plug connector*
5   *Sealed beam unit*
6   *Retaining ring*
7   *Headlamp mounting plate screws*

front wing and pushing the unit out of the wing.

28 Disconnect the wiring to the lamp holder to remove it from the vehicle.

29 To refit the lamp, press it firmly into the hole in the wing, but clean off any excess road dirt before doing so.

Tail, stop, flasher and reversing lamp assembly - removal and refitting

30 The procedure for this operation is described in Section 7, paragraphs 25 to 32. The extra light that is now required for the

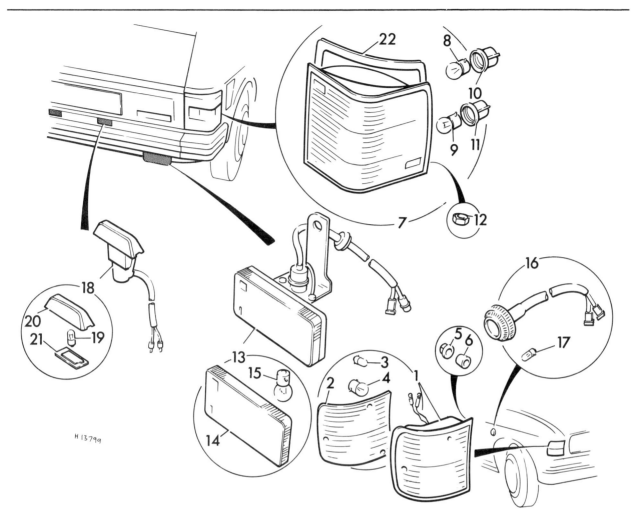

Fig. 13.29 Sidelights, flasher repeater and tail/rear/reverse lamp assemblies — Allegro 3 models (Sec 8)

1 Front sidelight and direction indicator assembly	13 Rear guard fog lamp
2 Lens	14 Lens
3 Sidelight bulb	15 Bulb
4 Flasher bulb	16 Side repeater flasher lamp unit
5 Bulb holder retaining nut	17 Bulb
6 Distance piece	18 Rear number plate lamp assembly
7 Rear lamp assembly	19 Bulb
8 and 10 Flasher and reversing lamp bulb and holder	20 Lens cover
9 and 11 Stop and tail lamp bulb and holder	21 Lens
12 Rear lamp holder retaining nut	22 Rubber seal

integral reversing light is provided by a dual filament bulb in each rear lamp assembly, which serves both the reversing and direction indicator lamps. In earlier models, the reversing lamps were separate units.

Rear fog guard lamp - removal and refitting
In accordance with EEC regulations, all new Allegro models are equipped with a red rear fog guard lamp. This is mounted beneath the rear bumper on the right-hand side.
31 To remove the lamp, first undo the right upper bumper mounting bolt and nut to which the lamp and mounting bracket are attached. The retaining nut is reached from within the boot (Saloon models) or beneath the load deck floor (Estate models).
32 Disconnect the wiring to the lamp. There are two push-in connectors coming from the loom near the right-hand rear lamp assembly. Note which wire fits into which connector before removing them.

33 Feed the wiring through the rear body panel and grommet, then remove the assembly from the car.
34 Refitting is the reverse procedure to removal.

Rear fog guard lamp - bulb renewal
35 Unscrew the two crosshead screws which retain the lens in place, and remove it.
36 The bulb is of the bayonet fitting type. Push in and twist to remove it.
37 Refit a bulb of a similar type and wattage to that which was removed.
38 Refit the lens and the two screws.

Rear number plate lamps - removal and refitting
39 The Series 3 models all have two rear number plate lamps. These are a push fit into the top surface of the bumper.
40 To remove the lamp, first disconnect the battery and then

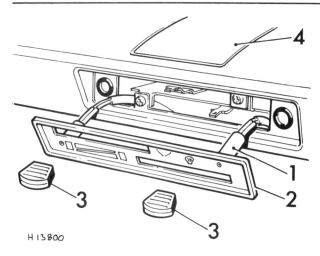

H 13800

Fig. 13.30 Heater control panel — bulb renewal (Sec 8)

1 Bulb holders	*3 Knobs*
2 Panel	*4 Ashtray space*

the wiring inside the boot (Saloon models) or under the load deck floor (Estate models). There are two push-in connectors coming from the wiring loom, one for each lamp.

41 From behind the bumper, push in the long retaining clips which hold the lamp into the bumper, then withdraw the lamp upwards from the bumper. Feed the wires through the grommet in the rear valance and remove the complete assembly.

42 Refitting is the reverse procedure.

Rear number plate lamps - bulb renewal

43 Remove the lamp as described in the previous paragraphs, but do not detach the wiring connector.

44 Separate the lamp assembly; the top and lens come away from the lamp holder and bulb. The lens is a loose fit, so can easily be lost.

45 Remove the bulb and replace it with a new one of the same type and wattage.

46 Fit the lens back into the top section, fit them both over the lamp holder and clip them together.

47 Refit the lamp to the bumper and push it firmly home so that the retaining clips locate under the bumper.

Heater control lever panel illumination - bulb renewal

48 Pull off the heater control lever knobs.

49 Remove the ashtray from the top of the dashboard as described in Section 12.

50 Insert one hand inside the ashtray space and push out the heater control panel. The bulb holders may now be pulled out of the panel. There is one bulb holder at either end. Remove whichever is faulty.

51 Withdraw the capless bulb from the holder and fit a new one of the same type and wattage.

52 Push the bulb holder back into the panel and refit the panel to the facia. It is a push-in fitting.

53 Refit the ashtray and heater lever knobs; check that the heater panel illumination comes on when the main lighting switch is operated.

Heater blower switch - removal and refitting

54 Disconnect the battery as a safety precaution.

55 Remove the heater cover and lower it away from the facia as described in Section 12, paragraphs 25 to 28.

56 The switch control knob is retained to the spindle by a stud located in the spindle. To remove the knob, first locate the small hole in the neck of the knob. Then insert a thin rod into the hole and push the stud in the spindle inwards so that the knob can be withdrawn.

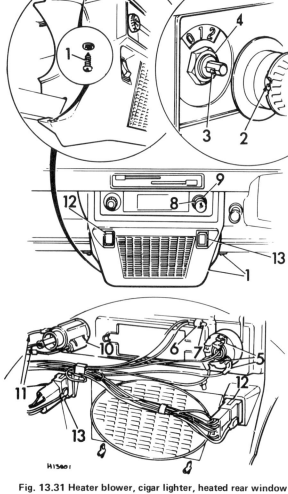

H13801

Fig. 13.31 Heater blower, cigar lighter, heated rear window and hazard switch arrangement (Sec 8)

1	*Heater cover retaining screws*	*7*	*Bulb*
2	*Hole in heater blower control knob*	*8*	*Cigar lighter*
		9	*Bezel*
3	*Stud in spindle*	*10*	*Bulb holder hood*
4	*Brass nut*	*11*	*Wiring to cigar lighter*
5	*Heater blower switch wiring*	*12*	*Hazard warning lights switch*
6	*Bulb holder*	*13*	*Heated rear window switch*

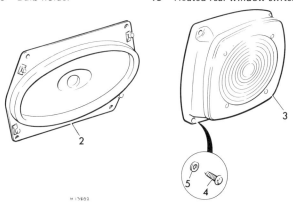

H 13802

Fig. 13.32 Radio speaker assembly (fitted to HL models) (Sec 8)

2	*Speaker*	*4*	*Screw*
3	*Pod*	*5*	*Washer*

57 Unscrew the brass retaining nut on the outside of the heater cover and withdraw the switch from the rear of the cover.
58 Disconnect the wiring from the fan switch, noting which wire fits where. A small diagram is the easiest way of remembering, even if there are only three wires.
59 Refitting is the reverse procedure to removal. Check, on refitting, that the blower fan works correctly.

Heater blower switch illumination - bulb renewal
60 Disconnect the battery as a safety precaution.
61 Remove the heater cover as directed in Section 12, paragraphs 25 to 28.
62 Pull the bulb holder out of the holder bracket.
63 Pull the bulb, which is of the capless type, out of the holder. Replace it with a new one of the same type and wattage.
64 Refitting is the reverse procedure to removal.

Cigar lighter - removal, refitting and bulb renewal
65 Disconnect the battery as a safety precaution.
66 Remove the heater cover as directed in Section 12, paragraphs 25 to 28.
67 Pull out the cigar lighter knob from the front of the cover.
68 Squeeze together the sides of the cigar lighter illumination bulb hood and remove the hood. The bulb and holder are now free. Pull the capless bulb out of the holder and replace it with a new one of the same type and wattage.
69 Disconnect the remaining wiring to the lighter unit, noting which wire fits where; use a diagram if necessary.
70 Unscrew the cigar lighter retaining bezel from the front of the heater cover and withdraw the lighter body from the rear of the cover.
71 Refitting is the reverse procedure to removal.

Hazard warning lights and heated rear window switches - removal and refitting
72 Disconnect the battery as a safety precaution.
73 Remove the heater cover as directed in Section 12, paragraphs 25 to 28.
74 Note which wires fit where on which switch and remove them.
75 Depress the spring retaining clip on the rear of the appro-

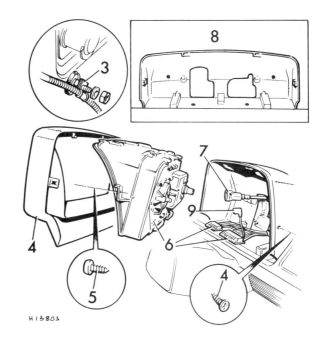

H13803

Fig. 13.33 Instrument panel removal — (Sec 8)

3 Speedometer cable bulkhead bracket
4 Cowl and retaining screw
5 Instrument panel retaining screw
6 Multi-plug connectors
7 Speedometer cable
8 Binnacle
9 Wiring connector for clock/tachometer

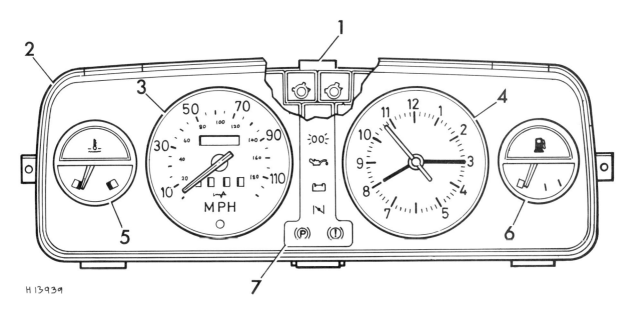

H13939

Fig. 13.34 Instrument panel — Allegro 3 L models (Sec 8)

1	Panel	3	Speedometer	5	Temperature gauge	7	Warning lights
2	Lens	4	Clock	6	Fuel gauge		

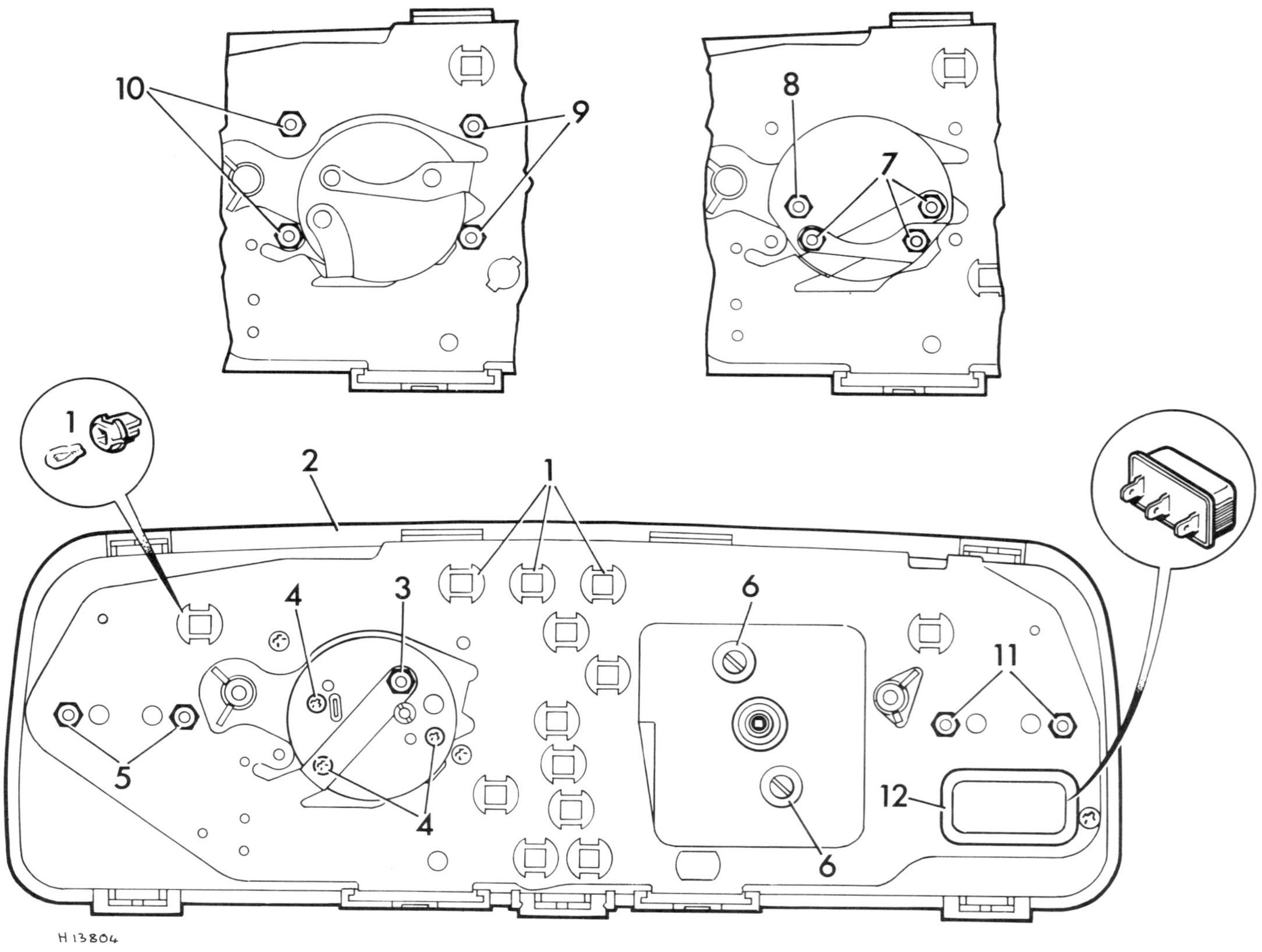

Fig. 13.35 Instrument panel — rear layout (Sec 8)

1 Bulb holders
2 Lens
3 Clock terminal nut
4 Clock retaining screws
5 Fuel gauge retaining nuts
6 Speedometer retaining screws
7 Tachometer printed circuit nuts
8 Tachometer retaining nut
9 Combined gauge — fuel section retaining nuts
10 Combined gauge — temperature section retaining nuts
11 Fuel gauge retaining nuts
12 Voltage stabiliser

H13804

priate switch, then push it out of the front of the heater cover and remove it.
76 Refitting the switches is the reverse procedure.

Radio fitting - general
77 In Allegro 2 and 3 models, provision is made in the heater cover for radio fitting. A panel is located between the cigar lighter and heater blower switch. The main front section of the heater cover has provision for fitting a single speaker, and is already made as a speaker grille.
78 In all Series 3 HL versions, a radio is fitted as standard equipment. This is a pushbutton, long and medium waveband receiver with a five section telescopic aerial mounted on the right-hand wing. In fact, all Allegro models now have a pre-drilled hole, covered by a flat black rubber plug, for radio aerial fitting in the right-hand front wing.
79 The HL models are also fitted with two speakers, one mounted on each side of the front passenger compartment below the dashboard.
80 If a radio is to be fitted, ensure before starting that its polarity is correct, or if of the dual polarity type, that the switch is changed to negative before fitting commences.

Radio - removal and refitting
81 Disconnect the battery as a safety precaution.
82 Remove the heater cover as directed in Section 12, paragraphs 25 to 28.
83 Disconnect the power supply to the radio at the in-line fuse holder. Push the narrower end of the holder in and twist it, then pull it out. Put the fuse in a safe place.
84 Disconnect the earth wire from the radio to the body.
85 Pull the aerial connector out of the socket on the rear of the radio.
86 Disconnect the wiring from the radio to the twin or single speakers. This is usually by a twin pin plug in the speaker wiring.
87 Pull off the volume and tuning control knobs, and the spacers, from the front of the radio.
88 Undo the retaining nuts on both spindle collars and remove them and the washers. Then withdraw the radio from the rear of the heater cover.
89 In Allegro 3 models, it may be easier to remove the heater blower switch lamp holder, as described earlier in this Section, so that the radio does not foul the wiring as it is withdrawn.
90 Refitting is the reverse procedure to removal.

Instrument panel - removal and refitting
91 Disconnect the battery as a safety precaution.
92 Undo the nut and washer which secure the speedometer cable to the stud on the rear bulkhead in the engine compartment.
93 Remove the screws in either side of the instrument binnacle and remove the instrument panel cowl. There are two clips which locate the top edge of the cowl against the binnacle. These must be released in order to remove the cowl.
94 Undo and remove the two self-tapping screws which retain the instrument panel to the binnacle. There is one screw on each side.
95 Ease the instrument panel forward and undo the speedometer cable knurled collar so that the cable can be released from the speedometer.
96 Then disconnect the two multi-plug connectors, noting which goes where.
97 Disconnect the wiring to the clock or tachometer, depending upon the model.
98 The instrument panel is now free to be removed.
99 Refitting is the reverse procedure to removal.

Instrument panel and warning lamp bulbs - renewal
100 Remove the instrument panel as described in the previous paragraphs.
101 Locate and identify the bulb which needs to be renewed.

102 Turn the bulb holder in the rear of the panel anti-clockwise and remove it from the panel.
103 Pull the bulb out of the holder (they are all capless bulbs) and push in a new one of the same wattage (see Specifications at the beginning of this Chapter).
104 Refit the holder and bulb into the instrument panel; secure it by rotating the holder in a clockwise direction.
105 Refit the instrument panel as already described.

Instruments - removal and refitting
106 Remove the instrument panel as described earlier in this Section.
107 Undo the six retaining clips and separate the lens assembly from the instrument panel.
108 The instruments may now be removed as required, but take care that the retaining bolts do not snag the printed circuit as the instruments are withdrawn.

Clock (all except HL models)
109 Unscrew the nut and lift off the tag from the printed circuit.
110 Remove the three crosshead screws which secure the clock in position.
111 Remove the clock from the front of the panel.
112 Refitting is the reverse procedure.

Speedometer
113 The speedometer is retained by two screws. Remove them and withdraw the instrument from the front of the panel.
114 Refitting is the reverse procedure.

Tachometer (HL models only)
115 There are four nuts on the rear of the tachometer. Three of them retain the printed circuit to the unit; the fourth locates the unit.
116 Remove all four nuts and withdraw the tachometer from the front of the instrument panel.
117 Refitting is the reverse procedure.

Fuel gauge (separate unit)
118 Remove the two retaining nuts and withdraw the instrument from the front of the instrument panel.
119 Refitting is the reverse procedure.

Temperature gauge (separate unit)
120 Remove the two retaining nuts and withdraw the instrument from the front of the instrument panel.
121 Refitting is the reverse procedure.

Combined fuel and temperature gauge
122 In basic models the fuel and temperature gauge is a combined unit fitted in the right-hand large instrument aperture.
123 Undo the four retaining nuts on the rear of the instrument panel and both gauges can be withdrawn simultaneously. If the temperature gauge only is to be removed this can be done, but the nuts which secure the fuel gauge must be slackened first to allow the necessary clearance. The reverse applies to the fuel gauge.
124 Take even greater care when removing only one of the instruments, as it will have to be withdrawn at an angle and this could very easily damage the printed circuit when the bolts are pulled through the terminals.
125 Refitting is the reverse procedure and again, great care must be taken. Do not forget to re-tighten the retaining nuts on the other gauge.

Voltage stabiliser - removal and refitting
126 Remove the instrument panel as described in this Section.
127 Withdraw the voltage stabiliser by pulling it out of the rear of the instrument panel.
128 Line-up the pins of the voltage stabiliser with the slots in the instrument panel and push it home to refit it.

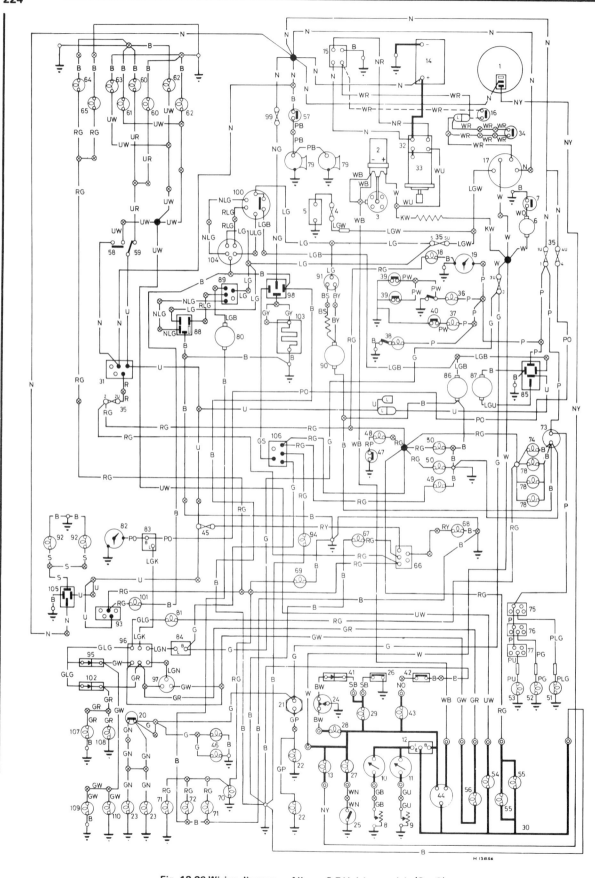

Fig. 13.36 Wiring diagram — Allegro 3 RH drive models (Sec 8)

Key to Fig. 13.36 Wiring diagram — Allegro 3 RH drive models (Sec 8)

1	Alternator
2	Ignition coil
3	Distributor
4	Line fuse — radio
5	Radio
6	Radiator fan motor
7	Radiator fan thermostat
8	Fuel gauge tank unit
9	Coolant temperature transducer
10	Fuel gauge
11	Coolant temperature gauge
12	Voltage stabilizer
13	Ignition/no-charge warning lamp
14	Battery
15	Starter solenoid relay
16	Automatic gearbox inhibitor switch — 1.7 models
17	Ignition/starter switch
18	Clock illumination lamp — HL models only
19	Clock — HL models only
20	Reverse lamp switch
21	Stop lamp switch
22	Stop lamp
23	Reverse lamps
24	Brake pressure differential switch
25	Oil pressure switch
26	Handbrake warning lamp switch
27	Oil pressure warning lamp
28	Brake failure warning lamp
29	Handbrake warning lamp
30	Printed circuit
31	Lighting switch
32	Starter solenoid
33	Starter motor
34	Automatic gearbox inhibitor switch — 1.3 models
35	Fusebox
36	Interior lamp
37	Luggage compartment lamp
38	Rear interior lamp
39	Interior lamp door switches
40	Luggage compartment switch
41	Diode — brake warning
42	Choke warning lamp switch
43	Choke warning lamp
44	Tachometer
45	Line fuse — front fog lamps
46	Automatic gearbox selector illumination lamp
47	Glovebox illumination lamp switch
48	Glovebox illumination lamp
49	Switch illumination lamp
50	Heater control illumination lamp
51	Roof lamp
52	Auxiliary roof sign lamp
53	Roof sign lamp
54	Headlamp main-beam warning lamp
55	Panel illumination lamps
56	Direction indicator warning lamp
57	Horn-push
58	Headlamp flasher switch
59	Headlamp dip switch
60	Headlamp dip beam
61	RH headlamp — inner
62	Headlamp main beam
63	LH headlamp — inner
64	LH sidelamp
65	RH sidelamp
66	Rear fog-guard lamp switch
67	Rear fog-guard warning lamp
68	Rear fog-guard lamp
69	Switch illumination
70	RH tail lamp
71	Number-plate illumination lamp
72	LH tail lamp
73	Cigar lighter
74	Cigar lighter illumination lamp
75	Roof lamp switch
76	Auxiliary roof sign switch
77	Roof sign switch
78	Switch illumination
79	Horn
80	Rear window
81	Hazard warning lamp
82	Clock — except HL models
83	Hazard warning flasher unit
84	Direction indicator flasher unit
85	Headlamp washer relay
86	Windscreen washer motor
87	Headlamp washer pump
88	Rear window wiper motor
89	Rear window washer and wiper switch
90	Heater motor
91	Heater switch
92	Front fog lamp
93	Front fog lamp switch
94	Heated rear window warning lamp
95	Diode — direction indicator warning lamp
96	Hazard warning switch
97	Direction indicator switch
98	Heated rear window relay
99	Line fuse — heated rear window
100	Windscreen wiper and washer switch
101	Front fog lamp warning lamp
102	Diode — direction indicator warning lamp
103	Heated rear window
104	Windscreen wiper motor
105	Front fog lamp relay
106	Heated rear window switch
107	LH front direction indicator lamp
108	LH rear direction indicator lamp
109	RH front direction indicator lamp
110	RH rear direction indicator lamp

Note: Not all items listed are fitted to all models.

Cable colour code

B	Black	P	Purple
G	Green	R	Red
K	Pink	S	Slate
LG	Light green	U	Blue
N	Brown	W	White
O	Orange	Y	Yellow

When a cable has two colour code letters the first denotes the
main colour and the second denotes the tracer colour.

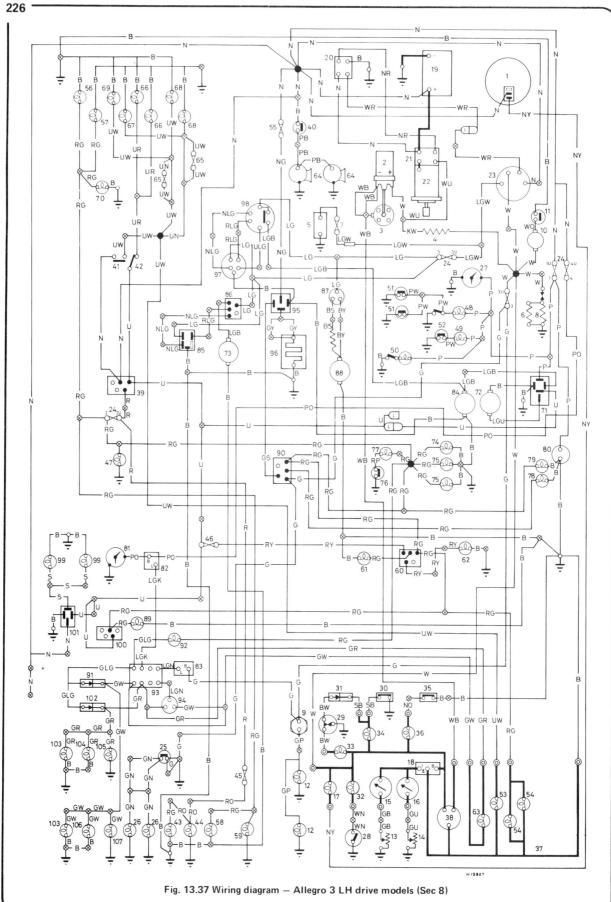

Fig. 13.37 Wiring diagram — Allegro 3 LH drive models (Sec 8)

Key to Fig. 13.37 Wiring diagram — Allegro 3 LH drive models (Sec 8)

1	Alternator
2	Ignition coil
3	Distributor
4	Ballast resistor (cable)
5	Radio
6	Suction chamber heater
7	Line fuse — radio
8	Induction heater
9	Stop lamp switch
10	Radiator fan motor
11	Radiator fan thermostat
12	Stop lamps
13	Fuel gauge tank unit
14	Coolant temperature transducer
15	Fuel gauge
16	Coolant temperature gauge
17	Ignition/no-charge warning lamp
18	Voltage stabilizer
19	Battery
20	Starter solenoid relay
21	Starter solenoid
22	Starter motor
23	Ignition/starter switch
24	Fusebox
25	Reverse lamp switch
26	Reverse lamps
27	Clock — HL models only
28	Oil pressure switch
29	Brake pressure differential switch
30	Handbrake warning lamp switch
31	Diode — brake warning
32	Oil pressure warning lamp
33	Brake failure warning lamp
34	Handbrake warning lamp
35	Choke warning lamp switch
36	Choke warning lamp
37	Printed circuit
38	Tachometer
39	Lighting switch
40	Horn-push
41	Headlamp flasher switch
42	Headlamp dip switch
43	Number-plate lamp
44	RH tail lamp
45	Line fuse — tail lamps
46	Line fuse — front fog lamps
47	Clock illumination — HL models
48	Interior lamp
49	Luggage compartment lamp
50	Rear interior lamp
51	Interior lamp door switch
52	Luggage compartment switch
53	Headlamp main-beam warning lamp
54	Panel lamps
55	Heated rear window
56	LH sidelamp
57	RH sidelamp
58	Number-plate lamp
59	LH tail lamp
60	Rear fog-guard lamp switch
61	Rear fog-guard warning lamp
62	Rear fog-guard lamp
63	Direction indicator warning lamp
64	Horn
65	Line fuse — headlamp (Italy only)
66	Headlamp dip beam
67	RH headlamp — inner
68	Headlamp main beam
69	LH headlamp — inner
70	Switch illumination lamp
71	Headlamp washer relay
72	Headlamp washer pump
73	Rear screen washer switch
74	Switch illumination
75	Heater control illumination lamps
76	Glovebox illumination switch
77	Glovebox illumination lamp
78	Heated rear screen warning lamp
79	Cigar lighter illumination lamp
80	Cigar lighter
81	Clock — except HL models
82	Hazard warning flasher unit
83	Direction indicator flasher unit
84	Windscreen washer motor
85	Rear window wiper motor
86	Rear window washer and wiper switch
87	Heater switch
88	Heater motor
89	Front fog lamp warning lamp
90	Heated rear window switch
91	Diode — direction indicator warning lamp
92	Hazard warning lamp
93	Hazard warning switch
94	Direction indicator switch
95	Heated rear window relay
96	Heated rear window
97	Windscreen wiper switch
98	Windscreen wiper and washer switch
99	Front fog lamp
100	Front fog lamp switch
101	Front fog lamp relay
102	Diode — direction indicator warning lamp
103	Direction indicator repeater lamp
104	LH front direction indicator lamp
105	LH rear direction indicator lamp
106	RH front direction indicator lamp
107	RH rear direction indicator lamp

Note: Not all items listed are fitted to all models.

Cable colour code

B	Black	P	Purple
G	Green	R	Red
K	Pink	S	Slate
LG	Light Green	U	Blue
N	Brown	W	White
O	Orange	Y	Yellow

When a cable has two colour code letters the first denotes the main colour and the second denotes the tracer colour.

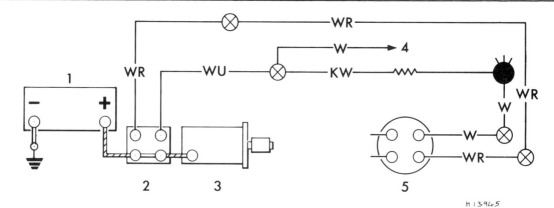

Fig. 13.38 Starter motor circuit — 1.1 and 1.3 models (Sec 8)

1	Battery	4	Ignition coil positive '+' terminal
2	Starter solenoid	5	Ignition/starter switch
3	Starter motor		

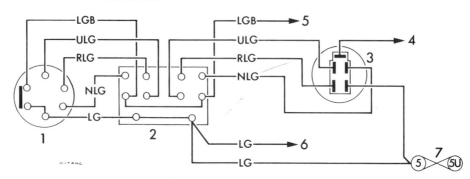

Fig. 13.39 Allegro 3 — Wiper circuit with delay unit fitted (Sec 8)

1	Windscreen wiper washer switch	4	Heater rear window relay	6	Heater motor
2	Windscreen wiper delay unit	5	Washer motor	7	Fusebox
3	Windscreen wiper motor				

9 Suspension and steering

General

1 Various modifications and additions have been introduced and these are all covered in the following paragraphs.

Steering wheel - Allegro 3 models

2 A new steering wheel has been introduced to replace the round one, which in turn replaced the original 'quartic' wheel, one of the 'original features' of the Allegro range when it was introduced in 1973. The new steering wheel is of the four-spoke variety with a soft padded rim.

Tyres - Allegro 3 (1.1 and 1.3) models

3 The Allegro 3 models are fitted with radial ply tyres. The 1.1, 1.3 and 1.3L Saloons have 145 - 13 whilst all other models are shod with 155 - 13 tyres. The various tyre pressures are given in the Specifications Section at the beginning of this Chapter.

Front wheel alignment

4 The front wheel alignment on Series 3 models has been altered and the front wheels should now toe-out as given in the Specifications Section.
5 Chapter 11, Section 37, may still be used with reference to front wheel alignment, but do not forget to use the new data.

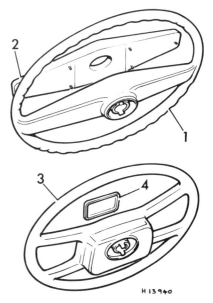

Fig. 13.40 Allegro steering wheels (Sec 9)

1	Round steering wheel — 2-spoke
2	Centre cushion pad
3	Round steering wheel — 4-spoke
4	Rectangular centre pad — basic models

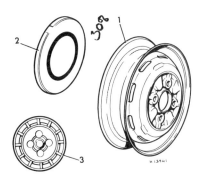

Fig. 13.41 Allegro 3 roadwheel and embellishers (Sec 9)

1   Roadwheel 4.5c x 13
2   Embellisher fitted to 1.1 and 1.3 standard models
3   Embellisher fitted to all L and HL models

Rear radius arm dimensions

6   The rear radius arm assembly dimension for Estate models varies from that for Saloon models. Dimension 'A' in Fig. 11.14 (Chapter 11) is 11.7 in (298 mm) for Estate models prior to the commission numbers given in the supplementary wiring diagrams in this Chapter, and 14.5 in (368 mm) for Estate models commencing at those commission numbers.

Roadwheels and embellishers

7   Various patterns of roadwheels and embellishers are fitted throughout the Allegro range. The 1100 and 1300 De Luxe and Super models are fitted with 4J x 13 wheels, whereas the Mk 3 models all have 4.5c x 13 roadwheels.

---

10 Gearbox and automatic transmission

Kickdown control linkage (automatic transmission) - checking and adjustment

1   Connect a tachometer to the engine.

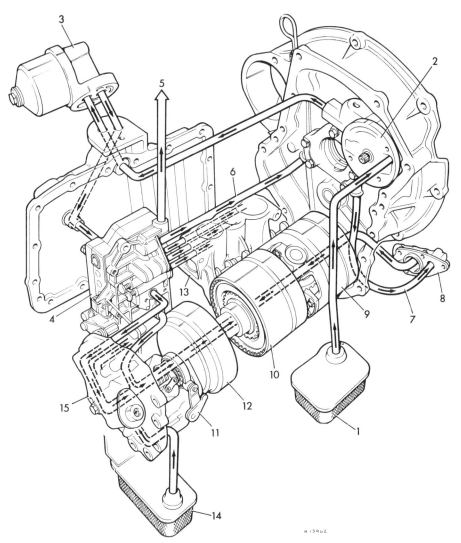

Fig. 13.42 Schematic diagram showing automatic transmission lubrication system and power flow (Sec 10)

1 Main oil strainer	*5 Engine oil feed*	*9 Gear train*	*13 Servo unit*
2 Oil pump	*6 Converter feed pipe*	*10 Top and reverse clutch*	*14 Auxiliary pump oil strainer*
3 Oil filter assembly	*7 Converter to low pressure valve feed*	*11 Governor*	*15 Governor housing*
4 Valve block	*8 Low pressure valve*	*12 Forward clutch*	

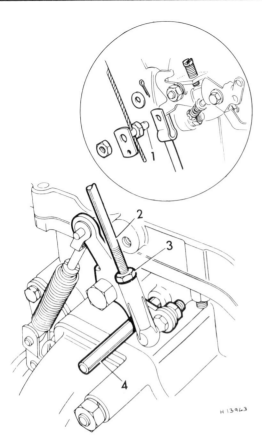

Fig. 13.43 Kickdown rod assembly (Sec 10)

1 Retaining pin
2 Kickdown rod
3 Locknut
4 ¼ in (6.0 mm) diameter checking rod

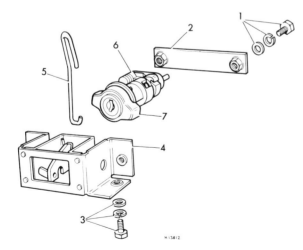

**Fig. 13.44 The alternative boot lid handle and lock assembly
(Sec 11)**

1 Bolt and washers (pivot plate)	4 Lock assembly
2 Pivot plate	5 Link arm
3 Bolt and washers (lock assembly)	6 Retaining ears
	7 Turn button handle

2 Run the engine until the normal running temperature is obtained and adjust the carburettor idling screw to give an idle speed of 750 rpm (refer to Chapter 3 if necessary).
3 Disconnect the kickdown control rod at the carburettor.
4 Insert a ¼ in (6 mm) diameter rod through the hole in the intermediate bellcrank lever and into the hole in the gearbox casing (see Fig. 13.43).
5 Now check that the kickdown rod can be refitted to the carburettor without having to pull the throttle lever or kickdown rod up or down to enable the retaining pin to be inserted.
6 If the retaining pin does not slide in easily, slacken the locknut on the kickdown rod and turn the rod until the correct length is obtained.
7 Reconnect the rod at the carburettor lever, tighten the locknut and remove the checking rod.
8 Test the operation of the kickdown facility as described in Section 23, Test No 9 of Chapter 6.

11 Body and fittings - Saloon and Estate models (1976 onwards)

Alternative boot lid handle and lock assembly (all models) - removal and refitting
1 Open the boot lid.
2 Loosen and remove the six screws securing the pivot plate and the lock assembly in position.
3 Lift away the pivot plate.
4 Disconnect the link arm from the turn button handle.
5 Press in the retaining ears on the turn button handle and withdraw the handle.
6 Remove the lock assembly.
7 Unhook the link arm from the lock assembly.
8 Refitting of the assembly is a reversal of removal, but ensure that the link arm and its attaching lever on the turn button handle are assembled on the left-hand side of the assembly.

Luggage compartment trim panel (Estate) - removal and refitting
9 Unlock and push the rear seat squab forwards.
10 Undo the securing clips and detach the luggage compartment side trim, starting at the front end.
11 Refitting is a reversal of the removal procedure.

Rear quarter trim panel (Estate) - removal and refitting
12 Remove the two screws attaching the rear end of the door seal retainer to the body sill.
13 Remove the bolt securing the seat belt reel to the body and detach the reel, spacer and locking plate.
14 Lift the rear seat cushion and remove the quarter trim panel lower edge securing screw. Unlock and lower the rear seat squab.
15 Remove the door seal from the body around the trim panel and detach the trim panel from the body flange. The panel may be removed after removal of the securing clips. The ashtray can be removed by detaching the spring clip.
16 Refitting is a reversal of the removal procedure.

Tailgate assembly - removal and refitting
17 For safety reasons, disconnect the battery.
18 Remove the two washer jet securing screws to release the jet from the tailgate, and detach the tube.
19 Remove the securing clips to release the tailgate inner trim panel.
20 Disconnect the two wires to the heated rear screen, and remove the washer tube and grommet from the tailgate.
21 Disconnect the wiring harness multi-plug from the wiper motor, and then pull each wire from the multi-plug. It will be necessary to insert a small screwdriver blade or other suitable instrument into the holes in the opposite side of the plug to depress the terminal blade retaining tongues. The holes are numbered on the front face of the multi-plug to enable correct re-connection. The black wire is connected to terminal 1, the

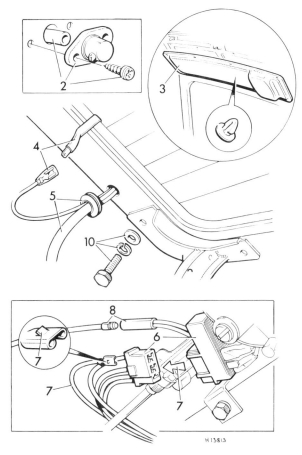

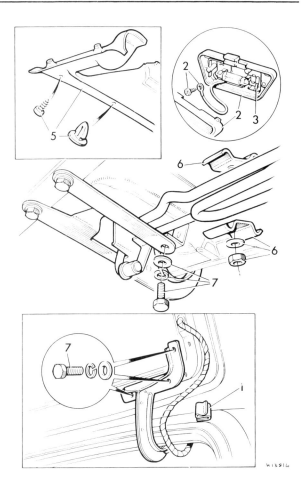

Fig. 13.45 Tailgate assembly (Sec 11)

2 Washer jet, tube and securing screw
3 Tailgate trim
4 Heater element terminal connection
5 Washer tube and grommet
6 Multi-plug connection
7 Terminal blade removal
8 Earth connection
10 Tailgate securing bolts

Fig. 13.46 Tailgate hinge assembly (Sec 11)

1 Clip   5 Hinge trim attachment
2 Lamp assembly   6 Torsion bar clamps
3 Feed wire   7 Hinge securing bolts

brown with green tracer to terminal 2, the green to terminal 4, and the red with green tracer to terminal 5.

22 Disconnect the heated rear screen earth wire at the snap connector.

23 Secure the detached multi-plug wires together with tape, tape the snap connector to the wiring harness and pull the wiring harness and rubber grommet from the tailgate.

24 The tailgate can be released from its hinges after removal of the six securing bolts.

25 Refitting is a reversal of the removal procedure. Ensure that all connections are made correctly.

Tailgate hinge - removal and refitting

26 Release the wiring harness clips or washer tube clips from the tailgate hinge.

27 Remove the rear roof lamp lens and two screws (earth wire attached to left-hand one) and remove the lamp from the hinge trim. Disconnect the feed wire from the lamp.

28 Supporting the tailgate open, remove the screws and clips to detach the hinge trim.

29 Release the two clamps from the tailgate hinge torsion bars by removing the two nuts.

30 Remove the securing bolts and remove the hinge.

31 Refitting is a reversal of the removal procedure.

Tailgate lock - removal and refitting

32 Remove the tailgate inner trim panel by removing the securing clips.

33 Disconnect the lock link from the outside handle.

34 Remove the three securing screws and remove the lock and link.

35 Disconnect the link from the lock lever, and remove the clip.

36 Refitting is a reversal of the removal procedure.

Tailgate handle - removal and refitting

37 Detach the tailgate inner trim panel by removing the securing clips.

38 Disconnect the lock link from the outside handle. Remove the securing nut and remove the outside handle.

39 Compress the bush retaining tongues and detach the link clip from the outside handle lever.

40 Refitting is a reversal of the removal procedure.

Heated rear screen (Estate) - removal and refitting

41 This is basically the same as that described in Chapter 12 for Saloon models. However, the wiper arm assembly will have to be removed for this operation.

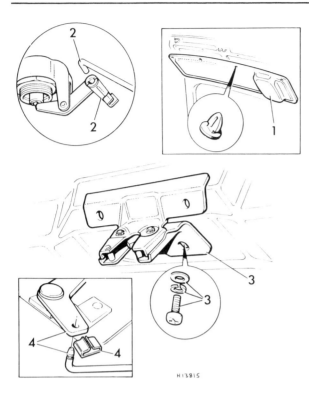

Fig. 13.47 Tailgate lock (Sec 11)

1 Tailgate trim	3 Lock securing screws
2 Lock link assembly	4 Link, lock lever and clip

Rear seat squab lock (Estate) - removal and refitting
42 Remove the rear seat squab by undoing the four bolts securing it to its hinges.
43 Remove the two catches and two lock covers after first removing the securing screws.
44 Detach the cover bead from the channel on the top and sides of the back panel of the squab. Raise the top edge of the seat squab cover, overlay and spring case to expose the lock mechanism.
45 Detach the control cable from the lock by removing the retaining collar.
46 The lock can be removed from the rear panel of the squab after removal of the four securing screws.
47 Refitting is a reverse of the removal procedure.

Rear seat squab lock control cable (Estate) - removal and refitting
48 Carry out the instructions given in paragraphs 42 to 45 inclusive.
49 Release the control cable from the control lever by rotating its end fitting ninety degrees to allow the lugs to pass through the shaped holes in the lever.
50 Refitting is a reverse of the removal procedure.

Rear seat squab lock control lever spindle (Estate) - removal and refitting
51 Carry out the instructions given in paragraphs 42 to 44 inclusive.
52 Push the control lever towards the top edge of the seat squab to release the control knob from the lever.
53 Push the control lever towards the bottom edge of the seat squab to release the lever from its spindle.
54 Remove the control spindle from the back panel of the seat squab by rotating it through 45°.
55 Refitting is a reverse of the removal procedure.

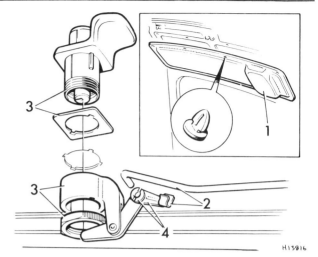

Fig. 13.48 Tailgate handle (Sec 11)

1	Tailgate trim	3	Handle assembly
2	Lock link	4	Bush and link clip

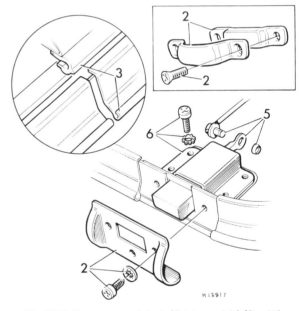

Fig. 13.49 Rear seat squab lock (Estate models) (Sec 11)

2	Lock cover and catch attachment
3	Cover bead attachment
5	Cable attachment
6	Lock securing screws

Rear seat assembly (Saloon models) - removal and refitting
56 To remove the rear seat cushion, press the centre of the lower edge of the cushion to the rear, thus releasing it from the clips on the floor panel.
57 Lift the cushion upwards and forwards to remove it.
58 With the cushion removed, it is now possible to reach the two, or four, retaining screws for the rear seat squab, which are located along the lower edge.
59 With the screws removed, lift the squab up vertically to release the rear of the squab from the clips along the rear bulkhead, just below the level of the parcel shelf.
60 Now the squab can be pulled forward to remove it from the car.

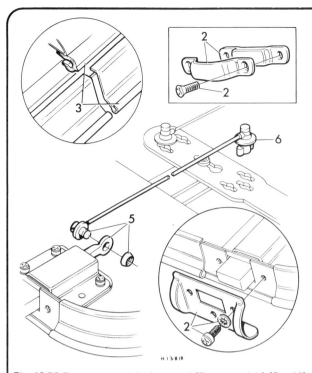

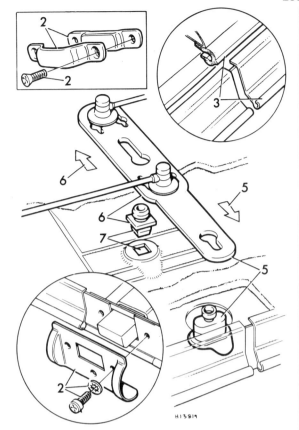

Fig. 13.50 Rear seat squab lock control (Estate models) (Sec 11)

2 Lock cover and catch attachment
3 Cover bead attachment
5 Cable attachment to lock
6 Cable attachment to control lever

Fig. 13.51 Rear seat squab lock control lever spindle
(Estate models) (Sec 11)

2 Lock cover and catch attachment
3 Cover bead attachment
5 Control knob release from lever
6 Control lever release from spindle
7 Spindle release from back panel

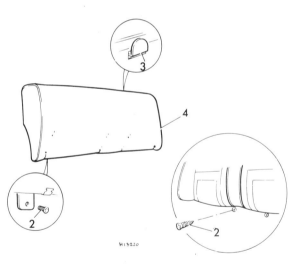

Fig. 13.52 Rear seat assembly (Saloon models) (Sec 11)

2 Squab retaining screws
3 Squab upper retaining clips
4 Squab

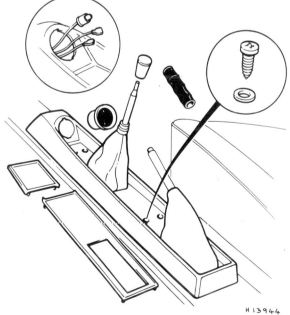

Fig. 13.53 Centre console assembly (Sec 11)

61 Refitting is the reverse procedure to removal. Make sure the cushion is properly located by the front clips.

Centre console (if fitted) - removal and refitting

62 For safety reasons, disconnect the battery.

63 Remove the front and rear finishing panels from the top of the centre console.

64 Twist off the handbrake lever grip and gearchange lever knob.

65 Remove the four screws and washers securing the console to the floor.

66 Lift up the front of the console and reaching underneath it, push out the clock.

67 Disconnect the wires and remove the bulb holder from the rear of the clock.

68 Pull the handbrake fully on and lift the console over the gearchange lever and handbrake lever.

69 Refit the centre console using the reverse of the removal procedure.

12 Body and fittings - Allegro 3 models (1979 onwards)

Facia panel - removal and refitting

1   Remove the instrument panel, as described in Section 8.

2   Remove the steering wheel, as described in Chapter 11.

3   Undo the two nuts and two screws which retain the choke control knob mounting panel to the main facia and cross rail.

4   Undo the two nuts and two screws which retain the auxiliary switch panel on the right of the steering column. One screw is located into the steering column and the other into the driver's door frame.

5   With all the nuts and screws removed, the two panels can now be lowered. There is no need to disconnect either the choke or auxiliary switches from their respective panels.

6   Remove the four crosshead screws which retain the heater cover to the facia and parcel shelf. Lower the cover with the switches and wiring intact.

7   Remove the ashtray from the top of the facia panel, as described later in this Section, then remove the knobs from the ends of the heater control levers.

8   Insert one hand into the ashtray space and push the heater control panel out of the facia. Then pull out the heater control bulb holders from the panel, and place the panel to one side.

9   Remove the two crosshead screws which retain the heater control lever quadrant to the facia panel.

10 Remove the two nuts which secure the facia panel to the centre brackets beneath the facia.

11 Then remove the four crosshead screws which retain the two brackets to the body, and remove them.

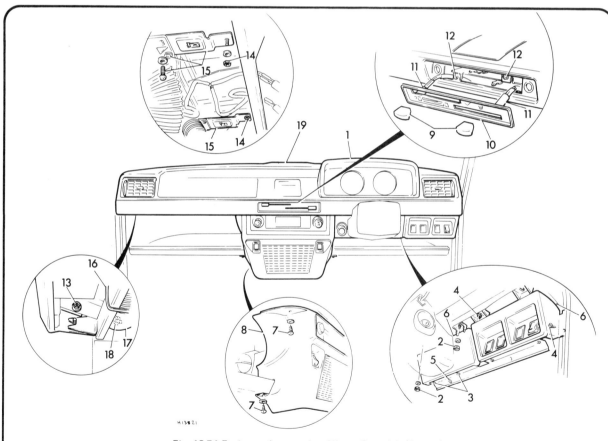

Fig. 13.54 Facia panel removal — Allegro 3 models (Sec 12)

1	Instrument binnacle	8	Heater cover	14	Nuts
2	Nuts	9	Heater control lever knobs	15	Brackets and retaining screws
3	Screws	10	Heater control panel	16	Trunking retaining clip
4	Nuts and screws	11	Heater control panel illumination bulbs	17	Face level vent tube
5	Screw	12	Quadrant retaining screws	18	Facia retaining nut
6	Switch panel	13	Nuts	19	Facia
7	Heater cover retaining screws				

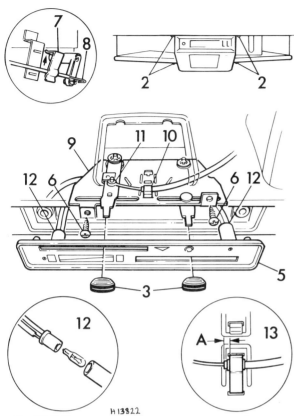

Fig. 13.55 Heater control lever and cable assembly (Sec 12)

2 *Heater cover retaining*	9 *Quadrant*
screws	10 *Cable clip*
3 *Heater control lever*	11 *Stud*
knobs	12 *Control panel bulb*
5 *Heater control panel*	*holders (Inset — bulb,*
6 *Quadrant retaining*	*holder and retainer)*
screws	13 *Dimension 'A' = 0.120 in*
7 *Spring clip*	*(3.0 mm) — correct*
8 *Cable end*	*position for outer cable*

12 Remove. the two nuts which secure the outer ends of the facia panel to the body side panels.

13 Undo the metal clips and withdraw the trunking from the face level vents at either end of the facia.

14 Undo and remove the two remaining retaining nuts (one at either end of the facia panel) behind the panel.

15 Lift the panel away.

16 Refitting is the reverse procedure to removal.

Glovebox lock and latch - removal and refitting

17 Remove the single screw which retains the stay to the glovebox lid.

18 Undo the single screw in each of the two hinges and remove the lid.

19 Carefully, support the lid and drill out the two rivets which retain the lock to the lid.

20 Unscrew the lock bezel and remove the lock from the lid.

21 Refitting will, of course, require the use of rivets to secure the lock to the lid. This is a simple job which your local garage should be able to do for you while you wait, if you do not possess a pop rivet gun of your own. Otherwise, refitting is the reverse procedure to removal, but do the riveting first, then refit the lock bezel.

Ashtray (facia) - removal and refitting

22 Open the ashtray, which is mounted in the top of the facia panel.

23 Depress the spring inside, until it touches the bottom of the tray. Then tilt the ashtray rearwards so that it is released from the facia.

24 Refitting is simply a matter of locating the rear end first and then pushing it home. To ease the relocation, depress the spring inside the ashtray.

Heater cover - removal and refitting

25 Disconnect the battery as a safety precaution.

26 Open the glovebox.

27 Unscrew the four crosshead screws which retain the heater cover to the facia and cross rail.

28 Lower the heater cover. If it is necessary to remove the cover completely, some or all of the following components (depending on the model) will have to be removed from the cover before this can be done.

    (a) *Heater fan control switch and illumination*
    (b) *Cigar lighter*
    (c) *Hazard warning light switch*
    (d) *Heated rear window switch*
    (e) *Radio or wiring to it, including aerial and speaker wires*

All these items are covered in Section 8.

29 Refitting is the reverse procedure to removal.

Heater control lever quadrant and cables - removal and refitting

30 Remove the heater cover, but only as far as is necessary to reach the heater unit itself. This is covered in the previous part of this Section.

31 Remove the ashtray, heater control lever panel and quadrant retaining screws as described in paragraphs 7 to 9.

32 The outer cables are held in position on the heater unit by spring clips. Lift up the spring clip to release the cable. Then free the hooked end of the inner cable from the heater operating lever.

33 Now carefully withdraw the heater lever quadrant from the facia with the cables still attached. The cables need to be fed carefully through the quadrant aperture, making sure that the ends do not become entangled with any other wiring behind the facia.

34 With the quadrant and cables removed, release the outer cable retaining clips and remove the cable from the clips. Then lift the inner cables off the studs on the control levers.

35 Refitting is basically the removal procedure in reverse. However, all the moving parts of the control lever quadrant should be lightly greased using an all-purpose grease.

36 When the heater control cables are refitted to the quadrant, the free end of the outer cable should project a maximum of 0.375 in (3.0 mm) from the spring retaining clip (see Fig. 13.55).

37 When refitting the outer cables to the heater unit, the following procedure must be used:

    (a) *Ensure that the control levers are in the 'OFF' position*
    (b) *Refit the inner cable ends to the heater unit levers*
    (c) *Pull the outer cable towards the remote control lever to tension the cable. Then, holding the cable in tension, snap the outer cable retaining clip into position on the heater unit. Whilst doing this, ensure that the control lever does not move at all*

38 With all the cables and quadrant refitted, check the operation of the cables and observe the movement of the heater control levers. They must have full movement. If they don't, check whether they have been refitted correctly and whether the outer cables were tensioned properly.

39 Finally, refit the heater control lever bezel and knobs, and the ashtray and heater cover.

Front spoiler - removal and refitting

40 All new models are fitted with a front air spoiler. This lightweight moulded air dam is designed to reduce the drag

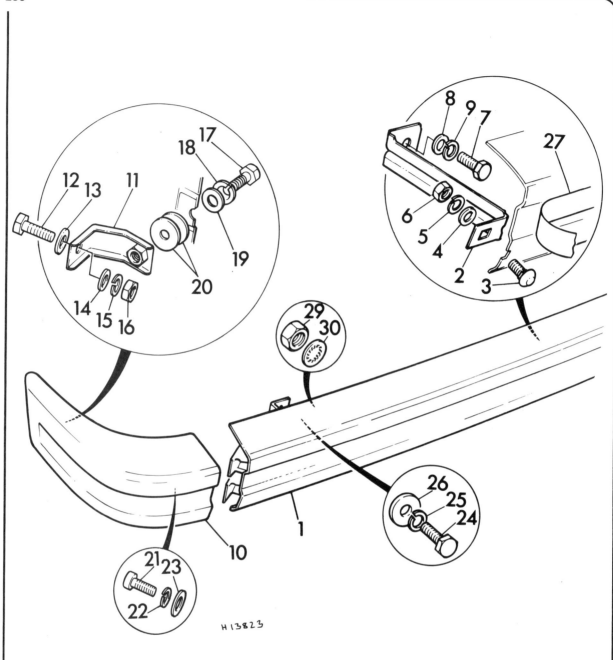

Fig. 13.56 Front bumper assembly (Sec 12)

1	Front bumper centre section	11	End section mounting bracket	21	Bolt
2	Main mounting bracket	12	Bolt	22	Spring washer
3	Bolt	13	Washer	23	Flat washer
4	Flat washer	14	Flat washer	24	Bolt
5	Spring washer	15	Spring washer	25	Spring washer
6	Nut	16	Nut	26	Spacer
7	Bolt	17	Bolt	27	Bright tape insert (HL models)
8	Flat washer	18	Spring washer	29	Nut
9	Spring washer	19	Flat washer	30	Lockwasher
10	Bumper end section	20	Rubber washer		

and thus improve fuel consumption by approximately 10%. It is the same type as is fitted to the Limited Edition Equipe versions of the Allegro 1750.

41 The spoiler is made in two halves. However, the right-hand spoiler helps retain the left-hand spoiler. Therefore, the right-hand spoiler can be removed and refitted without touching the left-hand one, but the right-hand one must be slackened off before the left-hand one can be removed.

42 Remove the two screws and the three bolts and nuts which retain the right-hand spoiler and remove it.

43 Remove the two screws and three bolts and nuts which retain the left-hand spoiler, then remove it.

44 Refit the left-hand spoiler first, but do not fully tighten the mounting bolts and screws.

45 Refit the right-hand spoiler and tighten up all the mounting bolts and screws for both spoilers.

Front bumper - removal and refitting

46 Remove the bolts which retain the end sections of the front bumper to the body. Do not lose the rubber washers.

47 Next, remove the bolts which secure the main section of the front bumper to the body. Lift the bumper away, and retrieve the spacer which is fitted between the bumper and its mounting bracket.

48 With the whole bumper assembly removed from the car, the end sections can be separated from the centre section by undoing the appropriate retaining bolts.

49 Refitting is the reverse procedure to removal. Do not forget to refit the appropriate washers and spacers which were removed.

Rear bumper - removal and refitting

50 Open the boot (or the tailgate) and disconnect the wiring to the rear number plate lamp at the plug-in connectors. In the Estate model, the load deck floor will have to be raised for this operation.

51 Undo and remove the two bolts, washers and mounting rubbers which secure the end sections of the bumper to the body.

52 Remove the four mounting bolts for the main section of the rear bumper. Note that the top bolt on the right-hand mounting bracket also retains the rear fog guard lamp. Disconnect the wiring, as directed in Section 8, and remove the lamp.

53 Remove the rear bumper.

54 The end sections of the bumper are each secured to the main section by two bolts and washers. These can be separated, if required, when the bumper has been removed.

55 To remove the number plate lamps, press in the retaining clips beneath the bumper and withdraw the lamps from the top edge bumper, as described in Section 8.

56 Refitting is the reverse procedure to removal. Don't forget to refit the rear fog guard lamp to the right-hand mounting bracket on reassembly. Check that both the number plate lamps and rear fog guard lamp operate correctly when they have been refitted.

Exterior mirror - removal and refitting

57 Remove the access cover from the mirror mounting bracket.

58 Remove the two screws which retain the mirror and arm assembly to the door, and remove the mirror.

59 Refitting is the reverse procedure to removal.

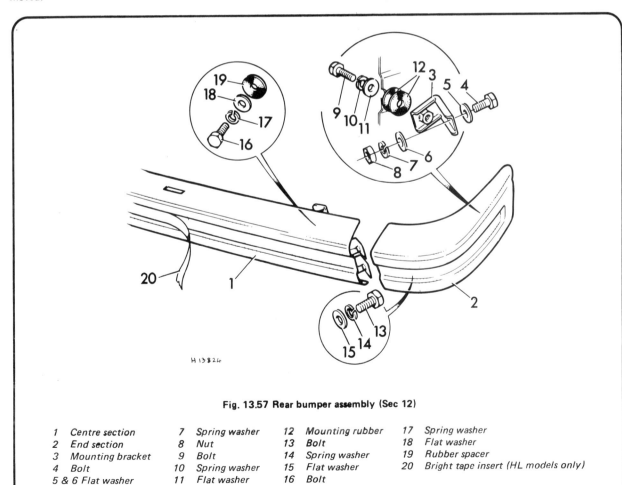

Fig. 13.57 Rear bumper assembly (Sec 12)

1	Centre section	7	Spring washer	12	Mounting rubber	17	Spring washer
2	End section	8	Nut	13	Bolt	18	Flat washer
3	Mounting bracket	9	Bolt	14	Spring washer	19	Rubber spacer
4	Bolt	10	Spring washer	15	Flat washer	20	Bright tape insert (HL models only)
5 & 6	Flat washer	11	Flat washer	16	Bolt		

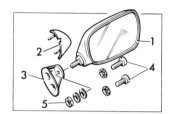

Fig. 13.58 Exterior rear view mirror assembly (Sec 12)

1   Mirror head   4   Retaining screws
2   Access cover   5   Mirror head retaining screws
3   Mounting bracket

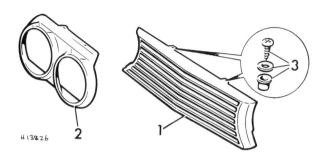

Fig. 13.59 Radiator grille assembly (twin headlamp models)
(Sec 12)

1   Grille
2   Headlamp trim surround
3   Grille retaining screw, washer and bush assembly

Child safety seats (Saloon models) - fitting

60 All new Allegro 3 Saloon models from March 1980 (Chassis No 186868) are fitted with four welded-nut anchorage points on the rear parcel shelf for mounting child safety seats.

61 All child safety seats can be fitted from inside the car. The parcel shelf boards are pre-drilled. All that needs to be done is to locate the holes by running your fingers over the rear parcel shelf vinyl covering; pierce the vinyl in the appropriate places. The bolts can then be inserted and screwed into the weld nuts beneath the shelf.

62 The normal rear seat belt anchorage points should be used for the lower mounting points. To locate these, remove the rear seat cushion, as described in Section 11.

Radiator grille (twin headlamp models) - removal and refitting

63 Open the bonnet and remove the headlamp surround trim on one side of the car, as described earlier in Section 8.

64 Remove the three grille retaining screws. There are two in the top and one in the lower edge.

65 The grille may now be lifted away and eased out from behind the remaining headlamp surround.

66 Refitting is the reverse procedure. It may be made easier if the other headlamp trim surround retaining screws are slackened for this part of the operation.

Conversion factors

Length (distance)

Inches (in)	X	25.4	= Millimetres (mm)	X 0.039	= Inches (in)
Feet (ft)	X	0.305	= Metres (m)	X 3.281	= Feet (ft)
Miles	X	1.609	= Kilometres (km)	X 0.621	= Miles

Volume (capacity)

Cubic inches (cu in; in³)	X	16.387	= Cubic centimetres (cc; cm³)	X 0.061	= Cubic inches (cu in; in³)
Imperial pints (Imp pt)	X	0.568	= Litres (l)	X 1.76	= Imperial pints (Imp pt)
Imperial quarts (Imp qt)	X	1.137	= Litres (l)	X 0.88	= Imperial quarts (Imp qt)
Imperial quarts (Imp qt)	X	1.201	= US quarts (US qt)	X 0.833	= Imperial quarts (Imp qt)
US quarts (US qt)	X	0.946	= Litres (l)	X 1.057	= US quarts (US qt)
Imperial gallons (Imp gal)	X	4.546	= Litres (l)	X 0.22	= Imperial gallons (Imp gal)
Imperial gallons (Imp gal)	X	1.201	= US gallons (US gal)	X 0.833	= Imperial gallons (Imp gal)
US gallons (US gal)	X	3.785	= Litres (l)	X 0.264	= US gallons (US gal)

Mass (weight)

Ounces (oz)	X	28.35	= Grams (g)	X 0.035	= Ounces (oz)
Pounds (lb)	X	0.454	= Kilograms (kg)	X 2.205	= Pounds (lb)

Force

Ounces-force (ozf; oz)	X	0.278	= Newtons (N)	X 3.6	= Ounces-force (ozf; oz)
Pounds-force (lbf; lb)	X	4.448	= Newtons (N)	X 0.225	= Pounds-force (lbf; lb)
Newtons (N)	X	0.1	= Kilograms-force (kgf; kg)	X 9.81	= Newtons (N)

Pressure

Pounds-force per square inch (psi; lbf/in²; lb/in²)	X	0.070	= Kilograms-force per square centimetre (kgf/cm²; kg/cm²)	X 14.223	= Pounds-force per square inch (psi; lbf/in²; lb/in²)
Pounds-force per square inch (psi; lbf/in²; lb/in²)	X	0.068	= Atmospheres (atm)	X 14.696	= Pounds-force per square inch (psi; lbf/in²; lb/in²)
Pounds-force per square inch (psi; lbf/in²; lb/in²)	X	0.069	= Bars	X 14.5	= Pounds-force per square inch (psi; lbf/in²; lb/in²)
Pounds-force per square inch (psi; lbf/in²; lb/in²)	X	6.895	= Kilopascals (kPa)	X 0.145	= Pounds-force per square inch (psi; lbf/in²; lb/in²)
Kilopascals (kPa)	X	0.01	= Kilograms-force per square centimetre (kgf/cm²; kg/cm²)	X 98.1	= Kilopascals (kPa)

Torque (moment of force)

Pounds-force inches (lbf in; lb in)	X	1.152	= Kilograms-force centimetre (kgf cm; kg cm)	X 0.868	= Pounds-force inches (lbf in; lb in)
Pounds-force inches (lbf in; lb in)	X	0.113	= Newton metres (Nm)	X 8.85	= Pounds-force inches (lbf in; lb in)
Pounds-force inches (lbf in; lb in)	X	0.083	= Pounds-force feet (lbf ft; lb ft)	X .12	= Pounds-force inches (lbf in; lb in)
Pounds-force feet (lbf ft; lb ft)	X	0.138	= Kilograms-force metres (kgf m; kg m)	X 7.233	= Pounds-force feet (lbf ft; lb ft)
Pounds-force feet (lbf ft; lb ft)	X	1.356	= Newton metres (Nm)	X 0.738	= Pounds-force feet (lbf ft; lb ft)
Newton metres (Nm)	X	0.102	= Kilograms-force metres (kgf m; kg m)	X 9.804	= Newton metres (Nm)

Power

Horsepower (hp)	X	745.7	= Watts (W)	X 0.0013	= Horsepower (hp)

Velocity (speed)

Miles per hour (miles/hr; mph)	X	1.609	= Kilometres per hour (km/hr; kph)	X 0.621	= Miles per hour (miles/hr; mph)

Fuel consumption*

Miles per gallon, Imperial (mpg)	X	0.354	= Kilometres per litre (km/l)	X 2.825	= Miles per gallon, Imperial (mpg)
Miles per gallon, US (mpg)	X	0.425	= Kilometres per litre (km/l)	X 2.352	= Miles per gallon, US (mpg)

Temperature

Degrees Fahrenheit (°F) $= (°C \times \frac{9}{5}) + 32$

Degrees Celsius (Degrees Centigrade; °C) $= (°F - 32) \times \frac{5}{9}$

*It is common practice to convert from miles per gallon (mpg) to litres/100 kilometres (l/100km), where mpg (Imperial) x l/100 km = 282 and mpg (US) x l/100 km = 235

Index